MESSIAEN PE
SOURCES ANL

For Yvonne Loriod

Messiaen Perspectives 1: Sources and Influences

Edited by

CHRISTOPHER DINGLE
Birmingham Conservatoire, UK

ROBERT FALLON
Carnegie Mellon University, USA

Routledge
Taylor & Francis Group

LONDON AND NEW YORK

First published 2013 by Ashgate Publishing

2 Park Square, Milton Park, Abingdon, Oxon OX14 4RN
711 Third Avenue, New York, NY 10017, USA

Routledge is an imprint of the Taylor & Francis Group, an informa business

First issued in paperback 2016

British Library Cataloguing in Publication Data
A catalogue record for this book is available from the British Library

The Library of Congress has cataloged the printed edition as follows:
Messiaen perspectives / edited by Christopher Dingle and Robert Fallon.
    volumes cm
 Includes bibliographical references and index.
   ISBN 978-1-4094-2695-0 (hardcover : alk. paper)
1. Messiaen, Olivier, 1908–1992—Criticism and
interpretation. I. Dingle, Christopher Philip, editor. II. Fallon, Robert, editor.
 ML410.M595M494 2013
 780.92—dc23

2013007758

ISBN 978-1-4094-2695-0 (hbk)
ISBN 978-1-138-24593-8 (pbk)

Bach musicological font developed by © Yo Tomita

Contents

List of Illustrations		*vii*
List of Figures and Tables		*ix*
List of Music Examples		*xi*
Acknowledgements		*xv*
Editors' Note		*xvii*

Introduction   1
Christopher Dingle and Robert Fallon

PART I   SOURCES

Perspectives on Sources   9
Christopher Dingle and Robert Fallon

1   Olivier Messiaen and the Prix de Rome as Rite of Passage   13
Laura Hamer and Christopher Brent Murray

2   Olivier Messiaen and *Portique pour une fille de France*   45
Lucie Kayas and Christopher Brent Murray

3   Formal Genesis in the Sketches for *Visions de l'Amen*   69
Yves Balmer

4   From Music for the Radio to a Piano Cycle: Sources for the
Vingt Regards sur l'Enfant-Jésus   85
Lucie Kayas

5   My Collaboration with Olivier Messiaen and Yvonne Loriod
on *Harawi*   101
Sigune von Osten

6   Olivier Messiaen's *Timbres-durées*   123
Christopher Brent Murray

7   From *Réveil des oiseaux* to *Catalogue d'oiseaux*: Messiaen's
Cahiers de notations des chants d'oiseaux, 1952–59   143
Peter Hill

8   In the Beginning Was The Word? An Exploration of the Origins of
       Méditations sur le mystère de la Sainte Trinité   175
       Anne Mary Keeley

Intermède

9   Yvonne Loriod as Source and Influence   197
       Christopher Dingle

PART II   INFLUENCES

Perspectives on Influences   213
Christopher Dingle and Robert Fallon

10   Messiaen and Mozart: A Love without Influence?   217
       Christopher Dingle

11   Messiaen and the Romantic Gesture: Contemplations on his Piano
       Music and Pianism   235
       Caroline Rae

12   Messiaen and the Problem of Communication   257
       Julian Anderson

13   Messiaen and *Art Sacré*   269
       Stephen Broad

14   Messiaen, the *Cinq Rechants* and 'Spiritual Violence'   279
       Philip Weller

15   Messiaen in Retrospect   313
       Hugh Macdonald

Appendix: Yvonne Loriod Discography   323
Christopher Dingle

Select Bibliography   *339*
Discography   *351*
Notes on Contributors   *353*
Index   *361*
Contents of Messiaen Perspectives 2: Techniques, Influence and Reception   *369*

List of Illustrations

1.1   Paul Dukas's letter of recommendation   20
1.2   Ministerial document listing the 1930 candidates for the Prix
de Rome competition   20

2.1   Dignitaries' stand, Gerland Stadium   50
2.2   The programme for the Marseilles version of *Portique*   51
2.3   General view of the Gerland Stadium with stage, orchestra, tents
for extras and amplification system   53
2.4   An image of the dress rehearsal for *Portique* in Lyon   54
2.5   The costume design for Joan of Arc by Jean Le Moal   54
2.6   The set design for the Orléans tableau by Jean Le Moal   55
2.7   Laurence Aubray as Joan of Arc during a rehearsal   56
2.8   Joan of Arc and her cavalry heralds   56
2.9   The living cathedral   57
2.10   An image from the coronation scene during which Messiaen's
Te Deum would have been heard   58
2.11   Pierre Schaeffer, Léo Preger and Jean Witkowski during a rehearsal
for *Portique pour une fille de France*   59
2.12   Jean Witkowski directing the orchestra in a rehearsal for *Portique*   59

5.1   Sigune von Osten rehearsing *Harawi* with Olivier Messiaen
and Yvonne Loriod, Bratislava, 7 December 1987   102
5.2   Letter from Yvonne Loriod to the author, 10 October 1988   103
5.3   Letter from Yvonne Loriod to the author, 28 May 1997   103
5.4   Letter from Yvonne Loriod to the author, 29 December 1987   104
5.5   Sigune von Osten rehearsing *Harawi* with Olivier Messiaen
and Yvonne Loriod, Bratislava, 7 December 1987   104
5.6   Sigune von Osten, Olivier Messiaen and Yvonne Loriod
after performing *Harawi*, Bratislava, 7 December 1987   120
5.7   Messiaen's dedication to the author in her score of *Harawi*,
Madrid 1988   120
5.8   Letter from Yvonne Loriod to the author, 6 December 1993   121

8.1   Illumination on parchment, unknown Netherlandish artist, from the
well-known early fifteenth-century illuminated manuscript *Très
Belles Heures de Notre Dame de Jean de Berry*   190

List of Figures and Tables

Figures

8.1	Information supplied in the publicity poster for the event at the Trinité	177
8.2	A summary of the theological elements in the *Méditations*	182
8.3	Chiastic structure of the *Méditations*	183
8.4	Textural and thematic relationships in the *Méditations*	184
8.5	Summary of overall musical structure of the *Méditations*	185
8.6	Music and theology in the fifth meditation	192

Tables

1.1	Placement of the candidates in the 1930 Prix de Rome competition	21
1.2	Candidates for the 1931 Prix de Rome competition	23
1.3	Voting record for the 1931 Prix de Rome competition	26
1.4	Formal structure of Olivier Messiaen's *La Sainte Bohème*	34
1.5	Formal structure of Olivier Messiaen's *La Jeunesse des vieux*	40
3.1	Three versions of *Visions de l'Amen* donated by Messiaen to the Bibliothèque Nationale de France in 1950	70
3.2	Forms of *Visions* in BnF Music Department Ms. 9138	73
6.1	Symmetrical permutations of the four *personnages* in sequences 1–24	133
6.2	Permutations and symmetries in Personnage A	135
6.3	Transformations of Personnage B	137

List of Music Examples

1.1 Harmonic reduction of the refrain from Messiaen's setting of
    La Sainte Bohème, bars 20–25   35
1.2 Melodic development in Messiaen's setting of *La Sainte Bohème*   36
1.3 Mixture of duple and triple pulsation in Messiaen's *La Sainte Bohème*
    (tenor solo, bars 109–112)   36
1.4 Messiaen's use of music from the *Pelléas and Mélisande* 'hair scene'   37
1.5 Thematic generators in Messiaen's early works   41
1.6 Piano reduction of the opening of *La Jeunesse des vieux* featuring
    parallel chords in octatonic modes, bars 5–9   41

2.1 The opening of Messiaen's *Te Deum*   63
2.2 The opening of Messiaen's *Impropères*   64

3.1 Ms. 9138, initial form of 'Amen de la Création', leaf 14, p. 4   75
3.2 The two *appel* motives   76
3.3 'Thème de la Création' in the formal plan for 'Amen de la Création'   77
3.4 *Visions de l'Amen*, 'Amen de la Création', bars 1–8, 'thème de la
    Création'   78
3.5 The 'joli thème B à la Mozart', main theme of the 'Amen du Désir'   80
3.6 Comparison of the carillon chords of the sketch and the final version   82

5.1 'La ville qui dormait', opening bars 1–3   105
5.2 'Bonjour toi', p. 10, system 2, bar 2   106
5.3 'Montagnes', p. 15, system 4   107
5.4 'Doundou tchil', p. 19, bars 2–4   108
5.5 'L'amour de Piroutcha', p. 30, last bar   109
5.6 'Répétition planétaire', p. 33, bar 1; p. 37, bars 4–5   110
5.7 'Répétition planétaire', p. 38, bar 1   111
5.8 'Syllabes', p. 56, bars 4–5   113
5.9 'Syllabes', p. 68, system 3 up to 2 bars before the end of the song   114
5.10 'L'escalier redit, gestes du soleil', p. 79, bars 2–5   115
5.11 'Amour oiseau d'étoile', p. 86, bars 3–4   116
5.12 'Katchikatchi les étoiles', p. 92, bars 3–4   117
5.13 'Katchikatchi les étoiles', p. 92, bar 5   118
5.14 'Dans le noir', end   118

6.1 Personnage A   130
6.2 Transcriptions of Sound E6 and 'The Wind in the Trees'   132

6.3   Interpolations in Personnage C, sequences 2, 6 and 10   138

7.1   Nightingale, Ms. 23077, p. 1   146
7.2   Nightingale, Ms. 23081, p. 10   147
7.3   Merle [noir], Ms. 23080   149
        (a) Page 6   149
        (b) Page 7   149
7.4   Notations at Orgeval and their use in *Réveil des oiseaux*   150
        (a) Loriot, Ms. 23080, p. 21   150
        (b) *Réveil des oiseaux*, fig. 40   151
7.5   Wood Thrush, Ms. 23036, p. 26, and appearance in *Oiseaux exotiques* 154
7.6   Bobolink, Ms. 23036   156
        (a) Page 15   156
        (b) Page 16   156
7.7   Nightingale, Ms. 23037, p. 25   158
7.8   Fauvette à Tête Noire notation and use in 'La Bouscarle'   160
        (a) Ms. 23040, p. 11   160
        (b) 'La Bouscarle', p. 12   161
7.9   23046, pp. 28 and 29 – motifs used for the Oystercatcher in
        'Le Courlis cendré' (see score, pp. 11 and 12)   162
7.10   Rouge-queue notation and use in 'Le Loriot'   163
        (a) 23085, p. 27   163
        (b) 'Le Loriot', p. 11   163
7.11   23049, p. 9   164

8.1   The principal themes of the communicable language in the
        Méditations   187
8.2   'Dieu est immense' is a variation of the 'Dieu' theme   187
8.3   The pedal part in 'le Souffle de l'Esprit' is based on the 'Dieu est
        immense' theme   188
8.4   The opening of 'le Souffle de l'Esprit' is a composite of transposed
        versions of 'Père' and 'Fils' from the first and seventh meditations   188
8.5   The 'Père' and 'Fils' themes move in contrary motion, except that
        their central notes move in parallel motion   191

10.1   First examples from 'Amen du Désir' and Mozart's 'Deh vieni,
        non tardar' (*Marriage of Figaro*) as quoted in *Traité III*, p. 249   226
10.2   Second examples from 'Amen du Désir' and Mozart's 'Deh vieni,
        non tardar' (*Marriage of Figaro*) as quoted in *Traité III*, p. 249 226
10.3   Opening of 'Entrée' from *Concert à quatre* and Mozart's 'Venite,
        inginocchiatevi' (*Marriage of Figaro*)   227
10.4   Passage from Commendatore scene of *Don Giovanni* as quoted by
        Messiaen in *Traité VII*, p. 139   231
10.5   Accord à Renversements Transposés, chord B, 5th transposition   231

| 10.6 | First accord à Resonance Contractée, transposition 1, chord B | 232 |
| 10.7 | Passage from Commendatore scene of *Don Giovanni* as quoted by Messiaen in *Traité VII*, p. 151 | 232 |

11.1	Messiaen *Visions de l'Amen*, 'Amen du Désir', bars 1–4	239
11.2	Concluding gestures of the Messiaen and Chopin sets of Preludes	243
	(a) Messiaen 'Un reflet dans le vent...', bars 199–202	243
	(b) Chopin Prelude no. 24, bars 73–77	243
11.3	Resonant effects in concluding cadences of Messiaen and Chopin	246
	(a) Messiaen 'Les sons impalpables du rêve...', bars 67–68	246
	(b) Chopin Nocturne op. 48, no. 2, bars 136–137	246
11.4	Climactic chordal resonances in Messiaen and Liszt	252
	(a) Messiaen *Visions de l'Amen*, 'Amen du Désir', bars 48–52	252
	(b) Liszt *Après une lecture de Dante*, bars 102–103	252
	(c) Liszt *Après une lecture de Dante*, bars 308–309	252

| 14.1 | *Rechant V*, end of Coda with the text 'dans l'avenir', showing also the parallel instance from the end of the Introduction ('dans le passé') | 294 |
| 14.2 | *Rechant III*, end of introduction, showing 'appoggiatura chords' with changing harmonies above a bass pedal | 312 |

Examples from Messiaen's *Préludes, Réveil des oiseaux* and *Visions de l'Amen* are published by Durand & Cie, Paris/United Music Publishers Ltd. England. Examples from Messiaen's *Catalogue d'oiseaux, Harawi, Méditations sur le mystère de la Sainte Trinité* are published by Editions Alphonse Leduc, Paris/United Music Publishers Ltd, England. The example from Messiaen's *Oiseaux exotiques* is published by Universal Edition A.G., Wien.

Acknowledgements

Two large, complex and international collections of this nature are clearly the product of a great many hands and eyes and we should like to thank all those involved in making these volumes possible. Our thanks first of all to the staff at Ashgate, which has published an impressive library of Messiaen scholarship for which all music scholars should be grateful. In particular, Heidi Bishop and Emma Gallon have shown immense patience, support and understanding of various surprises. We should also like to thank the proofreader, Sarah Price, and desk-editor, the indefatigable Barbara Pretty.

Many of the chapters within the two volumes have their seeds in the Messiaen 2008 International Centenary Conference at Birmingham Conservatoire and we should like to thank all of the delegates at this event for creating such a fertile atmosphere of intellectual exchange and for innumerable conversations that provided some of the hinterland to this collection. The Messiaen 2008 conference was generously supported by The British Academy. We are also grateful for support from colleagues at our respective institutions, notably Liz Reeve and Ronald Woodley from Birmingham Conservatoire and research assistants Matthew Brahm, Michael Ceurvorst and Devon Maloney as well as music librarian Kristin Heath at Carnegie Mellon University. In addition, colleagues at the University of Pittsburgh Department of Music, especially Anna Nisnevich, provided much inspiration.

Among the many ways in which Peter Hill has helped, we are especially grateful for his providing two pictures of Messiaen that appear as part of the cover illustration. We are also extremely pleased that Eric Prenshaw agreed to the inclusion of his photographs in the cover illustration, and would like to thank Yian Ling Cheong for the overall composition of the cover. Thanks should also go to Ruth Milsom for advice and support with many of the music examples. For Peter Hill's chapter, Madame Yvonne Loriod-Messiaen granted unrestricted access to the *cahiers* and to Messiaen's diaries and correspondence.

The greatest thanks, of course, should go to our marvellous contributors. Their scholarship is inspiring, while their understanding of sometimes infuriating requests is immensely appreciated. We hope we have done them justice. Finally, for their unstinting love and support, our families, especially William and Catherine Fallon, and Marie, Liz, Wilfred and Nathaniel Dingle.

Christopher Dingle and Robert Fallon

Alongside two pictures of Messiaen, the cover includes two photographs by Eric Prenshaw. These photos come from the 'Illuminating Messiaen' photography competition, sponsored by Duke Divinity School Initiatives in Theology and the Arts. Entrants were invited to listen to Messiaen's *Visions de l'Amen* and submit responses to the seven movements in the form of photography. The winners were displayed at King's College, Cambridge, UK and Duke Divinity School, USA, in conjunction with a concert performance of the work by Jeremy Begbie and Cordelia Williams.

The first photograph (the mountain) tries to capture the third movement, 'Amen de l'Agonie de Jésus'. In the garden, sweating with blood, we hear Jesus' agonized 'Let it be' to his Father: 'My Father, if this cup may not pass away from me, except I drink of it, thy will be done'. Christ bears the intensity of God's verdict on the world's wrongdoing. He cries out, laments, sighs, sweats blood. Only in this way can humanity be re-made.

The second photograph (the leaves) responds to the fifth movement, 'Amen des Anges, des Saints, du Chant des Oiseaux'. Transparent and effortless, the angels and saints offer their 'Amen' of praise to God in pure song. Nightingales, blackbirds, finches and warblers join the ecstatic vocal chorus of unselfconscious adoration.

Eric Prenshaw is a photographer who lives in Raleigh, NC, USA. He is a 2011 MDiv. Graduate from Duke Divinity School, where he studied with Dr Jeremy Begbie on issues regarding Theology and the Arts. Among other awards, he won four honourable mentions in the 'Illuminating Messiaen' photography exhibition. Eric currently serves as Minister of Children and Youth at Sunrise United Methodist Church. Inquiries can be directed to eprenshaw@gmail.com.

Editors' Note

Language

Where an English translation readily exists for a source, references are to that version. Similarly, the original French for quotations has generally been omitted where the source is readily available. The exception in both cases is where specific linguistic points are being made.

Technique de mon langage musical

Originally published in two volumes, text and musical examples respectively, Leduc has recently published single-volume French (1999) and English (2001) editions of *Technique de mon langage musical*. In the text, it is given simply as *Technique*, with specific references being to the music examples, which are numbered identically in every edition.

Traité de rythme, de couleur, et d'ornithologie

References to this are given as '*Traité*', followed by the volume number in Roman numerals, followed by the page reference as usual (e.g. *Traité VI*, p. 143).

Messiaen's Conversations with Claude Samuel

Page references are to Glasow's 1994 translation of Messiaen's 1986 conversations with Claude Samuel, given simply as *Music and Color*, as this is the most widely available English version. The exception is where the 1967 conversations (translated into English in 1976 by Felix Aprahamian) contain different material. Messiaen did not wish to appear as author of the conversations and, as a consequence, the author is given in the bibliography as Samuel.

Hill and Simeone

References to Peter Hill and Nigel Simeone's seminal work, called simply *Messiaen*, are given as 'PHNS', followed by the page number. References are to the English edition unless specified.

Yvonne Loriod

Messiaen's widow is referred to in the main text as Yvonne Loriod. Bibliographical references follow the source document. The variants are Yvonne Loriod-Messiaen, Yvonne Messiaen-Loriod and Yvonne Messiaen.

Capitalization and Orthography

Where possible, the capitalization of titles of works and movements follows that used by Messiaen where evidence exists for his clear preference. The editors have considered published scores, work lists, materials written in Messiaen's hand and the norms of French capitalization. There is no consistent norm we have followed, but rather have sought in each case to adopt the spelling that we think Messiaen would have preferred. This does not always follow any usual publishing convention, but it is our view that Messiaen's capitalization, despite the vagaries in orthography of his titles, is often revealing for the way in which it emphasizes (or de-emphasizes) key words. We point out especially that an ellipsis should always end the titles *Des Canyons aux étoiles...* and *Éclairs sur l'Au-Delà...* and the word 'Temps' is capitalized in the *Quatuor*.

Birds

When referring to the species itself, all words are capitalized. When referring to a title named after a bird, Messiaen's capitalization is followed.

Introduction

Christopher Dingle and Robert Fallon

> It's always dangerous to think you've got a great composer buttoned up. In
> Messiaen's case, there is much real thinking still to be done ... above all, not
> taking all Messiaen's own remarks about his music at face value.[1]

More than twenty years have now passed since Olivier Messiaen's death in 1992.
So much has been discovered and so much has changed in our understanding of
the man and his music that it is easy to forget how sparse the resources were at
that time. All the readily available music, books, articles and recordings could
fit comfortably onto a single shelf. In the field of scholarship since then, the
imperative identified by Roger Nichols for 'much real thinking', the need to get
beyond the composer himself, has increasingly borne rich fruit, including now the
chapters included in the two volumes of *Messiaen Perspectives*.

Since his death, Messiaen's output has become increasingly prominent in
musical life. Part of the growth in acceptance and recognition undoubtedly stems
from the 2008 centennial celebrations, but the worldwide exposure these prompted
seems only to have increased programming and recording of his music. That Renée
Fleming sang the orchestral version of *Poèmes pour Mi* in the broadcast opening gala
of the New York Philharmonic season in 2009 (and later recorded it) indicates the
extent to which Messiaen's music has entered the repertoire. Looking at some of the
numerous performances of his music around the world in 2012 and the first half of
2013, it is little surprise that works such as *Quatuor pour la fin du Temps*, *Turangalîla-
Symphonie*, *Oiseaux exotiques* and *Et exspecto resurrectionem mortuorum* crop up
with regularity. *Turangalîla* alone is on concert programmes in Tampere (Finland),
Miami, Essen (Germany), Berlin, Erlangen (Germany), Heidelberg, Hamburg,
Frankfurt, Ludwigsburg, Castilla y Leon (Spain), Taipai, Medellin (Columbia),
Birmingham, Aldeburgh (UK), London, Hiroshima, Madrid, Munich, Paris, Seattle,
Estonia, Weimar, London (again) and Frankfurt (again).[2] Even more noteworthy
than that global litany, perhaps, is that more challenging or difficult to mount works
are also featured. To take just two examples, *Chronochromie* is being given several
times by the Chicago Symphony Orchestra under Pierre Boulez and by the National

---

[1]   Roger Nichols, 'Messiaen: *Éclairs sur l'Au-Delà*', *Musical Times*, 135/1812 (February
1994): p. 117.

[2]   These are merely the performances listed on Malcolm Ball's Messiaen website
(www.oliviermessiaen.org) from the beginning of January 2012 until the summer of 2013.
It is entirely possible that there are others.

Orchestra of Belgium with Lothar Zagrosek, while *Des Canyons aux étoiles...* can be heard in performances by different ensembles in New York, Ann Arbor, Aspen and (back in New York) at Carnegie Hall. Meanwhile, Messiaen's music appears regularly in the recital programmes of students in conservatoires. That Durand have published an album entitled *Olivier Messiaen en treize morceaux pour piano* [Olivier Messiaen in thirteen pieces for piano] and Deutsche Grammophon a CD compilation called *Messiaen: Garden of Love's Sleep* underlines the extent to which the composer has moved beyond the specialist niche towards the mainstream of the classical music world. Even in jazz and pop, Messiaen has made a mark with Björk, Radiohead, and numerous other artists quoting his music, a remarkable achievement for any composer so soon after death.

Unsurprisingly, there has been a similar growth in scholarship about Messiaen. The publication of the final volume of Messiaen's *Traité de rythme, de couleur, et d'ornithologie* in 2002, then of Hill and Simeone's *Messiaen* in 2005, which drew upon access to the composer's personal archive, each marked a seminal moment in providing general access to his life and thought hitherto available to a select few.[3] In his call, quoted above, for much-needed thinking, Roger Nichols notes that this would follow 'in the footsteps most notably of Robert Sherlaw Johnson and Paul Griffiths'.[4] In other words, just two significant books on Messiaen in English were available in 1994, to which anyone else would have added Roger Nichols's own study. The German literature was no more extensive and even in France there was hardly an abundance of riches. Now those published in English alone since the appearance of Hill and Simeone's seminal book in 2005 would fill a bookshelf (see the Bibliography for full details):

- Siglind Bruhn, *Messiaen's Contemplations of Covenant and Incarnation: Musical Symbols of Faith in the Two Great Piano Cycles of the 1940s* (2007)
- Christopher Dingle, *The Life of Messiaen* (2007)
- Christopher Dingle and Nigel Simeone (eds), *Olivier Messiaen: Music, Art and Literature* (2007)
- Peter Hill and Nigel Simeone, *Olivier Messiaen: Oiseaux exotiques* (2007)
- Robert Sholl (ed.), *Messiaen Studies* (2007)
- Vincent Benitez, *Olivier Messiaen: A Research and Information Guide* (2008)
- Siglind Bruhn, *Messiaen's Explorations of Love and Death: Musico-Poetic Signification in the "Tristan Trilogy" and Three Related Song Cycles* (2008)
- Siglind Bruhn, *Messiaen's Interpretations of Holiness and Trinity: Echoes of Medieval Theology in the Oratorio, Organ Meditations, and Opera* (2008)
- Andrew Shenton, *Olivier Messiaen's System of Signs* (2008)
- Jon Gillock, *Performing Messiaen's Organ Music: 66 Masterclasses* (2009)
- Sander van Maas, *The Reinvention of Religious Music: Olivier Messiaen's Breakthrough Toward the Beyond* (2009)

---

[3]   Subsequent references to Hill and Simeone's *Messiaen* are given as 'PHNS'.

[4]   Roger Nichols, 'Messiaen: *Éclairs sur l'Au-Delà*...: p. 117.

- Judith Crispin (ed.), *Olivier Messiaen: The Centenary Papers* (2010)
- Andrew Shenton (ed.) *Messiaen the Theologian* (2010)
- Stephen Broad, *Olivier Messiaen: Journalism, 1935–39* (2012)
- Christopher Dingle, *Messiaen's Final Works* (2013)
- Gareth Healey *Messiaen's Musical Techniques: The Composer's View and Beyond* (2013)

Furthermore, in 2008 Caroline Rae updated Robert Sherlaw Johnson's classic book on the composer and feature articles on Messiaen have recently appeared in the world's top musicology journals.

To this abundance of recent scholarship, these two volumes stand out for presenting a wealth of new material and thinking that extends beyond the face value of Messiaen's remarks. Equally notable, though, is that, far from being the last word on the matter, the enclosed chapters tend to be the first detailed examinations of their respective avenues of enquiry. In some cases this is because material has not been generally available until now, in others because time was needed for a sense of historical perspective, and in others because the ideas are fresh. One charge that was levelled at Messiaen scholars in the past, with some justification, is of an insularity of thought. If this was symptomatic of both the viewpoint (from without and within) that Messiaen stood apart and a concurrent over-reliance on the composer's own explanations, the outward-facing nature of many of the contributions along with the broader frame of reference suggests that such a claim is becoming ever harder to substantiate.

The two volumes collect 29 chapters from an international and multilingual group of leading and emerging scholars of Messiaen. The chapters draw heavily, but not exclusively, from research presented at the Messiaen 2008 International Centenary Conference, organized by Christopher Dingle at Birmingham Conservatoire. However, these volumes are more than a simple set of conference proceedings; they also move beyond the theoretical divisions – rhythm, colour, ornithology and faith – that Messiaen himself espoused and much scholarship has adopted. Focusing on Messiaen's relationship with history – both his own and the history he engendered – the *Messiaen Perspectives* volumes convey the growing understanding of his deep and varied interconnections with his cultural milieux. Read from beginning to end, the five ways of examining Messiaen, which we have called *perspectives*, provide a chronological sequence of historiographical lenses in order of the creative lifecycle, from provenance to audience, or, in terms he would prefer, from genesis to revelation. *Messiaen Perspectives 1: Sources and Influences* explores the origins and cultural pressures that shaped Messiaen's music. By contrast, *Messiaen Perspectives 2: Techniques, Influence and Reception* analyses select compositions and the repercussions of his music. While each book offers a coherent collection in itself, together these complementary volumes elucidate how powerfully Messiaen was embedded in his time and place and how his relevance has not diminished today.

Many of the chapters range broadly across Messiaen's life and output while others look outward from him to the work of others. Some works or episodes of Messiaen's life are explored in detail, filling significant gaps, but several major works receive comment within *Messiaen Perspectives* as part of a broader context rather than as standalone case studies for they have already been explored elsewhere. So, while there is no specific chapter, for instance, on the opera *Saint François d'Assise*, anglophone readers can already find extensive information on this work in books, chapters or articles by Benitez, Bruhn, Dingle, Fallon, Griffiths and Camille Crunelle Hill, not to mention Hill and Simeone.[5] Similar lists can be produced for other major works, such as the *Quatuor*, *Turangalîla*, *La Transfiguration* or *Éclairs sur l'Au-Delà...*, and it is to be hoped that the literature specifically on each will continue to expand. Each perspective presented here shines a light on a particular facet of the composer. If we were French, it would have been sorely tempting to call these chapters 'regards', not that we could have culled nine of them to make the analogy complete. That said, prompted by the lightest movement of the *Quatuor pour la fin du Temps*, both books contain 'Intermède' (Interlude) chapters, placed between the principal parts, but related to them and the whole.

The perspectives contained within these two volumes both deepen and broaden our knowledge and understanding of Messiaen. An important feature is that several of the contributors write from the perspective of having performed the music at the highest level, with their professional practice informing their research, while Julian Anderson brings a composer's insights to Messiaen's creative imperatives in his chapter in the first volume. As with any scholarship, each discovery made, each issue addressed and each insight expounded suggests additional questions and lines of enquiry. In other words, it is fervently hoped that these chapters will act as a catalyst for further reflection, study and performance of Messiaen's music.

---

[5]   Vincent Benitez, 'Simultaneous Contrast and Additive Designs in Olivier Messiaen's Opera *Saint François d'Assise*', *Music Theory Online*, 8/2 (August 2002); Siglind Bruhn, *Messiaen's Interpretations of Holiness and Trinity: Echoes of Medieval Theology in the Oratorio, Organ Meditations, and Opera* (Hillsdale, NY: Pendragon, 2008); Christopher Dingle, 'Frescoes and Legends: The Sources and Background of *Saint François d'Assise*', in Christopher Dingle and Nigel Simeone (eds), *Olivier Messiaen: Music, Art and Literature* (Aldershot: Ashgate, 2007); Christopher Dingle, *The Life of Messiaen* (Cambridge: Cambridge University Press); Paul Griffiths, '*Saint François d'Assise*', in Peter Hill (ed.), *The Messiaen Companion* (London: Faber and Faber, 1995); Camille Crunelle Hill, 'Saint Thomas Aquinas and the Theme of Truth in Messiaen's *Saint François d'Assise*', in Siglind Bruhn (ed.), *Messiaen's Language of Mystical Love* (New York: Garland, 1998); PHNS; Nils Holger Petersen, 'Messiaen's *Saint François d'Assise* and Franciscan Spirituality', in Siglind Bruhn (ed.), *Messiaen's Language of Mystical Love* (New York: Garland Publishing, 1998).

Messiaen Perspectives 1: Sources and Influences

This first volume of perspectives falls into two parts that focus on the formation of several of Messiaen's works and the formation of Messiaen as an artist. Part I discusses key primary sources presented here for the first time. It is essentially chronological, the focus moving through Messiaen's career from the 1930s to the 1970s. The sources include not only scores and documents in archives, but also insight into performance practice. Part II presents insights into Messiaen's sources of inspiration, placing the composer within a broader historical and cultural framework than has hitherto been attempted. These chapters examine Messiaen's engagement across his life with a variety of traditions and artistic movements as seen through particular works, composers and compositional practices. In particular, for the concluding chapter, we deliberately sought a scholar from beyond the circles of Messiaen specialists and are delighted to print Hugh Macdonald's wide-ranging essay on how the composer fits into broader currents. The Intermède between the two parts is devoted to Messiaen's wife and principal interpreter, Yvonne Loriod. Following her death in 2010, this chapter inevitably carries an element of tribute to it, but it is intended neither as an extended obituary nor a comprehensive examination of her life and career. Rather, it seeks to examine her through the lens of this book's subtitle, for she stands as one of the greatest influences upon Messiaen and also became the principal source of information about and insight into him following his death. It is entirely appropriate, therefore, that this book should be dedicated to Yvonne Loriod, placing consideration of her impact literally at its centre and providing a discography of her commercial recordings as an appendix.

PART I
Sources

Perspectives on Sources

Christopher Dingle and Robert Fallon

Every scholar in music handles sources of one kind or another. Students learn early on about the difference between primary and secondary sources and, hopefully, that such status is not necessarily inherent to the source in question, but can depend upon the nature of the research. A newspaper review may be a secondary source for those studying a particular composer or performer, but a primary source for a specialist in music criticism. A facsimile copy of a composer's handwritten score or sketch, either as hardcopy or a pdf file, may be a primary source for someone looking at the musical materials of a work, where only the original, physical manuscript itself would count for a scholar trying to date it through the study of paper and ink types. Similarly, the CD transfer of Yvonne Loriod's 1946 recording of 'Regard de l'Esprit de joie' would count as a primary source for anyone analysing the performance on the recording,[1] where the captured sound is what matters, but for someone carrying out detailed discographical work, this is a secondary source and they would wish not just to hear, but to see (if possible) the original release, including the cover, the label on the disc itself and even the information etched onto the shellac.[2]

As important to note as the difference between primary and secondary sources is the disparate nature of sources that might be encountered. Alongside books, articles, scores, manuscripts, recordings and other artefacts, there are the more ephemeral sources such as non-recorded performances (arguably, aspects of those that are recorded) and, especially, the oral testimony of those directly involved with the subject of the research. Even when this material comes directly from the subject of the investigation – usually Messiaen in these volumes – it cannot necessarily be regarded as accurate and certainly not the only or whole truth. If talking about the impetus behind his works, the meaning behind passages or how he put them together, Messiaen is clearly the most authoritative source. Nonetheless, there are things left unsaid, because he did not wish or think or remember to say them, or because he was trying to put matters into terms that could generally be understood. When it comes to events, then (wilfully or not) Messiaen was as liable to misremember or partially recall as anyone else. Nonetheless, Messiaen's statements on anything to do with himself and his music demand to be taken seriously, even if experience has shown that some of his anecdotes should be taken with a large pinch of salt. The same could be said for those who were directly

---

[1]   EMI France 0946 385275 2 7 (2 CDs).

[2]   Pathé PDT 170 (78 rpm) Matrix nos: CPTX 748-1 (side 1), CPTX 749-1 (side 2).

involved in events in his life, who acted as witnesses or who worked with or were taught by him. However, in terms of reliability, and attendant challenges for scholars, there is a spectrum ranging from Messiaen's utterances, via Yvonne Loriod, numerous friends, colleagues, students, performers and independent witnesses to accounts such as Zdzisław Nardelli's *Otchłan ptaków* [Abyss of the Birds].[3] Nardelli was in Stalag VIIIA with Messiaen, and his book relates to their time there, but it is openly and clearly not a factual account, with the composer treated as a fictional entity, so nothing can be treated with certainty, and yet it is directly informed and shaped by life in the camp making it hard to dismiss entirely.

Whether they are historical fiction or a newly discovered manuscript, sources provide evidence for the scholar's argument. They may be credible or discredited, trivial or seminal, but sources are the stuff of understanding. With the many new sources presented and put to use in these pages, our understanding of Messiaen and his music grows handsomely.

These are exciting times for Messiaen scholars because a profusion of new sources has appeared in recent years, which, in itself, gives some indication of what more is to come in the course of time, once various logistical and bureaucratic barriers are overcome with regard to Messiaen's estate.[4] The posthumous publication of the composer's own *Traité* has had profound significance for our understanding of Messiaen's music and thought, as, of course, has the appearance of the scores for works from his final years, and some earlier ones, too. These were to be expected, as were one or two discoveries. What could not be anticipated was the extent to which Yvonne Loriod opened up her home and herself to scholars, resulting, notably, in Hill and Simeone's *Messiaen*. There is still some way to go before the Fonds Messiaen is properly archived and made accessible, and there has inevitably been something of a hiatus following Loriod's death in 2010, but information contained within Messiaen's appointment diaries, in letters and numerous other documents has profoundly transformed the understanding of the man and his music. Perhaps the richest resource of all is the vast number of *cahiers* containing Messiaen's birdsong notations, along with much other information, including preliminary sketches for some works. As is clear from Peter Hill's chapter, charting the developing relationship with birdsong material in an exploration of the *cahiers* from the 1950s, these will occupy scholars for years to come. As Hill outlines, the rationale underpinning the cataloguing of the *cahiers*

---

³   Zdzisław Nardelli, *Otchłan ptaków* [Abyss of the Birds] (Katowice: Wydawn, 1989).

⁴   Some notable examinations of Messiaen source materials include: Christopher Dingle, 'Frescoes and Legends: The Sources and Background of *Saint François d'Assise*', in Dingle and Simeone (eds), *Olivier Messiaen: Music, Art and Literature* (Ashgate, 2007); Robert Fallon, 'The Record of Realism in Messiaen's Bird Style', in Christopher Dingle and Nigel Simeone (eds), *Olivier Messiaen: Music, Art and Literature* (Ashgate, 2007); Peter Hill and Nigel Simeone, *Olivier Messiaen: Oiseaux exotiques* (Aldershot: Ashgate, 2007); PHNS; Rebecca Rischin, *For the End of Time: The Story of the Messiaen Quartet* (Ithaca, NY: Cornell University Press, 2003).

is far from clear at first glance. As a consequence, his chapter includes an appendix indicating the broad date and contents of each *cahier*; an invaluable resource that should save future scholars much time and bemusement.

There is still much that has not been seen. Most valuable will be the scores for various works that are known to have been written, but have never been published. For a long time, the title *Chœurs pour un Jeanne d'Arc* was little more than a puzzling entry in Messiaen's catalogue of works at the end of *Technique de mon langage musical*. The mystery was partially dispelled by Hill and Simeone, but, thanks to some excellent detective work, Lucie Kayas and Christopher Brent Murray provide a rich account of Messiaen's choral contributions to the Joan of Arc spectacle *Portique pour une fille de France*. The remaining 'missing' scores are generally very early works, and some, no doubt, have not survived. It is to be hoped, though, that the scores of pieces such as *L'Ensorceleuse* (Messiaen's Prix de Rome cantata), and *Le Banquet eucharistique* (the orchestral piece from which *Le Banquet céleste* was extracted) have not only survived, but will see the light of day before too long.

Alongside scores, sketches and other materials relating to the genesis of works are invaluable. Relatively few sketches appear to have survived from before the late 1950s, so Yves Balmer's careful investigation of sketch materials for *Visions de l'Amen* showing the evolution of significant themes for the work provides a fascinating snapshot of the creative process. Another such glimpse is afforded in Christopher Brent Murray's chapter, which outlines in detail Messiaen's only foray into the world of *musique concrète* with the composition of *Timbres-durées*.

The next major resource after the scores and sketches is the collection of recordings Messiaen made of his improvisations during Mass at the Trinité. Some of these appeared briefly on a two CD set, though, frustratingly given that this is music with a precise and specific source of inspiration in the texts of the day's celebration, no information was given at all about the dates or occasions for each improvisation. There are also the recordings of birdsong that Loriod made while Messiaen was taking notation in the field.

At the same time as material from Messiaen's personal archive has started to become available, archives of the Paris Conservatoire and other institutions with which Messiaen had contact during his long career have also begun to be consulted. Thanks to foraging in such places, Laura Hamer and Christopher Brent Murray chart Messiaen's participation in the Prix de Rome competition, examining both the process and the choruses that he wrote in the preliminary stages. Building on the excellent groundwork of Edward Forman,[5] Lucie Kayas examines the implications of new documents to provide further detail on the story of the genesis of the *Vingt Regards*. Similarly, Anne Keeley draws on the text of the sermon by Mgr Charles that inspired the *Méditations sur le mystère de la Sainte Trinité* and,

5   Edward Forman, '"L'Harmonie de l'Universe": Maurice Toesca and the genesis of *Vingt Regards sur L'Enfant-Jésus*, in Christopher Dingle and Nigel Simeone (eds), *Olivier Messiaen: Music, Art and Literature* (Aldershot: Ashgate, 2007).

as a consequence, repositions its theological focus. It is not surprising that such resources only started to be explored after Messiaen's death; why search among such things while the ultimate primary source is still available for consultation? Nonetheless, while grasping any excuse to visit Paris is understandable, there is much to be explored in the numerous places to which he travelled.

So these are exciting times for Messiaen scholars as there are still major discoveries to be made. However, it should also be recognized that it is also a critical period. This is in part because decisions are still be made about the estate that could have a profound impact on scholarship and broader knowledge of the composer. Even more crucial, though, is that the direct eye- and ear-witnesses will not be with us forever. There is an imperative to capture as much of these ephemeral sources as possible. Such testimonies may be problematic and partial, but evidence can only be assessed if it is gathered. The Institut National de l'Audiovisuel (INA) is to be applauded for recording a 6-hour-24-minute interview with Yvonne Loriod in 2002, a remarkable oral document made while she was still in full health. Similarly, Sigune von Osten, who worked very closely with Messiaen on performing *Harawi*, had the foresight to record her rehearsals with the composer and Yvonne Loriod. As is apparent in her chapter, there emerged an often radically different approach to performing the song cycle from that usually heard. As such, her testimony goes beyond the usual observations about performance for this is not just about a distinctive interpretation, but a different concept of approaching *Harawi* and, by extension, of understanding the possibilities of Messiaen performance practice.

The following chapters offer a good flavour of the range of materials that have become available or have been uncovered in the past decade. Taken as a whole, these eight perspectives on sources help especially to fill in the most pronounced lacunae of Messiaen's work, notably the first three decades of his career. These years also serve, of course, as sources for the remainder of his career, thus becoming influences. But that is for the second part of the book.

Chapter 1

Olivier Messiaen and the Prix de Rome as Rite of Passage

Laura Hamer and Christopher Brent Murray

The Significance of the Prix de Rome

Although often maligned, the Prix de Rome was one of France's most important artistic awards. Debussy's famous denigration of the competition as a 'useless tradition' is just one example of sentiment against it,[1] but the Prix de Rome brought the winner financial reward, official recognition, and critical exposure. Messiaen competed for this prestigious prize twice. In 1930 he failed to get past the *concours d'essai*; in 1931 he was more fortunate and progressed to the second round, but was not honoured with a prize. Drawing on the extant documentation held at the Institut de France, the manuscripts of Messiaen's *concours d'essai* competition entries in the Paris Conservatoire library, and contemporary press coverage, this chapter will examine Messiaen's engagement with the Prix de Rome competition and discuss the possible career advantages and restrictions that winning the Prix de Rome would have brought him. Although Messiaen's Prix de Rome cantatas were written hurriedly, under stressful conditions, and although the competition expectations seem to have placed certain restrictions on his style when compared to his free compositions, they are not unrepresentative of his music of this period. Many parallels, which will be discussed below, exist between the two choruses written for the *concours d'essai* and *Les Offrandes oubliées*, to say nothing of Messiaen's later works for choir and orchestra, including the *Trois Petites Liturgies de la Présence Divine* and, especially, the *Chant des déportés*.[2] Consideration of his Prix de Rome compositions, therefore, can add usefully to understanding of his compositional development.

---

[1] Claude Debussy, 'Concerts Colonne and Société des Nouveaux Concerts Spanish Music', *Société Internationale de Musique* (1 December 1913); cited in François Lesure (ed.), *Debussy on Music*, trans. Richard Langham Smith (London: Secker & Warburg, 1977), p. 303. For a nuanced examination of what might be termed the 'pros and cons' of the Prix de Rome as an institution, see the five contributions to 'Le prix de Rome: Modèle respecté ou cible des critiques?', the final section of Julia Lu and Alexandre Dratwicki (eds), *Le concours du prix de Rome de musique, 1803–1968* (Lyon: Symétrie, 2011), pp. 719–84.

[2] Please see the editors' note explaining the capitalization of the titles of Messiaen's works. For a full listing of Messiaen's musical works, see the appendix to *Messiaen Perspectives 2*.

Whilst the list of Prix de Rome laureates includes names that have sunk into total obscurity, winning the competition often represented the first step in a successful musical career, if not prolonged international renown. Famous winners of the Prix de Rome include Berlioz (1830), Gounod (1839), Bizet (1857), Massenet (1863), Debussy (1884) and, more recently, Dutilleux (1936). At the time of Messiaen's attempts, the winners of the Prix de Rome were entitled to four years of funded residency at the Académie de France in Rome (hereafter the Villa Médicis), which was intended to broaden their artistic horizons through exposure to Italian culture. They were also given the right to the title 'Premier Grand Prix de Rome', which could be written after the name in the space traditionally reserved for honours and degrees, indicating the elevated level of esteem that was attached to the award. For a young composer on the make, success in the Prix de Rome competition could be a considerable opportunity, and mark an important rite of passage from the student arena to the professional world.[3]

Messiaen was remarkably savvy with regards to establishing himself within the precarious musical profession. Nigel Simeone has demonstrated the proactive stance that Messiaen took in 1931 when applying for the coveted post of *titulaire* at the Trinité, the church where he was already working as a substitute organist: on hearing that the position was open (following the death of the previous incumbent Charles Quef on 2 July 1931), Messiaen lost no time in securing the support of senior musical figures, including Charles-Marie Widor, Marcel Dupré, Maurice Emmanuel, André Marchal, Charles Tournemire and Bérenger de Miramon Fitz-James, for his successful candidacy.[4] His position as a jury member for the Société Nationale de Musique from late 1931, and his slightly later involvement in creating the composers' groups and concert associations La Spirale and Jeune France provided ample opportunities for him to promote his own music and that of his friends. In the context of the steps that Messiaen took to advance his early career it appears likely that the opportunities that the Prix de Rome represented would have appealed to him greatly.

It must be noted, however, that as well as opportunities, winning the Prix de Rome also entailed a number of potential drawbacks. First, the obligatory residency at the Villa Médicis potentially undermined important musical contacts in France by effectively removing young composers from Paris. Messiaen, no doubt, would have been well aware of the frustrations that Berlioz and Debussy had experienced on account of this. Young French composers often found the high

---

[3]   For a thorough examination of the professional significance of the Prix de Rome during the final sixty years of its existence, see Rémy Campos and Aurélian Poidevin, '"Nous entrerons dans la carrier …"': Le prix de Rome, concours d'entrée des compositeurs dans la profession? 1906–1968', in Lu and Dratwicki (eds), *Le concours du prix de Rome de musique*, pp. 679–706.

[4]   For a detailed consideration of Messiaen's candidacy and appointment at the Trinité, see Nigel Simeone, '"Chez Messiaen, tout est prière": Messiaen's Appointment at the Trinité', *The Musical Times*, 145/1889 (Winter 2004): pp. 36–53.

temperatures of the long Roman summers unbearable.[5] Furthermore, as the Villa Médicis was unable to offer accommodation to couples, it was a competition rule that all candidates were to be unmarried. If Messiaen had continued to compete from 1932 onwards, he would have broken a promise to his employers at the Trinité and had to delay his marriage (22 June 1932) to the composer and violinist, Claire Delbos for several years.

The Prix de Rome Competition: Regulations and Traditions

Whatever its benefits and drawbacks, Messiaen twice competed for the Prix de Rome, an institution whose origins lie in the seventeenth century, when Louis XIV granted financial support to promising young artists to enable them to undertake a period of study in Italy. The Prix de Rome was formalized as an annual artistic competition by the Académie des Beaux-Arts following the establishment of the Institut de France in 1795 with the first Prix de Rome in musical composition being awarded in 1803.[6] During the years in which Messiaen took part in the competition, the Prix de Rome was organized by the Académie des Beaux-Arts, which was itself divided into five sub-divisions corresponding to various art forms: music, painting, sculpture, engraving and architecture.[7] Each of these five artistic disciplines had its own annual Prix de Rome competition until the prize was discontinued in 1968.

The competition for the Prix de Rome in musical composition opened each year in May with an eliminatory first round, the *concours d'essai*. The first round was judged by a specialist music jury, which consisted of the six musician members of the Académie des Beaux-Arts and three adjunct members, who were usually well-known composers. For this first round, the candidates were required to compose a vocal fugue plus a work for chorus and orchestra, based on a poem

---

[5]   Marguerite Canal (who won the Prix de Rome in 1920) received special dispensation from the Académie des Beaux-Arts, on health grounds, to leave Rome and return to Paris during especially warm periods.

[6]   For more detailed examinations of the origin, history and evolution of the Prix de Rome, see Alexandre Dratwicki, 'Une histoire du prix de Rome de Musique', Marie-Pauline Martin, 'Ouvrir le prix de Rome à la musique ou l'émulation des arts réunis: Enjeux et réalité d'une idée reepublicaine', and Julia Lu, 'Les origines du prix de Rome de musique: Genèse et fonctionnement sous l'Empire', all in Lu and Dratwicki (eds), *Le concours du prix de Rome de musique*, pp. 11–57, Eugène Bozza, 'This History of the "Prix de Rome"', *Hinrichsen's Musical Yearbook*, 7 (1952): pp. 487–94, and David Gilbert, 'Prix de Rome', in Stanley Sadie (ed.), *The New Grove Dictionary of Music and Musicians*, 2nd edition (London: Macmillan, 2001), Vol. 20, pp. 385–7.

[7]   The Académie des Beaux-Arts represents one of the five academies of the Institut de France, France's most important learned society. The other academies are: the Académie Française, the Académie des Inscriptions et Belles-Lettres, the Académie des Sciences, and the Académie des Sciences Morales et Politiques.

chosen by the specialist music jury. The competitors wrote the required works under strict examination conditions, over a period of several days, shut in the Palais de Fontainebleau in order to preclude the possibility of external help. Whilst at Fontainebleau they were provided with their own rooms with pianos in which to work and sleep, and where they were checked upon regularly, but shared meals and recreation. After reading the round 1 scores, the specialist music jury then chose up to six finalists to progress to round 2, the *jugement définitif*.

The round 2 candidates returned to their seclusion at the Palais de Fontainebleau for a further 30 days in order to compose a cantata setting of a second poem especially chosen by the Academicians. Paul Landormy and Joseph Loisel, in their entry on 'The Institut de France and the Prix de Rome' in the *Encyclopédie de la musique et dictionnaire du Conservatoire*, specified that the cantata text 'must provide material for a more or less developed air or solo for each role, for a duo and, if there are three roles, for a trio, not to mention the recitatives that link one scene to another'.[8] This offered scope for the musical tradition that the cantatas contained a prelude and several vocal numbers including soprano, tenor and bass solos, a duet and a trio. Landormy and Loisel commented that 'This music should be, as much as is possible, written for voices of contrasting register and be preceded by an instrumental introduction'.[9] After the 30 days of confinement at the Palais de Fontainebleau, and the official deposition of fair copies of the cantatas at the Académie des Beaux-Arts, the candidates had several weeks in which to prepare the presentation of their works (by vocal soloists to piano accompaniment) at the Institut de France, in the presence of the Academicians. Competitors were responsible for choosing their own singers and pianist, rehearsing their musicians and directing the final performance, although the influence and connections of their composition teachers may have often helped them in finding willing vocal soloists.

Auguste Mangeot gives a humorous account of the unfolding of the final round of the 1936 Prix de Rome at the Académie des Beaux-Arts:

> Au bout d'un mois de claustration, pendant lequel la plus grande distraction est d'aller lancer du pain aux carpes géantes, on boucle sa valise et chacun rassemble ses interprètes. Il en faut toujours trois: un soprano, un ténor et un baryton. Au début de juillet, les habits verts se rassemblent …. Ces neuf messieurs entendent les cantates, les discutent, puis émettent un premier vote.

---

[8]   'Cette scène devra donner matière à un air ou à un solo, plus ou moins développé, pour chaque personnage; à un duo et en outre à un trio, si la scène est à trois voix, ainsi que des récitatifs reliant les différents morceaux.' This, and later translations, when not indicated otherwise, are those of the authors. Paul Landormy and Joseph Loisel, 'L'Institut de France et le prix de Rome', in Albert Lavignac et Lionel de La Laurencie (eds), *Encyclopédie de la musique et dictionnaire du Conservatoire*, Part 2 (1920), p. 3491.

[9]   'La musique de cette scène, écrite, autant que possible, pour voix inégales, sera précédée d'une introduction instrumentale.' Landormy and Loisel, 'L'Institut de France et le prix de Rome', p. 3492.

Le lendemain "on remet ça", pour toutes les sections réunies, afin de ne pas priver les peintres, sculpteurs, architectes, graveurs et médaillistes de la passion brûlante de l'Emir pour l'épouse du Comte Renaud, engagé volontaire des Croisades. Au début, l'Institut est tout ouïe, mais quand l'émir revient pour la sixième fois, même s'il est frais rasé, on le trouve barbant.

Que voulez-vous! L'institut est une Institution qui veux ça et qui en revoudra jusqu'à l'extinction des siècles. Ensuite la foule des deux douzaines d'invités se disperse dans la cour ou va bouquiner le long des quais, et l'on vote. Au bout d'une petite demi-heure, on entend une voix qui, d'une fenêtre du premier étage crie, "Ça y est". Ça veut dire que le Tribunal rentre en séance.

[After a month of confinement during which the most amusing thing is to throw bread to the giant carp, [the candidates] pack their suitcases and gather their performers.[10] One invariably needs three: a soprano, a tenor and a baritone. At the beginning of July, the Academicians assemble in their green coats .... They listen to the cantatas, discuss them, and make an initial vote.

The following day, it is done all over again for all of the sections of the Institut, so that the painters, sculptors, architects, engravers and medallion-makers won't be deprived of the burning desire of the Emir for the wife of Count Renaud, a voluntary recruit for the Crusades. At the beginning, the Institut is all ears, but by the time the Emir returns in the sixth cantata, he's a crushing bore.

What do you expect? The Institut is an Institution. It wants things this way and will want them this way until the end of time. The twenty or so invited outsiders go to wait in the courtyard or read a book along the quays while the Academy votes. After about half an hour a voice calls '*Ca y est*' from a little window on the second floor. This means that the judges will announce their verdict.][11]

The Prix de Rome competition had a three-level award structure: *premier grand prix*, *premier second grand prix* and *deuxième second grand prix*. The judging of the competition was extremely complicated and involved two stages. First, there was the *jugement préparatoire* in which the specialist music jury proposed who they felt should be awarded the three prizes. All proposals made by the specialist

---

10   This 'distraction' was modified during the final round of the 1930 Prix de Rome when the five male candidates decided to throw to Fontainbleau's carp, not bread, but instead Yvonne Desportes, the only woman candidate that year. This hazing incident, possibly linked to another incident involving furniture broken by the six 1930 candidates, was denied to the press by the Fine Arts Minister of the time. Still, the minutes of the Academy meetings note that precautions were taken to prevent similar incidents the following year. The humorous photographs published in PHNS, p. 29, show nevertheless that the ambiance at Fontainebleau remained somewhat light-hearted.

11   Auguste Mangeot, 'Le prix de Rome', *Le monde musical* (31 July 1936): p. 208, as cited in Marguerite Sablonnière, *Le Conservatoire de Musique de Paris pendant l'entre-deux-guerres*, PhD thesis (École Nationale des Chartres, 1996), p. 209.

music jury, however, had to be ratified by the entire Académie de Beaux-Arts during the *jugement définitif* when all of the Academicians were entitled to vote.[12] Only the winning cantata of the *premier grand prix* was performed with a full orchestra on the day of the prize-giving. It was exceptionally unusual for a candidate to win the *premier grand prix* on their first attempt. Eventual winners of the *premier grand prix* usually participated at least twice, if not three to four times, working their way from admission to the second round to winning the two second prizes and then, perhaps, the *premier grand Prix de Rome*; this reality, with its parallel to the repeated attempts for receiving prizes in Conservatoire classes suggests that Messiaen was making progress from 1930 to 1931, and may have stood a fair chance of winning had he continued to try his luck in 1932 and 1933.[13] As with instrumental and written *concours* at the Conservatoire, candidates could only ever receive a higher prize in successive competitions, never an equal or lower one. It was generally acknowledged, moreover, that the awarding of a *premier second grand* prix heralded the candidate most likely to win the *premier grand prix* in the following year.

Messiaen and the Prix de Rome[14]

Messiaen entered the Prix de Rome competition for the first time in May 1930, at the end of his fourth year of composition studies at the Conservatoire, but before receiving his *premier prix* in composition on 23 June 1930. He would fail to get beyond the *concours d'essai*. Several of his compositions would soon be published by Durand, but apart from the Conservatoire orchestra's rather exceptional performance of his *Banquet eucharistique* in January 1930 and his first public Parisian organ recital in February 1930, Messiaen was still relatively unknown outside of Conservatoire circles. Potential candidates had to enrol at the Secretariat for the Académie de Beaux-Arts before 1 May, prove they were of

---

[12]   Usually the non-musicians deferred to and agreed with the first vote of their musician colleagues. Both the *jugement préparatoire* and the *jugement définitif* often involved several rounds of voting before decisions were reached regarding which candidates would be proposed for, or awarded, the prizes.

[13]   The experience of Messiaen's classmate from Paul Dukas's Paris Conservatoire composition class, Yvonne Desportes, may be taken as an instructive, classic example. She entered the Prix de Rome for the first time in 1929, when she did not get beyond the *concours d'essai*. In 1930 she progressed to the second round and won the *deuxième second grand prix*, in 1931 she won the *premier second grand prix* and in 1932 she obtained the *premier grand prix* itself. See Laura Hamer, *Musiciennes: Women Musicians in Interwar France*, PhD thesis (Cardiff University, 2009), pp. 162–8.

[14]   For a more extensive discussion of Messiaen's participation in the prix and an in-depth analysis of his choruses, see Christopher Brent Murray, *Le développement du langage musical d'Olivier Messiaen: Traditions, emprunts, expériences*, PhD thesis (Université-Lumière Lyon 2, 2010), pp. 192–226, 635–70.

French nationality (typically by providing an official copy of their birth certificate) and provide a letter of recommendation from 'a known artist' before being allowed to take part in the *concours*.[15] Most often, these 'known artists' were the candidate's composition or counterpoint teachers, usually former Prix de Rome recipients themselves.

Messiaen and his fellow candidates were sequestered at the Palais de Fontainebleau from 10 o'clock in the morning on Friday 2 May 1930 to compose 'a vocal fugue in at least four parts' on a subject by Georges Hüe and 'a chorus for at least four parts, with orchestra' upon a text composed of fragments from *La Sainte Bohème* by Théodore de Banville.[16] The fugues for the *concours d'essai*, written in the same academic style as those for the Conservatoire *concours* in fugue, were usually based on slightly longer subjects than those of the Conservatoire *concours* and thus generated much longer fugues. Still, Messiaen's fugues from 1930 and 1931 are quite traditional and present no remarkable variation from those of the other competitors and will not be discussed in the present chapter.[17] The sequestration in 1930 ended six days later, 8 May, at 10 o'clock in the morning. The musical composition chairs of the Academy judged the compositions at the Conservatoire at 9 o'clock in the morning on Saturday 10 May.[18]

Illustration 1.1 shows Paul Dukas's note approving the participation of five of the nine candidates for the competition, including Messiaen and also the eventual 1930 winner, Tony Aubin. Messiaen and Aubin were almost always mentioned together in the same breath during the 1930s and 1940s as the great hopes of their generation; however, although Aubin achieved considerable success as a composer, was appointed professor of composition at the Conservatoire in 1947 and elected to the Académie des Beaux-Arts in 1969, Messiaen has been better remembered by history.

Illustration 1.2 reproduces a ministerial document indicating the ages and teachers of the nine competitors for the *concours d'essai* of 1930. It is worth noting that Messiaen is the youngest of these candidates, has mistakenly been listed under his father's name (Pierre), and has submitted four letters of recommendation instead of the regular two. With the exception of Pierre Maillard, all nine candidates are presented as the students of Noël Gallon (then professor of fugue) and/or Paul Dukas. Table 1.1 shows the candidates for the Prix de Rome in 1930 and notes their placement. Pierre Maillard, Emile Marcelin, and Olivier Messiaen were eliminated after the first round.

---

[15] Landormy and Loisel, 'L'Institut de France et le prix de Rome', p. 3489.

[16] PHNS, p. 28. To give some generational context, Hüe received the Grand Prix de Rome in 1879, five years before Debussy received his Grand Prix de Rome in 1884.

[17] For an analysis and reproduction of Messiaen's fugues for the preliminary rounds of 1930 and 1931, see Murray, *Le développement du langage musical d'Olivier Messiaen*, pp. 116–18, 624–8.

[18] Archives Nationales, F[21] box 3531.

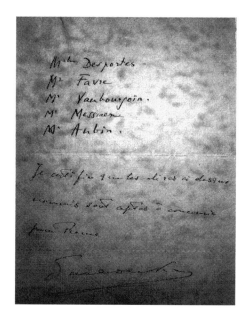

Illustration 1.1   Paul Dukas's letter of recommendation

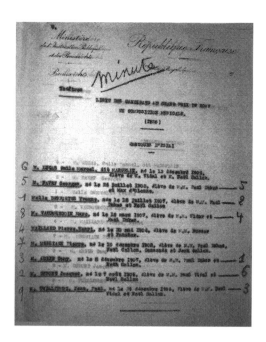

Illustration 1.2   Ministerial document listing the 1930 candidates for the Prix de Rome competition

Table 1.1   Placement of the candidates in the 1930 Prix de Rome competition

Candidate	Composition professor	Second round in 1930?	Highest Conservatoire composition prize	Highest Prix de Rome prize
Tony Aubin	Dukas	Yes	–	1ᵉʳ grand prix 1930
Yvonne Desportes	Dukas	Yes	1ᵉʳ prix 1931	1ᵉʳ grand prix 1932
Jacques Dupont	Vidal	Yes	2ᵉ prix 1931	1ᵉʳ grand prix 1931
Georges Favre	Dukas	Yes	–	–
Pierre Maillard	Büsser	No	–	–
Emile Marcelin	Vidal	No	2ᵉ prix 1933	2ᵉ grand prix 1932
Olivier Messiaen	Dukas	No	1ᵉʳ prix 1930	–
Marc Vaubourgoin	Dukas	Yes	–	1ᵉʳ second prix 1930
Jean Vuillermoz	Vidal	Yes	–	2ᵉ second prix 1932

Though the voting record of the Academicians has not survived, the study of the chorus manuscripts written by the eliminated candidates (conserved in the Médiathèque-Hector-Berlioz at the Paris Conservatoire) suggests a few reasons behind their choice. Marcelin atypically indicates his chorus 'in the style of an operetta chorus'; as one might expect, it does not have the serious tone of the other candidate's submissions. In Maillard's manuscript, the prosody and complexity of the counterpoint work against the text and would probably make it incomprehensible in a concert setting. His refrain ends with a repetition of the first line '*Avec nous l'on chante et l'on aime*' before jumping abruptly to a new texture. What is more, it is not certain that Maillard even turned in a fugue, for there is none to be found among the papers at the Conservatoire. Messiaen's chorus, as we shall see later in this chapter, is the only chorus of the nine submitted to tamper significantly with the order of the given text.

Although Messiaen did not proceed to the *concours définitif*, Gustave Samazeuilh's critical account of the 1930 Prix de Rome's final round includes an aside reminding the readers of the *Courrier musical* not to forget the two *premier prix* at that year's Conservatoire composition *concours*:

> Tandis que les lauréats savouraient, après tant d'émotions, la joie du succès, se prêtaient de la meilleure grâce du monde, dans la cours du palais Mazarin, aux félicitations de leurs parents et amis, aux assauts des photographes, aux interviews ... je ne pouvais m'empêcher de penser que deux des meilleures recrues de la classe de M. Dukas, M. Georges Hugon et M. Olivier Messiaen, titulaires du Prix de Composition, auteurs respectifs d'un Trio, d'un Quatuor à cordes, de Préludes pour piano, de Pièces pour orgue, où s'affirment des qualités du plus réconfortant augure, et qui semblent avoir tous deux, reçu des fées le présent précieux et rare d'une véritable nature, auraient eu aussi quelque droit

à ne pas être passés sous silence, victimes du huis clos réglementaire d'une épreuve qui ne demande pas, je vous en prie d'en être persuadés, une préparation moins sérieuse que celle du Prix de Rome.

[As the winners were savouring the joy of success after such a long and emotional trial, as they received congratulations from their friends and family in the courtyard of the Académie des Beaux-Arts and were assaulted by the journalists and photographers, I couldn't help but think of the two brightest talents from [Paul] Dukas' composition class: Georges Hugon and Olivier Messiaen. Both are recipients of the Composition Prize and the respective authors of a Trio and a *Quartet* for strings; *Préludes* for piano, and *Pièces* for organ, works which present the most reassuring and promising qualities. Both composers seem to have received the rare and precious gift of an individual nature and ought not to be overlooked in silence only because they participated in a [Conservatoire] *concours* that is closed to the public.[19] The reader should be reminded that the Conservatoire's composition *concours* is no less demanding than the Prix de Rome itself.][20]

Although it should be remembered that Samazeuilh was a close friend of Messiaen's composition teacher, Paul Dukas,[21] his statements about the difficulty of obtaining a Composition Prize at the Conservatoire were not exaggerated. In the 1920s the jury often decided to award no *premier prix* in composition at all. His observations underline the information noted in Table 1.1; unlike Messiaen, none of the recipients of prizes in the 1930 Prix de Rome had received a prize in composition.[22] His reference to Messiaen and Hugon as star pupils from Dukas's composition class is also significant as, in the late 1920s, Dukas strove to make attaining a *premier prix* in composition, as Messiaen did in 1930, as important as winning the Prix de Rome. This is in marked contrast to Widor's approach to the composition class, in which the clear focus was on preparing students to compete for the Prix de Rome. Significantly, perhaps, Messiaen did not often mention Widor when paying tribute to his Conservatoire teachers in later life.

---

[19]   Unlike the final round of the Prix de Rome.

[20]   Even the title of Samazeuilh's article indicates his scepticism concerning the Prix's usefulness in discerning the promising composers of the future: Gustave Samazeuilh, 'Le Concours de Rome 1930: Ce qu'il pourrait être, ce qu'il est' [The Concours de Rome 1930: What it could be, what it is], *Courrier musical* (15 July 1930): p. 477.

[21]   For more on this friendship, see Simon-Pierre Perret and Marie-Laure Ragot's biography, *Paul Dukas* (Paris: Fayard, 2007), especially pp. 64–6.

[22]   Unlike in the Prix de Rome competition, the best students entering the annual competitions in the various Conservatoire courses were awarded a *premier prix*, *second prix*, *premier accessit*, or *second accessit*. These 'prizes' were degrees of classification of accomplishment and not reserved for individuals – for example, there were 10 *premiers prix* among the women pianists in the *concours* of 1938.

By the time of the 1931 Prix de Rome competition, Messiaen was no longer a Conservatoire student, but he was still living at home with his father and younger brother. He worked as a cinema organist and as a substitute for Charles Quef on the organs at the Trinité.[23] Messiaen was among a dozen candidates in the first round, which opened on 30 April 1931 and was judged on 9 May. His choral setting of *La Jeunesse des vieux* [The Youth of the Elderly] by Catulle Mendès was judged sufficiently masterful to grant him a place among the six composers chosen for the final round, in the company of Henriette Roget, Henri Challan, Jacques Dupont, Émile Marcelin and Yvonne Desportes (Table 1.2).[24]

Table 1.2   Candidates for the 1931 Prix de Rome competition

Candidate	Composition professor	Second round in 1931?	Highest Conservatoire composition prize	Highest Prix de Rome prize
Henri Challan	Vidal/Büsser	No	–	1ᵉʳ second prix 1936
René Challan	Vidal/Büsser	Yes	1ᵉʳ prix 1935	1ᵉʳ grand prix 1935
Marcel Dautremer	Dukas	No	–	–
Yvonne Desportes	Dukas	Yes	1ᵉʳ prix 1931	1ᵉʳ grand prix 1932
Jacques Dupont	Vidal	Yes	2ᵉ prix 1931	1ᵉʳ grand prix 1931
Georges Favre	Dukas	No	–	–
Emile Marcelin	Vidal/Büsser	Yes	2ᵉ prix 1933	2ᵉ grand prix 1932
Olivier Messiaen	Dukas	Yes	1ᵉʳ prix 1930	–
Marcel Mirouze	Vidal/Büsser	No	1ᵉʳ prix 1934	–
Henriette Puig-Roget	Vidal/Büsser	Yes	2ᵉ prix 1932	1ᵉʳ second prix 1933
Marc Vaubourgoin	Dukas	No		1ᵉʳ second prix 1930
Jean Vuillermoz	Vidal	No	–	2ᵉ second prix 1932

The six candidates were shut away at Fontainebleau for 30 days between 15 May and 14 June 1931 to set the cantata text, *L'Ensorceleuse* [The Enchantress] by Paul Arosa.[25] The six cantatas were judged over two days: 3 July at the Conservatoire and 4 July at the Institut.

---

[23]   PHNS, pp. 48–52, chronicles the first performances of Messiaen's compositions during this period. A letter from Messiaen to his cousin Paul Mergier indicates that he played organs in two cinemas on the Place Pigalle between 1930 and 1931. BnF Mus. LA-MESSIAEN OLIVIER-2, Bobine 21574.

[24]   List of candidates for the 1931 Prix de Rome competition, *concours définitif*, Archives of the Institut de France, box 5E83.

[25]   Although officially chosen by *concours*, Arosa provided cantata texts for a number of years running: a list conserved at the Archives Nationales shows he was the author of

Arosa's text, set in Brittany, is reminiscent of the subject and atmosphere of Conservatoire director and member of the Institut, Henri Rabaud's 1924 one-act opera *L'appel de la mer* based on Rabaud's own translation and adaptation of Synge's *Riders to the Sea* (1904), with the mortal and menacing presence of the nearby sea and its appetite for local men.[26] *L'Ensorceleuse* is written for three characters: a young couple with a baby, Eva (soprano) and Yann (tenor), and a 70-year-old sailor, Joël (baritone).[27]

To summarize: It is evening, and the angelus can be heard ringing in the distance. Waiting in her seaside home for her husband to return, Eva laments the dangers of Yann's life as a sailor before singing a lullaby to her baby.[28] Yann comes home. To Eva's relief, he has decided not to set sail. Another tolling bell interrupts their ecstatic duet, throwing Yann into a dream-like state as he thinks of his sailing companions, soon to leave shore. He yearns to bid them farewell. Now singing of his love for the sea, Yann praises the mysterious forces of nature. Eva is distraught. Yann's *légende* is interrupted by the arrival of old sailor Joël, who has come to take Yann away. He explains that the fate of Yann's family has already been decided. Long ago, Joël promised Yann's father that he would make sure Yann did not betray the family pact with the sea. Defeated, Eva begins a prayer to both the sea and the Madonna. The two men join in and the prayer becomes a trio. The bell tolls again and the men leave. Eva collapses, in tears.[29]

---

the cantata texts for 1930, 1931, 1932 and 1933; the list ends in 1933 (Archives Nationales, AJ[37], box 386). The sheer number of texts provided by Arosa would seem to indicate that either the libretto *concours* was poorly advertised or that Arosa had an inside connection.

[26]   Henri Rabaud, *L'appel de la mer, drame lyrique en un acte sur la pièce* Riders to the Sea *de J. M. Synge*, French text and music by Henri Rabaud (Paris: Max Eschig & Cie, 1923).

[27]   Copies of the cantata text may be consulted in the archives of the Institute and in the Archives Nationales.

[28]   Two years later, in mid-March 1933, Messiaen made reference to his setting of the lullaby in a letter to the pianist Marcelle Soulage, noting that he'd rather not revive the lullaby from his cantata, remarking, 'It's too Fauré, too fake Breton' [C'est trop Fauré, trop faux-bréton]. Auction catalogue available at www.franceantiq.fr/slam/autographes, consulted in 2009.

[29]   In his review of the 1931 cantatas, Robert Brussel praises the inspirational potential of the new numbers that Arosa's text made possible while still respecting the 'outmoded genre' of the Prix de Rome cantata: 'a lullaby, and a sort of legend-vision that allows for the symphonic and vocal evocation of a marine cortège'. However, he continues: 'The only defect in Arosa's text is the fact that the conclusion is a scene without singing: Yann's departure represents a musical and poetic high point, but leaves a "temps froid" which in practical terms is detrimental to the immediate effect the scores.'

[Il y a là, mais sur un mode inhabituel au genre, tous les éléments, les ingrédients, pourrait-on dire, qui doivent entrer dans la composition d'une cantate destinée au concours de Rome ..., et cette fois, une berceuse et une sorte de vision légendaire qui permet d'évoquer à la fois vocalement et symphoniquement un cortège marin bien fait pour

The performers that Messiaen engaged and directed for the performance of his cantata were the soprano Georgette Mathieu, the tenor Louis Arnoult and the bass-baritone Louis Guénot, all members of the company at the Opéra Comique.[30] Messiaen himself played the two-hand piano reduction of the orchestral accompaniment, whereas some of the other candidates had chosen to reduce their scores for four hands.[31]

The specialist musical jury for the 1931 Prix de Rome consisted of the six elderly musician members of the Académie des Beaux-Arts not including the seventh, Charles-Marie Widor, who was the former teacher of some of the competitors: Alfred Bachelet (1864–1944), Alfred Bruneau (1857–1934), Georges Hüe (1858–1948), Gabriel Pierné (1863–1937), Henri Rabaud (1873–1949) and Gustave Charpentier (1860–1956), with André Bloch, Philippe Gaubert and Marcel Samuel-Rousseau serving as the three adjunct members.[32] The minutes of the Académie des Beaux-Arts reveal that Messiaen's cantata provoked no recorded commentary from them whatsoever. It is worth commenting in passing that the tone of the *procès verbaux*, which detail the judging of the Prix de Rome (in every discipline), is characterized

---

encourager l'inspiration du musicien. … Le seul défaut qui lui soit personnel réside dans le fait que sa conclusion comporte une scène muette: le départ de Yann qui, musicalement et poétiquement est fort à sa place, mais qui, pratiquement, crée hors de la scène un 'temps froid' préjudiciable à l'effet immédiat de chacune des partitions.] Robert Brussel, 'Le Concours de Rome', *Le Figaro* (6 July 1931): p. 5.

[30]   PHNS, p. 33. On p. 52, Hill and Simeone also indicate that Georgette Matthieu had given the first public performance of Messiaen's *La Mort du Nombre* under the direction of Nadia Boulanger just a few months earlier. There remains little trace of her career beyond these notes. Of the three singers cited, the tenor Louis Arnoult, not much older than Messiaen (born in 1901) had by far the most 'brilliant career' according to Jean Gourret and Jean Giraudeau. Arnoult was a contemporary of Messiaen's, studying at the Paris Conservatoire of Rabaud from 1924 to 1928 (Messiaen may very well have accompanied him as part of his duties in Estyle's accompaniment class). Arnoult debuted at the Opéra Comique the following year and at the Opéra de Paris in 1933, singing the role of Gonzalve in Ravel's *L'Heure espagnole*. He sang most frequently at the Opéra Comique, however, where he would remain part of the company until 1956. Messiaen's Joël, the Baritone-Bass Louis Guénot (1891–1968), while not as successful as Arnoult, nevertheless had a respectable career at the Opéra Comique where he sang from 1921 until at least 1939. Messiaen's choice may have been informed by the fact that Guénot was an original cast member for Rabaud's *L'appel de la mer*. K. J. Kutsch and Leo Riemens, *Großes Sängerlexikon, Vierte, erweitere und aktualisierte Auflage* (Munich: K. G. Saur, 2003), Vols 1, 3, pp. 157–8, 1878; Jean Gourret and Jean Giraudeau, *Dictionnaire des chanteurs de l'Opéra de Paris* (Paris: Albatros, 1982), pp. 153, 181.

[31]   As mentioned above, only the winning cantata was ever performed with a full orchestra, and only on the day of the official prize ceremony. It was normal practice for the piano reduction of the orchestral score to be used to accompany the cantatas at the *jugement définitif*.

[32]   The names of the jury are detailed in Paul Bertrand, 'Le Concours de Rome', *Le Ménestrel* (10 July 1931): p. 303.

by its extreme dryness; it would be much more noteworthy if recorded discussion of his entry did exist. The minutes for the *jugement préparatoire* typically record the votes cast for each category and detail which candidates the specialist jury intended to propose for the various prizes, with a very brief description of the outstanding attributes of their cantatas only. For example, the minutes for the 1931 *jugement préparatoire* record the result of months of labour and years of preparation in a few telegraphically expressed bland sentiments: 'It is decided to propose Mlle [Yvonne] Desportes for the *premier second grand prix* on the grounds: Cantata marked by a pretty musical sentiment, well managed, and well orchestrated.'[33] Likewise, the minutes for the *jugement définitif* merely recorded the votes cast by the entire Académie des Beaux-Arts for the three prizes and confirmed the names of the successful candidates.

The voting records for the 1931 competition do, however, reveal the presence of a few isolated supporters of Messiaen's cantata, though nobody seems to have thought his work was worthy of the *premier grand prix*. At the *jugement préparatoire*, his entry received one vote for the *deuxième second grand prix*, from the specialist musical jury.[34] The voting record reads as shown in Table 1.3.

Table 1.3   Voting record for the 1931 Prix de Rome competition

	First round	**Second round**	**Third round**
Mlle Roger obtains	3	3	3
M. Marcelin	2	3	1
M. Messiaen	1	–	–
M. Challan	2	3	1
Zéro [abstention]	1	–	–

In consequence, Mlle Roget will be proposed [to the non-musician Academicians] for the *deuxième second grand prix* with the commentary: <u>Musical cantata, pretty details.</u>*

* *'En conséquence*, Mlle Roget sera proposée pour le deuxième second grand prix avec le motif: <u>Cantate musicale, jolis détails.</u>'

At the *jugement définitif*, in which all the Academicians were entitled to vote, Messiaen obtained 6 votes for the *deuxième second grand prix* (against 13 for Henriette Roget, 3 for Émile Marcelin and 3 for René Challan). For the *premier second grand prix*, for which he had not even been considered at the *jugement préparatoire*, he took 3 votes (against 19 for Yvonne Desportes, 2 for Émile

---

[33]   'Il est décidé de proposer Mlle Y. Desportes pour le premier second grand prix avec ce motif: Cantate empreinte d'un joli sentiment musical, bien conduite et bien orchestrée.' Académie des Beaux-Arts, *Procès verbaux* (3 July 1931); Archives of the Institute de France.
[34]   Ibid.

Marcelin and 1 abstention).[35] The *premier grand prix* was eventually awarded to Jacques Dupont (now a forgotten figure), with Yvonne Desportes receiving the *premier second grand prix* and Henriette Roget the *deuxième second grand prix*.[36] The support for Messiaen divulged by the voting records is significant as it reveals that espousal for his music probably came from the non-musician Academicians, as it was at the *jugement définitif* that his cantata attracted the most votes (although it is also possible that some of the musical members may have revised their opinions after having heard the entries performed on the day of the *jugement définitif*).

It was not only amongst several of the Academicians that Messiaen won approval at the 1931 competition, as a number of the critics from the specialist music press present at the *jugement définitif* commented positively on his cantata (although the critics from the daily newspapers, including *Le Figaro*, *Le Monde* and *Le Matin* did not mention his entry). Paul Bertrand, the critic who covered the Prix de Rome competition for *Le Ménestrel* throughout the entire interwar period, praised Messiaen's talents and, whilst cautioning that he felt that dramatic music was not his forte, urged readers to take note of his name. Bertrand's account also makes valuable reference to the nature of Messiaen's musical writing, a tantalizing suggestion, at least until the day his heirs make the score of his cantata available for study:

> S'il est loin d'avoir écrit la meilleure cantate, M. Messiaen a néanmoins permis de démêler en lui une nature musicale hors pair. Seul, il a su, par l'âpreté, la grandeur et l'ampleur émouvantes de son prélude, créer quelque chose de l'atmosphère qui s'imposait, trouver un accent d'angoisse profonde pour l'appel de l'Eva et une impression déchirante pour l'adieu final. Et quel curieux développement du duo, avec ses descentes en quintes, et de la prière, avec la montée uniforme de ses trois accords, auxquels se superpose un dessin chromatique descendant!
>
> Mais, visiblement, M. Messiaen, qu'anime une vie intérieure intense, n'est plus l'aise dès qu'entre en jeu le conflit des faits et le choc des sentiments humains, et c'est pourquoi sa cantate donne une impression de déséquilibre un peu chaotique, non exempt d'ailleurs de monotonie. Néanmoins, retenons son

---

[35]   Académie des Beaux-Arts, *Procès verbaux* (4 July 1931); Archives of the Institute de France.

[36]   Roget did not win the 1932 Prix de Rome competition, as Hill and Simeone erroneously state (PHNS, p. 33). The 1932 competition was won by Yvonne Desportes; Académie des Beaux-Arts, *Procès verbaux* (2 July 1932); Archives of the Institute de France. The specialist music jury did, in fact, propose to award the *premier grand prix* to Roget at the 1934 *jugement préparatoire* (Académie des Beaux-Arts, *Procès verbaux*, 29 June 1934), although this decision was overturned at the *jugement définitif* (Académie des Beaux-Arts, *Procès verbaux*, 30 June 1934). The 1934 *premier grand prix* of the Prix de Rome was eventually awarded to the competition newcomer Eugène Bozza. See Laura Hamer, *Musiciennes: Women Musicians in Interwar France*, pp. 168–72.

nom. Il est douteux qu'il illustre la musique dramatique, mais je serais surpris qu'il ne se plaçât pas en haut rang dans la musique pure.

[Though he is far from having written the best cantata, it was nevertheless possible to sort out that he has an incomparably musical nature. He alone, through the sharpness, grandeur and volume of his prelude, managed to evoke something of the atmosphere that was called for. He also found just the right note of profound anguish for Eva's calls and the heart-breaking impression needed for the final adieu. And what a curious development in the duet, with its descending fifths, and in the prayer, with the uniform rising of those three chords, over which were superposed a chromatic descending line!

Still, though Messiaen clearly has an intense inner life, he is not at ease when conflicting actions and the clash of human sentiment come into play. This is why his cantata gave a certain impression of slightly chaotic imbalance that was not without some monotonous moments. Still, one should remember his name. Though it is unlikely that he will make a career writing music for the stage, I would not at all be surprised if he makes a name for himself in concert music.][37]

In *Le courrier musical*, Samazeuilh also predicted that Messiaen would be an important composer to watch and expressed outrage that he had not received a prize, reminding his readers once again that Messiaen had received the Composition Prize at the Conservatoire the previous year, ever emphasizing the equally prestigious nature of this honour. Samazeuilh's critique also provides interesting information about the elements essential to a 'winning' Prix de Rome cantata:

Mais il m'est impossible de souscrire à la sévérité du jugement de l'Institut, refusant toute récompense à M. Olivier Messiaen, élève de Paul Dukas, la nature la plus musicale du concours, la seule qui, à mon sens, ait donné à sa composition une construction poétique, qui y ait prouvé – en particulier dans son duo aux exquises inflexions qui eussent enchanté Emmanuel Chabrier – un don inventif de qualité rare. Titulaire du Prix de Composition en 1930, autrement significatif, sinon aussi renommé que le Concours de Rome, auteur de pièces d'orchestre, de chant et de piano, déjà justement appréciées des auditeurs de Concerts-Straram, de la Société Nationale et de la S.I.M. – ce qui n'a peut-être pas servi sa cause ici – il est possible que M. Messiaen soit peu familiarisé avec les roueries du métier de fabricant de cantates, que l'instrumentation, particulièrement délicate à réaliser, des dessins mouvants et complexes qu'il affectionne présente des imperfections, qu'il ait montré un insuffisant souci des oppositions tranchées, par quoi s'affirme, paraît-il, en ces milieux le futur homme de théâtre. Après comme avant le Concours de Rome 1931, M. Olivier Messiaen n'en reste pas moins un des meilleurs espoirs de sa génération, et un aussi honorable échec ne doit que l'encourager dans son travail, et lui assurer la sympathie de tous.

---

[37]   Bertrand, 'Le Concours de Rome': p. 304.

[I am unable to second the severity of the Institut's decision to deny recognition to M. Olivier Messiaen, a student of M. Paul Dukas. He has the most musical nature of all of the candidates and is the only candidate, in my opinion, to have given his composition a poetic structure. Messiaen showed his rare gift for invention in his duet in particular, where the exquisite inflections would have enchanted Emmanuel Chabrier. As a recipient of the Composition Prize in 1930 (an award which is equally significant, though not as renowned as the Concours de Rome), and as the author of works for orchestra and for voice and piano which have already been deservedly well-received by the audiences of the Straram Concerts, the *Société Nationale* and the S[*ociété*] I[*nternationale de*] M[*usique*] (perhaps more hindrance than help in the present situation) it is possible that M. Messiaen remains nevertheless unfamiliar with the tricks of the trade of cantata-makers, that the orchestration of the complex and shifting textures he so loves to create, and which is so difficult to realize, was imperfect. It is possible that he did not pay enough attention to the clearly defined oppositions, that attest in these circles to a future man of the theatre. After the Concours de Rome of 1931, just as before, M. Olivier Messiaen remains one of the greatest hopes of his generation. Such an honourable failure should serve both the general sympathy for his cause and to encourage him in his future work.][38]

Hill and Simeone quote a letter to Langlais of 3 August 1931 in which Messiaen himself stoically asserted that: 'My cantata was good as music, but inferior as theatre. So the judgment was very fair.'[39]

Messiaen's Renunciation of the Prix de Rome

The critics' words of encouragement fell upon deaf ears, however, as Messiaen never re-entered the Prix de Rome competition after 1931. (The opinions of the critics who were annually invited to attend the *jugement définitif* can be taken as a useful barometer of the Prix de Rome as they were in a good position to comment upon the relative talents of the candidates who regularly took part.) Perhaps even more encouraging was the small-scale support that Messiaen had gained amongst the members of the Academy. If Messiaen had continued to compete it is possible that this support may have grown large enough in subsequent years for him to win prizes. As already mentioned, and as Messiaen would have been fully cognizant, it was extremely rare for anyone to win the Prix de Rome outright on the first attempt. It generally took a composer several attempts, and determination to win

---

[38]   Gustave Samazeuilh, 'Le Prix de Rome', *Le courrier musical*, 15 July 1931: p. 461. Samazeuilh echoes Robert Brussel's consideration of Messiaen as 'one of the most remarkable musicians of his generation'. Brussel was also part of Dukas and Samazeuilh's circle of friends. Robert Brussel, 'Le Concours de Rome': p. 5.

[39]   Messiaen, letter to Langlais (3 August 1931); cited in PHNS, p. 34.

could represent a serious time commitment, often several years. If Messiaen had continued to compete, this long-term commitment would have had a number of serious consequences for his personal life.

It appears, however, that Messiaen had already renounced his hopes of winning the competition by August 1931. In early August 1931, the parish priest of the Trinité, Curé Hemmer, wrote Messiaen a letter that detailed certain reservations that he had about appointing him organist. Messiaen's interest in the Prix de Rome was a serious one:

> I am led to believe by various conversations about you, that you will be competing in the Prix de Rome and that in the highly desirable event of your winning, you would be away from Paris for two or even three years. I find it entirely natural that you should want to compete for the Prix de Rome: it would, I think, have a considerable impact on your artistic career, and the stay in Rome would enrich your artistic culture in general and the quality of your education. I am thus far from blaming you, or wanting to dissuade you, for your very worthy ambition. But success in that would again make your work at our *grand orgue* very intermittent.[40]

Messiaen responded to this concern in a letter dated 8 August 1931 in language that categorically surrendered his Prix de Rome ambitions in favour of the post at the Trinité: 'This objection cancels itself out: if I obtain the post at the Trinité, I will renounce the Prix de Rome.'[41] The evidence would appear unequivocal: measured against the honour and prestige of being appointed organist at a church that housed one of the finest (Cavaillé-Coll) organs in the world, not to mention the opportunity to employ his musical talents in the service of his devout Roman Catholic faith, the potential benefits of winning the Prix de Rome were, to Messiaen, negligible.

Messiaen's appointment as *titulaire* at the Trinité in September 1931, a post that he held for over 60 years, heralded the beginning of a very happy period in his life. It was marked by romantic as well as professional contentment and brought additional reasons for him to desist with the Prix de Rome, as 1932 was the year

---

[40]   Curé Hemmer, letter to Messiaen (undated, early August 1931); cited in Simeone, 'Chez Messiaen, tout est prière': p. 38. The other objections to appointing Messiaen that Curé Hemmer raised in his letter were the fact that Messiaen had not yet completed his military service (the undertaking of which may also have taken him away from away from Paris) and the general congregation's dislike of Messiaen's improvisations.

[41]   Messiaen, letter to Curé Hemmer (8 August 1931); cited in Simeone, 'Chez Messiaen, tout est prière': 42. Messiaen further assured the Curé that he would arrange to do his military service in Paris (when he eventually completed this he received special dispensation to undertake his duties as organist at the Trinité on Sundays). With regards to his modern style, he asserted: 'Do not think I am incapable of doing things that are not dissonant .... I can also be well-behaved and classical in style. I will adopt this and thus both you and the parishioners will be satisfied.' Ibid.

of his first marriage, to Claire Delbos. How and when Messiaen met Delbos, a student at the Schola Cantorum, remains a mystery, as they seemed to have kept their courtship a secret, but they married at the Église de Saint-Louis-en-l'Île on 22 June 1932. Messiaen's marriage precluded him from competing for the Prix de Rome after 1932, due to the single-status rule.

The Chorus of 1930: Messiaen's Setting of *La Sainte Bohème*[42]

Now that we have sketched the context and circumstances of Messiaen's involvement in the *concours de Rome*, let's turn to the surviving choruses from these competitions and consider their place in comparison to Messiaen's published works of the same period.[43] Unfortunately, due to complications in the succession of Messiaen's estate, it is currently not possible to consider Messiaen's cantata for the 1931 *concours définitif* (*L'Ensorceleuse*), which it is hoped will ultimately be found among the composer's papers. This said, the following discussion of his choral settings for the two *concours d'essais* sheds some light upon the musical style of his competition entries.

Théodore de Banville (1823–91) wrote *La Sainte Bohème* (the chorus text chosen for 1930) in 1847 and it was later published in his *Odes funambulesques*. This anacreontic ode to the Dionysian joys of bohemian life bears an epigraph borrowed from the end of George Sand's 1838 novel, *La dernière Aldini*, whose characters, according to Françoise Massardier-Kenney, were based on Franz Liszt and the Comtesse d'Agoult: 'he sang with a thundering voice to which we responded in chorus: *Vive la Bohème*'.[44] Banville's text can consequently be understood as the reworking of the ode sung by Sand's hero, the Venetian opera singer, Lélio, at the end of the novel. The musical connections to Sand's novel may have played into the Académie's choice, but Banville's text was too long for a preliminary round chorus and was accordingly cut. Conveniently, the verses with references to carousing and drink, the freeing of slaves and the glorification of Mother Nature over a Christian God were the ones to get the axe. Amusingly enough, this romanticized ode to the liberties of the artist's life was censored and then used as fodder for an academic and conformist state-sponsored competition.

Banville's ode is composed of five verses of ten octosyllabic lines following an ABBACCDEED rhyme scheme. The verses are separated from each other by

---

[42]   More detailed analyses of both choruses can be found in Murray, *Le développement du langage musical d'Olivier Messiaen*, pp. 205–26.

[43]   The manuscripts of Messiaen's choruses and fugues may be consulted at the Médiathèque-Hector-Berlioz of the Paris Conservatoire under D 8038 (1930) and D 8038 (1931).

[44]   'il chanta d'une voix tonnante à laquelle nous répondîmes en chœur: Vive la Bohème!' Françoise Massardier-Kenney, *Gender in the Fiction of George Sand* (Amsterdam, Rodopi, 1999), pp. 54–61.

a four-line refrain with an enclosed rhyme scheme that mirrors the beginning and end of the verses. The complete ode (plus a basic literal translation from the original French by Christopher Brent Murray) is presented below, with the Académie's cuts in italics.

La Sainte Bohème

Par le chemin des vers luisants,
De gais amis à l'âme fière
Passent aux bords de la rivière
Avec des filles de seize ans.
Beaux de tournure et de visage,
Ils ravissent le paysage
De leurs vêtements irisés
Comme de vertes demoiselles,
Et ce refrain, qui bat des ailes,
Se mêle au vol de leurs baisers:

Avec nous l'on chante et l'on aime,
Nous sommes frères des oiseaux.
Croissez, grands lys, chantez, ruisseaux,
Et vive la sainte Bohème!

Fronts hâlés par l'été vermeil,
Salut, bohèmes en délire!
Fils du ciseau, fils de la lyre,
Prunelles pleines de soleil!
L'aîné de notre race antique
C'est toi, vagabond de l'Attique,
Fou qui vécus sans feu ni lieu,
Ivre de vin et de génie,
Le front tout barbouillé de lie
Et parfumé du sang d'un dieu!

Avec nous l'on chante et l'on aime,
Nous sommes frères des oiseaux,
Croissez, grands lys, chantez, ruisseaux,
Et vive la sainte Bohème!

Pour orner les fouillis charmants
De vos tresses aventureuses,
Dites, les pâles amoureuses,
Faut-il des lys de diamants?
Si nous manquons des pierreries
Pour parer de flammes fleuries
Ces flots couleur d'or et de miel,
Nous irons, voyageurs étranges,
Jusque sous les talons des anges,
Décrocher les astres du ciel!

Blessed Bohemia

By the glowworm's path,
Gay friends with proud souls
Pass along the riverbank
With sixteen-year-old girls.
Beautiful figures and faces
They ravish the landscape
In their iridescent clothes
Like green damsels,
And this refrain, beating its wings,
Melds with their kisses' flight:

With us, it's singing and loving,
We are brothers of the birds.
Grow, great lilies, sing, brooks,
And long live blessed Bohemia!

Foreheads tanned by the vermillion summer,
Greetings, delirious bohemians!
Son of the chisel, son of the lyre,
Pupils full of sunlight!
The eldest of our ancient race
Is you, the vagabond of Attica,
Madly living without hearth or home,
Drunk on wine and genius,
Forehead smeared with dregs
and perfumed with a god's blood!

With us, it's singing and loving,
We are brothers of the birds
Grow, great lilies, sing, brooks,
And long live blessed Bohemia!

To decorate the charming jumble
Of your adventurous tresses,
Say, pale lovers,
Are diamond lilies necessary?
If we lack gems
To dress the flowery flames
Waves the color of gold and honey,
We'll go, strange voyagers,
To the angels' heels,
And unhook the stars from the sky!

Avec nous l'on chante et l'on aime,	With us, it's singing and loving,
Nous sommes frères des oiseaux.	We are brothers of the birds.
Croissez, grands lys, chantez, ruisseaux,	Grow, great lilies, sing, brooks,
Et vive la sainte Bohème!	And long live blessed Bohemia!

Buvons au problème inconnu,	*Let's drink to the unknown question,*
Et buvons à la beauté blonde,	*And drink to blond beauty,*
Et, comme les jardins du monde,	*And, like the gardens of the world,*
Donnons tous au premier venu!	*Give everything to the first comer!*
Un jour nous verrons les esclaves	*One day we'll see the slaves*
Sourire à leurs vieilles entraves,	*Smile at their former shackles,*
Et, les bras enfin déliés,	*And, with their arms finally untied,*
L'univers couronné de roses,	*The universe crowned with roses,*
Dans la sérénité des choses	*In the serenity of things*
Boire aux dieux réconciliés!	*Drink to the reconciled gods!*

Avec nous l'on chante et l'on aime,	*With us, it's singing and loving,*
Nous sommes frères des oiseaux.	*We are brothers of the birds.*
Croissez, grands lys, chantez, ruisseaux,	*Grow, great lilies, sing, brooks,*
Et vive la sainte Bohème!	*And long live blessed Bohemia!*

Nous qui n'avons pas peur de Dieu	*We, who are not afraid of God*
Comme l'égoïste en démence,	*Like the mad and selfish,*
Au-dessus de la ville immense	*Above the immense town*
Regardons gaîment le ciel bleu!	*Gaily watch the blue sky!*
Nous mourrons! mais, ô souveraine!	*We will die! But, O sovereign!*
Ô mère! ô nature sereine!	*O mother! O serene nature!*
Que glorifiaient tous nos sens,	*Glorifying all of our senses,*
Tu prendras nos cendres inertes	*You'll take our dead ashes*
Pour en faire des forêts vertes	*To make green forests*
Et des bouquets resplendissants!	*And resplendent bouquets!*

Avec nous l'on chante et l'on aime,	*With us, it's singing and loving,*
Nous sommes frères des oiseaux.	*We are brothers of the birds.*
Croissez, grands lys, chantez, ruisseaux,	*Grow, great lilies, sing, brooks,*
Et vive la sainte Bohème!	*And long live blessed Bohemia!*

Unlike his fellow competitors, Messiaen took the chance of further manipulating Banville's text, preferring to begin with the refrain instead of the first verse and effectively replacing the Strophe–Refrain–Strophe–Refrain (SRSR) form implied by the Institut's proposed text with a more symmetrical RSRSR (Table 1.4). It is possible that the jury did not appreciate his taking this liberty. In 1908, Nadia Boulanger had created a scandal by daring to challenge the Academy's authority in the *concours d'essai* when she produced an instrumental, rather than a vocal, fugue on the subject provided by Saint-Saëns, who was enraged by her boldness (and her implicit criticism of his fugal technique). Although she was allowed to progress to the *concours définitif* and was awarded the *deuxième second grand*

Table 1.4   Formal structure of Olivier Messiaen's *La Sainte Bohème*

Refrain	Strophe 1			Refrain	Strophe 2			Refrain
Allegro vivo	Allegretto			Allegro vivo	Allegretto			Allegro vivo
bars 1–29	30–48	49–64	65–77	78–106	107–122	123–145	146–168	169–209
Tutti SATB	Soprano Solo	Trio SSA	Trio SSA	Tutti SATB	Tenor Solo	Tutti SATB	Tutti SATB	Tutti SATB
E	B Mixolydian	F♯ Dorian	B Mixolydian	E	A♭ Mixolydian	Frequent modulations, fugatos		E

prix, she never achieved her ultimate goal of winning the *premier grand prix*, becoming instead a stark warning of the perils of disregarding the Académie's instructions.[45] The comparison of the competitors' various settings allows us to posit the implicit practices in this institutional genre of chorus-writing that had been instilled in the Conservatoire's latest crop of young composers. Each competitor's chorus includes a passage for solo tenor or solo soprano, not to mention a couplet or two set in a lightly contrapuntal fugato – Messiaen's chorus is no exception. Whereas Messiaen set up an opposition between the soprano solo in the first verse and the tenor solo in the second verse, Yvonne Desportes chose to write a true duet between soprano and tenor soloists, and Georges Favre favoured an alternation between tenor and bass soloists, a choice that seems most plausible due to the text's masculine, fraternizing tone. In the refrain, all of the competitors, like Messiaen, chose to employ a tutti orchestral texture and the complete SATB chorus singing homophonically.

Originally, Messiaen's manuscript seems to have counted some 32 pages, numbered in the composer's hand, but the 14th page is now missing. Happily, this hole (bars 85–92) occurs in the middle of the first repetition of the refrain and is easily reconstructed, since the music and orchestration on either side of this eight-bar lacuna are identical to the corresponding passages in the other iterations of the refrain. We may therefore assume that bars 85–92 are the same as bars 8–14.

Messiaen's setting of the refrain is a closed form of some 30 bars beginning and ending in E major, and firmly established by a double pedal on E and B in the first six bars. The refrain's four phrases correspond to the four lines of text, with the sopranos and tenors singing in octaves, the altos completing the harmony on common tones and the basses punctuating the ends of phrases. String tremolos and

---

trills in the winds activate the orchestral texture, lending density and intensity to the exclamation 'Vive la sainte Bohème' (Example 1.1).

Example 1.1   Harmonic reduction of the refrain from Messiaen's setting of *La Sainte Bohème*, bars 20–25

Throughout his setting, Messiaen avoids traditional tonic–dominant relationships and employs a number of other techniques typical of Debussy's 'drowning of tonality': suppression of the leading note, the use of the major chord on the seventh degree, exceptional resolutions for the dominant seventh chord, and extended dominant harmonies. From the opening, the tonal centre of E is blurred by a *balancement* between the fifths E–B and F♯–C♯. This rocking melodic movement between the first and second and fifth and sixth scale degrees anticipates the added seconds and sixths that surface later in the chorus, not to mention the development of a number of melodic elements based on the rocking motion.

Example 1.2 illustrates the development of a certain number of melodic motifs developed from the first chord, E major, with both an added second and sixth, a chord that also contains the shifting parallel fifths. In this figure, motivic accumulation and development can be resumed as B → D → E → G. Whereas the music of the refrain departs from and returns to a tonal centre of E, the strophes are far more modal and modulatory. Each of the first strophe's three parts begins with a stable passage in a single mode before departing to new territories through chromatic modulation. Despite using an abundance of dominant harmonies, Messiaen carefully avoids any semblance of a perfect cadence.

In the second strophe, Messiaen plays further with the binary and ternary divisions of different lengths of time, occasionally dividing each measure and beat in both two and three. The first phrase of the second strophe provides a clear example of such writing (Example 1.3). The duplets in the tenor solo melody and woodwinds are superposed over the cello's quavers; in a sense, this passage presents the superposition of $\frac{2}{4}$, $\frac{3}{4}$, and $\frac{6}{8}$ meters. Curiously, similar explorations of hemiola are found in a number of other competitors' choruses from 1930.

Other moments of note include a monodic passage for *a cappella* chorus at the end of the second strophe (bars 159–163) that anticipates the tutti monodies in octaves heard in the *Fantaisie* for violin and piano and allusions to certain passages of the *Trois Petites Liturgies* and the 'Danse de la fureur, pour les sept trompettes' from the *Quatuor pour la fin du Temps*.

Example 1.2   Melodic development in Messiaen's setting of *La Sainte Bohème*

Example 1.3   Mixture of duple and triple pulsation in Messiaen's *La Sainte Bohème* (tenor solo, bars 109–112)

A Reference to *Pelléas et Mélisande*

According to Marie-Louise Langlais, Messiaen is remembered by his classmate Rachel Brunschwig as having improvised in Dupré's organ class from 'little pieces of numbered paper upon which melodic formulas, modal turns and chord progressions, some of which were collected from Debussy's music'.[46] In *Technique* Messiaen confirms that his borrowing from Debussy began during his studies at the Conservatoire, showing in his examples 224–226 how a fragment of *Pelléas et Mélisande* was transformed to become a theme from the prelude 'Un reflet dans le vent' written in 1928 or 1929. It is not surprising, then, to hear Debussy-inflected writing in *La Sainte Bohème*, as it was composed the following year. Going beyond simple influence, it would seem that Messiaen knew Debussy's opera sufficiently well to reproduce certain passages during the sequestration of the 1930 preliminary round of the Prix de Rome without needing to consult a score. One sequence in particular, heard four times in the second strophe of Messiaen's setting, seems to have been consciously borrowed from *Pelléas et Mélisande*. This sudden rising motion and acceleration of the harmonic rhythm occurs in the tower scene of the third act, at the moment when Mélisande's hair falls from the tower and envelops Pelléas, who then deliriously winds it about his face and the surrounding vegetation: 'Je les tiens dans les mains, je les tiens dans la bouche... je les tiens dans les bras, je les mets autour de mon cou... Je n'ai jamais vu de cheveux comme les tiens, Mélisande' [I hold it my hands, I put in my mouth... I hold it in my arms, I wrap it around my neck... I've never seen hair like yours, Mélisande!...]. It hardly seems coincidental that Messiaen evokes this music at pitch when setting Banville's text on 'tresses aventureuses … flots couleur d'or et de miel' [adventurous tresses streams the colour of gold and honey]. Messiaen even seems to imitate the descending motive that follows Debussy's sequence (Example 1.4).

Example 1.4   Messiaen's use of music from the *Pelléas and Mélisande* 'hair scene'

---

[46]   Marie-Louise Jaquet-Langlais, *Jean Langlais: Ombre et lumière* (Paris: Combre, 1995), p. 51.

It should be added that this sequence is not a passing reference for Messiaen, for this academic, four-voice setting of Debussy's music is also found in Messiaen's four-part realization of lesson 20 from his *Vingt leçons d'harmonie*, as well as among his *Formules d'harmonie*, a series of four-part harmony examples given by Messiaen to students in his harmony class and conserved in Pierre Boulez's archives.[47] In short, Messiaen uses the same borrowed fragment in multiple contexts: an academic chorus, a harmony lesson and in examples for his harmony class.[48]

This sequence contains an ascending octatonic scale, and is indeed built around the octatonic collection, a collection that Messiaen would ultimately appropriate as his second mode of limited transposition. That said, the harmonies and progressions employed by Messiaen in *La Sainte Bohème* are generally less complex than those used in his first published compositions, written just before his first Prix de Rome chorus. This suggests that Messiaen, while not entirely forsaking his signature sound, tempered his modal language to conform to the expectations of the *concours*. The octatonic collection would again play a central role in the formal organization of Messiaen's Prix de Rome chorus for 1931, *La Jeunesse des vieux*.

The Chorus of 1931: Messiaen's Setting of *La Jeunesse des vieux*

On the morning of 30 April 1931, the competitors for the preliminary round received an abridged version of Catulle Mendès's (1841–1909) poem *La Jeunesse des vieux*, published in the 1895 collection *La Grive des vignes*. A Parnassian like Banville, Mendès's poetry and libretti were set to music by French composers such as Bizet, Bruneau, Chabrier, Debussy, Massenet, Messager and Satie. Although this text on the ephemeral joy of spring's return, which opens 'O, young men! You can hardly know our joy', seems an apt choice for the elderly members of the Institut, it is an unlikely subject for the young competitors, three of whom were young women. Again, passages had to be cut. This time the three quatrains dealing with the sensations of the young and the 'never-ending summer' of their amorous interest, were the ones to get the axe, leaving a text that deals exclusively with the springtime sensations of the elderly (reproduced below, with a basic literal translation by Christopher Brent Murray).

La Jeunesse des Vieux	The Youth of the Elderly
Ô jeunes hommes! notre joie,	O young men! Our joy
Vous ne la connaissez point,	You can hardly know,
De voir, comme un bouton rougeoie,	At seeing, like a reddening bud,
Le printemps qui point.	The coming spring.

---

[47] Conserved at the Sacher Stiftung in Basel, Switzerland, Mappe A 2a, 1.

[48] A number of other examples of Messiaen's reuse of Debussy's music will be addressed in a forthcoming book by Yves Balmer, Thomas Lacôte and Christopher Brent Murray dedicated to Messiaen's technique of thematic borrowing.

Quand le soleil, tout jeune, dore
Les toits hier pluvieux,
Une aube de jeunesse encore
Rit au cœur des vieux.

Il ranime, par la fenêtre
Que l'on se hâte d'ouvrir,
Du frisson de ce qui va naître
Ce qui va mourir;

Lui, par qui tant de fleurs écloses
Enchanteront les pourpris
Il évoque d'anciennes roses
À nos fronts flétris,

Et, quand l'or de sa gloire abonde,
Aux miroirs que nous fuyions
Nous fait la chevelure blonde
Avec ses rayons.

C'est pour nous qu'il chasse les brumes!
En l'hiver blanc de glaçons
Vous mêlez aux toux de nos rhumes
Des bruits des chansons;

Qu'il vente ou qu'il neige, n'importe!
Sans trêve, en vos jeunes cœurs,
Triomphe l'ardeur douce et forte
Des juillets vainqueurs;

Vous connaissez, lèvres ignées,
Les baisers jamais finis,
Même quand les fleurs sont fanées
Et vides les nids.

À ceux que l'hiver ensommeille
Il faut l'avril de retour
Pour qu'en eux s'ouvre, fleur vermeille
L'amour de l'amour.

Mais, alors, la douceur est telle
D'être si rare, on la sent
Si divine d'être mortelle
Presque en renaissant,

Que notre âme illusionnée
Ne voudrait pas changer pour
Votre été de toute l'année
Nos printemps d'un jour!

When the young sun gilds
The rainy roofs of yesterday,
The dawn of youth
Laughs anew in the hearts of the elderly.

It revives, through the window
We hasten to open,
A shiver of what will be born
Of what will die;

It, through so many blooming flowers
Will enchant the courtyards
It evokes bygone roses
To our withered brows,

And when the gold of its glory abounds,
In the mirrors from which we flee
It turns our hair blond
With its rays.

For us, it chases away the mists!
In the icy, white winter
You blend with the coughing of our colds
The noises of songs;

What does it matter if it blows or snows!
Without respite, in your young hearts
Triumphs the sweet and strong ardor
Of victorious Julys;

You know ignited lips,
Unending kisses,
Even when the flowers have faded
And the nests gone empty.

For those whom the winter makes slumber
The return of April is necessary
To open within them the vermillion flower
Of the love of love.

And, then, the sweetness is such
In being so rare, one feels it
So divine for its being mortal
Almost like being reborn,

That our deluded soul
Wouldn't exchange
Your year-long summer
For our one-day spring!

Messiaen's setting of *La Jeunesse des vieux* is far clearer and more respectful of the given text than that of *La Sainte Bohème* and is naturally structured around the eight quatrains he was given for his task. After a slow two-bar introductory melody in the cellos, a cell from which later harmonies and melodies are generated, the choir, divided in five parts, sings the first two quatrains accompanied by the entire orchestra. The same music returns at the end of the chorus, followed by a brief coda that repeats the opening cello melody. The central section, teeming with dominant ninth chords, can be clearly divided into four parts, each of which corresponds to the text of a quatrain (Table 1.5).

Table 1.5   Formal structure of Olivier Messiaen's *La Jeunesse des vieux*

A			B				A	
Intro	Quatrains 1–2	Trans.	Quatrain 3	Quatrain 4	Quatrain 5	Quatrain 6	Quatrains 7–8	Coda
Lent	*Bien modéré*	*Lent*	*Modéré*				*Bien modéré*	*Lent*
bars 1–2	3–21	22–23	24–32 a	33–44 b	45–53 a′	54–66 c	67–87	88–91
Cellos	tutti	cellos	soprano solo	quartet SSAA		tenor solo	tutti	cellos
A♭ with octatonic parallel chords			G♯	F♯	A	C♯ … B♭	A♭ with octatonic parallel chords	

La Jeunesse des vieux is more immediately comparable to Messiaen's published music of the 1928–31 period than is *La Sainte Bohème*. The technique of using a distinct, slow opening melody to serve as an intervallic and thematic generator for the entire chorus (a bit like a *thème donné* in the Conservatoire's organ improvisation classes) is also found in a number of other works (Example 1.5). The similarity between the opening cello melody of *La Jeunesse des vieux* and the passage for cellos at the beginning of *Les Offrandes oubliées* is particularly striking. Both of these works are in ABA form, and in both, Messiaen reuses the opening melody as a transition between parts A and B.

Another element typical of Messiaen's musical style that can be heard in *La Jeunesse de vieux* is the accompanying figure composed of parallel octatonic chords heard above the primary melody. In the opening section for the chorus, a basic diatonic progression is ornamented with parallel octatonic chords, a texture extremely reminiscent of Messiaen's later *Chant des déportés*. All three transpositions of the octatonic set are used in conjunction with the traditional harmonies with which they share the greatest number of common pitches (two of the three octatonic sets can be seen in Example 1.6).[49]

---

[49]   Allen Forte has noted a similar use of all three transpositions of the octatonic mode as a practice typical in Debussy's works: 'Debussy and the Octatonic', *Music Analysis,*

Example 1.5   Thematic generators in Messiaen's early works

Example 1.6   Piano reduction of the opening of *La Jeunesse des vieux* featuring parallel chords in octatonic modes, bars 5–9

Although both *La Sainte Bohème* and *La Jeunesse des vieux* were hurriedly written in stressful conditions and seem, stylistically speaking, more restrained than Messiaen's freely composed music of the same period, it is nevertheless clear that these works are very close to the rest of Messiaen's *œuvre*, particularly given the many parallels that can be drawn between the choruses and *Les Offrandes oubliées*, not to mention later works written for choir and orchestra such as the *Trois Petites Liturgies de la Présence Divine* and the *Chant des déportés*, with their simple textures in octaves for tutti choir, set against a colourful and shifting orchestral texture. Messiaen's Prix de Rome choruses are strange cases – half composition, half academic exercise. Though they will probably never become part of the repertoire in the way that Messiaen's other works have, they are nevertheless important examples of his early style and artistic efforts.

10/1–2 (March–July 1991): pp. 143–4, 153.

Conclusion: The Irresistible Appeal of Paris

Although winning the Prix de Rome could have brought Messiaen several opportunities that may have helped advance his early career, not least recognition, extensive press coverage, funding and the possibility of future commissions, the period of residency in Rome was unavoidable. Several French composers have commented upon the poisonous atmosphere that prevailed at the Villa Médicis. Debussy and Berlioz, both childhood heroes of Messiaen, famously disliked the environment. Debussy described the Villa Médicis as a cross between 'a cosmopolitan hotel, a private school, and a compulsory civilian barracks', and returned to Paris early, spending only a little over two years in Rome.[50] More recently, Messiaen's friend and classmate from Dukas's composition class, Elsa Barraine, who won the Prix de Rome in 1929, sent Dukas a letter shortly after arriving at the Villa Médicis in January 1930 in which she described the unpleasant atmosphere at the French Academy:

> We've become familiar with the Villa Médicis. Naturally, it takes time to get used to. The room attributed to us is tiny, not very clean, and damp. There are two and a half chairs, two beds, a table and two other pieces of furniture. You can't turn around. Happily, the Pleyel is good. We also have a sort of long and narrow space that serves as kitchen, storage space, bathroom and dining room. Happily there is a lot of fresh air and an admirable view of Rome. All of this would be nothing if the atmosphere between our fellow residents was more agreeable. But the young artists aren't very cheerful and they behave like nattering *concierges*: all of the conversations revolve around gossip and stories that go back to Berlioz. We stare each other down and the women peer at one another, sizing each other up. To top it all off, nobody agrees about paintings. It's an altogether charming atmosphere.[51]

---

[50]   Debussy, cited in Léon Vallas, *Claude Debussy: His Life and Works*, trans. Maire and Grace O'Brien (New York: Dover Publications, 1973), p. 31.

[51]   'Nous avons donc pris connaissance de la Villa Médici. Naturellement, il nous faudra du temps pour nous habituer. La chambre qui nous est échue est petite, pas très propre et humide. Il y a 2 chaises et demi. 2 lits. 1 table et 2 meubles. On ne peut pas se tourner. Heureusement que le Pleyel est bon. Nous avons aussi une sorte de [boyau] qui sert de cuisine-débarras-cabinet de toilette-salle à manger. Il y a heureusement beaucoup d'air et une vue admirable sur Rome. Tout cela ne serait rien si l'atmosphère générale était agréable entre camarades. Mais ce n'est pas gai, les jeunes artistes et ils ont plutôt l'air de pipelets: toutes les conversations générales roulent sur les potins et histoires en remontant à Berlioz – On se regarde en chien de faïence, les femmes se jaugent et s'épient avec des yeux méfiants, enfin personne ne peut se voir en peinture – c'est charmant.' Elsa Barraine, letter to Paul Dukas (15 January 1930); cited in Roger Nichols, *The Harlequin Years: Music in Paris, 1917–1929* (London: Thames and Hudson, 2002), p. 185. Reconsulted and retranslated to present a longer passage. (BnF musique, Lettres autographes W.48 (64) 'Lettres addressées à Paul Dukas', autograph letter from Elsa Barraine to Paul Dukas dated 15 January [1930]).

Although this letter was privately addressed to Dukas, it is not beyond reason to imagine that Barraine's close friends back in Paris, perhaps particularly those such as Messiaen who were also interested in the competition, may have been aware of her negative experiences in Rome.

In the early 1930s, Messiaen was an ambitious young composer who was proactive in establishing himself and promoting his own music through his involvement with a number of groups of composers and activity as a jury member of the Société Nationale de Musique. By 1931, winning the Prix de Rome might actually have been more detrimental than beneficial to him, as a period of extended residency in Rome may well have undermined important contacts and opportunities in Paris. Although Messiaen, like many Parisians, often professed to hate Paris, it was in all likelihood a better place to nurture his early career than Rome. All speculation over the possible benefits and drawbacks which winning the Prix de Rome would have brought Messiaen must, however, be purely academic, as his personal circumstances (appointment at the Trinité and marriage to Claire Delbos) precluded him from re-entering the competition after 1931.

Chapter 2

Olivier Messiaen and
Portique pour une fille de France

Lucie Kayas and Christopher Brent Murray

On 15 February 1941, Pierre Schaeffer's Association Jeune France was instructed by Pétain's secretary of youth affairs to organize pageants for a new national holiday, 11 May, celebrating French youth and veterans dedicated to the memory of Joan of Arc.[1] In mid-March 1941, Messiaen, Léo Preger and Yves Baudrier were asked to write incidental music for a stadium spectacle written by Pierre Schaeffer and Pierre Barbier. *Portique pour une fille de France* was an ambitious propagandist project combining theatre, dance, mime and massed movements of extras from various youth movements.[2] Though Olivier Messiaen's job in March and April of 1941 as a composer, pianist and administrator with Pierre Schaeffer's Association Jeune France is now common knowledge thanks to Peter Hill and Nigel Simeone's 2005 biography of Messiaen, the story of *Portique pour une fille de France* and Messiaen's involvement in the project remain relatively unknown – Messiaen never spoke of his experience with the Association Jeune France in interviews and little documentation on the details and circumstances of his lost compositions for *Portique* has previously come to light.[3] Using sources from the French National Archives, the archives of the French radio and military and a

---

[1] French National Archives, series AJ³⁹, box 83, dossier 'Fêtes et cérémonies', document 'Circulaire du 2e bureau du Sécrétariat genéral de la jeunesse, Objet: Organisation d'une fête de la jeunesse à l'occasion de la fête de Jeanne d'arc le 11 mai 1941'.

For a slightly different version of this chapter, written in French and more concerned with the role of Pierre Schaeffer, see Lucie Kayas and Christopher Brent Murray, 'Portique pour une fille de France: un mystère du XXe siècle', in Martin Kaltenecker and Karine Le Bail (eds), *Pierre Schaeffer: Constructions impatientes* (Paris: CNRS éditions, 2012), pp. 98–115.

[2] Pierre Barbier and Pierre Schaeffer, *Portique pour une fille de France* (Paris: Chiron, 1941). In a letter to Nadia Boulanger dated 14 March, Léo Preger, who arrived in Vichy on 12 March, confirms that he was asked to participate in the project but that the text by Schaeffer and Barbier was not yet complete. Bibliothèque Nationale de France, Music Department, Correspondence Preger-Boulanger, NLA 97, letters 010–078. Whereas Messiaen and Baudrier, both members of the original Groupe Jeune France were already in the Unoccupied Zone, Schaeffer probably knew Preger through Nadia Boulanger, with whom he had also taken lessons.

[3] PHNS, pp. 103–12.

number of private collections, we have been able to uncover a great deal about the history, content, music and meaning of *Portique pour une fille de France*. The essential points of this research are outlined in the following chapter and include a brief overview of Messiaen's activities in the spring of 1941, with his transition from prisoner of war to harmony professor; a history of the origins of the *Portique* project and its context as part of celebrating the new national holiday on 11 May; a description of the pageant with its cast of hundreds; and finally a look at the two recently rediscovered choral pieces written by Messiaen for the event.

Context: Messiaen's Journey from POW Camp to Conservatoire

Hill and Simeone indicate a 10 March 1941 letter from Messiaen to composer Claude Arrieu as the first sign of activity from Messiaen upon his return from captivity, with word of his new job with the Association Jeune France coming shortly afterward in a letter dated 12 March. Archival materials concerning Messiaen's military service further clarify the dates of Messiaen's movements during the spring of 1941.[4] To summarize, Messiaen was liberated from Stalag VIIIA in Görlitz on 10 February 1941. He was transported by train via a repatriation camp on the German–Swiss border and eventually arrived at a quarantine camp in Sathonay, near Lyon, on 16 February 1941, nineteen and a half months after being called up on 4 September 1939.[5] He was immediately demobilized, but probably spent three weeks in quarantine like his fellow prisoner, the cellist Étienne Pasquier.[6]

While Messiaen knew he had the job with the Association Jeune France on 12 March, his dossier for the job of harmony professor at the Conservatoire was received by the ministerial administration on 20 March, five days after the official deadline. This delay was overlooked thanks to Messiaen's status as a former prisoner of war, and his name was added to an impressive list of some

---

[4]   For more on these sources concerning Messiaen's military service, see Christopher Brent Murray, 'Nouveaux regards sur le soldat Messiaen', in David Mastin and Marine Branland (eds), 'De la guerre dans l'art, de l'art dans la guerre' special issue, *Textuel: Revue de lettres arts et cinéma de l'Université Paris VII*, 63 (2010): pp. 243–55. For more on Messiaen's nomination and the beginning of his Conservatoire teaching career, see Yves Balmer and Christopher Brent Murray, 'La classe de Messiaen: Retour aux sources', in E. Ducreux and A. Poirier (eds), *Une musique française après 1945?* (Lyon: Symétrie, forthcoming) and Yves Balmer and Christopher Brent Murray, 'Olivier Messiaen en 1941: À la recherche d'une année perdue', in M. Chimènes and Y. Simon (eds), *La musique à Paris sous l'Occupation* (Paris: Fayard/Cité de la musique, forthcoming).

[5]   According to the records of the Archives des victimes des conflits contemporains, Caen.

[6]   For Pasquier's account, see Rebecca Rischin, *Et Messiaen composa...* (Paris: Ramsay, 2006), pp. 146–7.

31 candidates.[7] Messiaen was proposed for nomination to his post as harmony professor after several rounds of voting by the *Conseil supérieur du Conservatoire* on 25 March, narrowly beating out his principal rival, Francis Bousquet.[8] Messiaen was also chosen over as his talented former classmates Maurice Duruflé and Tony Aubin who, in the following years, would be named to other Conservatoire posts in harmony and composition, respectively. A letter dated 28 March, cited by Hill and Simeone, indicates that Messiaen was aware of his preliminary nomination and that, barring a ministerial decision to override the *Conseil supérieur*'s vote, he would probably be shortly returning to Paris. Indeed, a letter communicating Messiaen's nomination does not seem to have reached the Fine Art and Youth Minister Louis Hautecœur's desk in Vichy until 17 April.

The delays for the official government paperwork confirming Messiaen's appointment and travel permit account for the date of his arrival in Paris. We can estimate Messiaen's return between the date of a card sent by Messiaen to Jacques Chailley, secretary to the Director of the Conservatoire, on 2 May and that of a letter mentioning Messiaen's return dated 10 May.[9] This second piece of correspondence is a letter from the Director's office thanking Alice Pelliot for services rendered as a substitute teacher for André Bloch's harmony class, which was to be taken over by Messiaen. Bloch had been set to retire, but, like several other elderly Conservatoire professors, his contract had been extended for the 1940–41 school year and, like them, he might well have continued teaching until after the end of the war were he not sent back into retirement in December 1940 following the enactment of Vichy's anti-Jewish legislation.[10] Pelliot, a solfège professor and Bloch's assistant at the Conservatoire upon the outbreak of war, taught Bloch's class during the interim from 26 December 1940 until Messiaen arrived in Paris and had also applied for Bloch's former position. Since Messiaen did not arrive in Paris before the harmony exams on 5 May, Pelliot also presented his future class to the exam jury.[11] Yvonne Loriod's memory of her first class with Messiaen on 7 May 1941 falls in the period between the harmony exams and

---

[7]   The record of the *Conseil supérieur*'s election of Messiaen is found in the French National Archives, F[21] 5322.

[8]   Francis Bousquet (1890–1942), veteran of the First World War, Grand Prix de Rome of 1923 and director of the Roubaix Conservatoire, wrote several angry letters to Louis Hautecœur following the nomination of the much younger and comparatively inexperienced Messiaen. He died in December of the following year.

[9]   Bibliothèque Nationale de France, Music Department, LAS Olivier Messiaen 10, and French National Archives, AJ[37] 427 letter 855.

[10]   Jean Gribenski, 'L'exclusion des juifs du Conservatoire', in Myriam Chimènes (ed.), *La vie musicale sous Vichy* (Brussels: Éditions Complexe, 2001), p. 145. See also Michèle Alten, 'Le Conservatoire de musique et d'art dramatique: Une institution culturelle publique dans la guerre, 1940–1942', *L'education musicale*, available at www.leducation-musicale.com/conservatoire.pdf.

[11]   French National Archives, AJ[37] 427, letter 474.

concours (which in 1941 took place on 8 June for the male students and 15 June for the female students).[12] Yvette Grimaud would receive a *premier prix* in this harmony *concours*, with Yvonne Loriod garnering a *second prix* – all thanks to the collective efforts of Bloch and Pelliot, topped off by a month of instruction from Messiaen.

Preparing for a Pageant

According to Hill and Simeone, it was probably at Neussargues during the time between his nomination and his actual arrival in Paris that Messiaen composed his part of the incidental music for the Joan of Arc pageants for 11 May, an event he missed attending due to his new duties at the Conservatoire. During the 1930s, Pierre Schaeffer was intensely involved in the Catholic scout movement, the *routiers*, so it is unsurprising to note that the text of *Portique pour une fille de France* by Schaeffer and Barbier is heavily influenced by the Joan of Arc-related writings of the Père Doncœur, creator of the *routier* movement, and more particularly by Léon Chancerel and his *Comédiens routiers*.[13] As the director of the newly created Association Jeune France, Pierre Schaeffer recruited within his network of scout theatre connections to organize the pageants and plays about Joan of Arc across Vichy at about the same time that Messiaen was liberated.[14] Schaeffer and Barbier's text borrows a number of details from the 1938 'jeu dramatique national' written by Léon Chancerel for the *Comédiens routiers*, *Mission de Jeanne d'Arc*, while also borrowing entire passages, including the stage directions, from *Présentation pour le procès de Jeanne d'Arc* by Robert Brasillach, essentially a translation in modern French of the transcript of Joan of Arc's trial.[15]

On 11 May 1941, according to the government's wishes, *Portique* was given in whole or in abridged form in dozens of locations, from major cities to small villages and the isolated youth labour camps of the *chantiers de jeunesse* that had replaced compulsory military service following the occupation. The largest and best-attended performances took place at the Gerland Stadium in Lyon and the Vélodrome Stadium in Marseilles with shorter versions and smaller-scale productions taking place in

---

[12]   PHNS, p. 145, as well as French National Archives, AJ[37] 535.

[13]   While evident to those familiar with the repertoire in question, this influence is clearly admitted by Schaeffer himself in his memoir, *Les antennes de Jéricho* (Paris: Stock, 1978), p. 275.

[14]   According to documents in the French National Archives, on 15 February the government requested the Association Jeune France to create pageants for 11 May. See F[21] 8098 and AJ[39] 83.

[15]   Léon Chancerel, *Mission de Jeanne d'Arc, célébration par personnages* (Paris: La Hutte, 1938). Robert Brasillach, *Le procès de Jeanne d'Arc*, nouvelle version présentée et ordonnée par Robert Brasillach (Paris: Alexis Bredier, 1932).

numerous locations across unoccupied France.[16] The incidental music by Messiaen, Preger and Baudrier is known to have been played at the two flagship performances conducted by Jean Witkowski in Lyon and Jean Giardino in Marseilles. Both men were important conductors in their respective cities.[17]

Though organizing large-scale performances throughout the *zone libre* in under three months was in itself a vast project, *Portique* was only part of the festivities for the national holiday declared by Pétain for 11 May.[18] The *Fête de Jeanne d'Arc* was intended to celebrate both the French homeland and the nation's youth, just as Joan of Arc had been appropriated as a symbol for both the Vichy incarnation of the veteran's organization, the *Légion française de combattants*. Already in the 1930s, Joan of Arc had become an increasingly important figure of focus for French Catholic youth movements.

The official programme, clearly spelled out by the authorities and communicated at the local level by regional prefects, was nearly identical from town to town. Typically the day began with a solemn ceremony involving the *Légion des anciens combattants*, in which veterans might lay a wreath on a monument to war dead, frequently a statue of Joan of Arc. In many cases this ceremony took place before the local town hall where the image of the Maréchal had officially replaced that of Marianne a few weeks before. Later in the morning, a Mass dedicated to the country's youth was pronounced, preferably outdoors. Finally, a pageant centred on Joan of Arc, also outdoors, was given during the afternoon.

In Lyon, the wreath laying took place on the Jeanne d'Arc statue at the Place Puvis de Chavannes in the heart of the bourgeois sixth arrondissement. The Mass for Lyon's youth was pronounced on the Parvis de Saint Jean before the cathedral in old Lyon, where the service was amplified and broadcast on loudspeakers to the young men and boys standing outside – the young women and girls of the youth movements were seated inside. The youth and their families were then called upon to watch and

---

[16]   In Vienne, for example, *Lyon-Soir* reports a version of *Portique* to be given in the town's imposing Roman amphitheatre composed of four of the ten tableaux of *Portique*. 'Pour Jeanne d'Arc à Vienne', *Lyon-Soir* (9 May 1941). Schaeffer and Barbier's text is itself followed by advice on how to scale down the production and its staging.

[17]   Witkowski had a special relationship with the music of Messiaen, as the conductor of the Lyon première of *Les Offrandes oubliées* in Lyon in 1933. He would ultimately direct the Lyon première of the *Trois Petites Liturgies* as well. See Yves Ferraton, *Cinquante ans de vie musicale à Lyon: Les Witkowski et l'Orchestre Philharmonique de Lyon, 1903–1953* (Trevoux: Editions Trevoux, 1984).

[18]   One such cultural event commemorating Joan of Arc took place at the Paris Conservatoire. Like the *Portique,* it involved members of both Messiaen's group Jeune France as well as Schaeffer's Association Jeune France. The event presented *Jeanne d'Arc,* an oratorio in seven parts with music by Louis Beydts, Georges Dandelot, Raymond Loucheur, Tony Aubin, Jacques Chailley, Pierre Capdevielle and André Jolivet. First presented in a radio broadcast in early May 1941, Charles Münch revived the work at the Concerts de la Conservatoire on 28 April 1942. For more information, see hector.ucdavis. edu/sdc/programs/Pr115.htm.

Illustration 2.1   Dignitaries' stand, Gerland Stadium

participate in *Portique pour une fille de France* at 3 o'clock in the afternoon in the Gerland Stadium. The pageant, like the morning Mass, was amplified and broadcast on loudspeakers to render it audible to the thousands of spectators in the stands. Photographs from the period show the dignitaries' stand decorated with rosettes and bunting (Illustration 2.1). A loudspeaker can be seen in the foreground.[19] Some 40 loudspeakers were needed to amplify the orchestra and actors' voices and were distributed around the track of the stadium at regular intervals.[20]

A closer look reveals the government officials, clergy and military officers who attended *Portique* in Lyon, as they did in all of the state-sponsored spectacles on 11 May. The scale of the pageant in Lyon called for the attendance of powerful figures: Vichy's finance minister, Yves Bouthillier, Cardinal Gerland and several army generals. According to several newspapers, Bouthillier's late arrival, announced at the intermission, was received with 'unanimous cries of *Vive Pétain* from the entire stadium'.[21] With seats at just one franc for the members of youth movements, and comparatively cheap seats for the general public, photos of the event show that Gerland Stadium was full to capacity, with some 15,000 to 50,000

---

[19]   This and other photos in this chapter are from the personal collection of André Gervais, the director for the Lyon version of *Portique*. Our profound thanks go to his daughter for generously sharing her father's photo collection.

[20]   André Fabre, 'Portique pour une fille de France', *Lyon-Soir* (7 May 1941): p. 3.

[21]   See for example, *Le Progrès* (12 May 1941).

Illustration 2.2   The programme for the Marseilles version of *Portique*

spectators depending upon the source, with most newspapers reporting about 35,000.[22] A programme from the Marseilles version of *Portique* is conserved in the French National Archives (Illustration 2.2). The watercolour of Joan of Arc on the programme's cover is the work of the set designer Guillaume Monin.

The programme opens by citing an exhortation from Maréchal Pétain: 'We shall maintain and enlarge, if possible, the tradition of high culture that stands behind the very idea of our Nation (*Patrie*)'.[23] Bromides referring to 'high culture' in the programme aside, the declared artistic project of the Association Jeune

---

[22]   In Gerland Stadium, Lyon, seats cost 5 to 10 francs, 40 francs for the *tribune d'honneur*, compared to the Vélodrome Stadium in Marseilles where they cost 1 or 2 francs and 20 francs for the *tribune d'honneur*. The high estimate of 50,000 spectators is quoted by Association Jeune France propaganda report, which probably inflated the figure in the hopes of preserving their association, already menaced with dissolution by the government at the time of the report's drafting.

[23]   'Nous maintiendrons, nous élargirons s'il se peut, une tradition de haute culture qui fait corps avec l'idée même de notre Patrie'. This citation appears to be taken from an article signed by Pétain and published in the summer of 1940. Philippe Pétain, 'Réforme de l'éducation nationale', *La revue des deux mondes* (15 August 1940).

France was that of tearing down intellectual and class barriers and favouring mass participation and general education in popular arts and folklore.[24]

Staging *Portique*: Medieval Pastiche, Anachronism and Scout Theatre Traditions

Portique is divided into two parts, each composed of five *tableaux*. The first part deals essentially with Joan's girlhood and military exploits, taking the audience through her participation at the battles of Vaucouleurs and Orléans to the coronation of Charles VII in Reims. The second part depicts Joan's captivity, trial and execution. The weather was inclement across southern France on 11 May 1941: the Marseilles production was hindered by the mistral, and it would seem that rain interfered with the Lyon version of *Portique*. After a particularly heavy deluge during the intermission, extensive cuts were made to the second half. Indeed, the only surviving photographs of the second part of the spectacle depict the tenth and final tableau where Joan is burned at the stake.

Illustration 2.3 shows a general view of the playing field. Note that the stage was a simple square-shaped podium with flights of steps on the front and back, and a ramp on either side. At each corner of the stage were flagpoles bearing pennants with the seven stars of the Maréchal. More importantly, these poles served to suspend the microphones of the sound system. The spoken choir and the handful of actors with speaking roles were limited to the amplified area defined by the stage and its microphones. A square of potted plants demarcated the area reserved for the orchestra and choir.

The narrator, or 'messenger' was positioned in the centre of the stage. During the coronation scene the messenger transformed into a radio announcer, narrating the massed movements of the hundreds of extras in an anachronistic language that Schaeffer borrowed from contemporary radio broadcasts. Two *coryphées*, or coryphæi, the term for the leader of a Greek chorus, were stationed in towers on either side of the stage. A device borrowed from Léon Chancerel's *Mission de Jeanne d'Arc*, the *coryphées* are present for the entire length of the drama. Like the messenger, they commented upon the action in a Manichean dialogue: one cheering on Joan of Arc, the other deriding her. A similarly divided spoken chorus (such spoken choruses were a popular device in scout theatre) dressed in white, provided the 'voice of the people' and further developed certain of the *coryphées*' views. A great number of white conical tents were planted on either side of the stage. Like the *coryphées*, one side represented the camp of the French army, the

---

[24] For an overview of the Association Jeune France, see Véronique Chabrol, 'L'ambition de "Jeune France"', in Jean-Pierre Rioux (ed.), *La vie culturelle sous Vichy* (Brussels: Editions Complexe, 1990), pp. 161–78 and Philip Nord, 'L'expérience de Jeune France', in Karine Le Bail and Martin Kaltenecker (eds), *Pierre Schaeffer: Constructions Impatientes* (Paris: CNRS Editions, 2012), pp. 86–97.

Illustration 2.3   General view of the Gerland Stadium with stage, orchestra, tents
for extras and amplification system

other that of Joan's eventual captors, the English. These tents, along with some
horses and their riders, were loaned to the Association Jeune France for use in the
pageant by the French army. The tents also served to hide the hundreds of child
extras when they were not acting out massed choreographies on the playing field.

In Illustration 2.4, a photograph probably taken during the dress rehearsal
on 10 May, the set-up for the sound system and the details of the set and props
are clearly visible, including the towers for the *coryphées* and the maypole-
like tree featured in the second tableau, 'Domrémy'. The sets and costumes
for *Portique* were the work of the artist Jean Le Moal, member of a group of
artists that would be dubbed the 'Nouvelle école de Paris' a few years later
(Illustrations 2.5 and 2.6). The material shortages of the day are apparent when
one compares Le Moal's drawings for Joan's costume and the Chirico-esque sets
with photographs of the Association Jeune France's attempt to realize them.[25]

---

[25]   Our sincere thanks to Anne Le Moal, the daughter of Jean Le Moal, for generously
allowing us to use these images of her father's work. Certain sources attribute the costume
and set design of *Portique* to the set-builder, Edmé Lex, or the costume atelier director,
Yvonne Leenhardt. For the production in Lyon, the costumes and sets seem to have been
entirely conceived by Jean Le Moal.

Illustration 2.4   An image of the dress rehearsal for *Portique* in Lyon

Illustration 2.5   The costume design for Joan of Arc by Jean Le Moal

Illustration 2.6   The set design for the Orléans tableau by Jean Le Moal

Raymond Cogniat would write of Le Moal's sets:

> The traditional backdrop with its painted canvas and artifices does not hold up
> in an outdoor setting. All that counts outdoors are constructions with depth and
> a clear delimitation of the stage. Even the use of colour must be modified – an
> overly colourful or detailed set can be confusing. The essential thing is to create
> a set with neutral tones and constructions of considerable size. Upon the stage
> reduced to its essentials, the players' movements stand out in clear relief – for
> in contrast to the sets, the costumes and props can and even must be extremely
> colourful, becoming mobile points that propel and clarify the action.[26]

The only actor among the professionals playing the four leading roles identified
by newspaper accounts was Laurence Aubray, who played Joan. She was 22 in
1941. In Illustration 2.7 Aubray is seen rehearsing the second tableau, 'Domrémy',
surrounded by the young extras playing village girls.

In Illustration 2.8 Aubray is accompanied by her heralds, non-speaking roles
played by members of the French cavalry. They have just dismounted from
their horses and wear their standard-issue riding boots and jodhpurs under their
costume. (It is possible to recognize the heralds thanks to the costume sketches
interspersed in the text of *Portique*.)

---

[26]   Raymond Cogniat, 'En zone non-occupée', in Michel Florisoone, Raymond
Cogniat and Yves-Bonnat (eds), *Un an de théâtre, 1940–1941* (Lyon: Les éditions de la
France nouvelle, 1942), p. 29.

Illustration 2.7   Laurence Aubray as Joan of Arc during a rehearsal

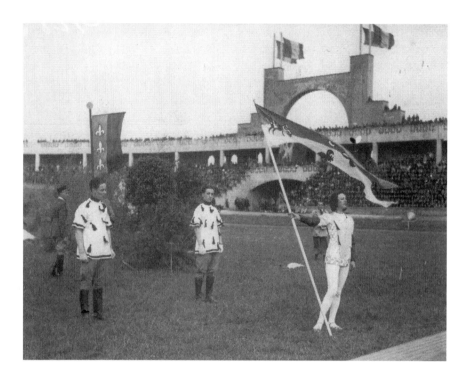

Illustration 2.8   Joan of Arc and her cavalry heralds

Illustration 2.9   The living cathedral

The coronation scene represented a key moment in the mass movements of
the hundreds of *figurants*. These extras – a mix of scouts, youth labourers from
the *chantiers de jeunesse* and soldiers – formed the outlines of the cathedral
(Illustrations 2.9 and 2.10).[27] The image of these living stones of the Eternal
Church made up of chosen believers, an image also behind Messiaen's *Apparition
de l'Église éternelle*, is of course close at hand. In a sense, this scene is the literal
incarnation of one of Vichy's goals for the *Fête de Jeanne d'Arc*: to inspire France's
youth to come together in the interest of the common good to rebuild France.

In general, the period's newspapers fail to mention the degree to which the
weather interfered with the pageant. The reviews are positive, patriotic and banal –
hardly surprising given the role of the state in the staging of the day's activities
and its control of the press. Still, a few journalists reproached problems with the
sound system, the slow coordination of the mass movements and the script's
anachronisms.

---

[27]   Gervais described the choreography to a newspaper reporter for *Le Journal*, a Lyon
newspaper: 'For the scene of the coronation, for example, the line of soldiers will create the
nave with a deployment of flag-bearers marking the outline of the apse of Reims cathedral
where the cortège of lords, the King and Jeanne will enter.' Stéphane Faugier, 'Portique
pour une fille de France', *Le Journal* (9 May 1941): p. 2.

Illustration 2.10   An image from the coronation scene during which Messiaen's
              Te Deum would have been heard

The Music of *Portique*

Considered lost until very recently, the musical numbers for *Portique* were
previously only known through indications in the text by Schaeffer and Barbier,
and, of course, Messiaen's mention of 'Chœurs pour une *Jeanne d'Arc* (Neussargues,
Cantal, 1941) (Pour un grand chœur et petit chœur mixte, a capella) *Te Deum –
Impropères*' in his list of works at the end of *Technique de mon langage musical*. Hill
and Simeone cite letters from Messiaen to his wife Claire Delbos in the spring of
1941 that seem to confirm that, as mentioned above, he did indeed write the choruses
for *Portique* during one of his visits to Claire at her parents' property at Neussargues,
where she had been living with their son Pascal since the beginning of the war.

  According to Jean Witkowski's agenda, two musical rehearsals for *Portique*
took place at Gerland Stadium on the morning of 5 May and afternoon of 10 May
(Illustration 2.11).[28] Thanks to the single newspaper that gives a detailed account
of the music for *Portique*, we know that there were some 200 choristers (probably
singing not from the stage, but from the musicians' area, to judge from photographs),
but that the orchestra counted about 25 musicians (see note 30). In Illustration 2.12
one can see a few of the instruments, including a grand piano, a clarinet, an oboe, a

---

[28]   Personal communication from Jean Witkowski's son, Ivan M. Witkowski.

Illustration 2.11 From left to right: Pierre Schaeffer, Léo Preger and Jean Witkowski during a rehearsal for *Portique pour une fille de France*

Illustration 2.12 Jean Witkowski directing the orchestra in a rehearsal for *Portique*

flute doubling the piccolo, an abandoned bassoon and a sort of saxhorn or Wagner tuba. The ensemble seems to have been composed of local professionals.

The journalist and music critic Henry Fellot gives abundant praise to the music of all three composers and seems to be the only journalist to note the contributions of each in any detail:

> The musical programme began by a somewhat anachronistic rendering of a fragment of [Méhul's] *Chant du départ* (in the fifteenth century!), followed by a touching *Déploration*, a vocalise on prolonged 'Ahs!' proclaimed by a mournful choir of refugees; this gripping page was written by M. Preger, to whom we also owe a charming little *Marche* of pastoral character dominated by the woodwinds which accompanies the recognition of the King by Joan, as well as a powerful *Chant des Bâtisseurs* (for *a capella* choir in Gregorian style) which precedes the grandiose coronation ceremony at Reims.
>
> Here M. Baudrier takes the scene, if we dare speak in such terms, with the magnificent, *Marche du Cortège du Sacre*, which precedes the sumptuous and sonorous *Te Deum* by M. Messiaen. We hear the latter musician a second time in the very modern *Impropères*, where Joan, condemned and imprisoned, painfully questions the people of France for whom she has sacrificed herself.
>
> Joan climbs upon the pyre. Once again, the music of M. Baudrier translates with striking veracity the scene where the Bishop Cauchon follows the patron saint of France, sobbing, pleading, and imploring, as though he were trying to join her. Here again there is music, but that of M. Preger, which closes the drama with the 'Seven Words of Joan' mounting her Calvary and uttering to men and to the heavens, before dying, the immortal words of her glorious agony.
>
> One can only admire the unity of vision that permitted the three composers who successfully created this score to give it a generally uniform style. The execution, under the direction of M. Jean Witkowski, was excellent and worthy of the splendid spectacle, of which the music was not the least of its qualities.[29]

> [Le programme musical commence par une assez anachronique exécution d'un fragment du *Chant du Départ* (au XVᵉ siècle!), suivi d'une émouvante déploration, vocalisé sur des 'Ah!' prolongés clamée par un Chœur douloureux de Réfugiés; cette page saisissante est de M. Preger, à qui l'on doit également une charmante petite *Marche* de caractère pastoral, où dominent les 'bois', et qui accompagne la reconnaissance du Roi par Jeanne, ainsi qu'un puissant *Chant des Bâtisseurs* (Chœur *a capella* en style grégorien), qui précède la cérémonie grandiose du Sacre de Reims.
>
> C'est alors que M. Baudrier entre en scène, si nous osons ainsi parler, avec la magnifique *Marche du Cortège du Sacre*, qui précède le somptueux et sonore *Te Deum* de M. Messiaen. Nous retrouvons ce dernier musicien dans la page, très

---

[29]   Henry Fellot, 'La Partition de MM. Yves Baudrier, Léo Preger et Olivier Messiaen', *Lyon-Soir* (14 May 1941): p. 3.

moderne des *Impropères*, alors que Jeanne, prisonnière et condamnée, interroge
douloureusement le peuple de France pour lequel elle s'est sacrifiée.

Jeanne monte à son supplice. Et, de nouveau, la musique de M. Baudrier,
traduit avec une frappante vérité la scène où l'évêque Cauchon suit la sainte de
France, sanglotant, suppliant, implorant son pardon, comme s'il cherchait à la
rejoindre.

Et c'est encore la musique, mais celle de M. Preger, cette fois, qui conclut le
drame, avec *Les Sept Paroles de Jeanne*, gravissant son calvaire et lançant aux
hommes et vers le ciel, avant de mourir, les mots – immortels, ceux-là – de sa
glorieuse agonie.

On ne peut qu'admirer l'unité de vues qui a permis aux trois musiciens, qui
ont mené à bien cette partition, de lui donner un style général uniforme.

L'exécution, sous la direction de M. Jean Witkowski, a été excellente et
digne de la splendide manifestation du Stade, dont la partie musicale ne fut pas
la moindre attraction.]

Fellot's notes seem to indicate that Preger, like Messiaen, also resorted to the use
of plainchant, and that perhaps all three composers had received some sort of
aesthetic directive from the Association Jeune France's administrators. Indeed, as
we shall explain further, the music composed by Messiaen for *Portique* does not
bear the marks of his style, apart from its abundant paraphrase of plainchant.

Popular and traditional songs were an important part of the pageant. The
Chant du départ mentioned by Fellot at the beginning of the show must certainly
have seemed odd in this context, as Fellot suggests. Written by Nicolas Méhul to
words by Marie-Joseph Chénier, the *Chant du départ* became an anthem during
the Empire, and later galvanized French troops during the First World War. Also
of note are the traditional round (one often used by Debussy), 'Nous n'irons plus
au bois' sung by the little girls in the tableau 'Domrémy' as well as the refrain,
'Orléans, Beaugency, Notre-Dame de Cléry' heard in the sixth tableau, 'Prologue
du chœur'. The latter tune is not entirely inauthentic for its origin, the 'Carillon
de Vendôme', dates back to the days of Joan of Arc. Still, all of these choices
correspond as much to the popular origins of Joan of Arc as they do to the aesthetic
ideals of the *Révolution nationale*.

Lucie Kayas's recent rediscovery of the choral parts for the music written by
Preger and Messiaen in the archives of Radio France has allowed us to get a better
idea about the true musical nature of Messiaen and Preger's contributions.[30] All

---

[30]   Olivier Messiaen, 'Impropères', Radio France, Cb 559, 'Te Deum', Radio France,
Cb 560, Léo Preger, 'Chant des réfugiés', Radio France, Cb 561, 'Nous bâtissons la
cathédrale' [sic], Radio France Cb. 562, 'Choral final', Radio France, Cb. 563. Preger's
instrumental music has yet to be found, but Pierre Gaucher has been kind enough to share
the following information on Baudrier's contributions from his forthcoming book *La Jeune
France, 1936-1945: Une ambition collective* (Lyon: Symétrie, forthcoming), based on this
2001 PhD thesis *De la Spirale à la Jeune France, 1935-1945*, Université de Tours, here

of the parts bear the words, 'Copying realized by the roneotype service of the Maîtrise Jeune France of Lyon'. This music includes the 'Chœur des réfugiés' by Preger that corresponds to the 'hummed and wordless melody' indicated in the 'Domrémy' tableau and is written for a mixed four-part choir. Preger's second chorus, 'Nous terminons la cathédrale' was sung at the beginning of the fifth tableau, the 'Sacre' described above. It is written in the syllabic style of a traditional folksong, and is harmonized for three voices (soprano, alto, with the tenor and bass singing together). The chorus is rather modal, which perhaps explains why Fellot associated it with a neo-Gregorian style. Preger's third contribution, the 'Choral final' also serves as Joan's final words in the tenth tableau, which portrays her as a Christ-like martyr whose seven last words paraphrase those of Christ on the cross.

In being assigned, or perhaps in having chosen, the *Te Deum* and the *Impropères* for his musical contribution to *Portique*, Messiaen took charge of setting the two truly religious texts of the work, both sung in Latin in a quasi-liturgical style. Illustration 2.10 is an image from the moment during the performance when the *Te Deum* was presumably heard. Messiaen chose to employ plainchant-like writing, treating the *Te Deum* like a responsorial alternating between the large and small choirs in three voices (soprano, tenor and bass). Messiaen confides the intonation of the Gregorian *Te Deum* to the basses first, leading to a melismatic continuation of the melody in all three voices (Example 2.1). He groups verses 2 to 13 in pairs, with the large choir singing the plainchant in unison and the small choir responding polyphonically and, at certain moments, putting a melismatic emphasis on important words like 'sanctus' or 'laudat'.

The *Impropères* usually accompany the veneration of the crucifix in the Good Friday liturgy, and their choice once again accents the parallelism constructed by Schaeffer and Barbier between the Passion of Christ and that of Joan of Arc. This music accompanies the first scene of *Portique*'s tenth and final tableau, and is written in the same responsorial style as the *Te Deum*, alternating with the spoken reproaches addressed by Joan to those who have betrayed her. If Fellot found that Messiaen's *Impropères* were 'very modern', it is probably because of the harmonic use of the dissonant major second given to the tenors in the recitations for small choir (Example 2.2).

The music written for *Portique* is typical of music created for mass spectacles: *a cappella* choruses singable by amateurs, use of popular and liturgical references

translated into English: 'A manuscript kept in the papers of Yves Baudrier, described by his late wife, Christiane (who lived out the end of her days in a Paris convent), indicates the instrumentation of Baudrier's contribution: 8 violins, 3 double basses, 1 flute, 2 oboes, 2 clarinets, 2 bassoons, 2 trumpets, 2 trombones, 1 tuba, piano and percussion. The titles and lengths of each piece are indicated as follows: Broad Introduction (1' ½), Fanfare (20"), King's Cortege (1' ½), Jeanne's Sadness (1'), Cauchon's Remorse (1'), Tumult (1'). Yves Baudrier indicated that this music was written in a "voluntarily simple and popular style" and that the score had been deposited with the publisher Billaudot.' Our sincere thanks go to Pierre Gaucher for allowing us to cite from his forthcoming work.

Example 2.1   The opening of Messiaen's *Te Deum*

to reinforce the feeling of belonging to a national and religious community and instrumental music for winds written to be audible outdoors.

Beyond *Portique*

Despite the numerous versions of *Portique* given simultaneously throughout France on 11 May 1941, the play was forgotten in favour of other projects when it came time to mark the national Joan of Arc holiday the following year. Much had changed over the course of a year, and the Association Jeune France was no longer in existence. With the intensification of Vichy's collaboration, Schaeffer's association was disbanded by Vichy at the beginning of 1942 for being a suspected haven for Christian-Democrats and individualism.[31]

René Rémond effectively sums up the symbolism that would continue to link Joan of Arc to Maréchal Pétain for the duration of the war:

---

[31]   On the dissolution of the Association Jeune France, see Michel Bergès, *Vichy contre Mounier* (Paris: Economica, 1997), and Chabrol, 'L'ambition de "Jeune France"', p. 176.

Example 2.2   The opening of Messiaen's *Impropères*

At the lowest moment of the Hundred Years' War, whose suppressed memory now re-emerged, God sent a shepherdess to deliver Orléans and consecrate the King's legitimacy. In 1940, he singled out the Maréchal. The parallel between Joan of Arc and Pétain, between the young girl and the old soldier, would inspire a sanctimonious literature where vacuity rubbed elbows with the desire to maintain hope in the homeland, a desire that would corrupt the spirit of certain patriots.[32]

[Aux pires moments de la guerre de Cent Ans dont les souvenirs remontent alors à la surface, Dieu a suscité une bergère pour délivrer Orléans et consacrer la légitimité du souverain. De même, en 1940, il a tenu en réserve le Maréchal. Le parallèle entre la bonne Lorraine et Pétain, entre la jeune fille et le vieux soldat, inspirera une littérature édifiante où la niaiserie bêtifiante côtoie la volonté de ne pas désespérer de la patrie, et conduira certains patriotes aux dévoiements de l'esprit.]

Vichy's move to appropriate Joan of Arc as a Christian and nationalist symbol was, of course, just one of many such attempts made over the course of French history. Though today Joan of Arc is most frequently appropriated by the far-right Front National of Jean-Marie and Marine Le Pen, a rarely cited interview with Messiaen on the subject of his admiration for Général de Gaulle reveals how easily Joan of Arc could be associated not only with the likes of Pétain, but also de Gaulle. The unidentified interviewer's words are in italics, and we reproduce a large portion of the interview, a very rare example of Messiaen voicing a political opinion. This also would seem to be the only time Messiaen evoked the figure of Joan of Arc in his interviews, in spite of his music for the Joan of Arc pageant described above.

Wasn't de Gaulle's claim, 'Je suis la France', one of the main things people reproached him for? Does his claim seem normal to you?
It's entirely normal. In a nation, there needs to be – and a nation is something extraordinarily complex and alive, it's not a convention, it's a whole group of people who came together little by little, who thought in the same way, and who had the same hopes and desires – there needs to be a man who embodies all of that. Basically, the kings of France were nothing else. They said, 'We are France', and maybe it wasn't all that bad. That said, I'm not a political man, and I never was part of Action Française, of course, but I do think that one man can embody a nation's destiny.

Embodying France means embodying its history, as you've just said; but doesn't it also involve embodying a certain spiritual ideal?
Certainly. France is also something physical. There's a spirit running through our flesh. Look how varied France is! Look at the different provinces! There

---

[32] René Rémond, *Notre siècle* (Paris: Fayard, 1991), p. 262.

are the mountains and the ocean, vineyards, fields, and forests.[33] We have a bit of Spain, a bit of Germany, a little bit of Switzerland and also of Italy and England – yet it's all France and it's unique in the world. And this varied France, this France of so many different faces and landscapes exists in and of itself. It's irreplaceable.

But this link that unifies so many provinces into a single nation, isn't it the desire to build something spiritual [for humanity]?
I'll answer your question as a Christian. Again, I'm not a political man. But I'm Catholic, and I've studied theology. It's only as a believer that I want to talk to you: it should not be forgotten that General de Gaulle was also a believer. I'd also like to evoke a figure, one very close to de Gaulle, one that was also a symbol who embodied France: I want to talk about Joan of Arc. At one time, Joan of Arc represented a movement of French spirituality. Because there is indeed such a movement, full of hope and faith, equal to similar movements in Spain, for example, and which is an important part of France.

And for you, de Gaulle embodied that movement?
De Gaulle was one person who embodied that aspect of France. There were others of course, but he embodied it.[34]

[L'une des grandes choses que l'on reprochait à de Gaulle, n'était-ce pas qu'il prétendait: 'Je suis la France'? Vous, cela vous semble normal?
Tout à fait! Tout à fait normal. Il faut bien qu'il y ait dans un pays – et un pays, c'est quelque chose d'extraordinairement complexe et vivant, ce n'est pas une convention, c'est tout un ensemble de gens qui se sont réunis peu à peu, qui ont pensé de la même façon, qui ont eu les mêmes désirs et les mêmes espoirs – il faut bien qu'il y ait un homme qui incarne tout cela. En somme, les rois de France n'étaient pas autre chose; ils disaient: 'Nous sommes la France' – et ce n'était peut-être pas plus mal. Cela dit, je ne fais pas de politique, je n'ai jamais été de l'Action Française, bien entendu – mais je pense que quelqu'un peut effectivement incarner le destin d'un pays.

Incarner la France, c'est incarner son histoire comme vous venez de le dire; mais est-ce que ce n'est pas aussi incarner un idéal spirituel?
Certainement; car la France est aussi quelque chose de charnel. Il y a un esprit qui court dans toute chair. Voyez comme la France est variée! Voyez les provinces françaises! Il y a la montagne et l'océan, les vignobles, les champs, la forêt.

---

[33]   This vision is clearly linked to the landscapes of *Catalogue d'oiseaux* and its ornithological portrait of France.

[34]   Olivier Messiaen, 'Des Paroles d'esprit: Entretien avec Olivier Messiaen', in Michel Casenave and Olivier Germain Thomas (eds), *Charles de Gaulle* (Paris: Editions de l'Herne, 1975), pp. 44–5.

Nous avons un peu de l'Espagne, un petit peu de l'Allemagne, un petit peu de la Suisse, et puis aussi de l'Italie et de l'Angleterre – et pourtant c'est la France, et elle est unique au monde. Et cette France variée, cette France si différente de visages, et de paysages, elle existe par elle-même et on ne peut pas la remplacer.

Mais ce lien, si justement, qui unit tant de provinces en une seule nation, n'est-ce pas une volonté de bâtir pour l'homme quelque chose qui atteigne au domaine spirituel?
Je vais vous répondre en chrétien. Encore une fois, je ne fais pas de politique. Mais je suis catholique, j'ai étudié la théologie, et c'est seulement en croyant que je voudrais vous parler: il ne faut pas oublier que le général de Gaulle était aussi un croyant. Eh bien! j'aimerais évoquer une autre figure qui est si proche de de Gaulle, et qui était elle aussi un symbole, et qui a elle aussi incarné la France: je veux parler de Jeanne d'Arc. Jeanne d'Arc a représenté à un moment donné le courant spirituel français. Car il existe bien un tel courant, traversé d'espérance et de foi, à l'égal du courant espagnol, par exemple, et qui fait partie de la France.

Et de Gaulle, pour vous, a incarné ce courant?
De Gaulle a incarné cet aspect de la France. C'en était un. Il y en avait d'autres, bien sûr, mais il l'a incarné.]

Of course, it is hardly surprising that, in later years, Messiaen preferred to associate Joan of Arc with Général de Gaulle instead of Maréchal Pétain. Beyond an obvious desire to forget the war years, the great international renown that Messiaen came to enjoy as he gradually assumed the unofficial title of France's best-known living composer came, in part, through state support during de Gaulle's years in power at the beginning of the Fifth Republic. Still, it is worth remembering that Messiaen, like so many politicians and artists who would subsequently turn their backs on the Vichy regime, dallied for a fleeting moment on the fringe of the *Révolution nationale*.

Chapter 3
Formal Genesis in the Sketches for
Visions de l'Amen[1]

Yves Balmer

On 10 June 1950, seven years after the première of *Visions de l'Amen* at the Concerts de la Pléiade,[2] Olivier Messiaen donated three different versions of *Visions de l'Amen* to the Paris Conservatoire's library, a collection that had just become the property of the newly founded Music Department of the Bibliothèque Nationale de France.[3] This gift was recorded in a donation ledger under the numbers 3746, 3747, and 3748, as clarified in Table 3.1.

The numbering of the manuscripts and donations in the library records correspond to the chronology of their creation as noted by Messiaen himself in blue ink on the title page inscription of the printed edition:

> Copy given to the Music Department of the Bibliothèque Nationale, Bibliothèque du Conservatoire at the same time as the sketch and autograph manuscript versions of *Visions de l'Amen*. This is the definitive version of the work (including the tempo indications, dynamics, fingerings, pedal markings,

---

[1] Translated from the French by Christopher Brent Murray. When not indicated otherwise, translated citations are Murray's.

[2] For information on the première of *Visions de l'Amen* and the Concerts de la Pléiade, see Nigel Simeone, 'Messiaen and the Concerts de la Pléiade: "A kind of clandestine revenge against the Occupation"', *Music and Letters*, 81/4 (November 2000): pp. 551–84; Yves Balmer, *Edifier son œuvre: Génèse, médiation, diffusion de l'œuvre d'Olivier Messiaen*, PhD thesis directed by Joëlle Caullier (Université Charles-de-Gaulle Lille 3, 2008), pp. 43–51; 'Présentation des Concerts de la Pléiade' (February 1943, one sheet, printed recto only), *La lettre de la Pléiade*, no. 25 (August–September 2006): p. 3. *La lettre de la Pléiade* is a special publication for the clients of Gallimard's eponymous collection (available at www.gallimard.fr/collections/pleiade.htm). See also Paris, Bibliothèque Nationale de France, Music Department, Fonds de la Pléiade, Rés. Vm, dos. 70. Yves Balmer and Christopher Brent Murray, 'Olivier Messiaen en 1941: À la recherche d'une année perdue', in M. Chimènes and Y. Simon (eds), *La musique à Paris sous l'Occupation* (Paris: Fayard/Cité de la musique, forthcoming).

[3] For more on the music collections of the Bibliothèque Nationale de France, see François Lesure, 'The Music Department of the Bibliothèque Nationale, Paris', *Notes*, 35/2 (December 1978): pp. 251–68.

articulations, phrasing, and accents) and the text of its Preface. Paris, 10 June 1950. Olivier Messiaen[4]

Table 3.1   Three versions of *Visions de l'Amen* donated by Messiaen to the Bibliothèque Nationale de France in 1950

Donation 3746

Working autograph score in pencil, *Visions de l'Amen* pour 2 pianos par Olivier Messiaen. Catalogued under Cons. Ms. 9138. 320 × 230 mm.

The Bibliothèque Nationale's card catalogue indicates, '7 fascicules and 6 pages of text (each fascicule has an original page number that does not take into account the sketches and variants which are often crossed out or erased). The whole is contained in a folder which bears traces of sketches for Amen no. IV.'

The mode of conservation was changed in order to spare the 'folder which bears traces of sketches for Amen no. IV' so that today, Ms. 9138 is made up of 8 'fascicules' (one of which is this former folder). The other fascicules are also protected by a folder of manuscript paper which also bear traces of sketches for *Visions de l'Amen*.

Donation 3747

Clean autograph copy in blue ink with preface, *Visions de l'Amen* pour 2 pianos par Olivier Messiaen. Catalogued under Cons. Ms. 9139. 350 × 270 mm. (2 liminal pages, 72 pp. of musical manuscript, 7 pp. of text.) The Bibliothèque Nationale's card catalogue notes, 'An autograph annotation in pencil indicates that the final state of this manuscript is that of the Durand printed edition. This manuscript presents a few variants with that edition … and some corrections in pencil'.

Donation 3748

Printed score, Olivier Messiaen, *Visions de l'Amen*, (Paris: Durand, 1950), [6]–99 pp. Signed and dedicated by the composer. Catalogued under Cons. Ms. 2450.

Astonishingly, musicologists interested in Olivier Messiaen's music have overlooked these freely accessible documents – regrettably so, for their analysis affords a rare glimpse of Messiaen's atelier in the early 1940s.[5] Each of the three sources provides precious information about the different phases of *Visions de*

---

[4]   Olivier Messiaen, *Visions de l'Amen* (Paris: Durand, 1950), copy conserved in Paris, Bibliothèque Nationale, Music Department, Cons. Rés. 2450. 'Exemplaire donné au département de la musique de la Bibliothèque Nationale, Bibliothèque du Conservatoire – en même temps que le brouillon et le manuscrit autographes des "*Visions de l'Amen*". Il constitue la version définitive de l'œuvre (quant aux indications de mouvements, de nuances, de doigtés, de pédale, de legato-staccato, et d'accentuation), et du texte de la Préface. Paris, 10 juin 1950. Olivier Messiaen'

[5]   These sources are all but absent from all of the major bibliographies and research resources on the composer, including Nigel Simeone, *Olivier Messiaen: Catalogue of Works* (Tutzing: Hans Schneider, 1998), pp. 80–82, and PHNS, p. 402. Only Vincent Benitez mentions this source in incomplete form, *Olivier Messiaen: A Research and Information Guide* (New York and London: Routledge, 2008), p. 15.

l'Amen's composition, not to mention a number of revelations about Messiaen's working methods, a blind spot in research on the composer due to the inaccessibility of his sketches. Among other things, these sketches reveal details about the origins of Messiaen's musical material, including compositional and formal ideas, pianistic textures, use of rhythmic pedals and the tonal or modal framework of his material. Also observable is the finalization – with the assistance of Yvonne Loriod during their first rehearsals together – of the work's sonorous structures, dynamics, tempi and fingerings.[6] The current chapter is principally concerned with formal questions in *Visions de l'Amen*, and more specifically, with what can be learned about the work's formal genesis by studying the sketches in the above-described Ms. 9138.

Ms. 9138 is an eminently difficult document to study. Its current form and order were determined at the time of Messiaen's donation. The pages of this manuscript served two different functions and show traces of two different stages of composition – the pages of the pencil working score are contained inside folders made from leaves of manuscript paper that bear sketches, fragments of text, notes, plans, chords and rhythms – all elements that make up sketches for *Visions de l'Amen*. These sketches are incomplete. Only those found on the leaves used as folders for the pencil score have survived. These sketches – primarily those on leaves 5, 10, 14, 17 and 23 – are the sources used in the present study.[7]

Messiaen and the Question of Form

In his writings, Messiaen expends little energy on formal questions. In *Technique* he presents his musical language as one where form plays a secondary role, a 'language considered from a triple point of view: rhythmic, melodic, and harmonic'.[8] *Technique* does nevertheless include a few short chapters in which form is at the heart of Messiaen's considerations, including Chapter XII ('Fugue, Sonata, Plain-Chant Forms') and to a lesser degree, Chapters X ('Melodic Development') and XI ('Lied Phrase, Ternary and Binary Phrases'). In Chapter XII, Messiaen explains how he conceives form, and the various paragraphs of this

---

[6]   Beyond the present article, the author's university and conservatoire dissertations are partially dedicated to the analysis of the *Visions de l'Amen* manuscript. Yves Balmer, *Edifier son œuvre*, pp. 29–205; Yves Balmer, *Comment compose Messiaen? Analyse génétique des brouillons de* Visions de l'Amen, research thesis under the direction of Michaël Lévinas (CNSMDP, 2008). Balmer is preparing an analysis and facsimile edition of Ms. 9138 and the first clean pencil copy of *Visions de l'Amen* belonging to Durand. The latter document predates BnF Ms. 9139 (Paris: Société Française de Musicologie, forthcoming).

[7]   For a detailed description of the organization and content of Ms. 9138, see Balmer, *Edifier son œuvre*, pp. 55–61.

[8]   *Technique*, 'Preface'.

section reveal what he considers to be the defining factors of the fixed forms he examines, including fugue, sonata, sequence, kyrie, psalmody and vocalise.

When writing on fugue, Messiaen affirms that 'without constraining ourselves to making regular fugues, we shall keep the most essential parts of them: the episode and the stretto'.[9] By this, Messiaen indicates that he has chosen to keep modes of composition anchored in tradition, inherited from past generations and defined by their technical demands. The same is true for the sonata, of which Messiaen keeps only the development.[10] In the case of both fugal and sonata forms, Messiaen maintains formal schemas, manners of writing and a manner of thinking about music that is rooted in tradition, while refusing to embrace fully the traditional forms on their own terms.

In the context of his thoughts on sonata form, Messiaen analyses the fifth movement of his *La Nativité*, 'Les Enfants de Dieu':

a. First element over a dominant pedal in B major. Development by amplification of the second measure of the theme.
b. A great fortissimo cry, upon a sort of schematic augmentation of the theme.
c. A tender phrase, forming the conclusion, established over a tonic pedal in B major.[11]

The form of this analysis is similar to certain sketches for *Visions de l'Amen* in that it is a succession of juxtaposed compositional elements. These elements are clearly separated from one another. They are developed using unique, systematic techniques and they are never interwoven with one another or contextualized.

Paradoxically, this separation of elements appears most clearly in Messiaen's presentations of his techniques for development, in which the logic is not transformational (as is usually the case in developments) but one of succession. This is clearly demonstrated in the titles of the third and fourth paragraphs of Chapter XII: 'Development of Three Themes, Preparing a Final Issued From the First' and 'Variations of the First Theme, Separated by Developments of the Second'.[12]

Messiaen himself admitted that he rarely addressed questions of musical form in his own writings, even affirming that he had 'spoken little' of his own conception of musical form in his classes at the Conservatoire in a letter to Michèle Reverdy congratulating her on the publication of her *L'œuvre pour piano d'Olivier Messiaen*.

> I think your book, with Leduc's beautiful presentation, is perfect as it is. It is always very accurate from a rhythmic and harmonic point of view. You also haven't forgotten about color, and everything concerning writing for the piano.

---

[9]   Ibid., Chapter XII, opening.
[10] Ibid., Chapter XII, section 2.
[11] Ibid., Examples 153–4.
[12] Ibid., Examples 156–60 and 161–9.

But above all, the study of form seems to be the most original and developed aspect of your work – this has never been done before, and *I myself have spoken little about it to my class* [my emphasis].[13]

What follows will show that, although Messiaen rarely wrote or spoke publically about form, paradoxically, formal considerations are omnipresent in the sketches for *Visions de l'Amen*. This parameter constitutes a central concern of Messiaen's work as a composer.

Form in Messiaen's Sketches: Composition or Juxtaposition?

The first and most basic revelation of the sketches for *Visions de l'Amen* is that Messiaen reflected a great deal on form. Formal schemas make up a major part of the surviving sketches. Many of Messiaen's notes in the sketches are explicitly related to the form of the work in progress, either to the cycle as a whole (leaf 10, page 3) or the form of the individual movements themselves. Messiaen also uses the word *forme* in the title he gives to three of his formal sketches.

Messiaen's formal sketches can be compared to a sequence of events. The plan is written out in words, and these sections seem interchangeable due to the fact that the connection between them is purely arbitrary, not the product of an organic thematic logic. Table 3.2 indicates Messiaen's notes on form in Ms. 9138.

Table 3.2   Forms of *Visions* in BnF Music Department Ms. 9138

Location	Messiaen's indications on the page of sketches
leaf 14, p. 4, upper half	Amen de la Création
leaf 14, p. 4, lower half	*Amen de la Consommation*
leaf 14, p. 3, entire page	Pour Amen du Désir: (forme complète – <u>adoptée</u>)
leaf 10, p. 3, lowest fifth	'Visions de l'Amen' – en 5 morceaux: [primitive general form]
leaf 5, p. 3, upper third	<u>Forme de Amen de planète</u>

---

[13]   Letter from Olivier Messiaen to Michèle Reverdy, 7 August 1978, personal archives of Michèle Reverdy. The author would like to express his profound gratitude to Michèle Reverdy for allowing him to consult and cite her letters from Messiaen. 'Tel [votre ouvrage] est, avec la belle présentation des éditions Leduc, je le trouve absolument parfait. C'est toujours très exact au point de vue rythmique et harmonique. Vous n'avez pas oublié les couleurs, vous avez pensé à tout ce qui concerne l'écriture de clavier, et surtout, l'étude des formes me semble être la chose la plus originale et la plus poussée: en effet, elle n'a jamais été fait par personne, et j'en ai moi-même peu parlé à ma classe.'

There are no surviving formal sketches for three of the seven *Visions de l'Amen*. Unfortunately, the haphazard manner in which these sketches came to be conserved in the collections of the Bibliothèque Nationale de France, as simple folders and not as sketches in their own right, prevents us from drawing any conclusions that might shed light on these movements. The surviving formal sketches emphasize that, for Messiaen, a musical form is written out and is made up of various sections that follow one after another, and is planned before the act of realizing the music beyond its mere themes. Apart from the plan for the 'Amen du Désir' these plans were not written after the music was composed, but were preliminary sketches. Here, form is a succession of moments, and these moments are not derived or developed from the compositional material. Their succession is paratactical and carried out without resorting to any sort of transitional material. These formal sections are separated by double bars, often preceded by a fermata, as can be seen in Example 3.1.[14]

Formal Genesis in 'Amen de la Création'

The sketch of the initial form of 'Amen de la Création' is found on leaf 14, p. 4 of Ms. 9138 (Example 3.1). This sketch bears the heading '<u>Amen de la création</u>' with a lower-case c. The main interest of this vestige resides in the numerous differences between it and the final version of the movement. It would even be more accurate to speak not of differences, but radical modifications, for the final version of the movement has almost nothing to do with the project that Messiaen initially set down. The sketch for 'Amen de la Création' – a form in eight sections with two main themes and a refrain that Messiaen labels *appel* (a call, a cry) – is much longer and contains more thematic material than the final version. The initial thematic abundance of the sketch is replaced in the final version by a strikingly monothematic block. The '*thème de la création*', a chorale, is repeated in a single, dramatic crescendo in the second piano, while the first piano accompanies this music with a 'carillon' of chords.

No intermediate sketches, realized versions, or even fragmentary sketches of a realization of Messiaen's first plan for 'Amen de la Création' is conserved among the sketches of Ms. 9138. Still, this formal sketch is detailed enough to allow for an analysis that reveals the meaning and place of formal considerations in Messiaen's creative process.

---

[14]   A similar practice can be observed in Messiaen's sketches for an abandoned work in the margins of his manuscript for the *Deux Monodies en quarts de ton*. See Christopher Brent Murray, *Le développement du langage musical d'Olivier Messiaen: Traditions, emprunts, expériences*, PhD thesis (Université-Lumière Lyon 2, 2010), pp. 422–5.

Example 3.1   Ms. 9138, initial form of 'Amen de la Création', leaf 14, p. 4

The Sketch Materials

When Messiaen sketched out his formal plan, he divided it into eight parts and anticipated using three different themes as his material: an *appel* used in sections 1 and 4, reprised in section 7; a 'th[ème] A' used in sections 2, 5 and 8; and a 'th[ème] B' to be used in sections 3 and 6.

The *appels* of sections 1 and 4 are related to one another. Each is four measures long and has the same rhythmic organization. The *appel* of section 4 inverts certain intervals of the *appel* in section 1 (Example 3.2).

Example 3.2   The two *appel* motives

In the sketch, these elements are presented without harmonies, but Messiaen indicates both the pitches and rhythms of the *appels*, which is not the case for the other two themes in this sketch. Their rhythmic and melodic structures are highly reminiscent of monodies in other works by Messiaen. Both *appels* (indicated '*lent*' for 1 and *fff* for both 1 and 4) are perfectly typical of Messiaen's musical language.

Messiaen notes that he will reuse both *appels* in section 7 ('*ensuite appels 1 et 4*'), defining at this point in the sketch their character as *appels*. This term, whose connotations include brass fanfares invoking the solemn and the grandiose, reveals that Messiaen had a very different idea in mind for the nature of his movement at the time he wrote the initial sketch. The first sketch of 'Amen de la Création' began with a grand inaugural gesture, a triumphant glorification of the Creation, whereas Messiaen ultimately chose to begin with a nearly inaudible pianissimo, illustrating a very different idea about the nature of the Creation.

The *appels* were not kept in the final version of the movement, and there is no trace of the reasons for their rejection in the surviving sketches, but their relation by partial inversion, and the fact that they are derived from Adam de la Halle's 'Jeu de la feuillée' suggests there were steps in the compositional process predating the surviving sketches. The removal of these elements from not only the movement but the entire cycle of movements raises other questions, particularly because the *appels* are found among the catalogue of themes that appear in *Technique* (Example 141), which would seem to indicate something of their importance to Messiaen. It should be noted that the name of Adam de la Halle appears in the sketches alongside that of Rameau, references that confirm the sources of Messiaen's music and that point to a recurrent creative technique.[15]

_____

[15]   This is the subject of a forthcoming book by Yves Balmer, Thomas Lacôte and Christopher Brent Murray, working title *Les techniques du langage musical d'Olivier Messiaen* (Lyon: Symétrie, forthcoming) as well as the second part of Murray, *Le développement du langage musical d'Olivier Messiaen*. As to the thematic origins of *Visions de l'Amen*, see Balmer's forthcoming facsimile edition of the *Visions de l'Amen* sketches.

Thème A, Future 'thème de la Création'

In the above-mentioned formal plan, the theme for section 2 is labeled 'th[ème] A', a theme that Messiaen would later dub 'thème de la Création'.[16] This theme is harmonized, and its rhythmic notation is minimal but clear on the whole. The long notes and the penultimate crochet are also clearly indicated (Example 3.3).

Example 3.3   'Thème de la Création' in the formal plan for 'Amen de la Création'

The marking 'lent et mystérieux' at the head of the 'thème de la Création' appears even in this very early stage of composition (Ms. 9138), although it would later evolve to read 'Très lent, mystérieux et solonnel' in the first clean pencil version (also in Ms. 9138).

The theme is fixed from this early moment in the formal genesis of the work and undergoes no further modifications, although Messiaen's working notes seem to show that the musical material presented on three staves represents only a fragment of the theme's intended development: Messiaen notes 'etc. complete modulating phrase in *E* and in *C major*' and 'second conclusion, end of the phrase'.[17] Messiaen indicates the tonal trajectory that will be taken to constitute the whole of the theme and the second phrase of music is marked as 'fin de la phrase', suggesting that the staves of music do not connect to one another. Also, one can make out the erased note '2e conclusion' above Messiaen's note 'fin de la phrase'.

As a whole, these clues show that Messiaen had originally imagined a longer, more developed and modulating phrase, one that eventually might have a number of different endings. None of this is found in the final version of the work, where the 'thème de la Création' is identical to the contours set down by the composer in the sketch on leaf 14, p. 2 (Example 3.4).

It goes without saying, then, that the melodic structure of the movement evolved a great deal between the sketch and the final version, with Messiaen eliminating

---

[16]   *Traité III*, p. 233. Messiaen's analysis of *Visions de l'Amen* can be found on pp. 229–75.

[17]   'etc. phrase complète modulant en *mi* et – et en *ut majeur* – ', '2ᵉ conclusion, fin de la phrase'.

Example 3.4   *Visions de l'Amen*, 'Amen de la Création', bars 1–8, 'thème de la
               Création'

the *appels* and simplifying 'thème A' by abandoning his initial plan to extend and
modulate it. In the same manner, Messiaen also planned on using a 'thème B' that
he also ultimately eliminated.

Thème B, Future Material for the 'Amen du Désir'

The 'thème B' is an enigmatic part of Messiaen's formal sketch (reproduced
in Example 3.1). Messiaen does not bother to write it out, and refers only to a
theme from his *Traité* (his way of referring to *Technique* in the sketches):[18]

---

[18]   The relationship between the sketches for *Visions de l'Amen* and the *Traité*, which
would ultimately become *Technique de mon langage musical*, is a subject that merits
a detailed study of its own. It should be pointed out that Messiaen repeatedly refers to
examples from the *Traité* throughout his sketches. To judge from the difference between
their numbering and the numbering of the examples in the final published version of
Technique, the *Traité* was a shorter, earlier version of *Technique*. This casts doubt on the
chronology of both *Visions de l'Amen* and *Technique* as recounted in PHNS (pp. 119–20):
'It was during this vacation [summer 1942] that Messiaen later said he wrote much of
Technique de mon langage musical, though earlier diary entries indicate that some of his
ground-breaking treatise was already in existence before this date: he almost certainly used
this summer to put the book into its final form. Messiaen was back in Paris at the start of
October. By the middle of the month, he was putting the finishing touches to *Technique
de mon langage musical*: "finish Traité and give it to Leduc with list of subscribers for its
publication". Although Hill and Simeone make no further reference to Messiaen working
on *Technique*, a major source of musical examples in *Technique* is *Visions de l'Amen*,
which, according to Hill and Simeone, was started during the autumn of 1942 (p. 120) after
Technique was supposedly in 'its final form'. Faced with this contradiction, two connected
hypotheses need to be considered. The first is that *Technique* was probably considerably
reworked between its 1942 version and the published version of 1944. The second is that
the *Visions de l'Amen*, which were premièred in 1943, were composed, in whole or in
part, before Messiaen received the commission from Denise Tual and the Concerts de la
Pléiade at the end of 1942. This second hypothesis is more or less confirmed in a short
text by Denise Tual, 'Itinéraire des concerts de la pléiade', typescript, Paris, Bibliothèque
Nationale de France, Music Department, Rés. Vm, dos 70 (1), p. 7. 'At the time I got in
contact with him, and when he offered the *Visions de l'Amen*, a work *in progress* for piano

'3) ensuite th[ème] B (le ~~joli~~ th[ème] à la Mozart par +46 du Traité) Transposé en la majeur'. The study of the sketches clearly demonstrates (and for the first time) that Messiaen himself used *Technique* as a reference during his own compositional process, at least for *Visions de l'Amen*. In spite of this lack of musical notation, Messiaen describes the theme in four manners:

- According to personal taste: Messiaen likes this music. It is a 'pretty' theme. (One is led to wonder what 'pretty' means to a composer such as Messiaen.)
- Stylistic reference: 'à la Mozart'.
- Harmony: Messiaen notes one of the most fundamental tonal progressions, the resolution of a dominant seventh chord in third inversion (known as the 'chord of the tritone' in French [+4]) to a first inversion tonic chord (known as the 'chord of the sixth' [6])
- Transposition and tonality: this theme will be transposed to A major, which would seem to indicate that the example in the *Traité* is in another key.

In the initially planned form for 'Amen de la Création', 'thème B' is noted as reappearing in the sixth section, '6) puis th[ème] B avec cascades d'accords (plus trilles et arpèges) en mode 3 [D^{+4}] et un mode 2 [C$\sharp^6$] voir cet effet dans Traité'. Here Messiaen again refers to the *Traité*, this time without referencing Mozart. The harmony is the same, but is specified (the progression of +4 to 6, resolving to A major), and this time Messiaen describes the accompaniment, a 'cascade of chords' that will serve as a variation for the second presentation of the theme. The harmonies of this cascade are specified, two superposed modes, an 'effect' that appears 'in the Traité'.

In spite of its brevity, the sketch for 'thème B' provides enough information to identify the motive elsewhere. Thanks to a series of comparisons and some deductive reasoning, it can be affirmed that 'thème B' forms the material that would later become the main theme of 'Amen du Désir' (Example 3.5).

Messiaen's description of the first theme of 'Amen du Désir' in *Technique* also evokes Mozart's influence: 'Melodic contours somewhat like Mozart [*un peu "Mozart"*]. The harmonies of the lower staff are simple and tonal; the modes mingled there suffice to communicate to them infinite tenderness and divine love.'[19] What is more, beyond the 'un peu Mozart' in *Technique*, Messiaen further defines the source of this theme in the *Traité*:

---

which would require the paying of copyist's fees, he asked me if the Pléiade could pay these costs, and I reassured him that this would be possible. And so, the *Visions de l'Amen* were a commission.' [À l'époque où je me mis en rapport avec lui, et où il me proposa les *Visions de l'Amen*, une œuvre pour piano, *encore inachevée*, et qui nécessitait des frais de copie, il me demanda si la Pléiade pouvait les assumer, je le rassurai. Les *Visions de l'Amen* ont donc été une commande.] The emphasis is the author's.

19 *Technique*, example 370.

Example 3.5   The 'joli thème B à la Mozart', main theme of the 'Amen du Désir'

The ecstatic, tender theme – First period, 4 measures. The first melodic contours [example] are reminiscent of Mozart (Susanna's aria, *Marriage of Figaro*) [example]. The falling sixth in the third measure is also Mozartian. ... Also note the new Mozartian contour in the penultimate measure [example] which recalls Mozart (Susanna's aria).[20]

Not only does the main theme of 'Amen du Désir' have its roots in a Mozartian model, like the planned 'thème B' for the 'Amen de la Création', but the harmony of Mozart's music also corresponds to that planned for 'thème B': a dominant seventh chord in third inversion (C–D–F♯–A) and its resolution to a tonic triad in first inversion with an added sixth (B–D–E–G), as Messiaen noted, '+4 6'. Thus, Messiaen's own auto-analytical writings confirm that the 'joli thème à la Mozart' described in the sketches for 'Amen de la Création' would ultimately become the first theme of the 'Amen du Désir'.

Although the description of the themes and their analyses by Messiaen seem to correspond, another question remains. In his sketch for 'Amen du Désir',[21] Messiaen notes the incipit of the theme and indicates the *Traité*: 'voir ex. 169

---

20   *Traité III*, p. 249. The emphasis is Messiaen's.
21   Bibliothèque Nationale, Music Department, Ms. 9138, leaf 14, p. 2.

Ter complet'.[22] If the hypothesis about the identity of 'thème B' in the 'Amen de la Création' formal sketch is well founded, this second occurrence would seem to indicate that Messiaen used multiple modes of cross-referencing to indicate his thematic material. On one hand, in 'Amen de la Création' we observe a cross-reference without musical notation to an unnumbered theme in his *Traité* that is associated with Mozart. On the other hand, in 'Amen du Désir' we observe a cross-reference with a musical incipit to a numbered theme in the *Traité* without any mention of Mozart.

Beyond this, the thematic cross-referencing to the *Traité* in the sketches can also be seen in the note on the transposition of 'thème B'. In *Technique*, the 'à la Mozart' theme is noted in G major. 'Amen de la Création' is in A major, so Messiaen notes in his sketch that the theme will have to be 'tranposed to A major'. This would not only seem to indicate Messiaen's consciousness of the key in which the theme is noted in his draft of *Technique* (the *Traité*), but what is more, it would seem that the example that once bore the number '169 *ter*' became example 370 in the final version of *Technique*. This corroborates the observations made in note 18 concerning the difficulties in dating the creation of *Technique*.

The discovery of a link between the 'joli thème à la Mozart' in the sketches for the 'Amen de la Création' and the first theme of 'Amen du Désir' suggests two possible hypotheses about Messiaen's compositional decisions. Perhaps Messiaen hoped to unify the cycle of movements by using the theme in both 'Amen de la Création' and 'Amen du Désir' as he already does with the 'thème de la Création' that is heard throughout the cycle, and as the sketches show that he initially intended to do by using the *appel* in both the 'Amen de la Création' and the 'Amen de la Consommation'.[23] Or perhaps he both planned and wrote 'Amen du Désir' after already having abandoned the first version of 'Amen de la Création' and chose to save the 'joli thème à la Mozart' he cut from 'Amen de la Création' by using it in a new movement. This second proposition would help to explain the addition of a movement to a work that Messiaen had initially conceived in five movements.[24]

The Carillon

Finally, the carillon is an essential element of the final version of 'Amen de la Création'. Indeed, it is the only music played by the first piano, superposed over

---

[22] In French, when a series of numbers (such as house numbers) is already in place the addition of the words 'bis' (second) and 'ter' (third), allow for insertions without renumbering.

[23] Balmer, *Edifier son œuvre*, pp. 82–5.

[24] Balmer, *Edifier son œuvre*, pp. 94–9. The first version of *Visions de l'Amen* in five movements included, 'Amen de la Création', 'Amen des étoiles, de la planète à l'anneau', 'Amen de l'agonie de Jésus', 'Amen des Anges, des saints, du chant des oiseaux', and 'Amen de la Consommation'. Messiaen later added 'Amen du Désir' and 'Amen du jugement'.

the 'thème de la Création' in the second piano. Although the carillon theme is present in the sketches for 'Amen de la Création', it plays a minor, thematically unimportant role. Messiaen notes only, '8) reprise fin du th[ème] A *ff* avec au dessus un carillon sur "accords en 4tes"' (see the bottom of Example 3.1). The word *carillon* itself is found just before the end of the sketch and only appears once. In the sketches, the carillon is composed of only two chords, whereas in the final version, Messiaen decided upon a motive using between three different chords. The two chords found in the sketch become the second and third chords of the final version. Messiaen generates the first chord in the final version by transposing the first chord of the sketches up a major second (Example 3.6).

Example 3.6   Comparison of the carillon chords of the sketch (left) and the final version (right)

The carillon theme goes from playing a minor role in the sketches to becoming an essential component of the entire movement. This new importance would seem to coincide with the decision to abandon both the *appels* and 'thème B'.

Conclusion: Form, Aesthetics, Meaning

Beyond the material he planned on using and then abandoned, Messiaen's imagined form of 'Amen de la Création' in his sketches tells us a great deal about his methods and manner of writing music. In *Visions de l'Amen* he wrote out his plan in words, conceiving his composition in separate sections. Each of these sections is introduced with terms typically used to navigate lists and indicate temporal transition (*ensuite*, *puis*, *et*, etc.). Moreover, Messiaen reiterates the chronological nature of his conception of form by numbering each of the sections he has already described in words. The formal sketch for 'Amen de la Création' is an unexpected confirmation of Boulez's famous comment, '[Messiaen] doesn't compose, he juxtaposes'.[25] This manuscript source allows us to see the essence of Messiaen's ideas on formal construction. In this earliest trace of the movement's genesis, one that Messiaen abandoned and that is consequently unaffected and untouched by further compositional efforts, it is quite clear that Messiaen initially conceived the movement as a series of juxtaposed sections.

The form described in the sketch studied here never saw the light of day; Messiaen changed his project a great deal. I have found no clues as to the reasons

---

[25]   Pierre Boulez, *Stocktakings from an Apprenticeship*, trans. Stephen Walsh (Oxford: Clarendon, 1991), p. 49.

for this change, and no trace exists of the passage from the sketch to the final version. Still, the existence of this sketch leads me to raise some questions. Did Messiaen change the form of 'Amen de la Création' for aesthetic reasons? Had he already decided upon the programme of the movement at the time he made his first formal sketch?

The initial form for the movement is bi-thematic and influenced by romantic models with their notions of re-exposition, variation, contrast and grandiose conclusion. This romantic model is quite distant from the musical idea described in Messiaen's preface for the final version of the movement: 'The entire movement is a crescendo. It begins with an absolute pianissimo, in the mystery of that primitive nebula that already contains all of the power of light, all of the bells that quiver in that light – light and as a consequence, Life.'

'Amen de la Création' evolved from a form whose grammar was anchored in tradition to something far more evocative. Messiaen abandoned fragmentary organization by opposition of themes (that of the sketch) and chose an eminently teleological form. In the final version, Creation is no longer a series of events, but rather a path, a *becoming*, a broad litany that advances, growing in intensity, exploring the varied registers of the piano, ornamented with the superposition of a rhythmically complex carillon. The initial idea of a powerful, radiant Creation is replaced by a Creation that looks towards the future, where the end is more glorious than the beginning, where the Omega outshines the Alpha.

There remains the question of the link between music and meaning in Messiaen's art. Messiaen's initial idea generated a form and some musical material. Then a change in his ideas led to a modification of the form that conserved part of the material. If, as it seems, the idea to make 'Amen de la Création' a single grand crescendo came after the idea to write a movement about the Creation, it would seem that there was, in the beginning, no direct correlation between the title and the proposed form, or that Messiaen's theological ideas about the nature of Creation – or the best way to musically illustrate Creation – changed after his initial sketch for the movement. To understand better the formal changes in the 'Amen de la Création' it would be useful to combine the study of Messiaen's sketches and manuscripts with what Messiaen might have read on the subject of Creation, either in the writings of Ernest Hello, whose imagery Messiaen found extremely suggestive, or in other sources in Messiaen's personal library.[26] This kind of investigation provides an opportunity for Messiaen scholars specializing in different sorts of sources, in different aspects of Messiaen's life and music, to cross-pollinate their knowledge and further our understanding of his compositional process and musical thought.

---

[26]   For example, Messiaen described Hello's *Paroles de Dieu* as 'an extraordinary book that develops an entire symbolism from the Scripture'. Brigitte Massin, *Olivier Messiaen: Une poétique du merveilleux* (Aix-en-Provence: Alinea, 1989), p. 155. See Yves Balmer, 'Religious Literature in Messiaen's Personal Library', in Andrew Shenton (ed.), *Messiaen the Theologian* (Farnham: Ashgate, 2010), pp. 15–27.

Chapter 4

From Music for the Radio to a Piano Cycle: Sources for the *Vingt Regards sur l'Enfant-Jésus*

Lucie Kayas

The strange genesis of Messiaen's *Vingt Regards*, first conceived as an accompaniment for a radio play by Maurice Toesca, has received close investigation in studies by Edward Forman and Siglind Bruhn.[1] In addition to these studies, two new sources have led to the need for the present synthesis that reconstructs more precisely how, during the first half of 1944 in occupied Paris, Messiaen came back to the subject of Christ's Nativity, which had previously inspired *La Nativité du Seigneur*, written in 1935.

Eclectic Sources Found in the Author's Note

If we carefully analyse the note published as preamble to the score that Messiaen used to read between the pieces during the first performances of the *Vingt Regards*,[2] the lecture given in the Musikhochschule in Saarbrücken in 1954 (later printed in the *Traité*)[3] and the text written in 1978 for the concerts given in honour of the composer's 70th birthday,[4] we notice two types of indications, referring to both literature and visual arts and eventually to music. In the second paragraph of the Author's Note, after having explained where and how the Theme of God is used, Messiaen mentions several sources of inspiration, including 'bird songs, chimes, spirals, stalactites, galaxies, photons, and texts by Dom Columba Marmion, Saint Thomas, Saint John

---

[1]   Edward Forman, '"L'harmonie de l'Univers": Maurice Toesca and the Genesis of *Vingt Regards sur l'Enfant-Jésus*', in Christopher Dingle and Nigel Simeone (eds), *Olivier Messiaen: Music, Art and Literature* (Aldershot: Ashgate, 2007); Siglind Bruhn, *Messiaen's Contemplation of Covenant and Incarnation: Musical Symbols of Faith in the Two Great Piano Cycles of the 1940s* (Hillsdale, NY: Pendragon Press, 2007).

[2]   Olivier Messiaen, 'Note de l'auteur' in *Vingt Regards sur l'Enfant-Jésus* (Paris: Durand, 1947).

[3]   *Traité II*, pp. 437–509.

[4]   [Unsigned], *Hommage à Olivier Messiaen* (Paris: La Recherche Artistique, 1978), pp. 43–7.

of the Cross, Saint Theresa of Lisieux, the gospels or from the missal'. Later on, he comes back to Dom Marmion's *Le Christ dans ses mystères* and Maurice Toesca's *Douze Regards*. These could be considered as theological and literary sources. Then, reading the details given for each movement, the following inscriptions by Messiaen can be traced to quotations from the Bible or the missal, such as:

- 'Regard du Père': 'This is my Son, the Beloved, with whom I am well pleased' (Matthew 3:17/Mark 1:11).
- 'Regard de la Croix': 'You will be a priest' (Psalm 110:4). [In the Bible: 'You are a priest for ever'; in Marmion:'You are a priest for eternity' (p. 85).]
- 'La Parole toute puissante': 'The Son sustains all things by his powerful word' (Hebrews 1:3).
- 'Regard des Anges': 'God makes his angels winds and his servants flames of fire' (Psalm 104 and Hebrews 1:7).
- 'Par Lui tout a été fait': 'All things came into being by him, and without him not one thing came into being' (John 1:3).[5]
- 'Regard de l'Onction terrible': 'Therefore God, your God, has anointed you with the oil of gladness beyond your companions' (Psalm 45:7).[6]
- 'Je dors, mais mon cœur veille': 'I sleep, but my heart is awake' (Song of Songs 5:2).

In 'Je dors, mais mon cœur veille', Messiaen also refers to the *Fioretti* of Saint Francis (LIII, 'Of The Second Consideration Of The Sacred, Holy Stigmata'). In the 'Note de l'Auteur', he writes: 'Ce n'est pas d'un ange l'archet qui sourit, – c'est Jésus dormant qui nous aime dans son Dimanche et nous donne l'oubli…' [It is not the bow of an angel that smiles, – it is the sleeping Jesus who loves us on his day of rest and gives us oblivion…]. The passage adapted from the *Fioretti* reads: 'l'Ange poussa l'archet sur la viole et fit une note si suave, que s'il avait continué en tirant l'archet, on serait mort de joie…' [the Angel drew his bow across the viol producing so sweet a sound that, if he had continued to play, all who heard him would have died of joy…].[7]

---

[5]   The French here is 'Toutes choses ont été faites par elle, et rien de ce qui a été fait n'a été fait sans elle'; 'Elle' refers to 'la Parole' (the Word). As the first verse of John states that 'la Parole était Dieu', the title derives indirectly from John 1:1.

[6]   See Messiaen's own commentary in *Hommage à Olivier Messiaen*, p. 47: 'C'est là cette Onction unique, inouïe, terrifiante, dont parle le Psaume 45'. It is interesting to note that in Messiaen's interpretation, he refers to the oil used for anointing as 'awesome unction' ('awesome' here carrying its original meaning rather than more recent colloquial usage).

[7]   The image of the musician angel arises from this passage. Viewing Maurice Denis's picture in the edition of the *Fioretti* owned by Messiaen, it is hard not to think of his first wife Claire Delbos playing the violin for Messiaen as for Saint Francis. See *Les Petites Fleurs de Saint François*, trans. André Pératé, illustrations by Maurice Denis (Paris: Librairie de l'Art Catholique, 1926), p. 246. This was Messiaen's edition.

Finally, Messiaen also indicates pictures or artists having inspired his music such as the painter De Chirico for 'Regard du Temps', a painting of the Virgin adoring her Son in the womb for 'Première Communion de la Vierge', an engraving of Mary, Jesus and the 'little sister' Thérèse for 'Le Baiser de l'Enfant-Jésus' and an old tapestry for 'Regard de l'Onction terrible'.[8] In 1978, Messiaen added Michelangelo's *Last Judgement* for 'Regard des Anges'. If we go back to literary sources, two names require more development: Maurice Toesca and Dom Marmion, both almost forgotten today even in France.

Maurice Toesca(1904–98), Police Officer and Writer in Occupied Paris and His Correspondence with Messiaen

Peter Hill and Nigel Simeone's biography of Messiaen has told us that Toesca's name occurs several times in Messiaen's diaries for 1944.[9] However, nothing can be found recalling *Douze Regards* either among the more than 25 items published by Toesca or in his archives held at the IMEC (Institut Mémoire de l'Édition Contemporaine/Institute for the Memory of Contemporary Writers) in Caen (France). His 1975 memoir, *Cinq ans de patience*,[10] includes several references to Messiaen and his music for the year 1944 and in Caen there is a file called *Nativité* that offers much material to help us understand what Messiaen owes to Toesca.

Born in 1904 in Confolens (Charente), Maurice Toesca was a student of the French philosopher Alain (aka Émile Chartier) at the Lycée Henri IV in Paris before entering the French administration, as mentioned in the obituary published in *Le Monde* on 3 February 1998.[11] In a letter in response to this article, historian Jean-Marc Berlière pointed out Toesca's exact duties:

> Sub-prefect of the Côtes-du-nord, Meurthe et Moselle, then of the Aisne, Toesca was appointed police Superintendant in charge of the Somme, the Ardennes and the Oise …. In June 1942, Maurice Toesca moved to Paris to work with Amédée Bussière, prefect of the Somme designated by Laval. He was officially sent on secondment by the police prefect in September. Toesca becomes his 'directeur de cabinet' and remained in this position until the insurrection of 19 August 1944 (in fact 30 July).

> [Sous-préfet des Côtes-du-Nord, de Meurthe-et-Moselle puis de l'Aisne, nommé intendant de police chargé du service régional de police de la Somme, des Ardennes et de l'Oise …. Maurice Toesca suivit à Paris en juin 1942 Amédée

---

[8]   See the 'Note de l'Auteur' in the published score.

[9]   PHNS, pp. 134–41.

[10]   Maurice Toesca, *Cinq ans de patience* (Paris: Emile-Paul, 1975).

[11]   [unsigned], 'Maurice Toesca: Essayiste et romancier', obituary, *Le Monde*, 3 February 1998: p. 11.

Bussière, préfet de la Somme nommé par Laval. Officiellement détaché auprès du préfet de police en septembre, Maurice Toesca est son directeur de cabinet: il le restera jusqu'à l'insurrection du 19 août 1944.][12]

Toesca appears to be a controversial man, compromised by working with the German occupying forces but trying nevertheless to help some of his Jewish acquaintances, including the poet Robert Desnos. This intercession caused Toesca's departure from the Paris Préfecture at the end of July 1944, as we can read in his memoires:

30 July 1944

Thanks to a very faithful police inspector from Alsace who is in charge of the liaison with the rue des Saussaies, I found out yesterday evening that it was my turn to be arrested. ... I have made up my mind: either I officially quit my position within twenty-four hours or I join the Maquis. As I do not want to look like a last minute resistant, I told M. Bussière that I would voluntarily – almost secretly – stay on his side. The main thing for me is to let the Germans know that I am no longer on the staff of the Prefecture.

[30 juillet 1944

J'ai su hier soir, par un inspecteur de police alsacien, très dévoué, qui assure la liaison avec la rue des Saussaies, que mon tour était venu d'être arrêté. ... Ma décision est prise: ou bien je quitte officiellement mon poste dans les vingt-quatre heures, ou bien je prends le maquis. Comme je ne veux pas avoir l'air de jouer les résistants de la dernière heure, j'assure M. Bussière que je resterai néanmoins auprès de lui, à titre bénévole et quasi clandestin. L'essentiel pour moi est de faire savoir aux Allemands que je n'appartiens plus au personnel du Ministère de l'intérieur.][13]

According to *Cinq ans de patience*, Toesca attended a performance of *Visions de l'Amen* at Guy-Bernard Delapierre's house on 20 July 1944, and he already knew the *Quatuor pour la fin du Temps* from 8 June, as shown by an enthusiastic letter to the composer.[14] But the first contact between the two men goes back to February 1944, as Messiaen's letter to Toesca on 4 February shows:

---

[12]   Jean-Marc Berlière, 'L'autre Maurice Toesca', *Le Monde* (13 February 1998): p. 11.

[13]   Toesca, *Cinq ans de patience*, pp. 311–12.

[14]   Letter from Maurice Toesca to Olivier Messiaen, 8 June 1944, quoted in English, with French original in a footnote, in Forman, '"L'harmonie de l'Univers"', pp. 13–14.

Dear Friend,

Many thanks for your phone call. Thank you for agreeing to deal with this fine subject. Here, with all my gratitude, is the promised page. It is taken from *Le Christ dans ses mystères* by Dom Columba Marmion, in a section dedicated to Christmas which starts with this sentence from John: '*To all those who received him* (by faith), *who believed in his name, he* (the Word) *gave the power to become children of God*'.

　　See you soon – once I am finished with the orchestration I'm doing at the moment, I'll visit you.

Olivier Messiaen

[Cher Ami,

Merci pour votre coup de téléphone. Merci de vouloir bien traiter ce beau sujet. Voici donc, avec toute ma reconnaissance, la page promise. Elle est extraite du 'Christ dans ses mystères' de Dom Columba Marmion, et s'y situe dans un passage sur la Noël qui commence par cette phrase de l'Evangile selon Saint Jean: 'A tous ceux qui l'ont reçu (par la foi), il (le Verbe) a donné le pouvoir de devenir enfants de Dieu.'

　　A bientôt – dès mon présent travail d'instrumentation terminé, j'irai vous voir.

Olivier Messiaen][15]

Messiaen was actually working on the *Trois Petites Liturgies* at the time.

　　Receiving this letter, Toesca wrote of his excitement in the unpublished part of his memoir:

> Got this morning a note from Messiaen. All the elements of my Nativity that I have mentioned to him are exciting me. What we want to say on this subject is not insignificant, but one needs to find the right tone. Not the tone of the Bible nor of the Gospels.
>
> [Reçu ce matin un mot de Messiaen. Je précipite en moi les éléments de la Nativité dont je lui ai parlé. Ce qu'on a à dire sur ce sujet n'est pas mince, mais il faut trouver le ton. Pas celui de la Bible. Pas celui des Evangiles.][16]

Toesca's description of his meeting with Messiaen at the performance of *Visions de l'Amen* at Delapierre's house shows his continued faith in their collaboration:

---

[15]　Letter from Olivier Messiaen to Maurice Toesca, Caen, IMEC, Fonds Toesca.

[16]　Maurice Toesca, *Mémoires dactylographiées* (Caen: IMEC, Fonds Toesca, n.d.).

I arrived on the doorstep just at the same moment as Messiaen. We exchange civilities. Our smiles express the complicity of mutual understanding; we think of the same things; we understand each other. I told him: 'Here are my words'. He replied: 'I'll give you my sounds'. He has already composed eleven piano pieces for our radiophonic essay *Les Douze Regards*.

[J'arrive sur le seuil en même temps que Messiaen. Nous échangeons des amabilités. Nos sourires ont la complicité de l'entente; nous pensons aux mêmes choses; nous nous comprenons. Je lui ai dit: 'Voici mes mots', il me répond: 'Je vous donnerai mes sons'. Pour notre essai radiophonique *Les Douze Regards*, il a déjà composé onze pièces de piano. J'ai hâte de les entendre.][17]

On 9 September, Toesca writes again:

Olivier Messiaen calls me on the phone. His voice is exultant: he has finished his musical accompaniment for the *Douze Regards*. I congratulate him. 'I am sorry', he says, 'for I have exceeded the limits given for the composition; I thought I would use up the commentaries within twelve piano pieces but yesterday evening I completed the 24th one;[18] this work is as important as the *Préludes*.'

[Olivier Messiaen m'appelle au téléphone. Sa voix triomphe: il a terminé son accompagnement musical pour *Douze Regards*. Je l'en complimente. 'Je m'excuse, dit-il, d'avoir dépassé les limites de la composition; j'avais pensé épuiser les commentaire en dix ou douze pièces pour piano et j'ai achevé hier soir la vingt-quatrième; c'est une œuvre de l'importance des Préludes, par exemple.'][19]

We now need to understand how this 'essai radiophonique' came about, as described in a letter from Henry Barraud to Toesca a year later, on 8 February 1945:

Please believe that there is no way that the Radio would fail to honour the agreement it had with you and your collaborator Olivier Messiaen. These commissions came from the former director and under the present conditions were quite unknown to me. … After having examined the case, I understand that they have been ordered on a special credit … managed by the Administrative services at the request of the Music Department.

[Croyez bien qu'il n'est pas question un instant que la Radiodiffusion ne fasse pas honneur aux engagements qu'elle a pris avec vous et avec votre collaborateur, Olivier Messiaen. Ces commandes avaient été passées par la précédente direction

---

[17] Toesca, *Cinq ans de patience*, p. 298.

[18] Toesca's memory is not totally reliable for there are only 20 *regards*; he may have confused their number with Chopin's 24 *Préludes*.

[19] Toesca, *Cinq ans de patience*, p. 348.

et dans des conditions mal connues de moi. ... A l'examen, je vois que ces commandes ont été faites sur un crédit tout à fait spécial ... qui était géré par le Service administratif et sous le contrôle de la Direction de la musique.][20]

It was, therefore, not Barraud himself who commissioned the piece but his forerunner Henry Büsser.

The Context of Occupied Paris and the Studio d'Essai

The formulation 'essai radiophonique' strongly recalls Pierre Schaeffer's Studio d'Essai inaugurated on 1 January 1943. Schaeffer's staff included Maurice Martenot and Albert Ollivier, whom he knew from the Association Jeune France in Vichy, together with René Bourdariat for the production, whose name – according to Hill and Simeone – appears in Messiaen's diary on 16 November: 'Look at the cut version of the *Regards* and the texts, for the Studio d'Essai, with Bourdariat, Toesca and Delapierre.'[21] So, the next question is: why did Schaeffer, who entered the Resistance in August 1943, address such a controversial personality as Toesca and associate him with Messiaen? The answer is probably in the ambiguous attitude of Schaeffer – described by Karine La Bail as 'vichysto-résistant' – who worked at the same time with members of the Front national des musiciens (such as Barraud, Barraine and Désormière) and with compromised artists such as Florent Schmitt and Cortot producing what Karine Le Bail calls 'des émissions écrans' (screen broadcasts) in order not to be troubled by his administration.[22]

Schaeffer's archives[23] show that for the second half of 1944, he had a plan for 'a series of tributes lasting 40 minutes, to poets or writers who have inspired contemporary musicians'.[24] We also know that Yvonne Loriod recorded an entire concert for the Studio d'Essai broadcast on 14 March including three of Debussy's *Études*, *Trois danses rituelles* by Jolivet, three of Messiaen's *Préludes*, Four Pieces op. 3 by Kodály and Bartók's Sonata. So, it is probably thanks to the Studio d'Essai and the relationship between Messiaen, Loriod and Schaeffer that Messiaen and Toesca happened to work together on a Nativity project.

---

[20]   Letter from Henry Barraud to Maurice Toesca, 9 September 1944, Caen, IMEC, Fonds Toesca.

[21]   Messiaen's personal archive: 'Voir avec Bourdariat, Toesca et Delapierre découpage des Regards avec la pièce pour le Studio d'essai'. This information was kindly provided by Nigel Simeone.

[22]   See Karine Le Bail, *Musique, pouvoir, responsabilité: La politique musicale de la radiodiffusion française, 1939–1953*, PhD diss. (Paris: Institut d'Études Politiques de Paris, 2005).

[23]   Caen, IMEC, Fonds Schaeffer.

[24]   Ibid.

Toesca's *Nativité*

If we believe Messiaen, he was the person who asked Toesca to write words for him, so we can suppose that the Studio d'Essai first thought of Messiaen, who asked for a writer in order to get an appropriate radiophonic text for his music. Someone might have suggested Toesca, who called the composer and accepted the challenge. This version fits with the nature of Schaeffer's project.

In a later letter to the German musicologist Hans-Dieter Clausen from 15 September 1960, Toesca gives his own version of the story:

> It is true that Messiaen composed his *Vingt Regards* starting from a *Nativity* that I wrote that was intended to be called *Les Douze Regards*. It happened as follows: French Radio decided to broadcast one of my works. This work needed a musical illustration and Messiaen was chosen by the Director of the radio station. So I got in touch with Olivier Messiaen. … Messiaen was asked to write half-an-hour of music; but when he finished his work, he had written more than two hours of music!

> [Il est exact que Messiaen a composé ses *Vingt Regards* en partant d'une *Nativité* que j'ai écrite, et qui devait à l'origine porter comme titre 'les Douze Regards'. Voici comment cela s'est passé: La Radiodiffusion française avait décidé de monter sur l'une de ses antennes mon œuvre. Cette œuvre appelait une illustration musicale. Messiaen fut choisi par le Directeur de la chaîne radiophonique. J'entrai donc en relation avec Olivier Messiaen. … Messiaen devait écrire une demi-heure de musique; mais lorsqu'il eut terminé son travail, il en avait composé près de deux heures!][25]

According to the documents, this appears as an embellished version, for obviously Messiaen was the first to be approached by Radiodiffusion Française.

The text produced by Toesca exists in a typed version in his archives,[26] together with its first edition in *La revue hommes et monde* from January 1949.[27] Famous writers such as Maurice Allais, Jean Cocteau, Julien Green, Joseph Kessel, André Maurois, Marcel Pagnol or Jules Romains were contributors to this short-lived publication.

Toesca's *Nativité* is a kind of Christmas tale recalling the faux-naïf style of Ramuz's *Histoire du soldat*. Divided into nine parts (reworked into eight for the edition in the *Revue*), the *Nativité* mixes dialogues with descriptions and involves ten characters: First Woman, Second Woman, A Man, The Herald, A Centurion, Joseph and Mary, a Herdsman, his wife, and his daughter Judith:

---

[25]   Letter from Maurice Toesca to Hans-Dieter Clausen, Paris, 15 Septembre 1960, Caen, IMEC, Fonds Toesca.

[26]   Caen, IMEC, Fonds Toesca.

[27]   Toesca, 'La Nativité', *La revue hommes et mondes,* no. 39 (January 1949): pp. 119–38.

1. The Herald announces Herod's order to take a census of the population. Joseph and Mary leave for Bethlehem, followed by the star.
2. Birth of the baby.
3. Dialogue between the ox and the donkey.
4. A herdsman comes with his wife and daughter to visit Jesus.
5. Three shepherds enter to honour the newborn child.
6. Adoration of the Three Kings.
7. Three angels miraculously enter through the roof and announce Jesus' final sacrifice.
8. Everybody is asleep, except Mary. She prays and waits for her son's first look at her.
9. Mary too is asleep. Only silence.

Toesca followed the scenes suggested by the Marmion quotation sent by Messiaen and developed the story in the naive manner of a Christmas tale having the animals speak. It is useful to see the quotation Messiaen sent in full:

> And how ought we to receive Him? By faith: *His qui credunt in nomine ejus.* It is to those who – believing in His Person, in His word, in His works – have received this Child as God, that it has been given, in return, to become themselves children of God: *Ex Deo nati sunt.*
>
> Such is, in fact, the fundamental disposition that we must have so that this 'admirable exchange' may produce in us all its fruits. Faith alone teaches us how it is brought about; wherein it is realized; faith alone gives us a true knowledge of it and one worthy of God.
>
> For there are many modes and degrees of knowledge.
>
> 'The ox knoweth his owner, and the ass his Master's Crib', wrote Isaiah, in speaking of this mystery [Is 1:3]. They saw the Child lying in the crib. But what could they see? As much as an animal could see: the form, the size, the colour, the movement – an entirely rudimentary knowledge that does not pass the boundary line of sensation. Nothing more.
>
> The passers-by, the curious, who approached the stable-cave saw the Child; but for them He was like all others. They did not go beyond this purely natural knowledge. Perhaps they were struck by the Child's loveliness. Perhaps they pitied His destitution. But this feeling did not last and was soon replaced by indifference.
>
> There were the Shepherds, simple-hearted men, enlightened by a ray from on high: *Claritas Dei circumfulsit illos* [Lk 2:9]. They certainly understood more; they recognised in this Child the promised Messiah, long awaited, the *Exspectatio gentium* [Gen 49:10]; they paid Him their homage, and their souls were for a long time full of joy and peace.
>
> The Angels likewise contemplated the Newborn Babe, the Word made Flesh. They saw in Him their God; this knowledge threw these pure spirits into awe and wonderment at such incomprehensible self-abasement: for it was not

to their nature that He willed to unite Himself: *Nusquam angelos*, but to human nature, *sed semen Abrahae apprehendit* [Heb 2:16].

What shall we say of the Blessed Virgin when she looked upon Jesus? Into what depths of the mystery did her gaze penetrate – that gaze so pure, so humble, so tender, so full of bliss? Who shall be able to express with what lights the soul of Jesus inundated His Mother, and what perfect homage Mary rendered to her Son, to her God, to all the states and all the mysteries whereof the Incarnation is the substance and the root.

There is finally – but this is beyond description – the gaze of the Father contemplating His Son made flesh for mankind. The Heavenly Father saw that which never man, nor angel, nor Mary herself could comprehend: the infinite perfections of the Divinity hidden in a Babe... And this contemplation was the source of unspeakable rapture: Thou art My Son, My beloved Son, the Son of My direction in Whom I have placed all My delights... [Mk 1:2; Lk 3:22].

When we contemplate the Incarnate Word at Bethlehem, let us rise above the things of sense so as to gaze upon Him with the eyes of faith alone. Faith makes us share here below in the knowledge that the Divine Persons have of One Another. There is no exaggeration in this. Sanctifying grace makes us indeed partakers of the divine nature. Now, the activity of the divine nature consists in the knowledge that the Divine Persons have the One of the Other, and the love that they have One for the Other. We participate therefore in this knowledge and in this love. And in the same way as sanctifying grace having its fruition in glory will give us the right of seeing God as He sees Himself, so, upon earth, in the shadows of faith, grace enables us to behold deep down into these mysteries through the eyes of God: *Lux Tuae claritatis infulsit* (Preface for Christmas).[28]

[Et comment devons-nous le [le Don de Dieu] recevoir? – par la foi: *His qui credunt in nomine ejus*. C'est à ceux qui, croyant en sa personne, en sa parole, en ses œuvres, ont reçu cet enfant comme Dieu, qu'il a été donné, en retour, de devenir eux-mêmes enfants de Dieu: ex Deo nati sunt.

Telle est, en effet, la position fondamentale qu'il nous faut apporter pour que cet admirable échange produise en nous tous ses fruits. Seule, la foi nous en fait connaître les termes et la manière dont il se réalise; seule, elle nous fait pénétrer dans les profondeurs de ce mystère; seule, elle nous en donne une vraie connaissance digne de Dieu.

Car il y a bien des modes et des degrés de connaissance.

'Le bœuf et l'âne ont connu leur Dieu', écrivait Isaïe, en parlant de ce mystère. Ils voyaient l'enfant couché dans la crèche. Mais que voyaient-ils? Ce que peut voir un animal: la forme, la grandeur, la couleur, le mouvement – connaissance toute rudimentaire qui ne franchit point le domaine de la sensation. Rien de plus.

---

[28] Dom Columba Marmion, *Christ in His Mysteries: Spiritual and Liturgical Conferences* (St Louis, MO: Herder, 1931), available at www.cin.org/marmion.html.

Les passants, les curieux qui se sont approchés de la grotte ont vu l'enfant; mais pour eux, il était semblable à tous les autres. Ils ne sont pas allés au-delà de cette connaissance purement naturelle. Peut-être ont-ils été frappés de la beauté de l'enfant? Peut-être ont-ils plaint son dénuement? Mais ce sentiment n'a point duré, et l'indifférence a bientôt repris le dessus.

Il y a les bergers, cœurs simples, 'éclairés d'un rayon d'en haut': *Claritas Dei circumpulsit illos.* Ils ont compris assurément davantage; ils ont reconnu en cet enfant le Messie promis, attendu, l'*Exspectatio gentium*; ils lui ont rendu leurs hommages, et leurs âmes ont été pour longtemps remplies de joie et de paix.

Les anges également contemplaient le nouveau né, Verbe fait chair. Ils ont vu en lui leur Dieu; aussi cette connaissance jetait ces purs esprits dans la stupeur et l'admiration d'un abaissement si incompréhensible: ce n'est pas à leur nature qu'il a voulu s'unir, *nusquam angelos*, mais à la nature humaine, *sed semen Abrahae apprehendit.*

– Que dirons-nous de la Vierge, quand elle regardait Jésus? A quelle profondeur du mystère pénétrait ce regard si pur, si humble, si tendre et si plein de complaisance! On ne saurait exprimer de quelles lumières l'âme de Jésus inondait alors sa Mère, et quelles sublimes adorations, quels hommages parfaits Marie rendait à son fils, à son Dieu, à tous les états et à tous les mystères dont l'Incarnation est la substance et la racine.

Il y a enfin – mais ceci est inénarrable – le regard du Père contemplant son Fils, fait chair pour les hommes. Le Père céleste voyait ce que jamais ni homme, ni ange, ni Marie elle-même ne comprendront: les perfections infinies de la divinité qui se cachaient dans un enfant.... Et cette contemplation était la source d'un ravissement indicible: 'Tu es mon Fils, mon Fils bien-aimé, le Fils de ma dilection, en qui j'ai mis toutes mes complaisances.' ...

Lorsque nous contemplons à Bethléem le Verbe incarné, élevons-nous au-dessus des sens, pour ne regarder que des yeux de la foi. La foi nous fait participer ici-bas à la connaissance que les divines Personnes ont l'une de l'autre. Il n'y a point en ceci d'exagération. La grâce sanctifiante nous rend, en effet, participants de la nature divine; or, l'activité de la nature divine consiste dans la connaissance et l'amour que les personnes divines ont l'une de l'autre, l'une pour l'autre; nous participons donc à cette connaissance. Et de même que la grâce sanctifiante s'épanouissant dans la gloire nous donnera le droit de contempler Dieu comme il se voit; de même, sur la Terre, dans les ombres de la foi, la grâce nous donne de regarder les profondeurs des mystères par les yeux de Dieu: *Lux Tuae claritatis infulsit.*][29]

We already identify here different possible looks or *regards*: those of the shepherds, the angels, the Virgin and the Lord. However, is it possible, starting with this text,

---

[29]   Letter from Messiaen to Toesca, 4 February 1944; the quotation is from Dom Columba Marmion, *Le Christ dans ses mystères* (Namur, Belgium: Abbaye de Maredsous and Paris: Desclée de Brouwer, 1919), pp. 143–4.

to reconstruct what Messiaen's *Douze Regards* could have been, among the 20 we know? Two autograph manuscripts of Messiaen's *Vingt Regards* now kept in two different banks in Paris bring an answer to light: one of 84 pages in pencil, and a fair copy of 130 pages in purple ink.[30] The summary of the pencil version reads as following:

p. 1	Regard des prophètes
p. 4	Le regard de la Vierge 'bien'
p. 8	Le regard du fils sur le fils 'bien'
p. 13	Le regard des Anges 'bien'
p. 17	Le regard du Père 'bien'
p. 19	Le regard de l'Etoile 'bien'
p. 20	Le regard du Temps 'bien'
p. 22	Le regard de la Croix 'bien'
p. 24	Le regard de l'Eglise d'Amour
p. 33	Le regard de l'onction terrible 'bien'
p. 38	Le regard du silence 'bien'
p. 41	L'esprit de joie 'bien'
Le regard de l'échange (rayé) (extrait)	
p. 50	Le regard de l'échange 'bien'
p. 52	La Parole toute puissante 'bien'
pp. 55, 56, 57, 58 (à l'envers)	Première Communion de la Vierge
p. 59	Regard des hauteurs 'bien'
p. 61	Baiser de l'Enfant Jésus 'bien'
p. 68	Noël
p. 71	Je dors mais mon cœur veille 'bien'
p. 75	Par lui tout a été fait

This order is quite different from the printed score and we can see that all the pieces including the word *regard* in their title (except 'Regard des hauteurs') are at the beginning. This suggests that Messiaen started with the pieces closely related to Toesca's texts and added his own musical commentaries. We now can examine according to what logic the change of the order was made and how the new pieces were conceived. This leads back to Dom Columba Marmion.

Dom Columba Marmion (1858–1923) and *Le Christ dans ses mystères*

Born in Dublin of an Irish father and a French mother in 1858, Joseph Marmion studied theology in Rome where he was ordained a priest in 1881. He then became a monk at the Benedictine Abbey of Maredsous (Belgium) under the name of

---

[30]   I would like to thank Catherine Massip, former manager of Music Department at the Bibliothèque Nationale de France, for having provided the description of the manuscript in pencil. The manuscript is currently inaccessible.

Columba Marmion in 1886. Abbot of Maredsous from 1909 to his death in 1923, he was beatified by the Catholic Church in 2000.

Le Christ dans ses mystères [*Christ in His Mysteries*] was first published in 1919. It is a collection of 'spiritual speeches' given by Marmion, his two other major books being *Le Christ vie de l'âme* (1917) and *Le Christ idéal du moine* (1922).[31] *Le Christ dans ses mystères* consists of 20 chapters (is this a coincidence?) distributed among three parts:

- Preliminary Talks [Conférences préliminaires]
- Book I: The person of Christ [La personne du Christ]
- Book II: The mysteries of Christ [Les mystères du Christ]

In Book II, 'Les mystères du Christ', Marmion develops several ideas obviously borrowed by Messiaen in order to build the dramaturgy of his musical commentaries on the Nativity. Here the justification can be found for Messiaen's placing the 'Regard du Père' at the very beginning of the cycle: 'The Father now gazes upon his incarnate Son. ... The first gaze towards Christ, the first love that enfolds him is the gaze of the love of his Father.'[32] We also find the idea of 'L'échange', inspired by the Antiphon for the Circumcision, 'O admirabile commercium': 'Let us stop for a moment to admire, with the Church, this exchange between the creature and the Creator, between heaven and earth; this exchange is at the heart of the mystery of the Nativity'.[33] In the poems written when he was in jail in Toledo, the mystic Saint John of the Cross also uses this term, writing, 'and the Mother was overwhelmed by the sight of this exchange'.[34] Marmion further develops the idea of the Crucifixion being already present in the crib: 'It is in the crib that he began the life of suffering that he wished to live for our sake and whose end is at Golgotha'.[35] This helps us understand the 'Regard de la croix' and 'Regard de l'Onction terrible'.[36] Marmion also mentions the subjects of the 'Première communion de la Vierge' and the 'Regard de la Vierge'. Between the Annunciation and the Nativity, he says: 'Illuminated by a light from above, Mary was prostrated

---

[31]   These books were first published as follows: Dom Columba Marmion, *Le Christ vie de l'âme* (Namur, Belgium: Abbaye de Maredsous, 1914); *Le Christ dans ses mystères: Conférences spirituelles* (Namur, Belgium: Abbaye de Maredsous and Paris: Desclée de Brower, 1919); and *Le Christ idéal du moine: Conférences spirituelles sur la vie monastique et religieuse* (Namur , Belgium: Abbaye de Maredsous and Paris: Desclée de Brower, 1922).

[32]   Marmion, *Le Christ dans ses mystères*, p. 129.

[33]   Ibid., p. 127.

[34]   'Et la mère était pâmée de voir un tel échange', from No. 9, 'De la Nativité' in Saint Jean de la Croix, *Poésies* (Paris: Flammarion, 1993), p. 167.

[35]   Marmion, *Le Christ dans ses mystères*, p. 138.

[36]   The unction refers to the chrism used for anointing during baptism.

in front of her Son'. Marmion goes on: 'From her first gaze at the Infant Jesus, the Virgin inwardly prostrated in an adoration whose depth we cannot fathom.'[37]

So we now understand how the reading of Dom Marmion influenced Messiaen's own concept of the Nativity. In his *Traité*, Messiaen explains more about the symbolic structure of the whole cycle:

> The pieces are organized by contrasts of tempo, intensity of colour – and also for symbolic reasons.
>
> The Regards dealing with God are distributed in fives (I, V, X, XV, XX). 'Regard de la Croix' bears the number VII (7, perfect number) because Christ's sufferings on the cross have restored the order troubled by sin. 'Regard des Anges' bears the number XIV (twice 7) for the Angels' grace has been confirmed. The 'Regard du Temps' bears the number IX: Time has seen born within him one who is eternal, trapped in the 9 months of pregnancy that other children experience. The 'Regard de l'Onction terrible' bears the number XVIII (twice 9): Divinity is spread on mankind by Christ, the only Son of God: this awe-inspiring unction, this choice of a certain flesh by the terrible Majesty suggests both the Incarnation and the Nativity. Two pieces speak of Creation and of the Divine government or support of all things, and of unceasing Creation. These are number VI 'Par Lui tout a été fait' (six is the number of the Creation) and number XIII 'La Parole toute-puissante'.[38]

The confrontation of Toesca's *Nativité*, Marmion's *Christ dans ses mystères* and Messiaen's comments make clear that the composer proceeded in several steps, starting from the commission of incidental music and ending up with a strongly structured piano cycle.

A final question remains: is it possible to find out Messiaen's inspiration for eight more pieces after having conceived 'Douze Regards' for the radio? The visual sources mentioned by the composer offer new leads.

Visible and Invisible Sources of Inspiration

As mentioned in the introduction, Messiaen's 'Note de l'Auteur' for the *Vingt Regards* offers five visual sources, as identified and described below:

- IX. 'Regard du Temps' presents the short, cold and strange theme of Time, which is compared with 'the egg-shaped heads of Chirico' characteristic of the painter's surrealist period.
- XI. 'Première Communion de la Vierge' refers to 'a tableau in which the Virgin is shown on her knees, withdrawn in herself – a luminous halo over

---

[37]　Marmion, *Le Christ dans ses mystères*, p. 172.

[38]　*Traité II*, p. 438.

her Womb. Her eyes closed, she adores the Fruit hidden within her'. This could be some Renaissance painting in the style of Jean Bellegambe's *Vierge de l'immaculée conception* from the Douai Museum.

- XV. 'Le Baiser de l'Enfant-Jésus' was inspired by a pious and naïve engraving representing 'the infant Jesus leaving the arms of His Mother to embrace little Theresa', in fact Saint Theresa of Lisieux. This picture, showing Sister Theresa coming from the garden with flowers, belongs to the collection of the Lisieux pilgrimage and is held in the Messiaen Archive.[39]

The note also refers to Saint Theresa's writings to Mother Agnès recalling the day of her First Communion: 'Oh how sweet was Jesus' first kiss upon my soul! ... For a long time, Jesus and poor little Theresa had looked at each other and understood each other. On this day it was no longer a look but a fusion.'[40] Later Saint Theresa writes: 'My childish wishes have vanished. Of course, I still love to decorate little Jesus' altar with flowers, but now that He has given me the flower I wished for, sweet little Cécile, I am offering her to Him as my most beautiful bouquet'.[41] This was about the time of Saint Theresa's First Communion: she was actually called Saint Theresa of the Infant Jesus, which explains how Messiaen's imagination connected Jesus with Saint Theresa. The Theme of Love appears in this *regard*, developed in its next appearance, in 'Je dors mais mon cœur veille'. Could Yvonne Loriod – the dedicatee of the *Vingt Regards* – have been a carefully hidden source of inspiration in this music of love? In a draft version of the Author's Note, Messiaen wrote: 'Mysterious circumstances pressed me to write this work: I dedicate it to Yvonne Loriod (whose technique equals her genius ... and who understood my mission)'.[42] Both 'Le Baiser de l'Enfant-Jésus' and 'Je dors mais mon coeur veille' show a very idiomatic, quite romantic writing for the piano, which also suggests the influence of Loriod's technique. Another document confirms this hypothesis:

---

[39] I would like to thank Peter Hill for providing this information when we met in Birmingham for the Messiaen 2008 Centenary Conference. He mentioned that he saw the picture in Paris when visiting Yvonne Loriod.

[40] 'Ah! qu'il fut doux le premier baiser de Jésus à mon âme! .... Depuis longtemps, Jésus et la pauvre petite Thérèse s'étaient regardés et s'étaient compris .... Ce jour-là, ce n'était plus un regard mais une fusion', in Thérèse de l'Enfant-Jésus, *Manuscrits autobiographiques* (Paris: Seuil, 2006), pp. 92–3.

[41] 'Mes désirs enfantins sont envolés, sans doute j'aime encore à parer de fleurs l'autel du petit Jésus, mais depuis qu'il m'a donné la fleur que je désirais, ma Céline chérie, c'est elle que je lui offre comme mon plus ravissant bouquet.' Ibid. p. 205.

[42] Draft for the 'Note de l'auteur'. 'Des circonstances mystérieuses m'ont poussé vers cette œuvre: je la dédie à Yvonne Loriod (dont la technique égale le génie et qui a compris ma mission).' This information was provided by Nigel Simeone in a speech given at the Festival Messiaen au pays de la Meije in July 2006, '"L'Esprit de joie": Olivier Messiaen et ses *Vingt Regards*'.

Finally, this work contains several special traits and effects – a little revolution in piano writing – that I certainly never would have made if I had not heard Yvonne Loriod's first concerts and had the good fortune myself of being a pianist.

[Enfin elle [cette oeuvre] contient nombre de traits et d'effets pianistiques spéciaux – petite révolution dans l'écriture du piano – que je n'aurais certainement jamais réalisés si je n'avais pas entendu les premiers concerts d'Yvonne Loriod et eu la chance d'être moi-même pianiste.][43]

- XIV. 'Regard des Anges' has a description of a 'birdsong swallowing blue'[44] that refers to Michelangelo's *Last Judgement* in the Sistine Chapel. Here we can see athletic angels playing the trombone: this recalls – or perhaps inspired – the theme played by the left hand bars 14–18. This reference demonstrates that in Messiaen's theological thought, not only the Crucifixion but also the Last Judgement and Saint John's Revelation are already contained in the Nativity.
- XVIII. 'Regard de l'Onction terrible' confirms such an observation. In this last visual source, which is also the oldest, Messiaen states: 'An old tapestry shows the Word of God in battle. ... We only see two hands on the hilt of the sword which they brandish amid the flashing lightening'.[45] We know that Messiaen had the Angers Tapestry of the Revelation in mind, specifically image no. 73, 'Le Christ charge les bêtes', as Siglind Bruhn has previously suggested.[46]

In sum, we can say with certainty that Messiaen first wrote 12 – or even 13 – *regards* for Toesca's *Nativité* as a commission from the Radiodiffusion Française for Pierre Schaeffer's Studio d'Essai. Enthused by the subject, he then embarked on a larger project, developing his own concept of the Nativity inspired at the same time by Dom Marmion, Saint Thérèse of Lisieux, Saint John of the Cross, the Revelation, pictures he loved and, of course, Yvonne Loriod's fantastic gifts as a pianist. From all this, Messiaen built a musical architecture fitting with both his musical and theological thought, constructing a mosaic of musical images or visions on the Nativity.

---

[43] Draft for the 'Note de l'Auteur', ibid.

[44] Messiaen, 'Note de l'Auteur'.

[45] Ibid.

[46] Siglind Bruhn, *Messiaen's Contemplations*, p. 250: 'As Yvonne Loriod told me in 1994, Messiaen visited Angers several times. There can be no doubt that he saw all the panels accessible to visitors, but he probably also studied the documentation that identifies the biblical verses on which each panel is based.'

Chapter 5

My Collaboration with Olivier Messiaen and Yvonne Loriod on *Harawi*

Sigune von Osten

Preface

The soprano Sigune von Osten worked with Olivier Messiaen during his final years from 1987 until one of his last concerts at the Bruckner Festival in Linz, Austria, in November 1991. She performed *Harawi* and the orchestral version of *Poèmes pour Mi* in Prague, Bratislava, Metz, Madrid and Linz with Messiaen and his wife, Yvonne Loriod, and additional performances had been planned before the composer's death.

Sigune von Osten met the composer and Yvonne Loriod in 1986 at the Beethoven festival in Bonn, which had been dedicated to Messiaen that year. There she performed *Chants de terre et de ciel* and *Poèmes pour Mi* in the piano version.

In 1987, Sigune von Osten worked with Messiaen and Yvonne Loriod on *Harawi* for the first time and gave her first concert with them on 7 December 1987 in the Philharmonia, Bratislava, accompanied by Yvonne Loriod at the piano. With the permission of Messiaen and Yvonne Loriod, Sigune von Osten recorded the three rehearsals and the concert on cassette. This article is based on these recordings. All quotations (originally by Messiaen in French) are taken from the cassettes during the rehearsals on 5 and 6 December 1987 in Smetana Hall, Prague, and digitalized at the request of Sigune von Osten in 2007 by sound master Joachim Hütteroth, Hergersweiler, Germany.[1]

Introduction

During the three rehearsals before the concert, we developed many changes to the original 1945 score of *Harawi*. According to what Messiaen explained there,

---

[1]   The excerpts are from letters of Yvonne Loriod to Sigune von Osten, and the dedications by Messiaen are in her score of *Harawi*. The photos were taken by Juraj Bartos during the general rehearsal and the concert in the Philharmonia, Bratislava, 7 December 1987. Yvonne Loriod: 'Elles [the photos] sont magnifiques et nous rappellent un moment privilégié de notre première rencontre' (letter from 27 July 1988). All these (and additional documents) are privately owned by Sigune von Osten.

the images and visions he had in mind when he composed *Harawi* required an enormous variety of different colours and sounds beyond the classically trained voice. Therefore, I offered my voice in various ways: for some songs, the usual *bel canto*; for others, a more natural style in the sense of singing with non-vibrato elements as in folk singing; for yet other songs, special sound elements and Sprechstimme.

Almost none of these vocal creations and expressions can be found written in the score. Only the personal dialogue with Messiaen himself, connected with my experience of contemporary and experimental vocal music at that time, led to a new interpretation of *Harawi*. After our first concert, he paid me a wonderful compliment in the newspaper *Pravda*:

> The cycle *Harawi*, extremely demanding for the interpreter, has received new dimensions of expression thanks to Sigune von Osten. It was a miracle. Her metamorphosis of my work has passed all my expectations and has added extraordinary creative moments to all former interpretations.[2]

Illustration 5.1   Sigune von Osten rehearsing *Harawi* with Olivier Messiaen and Yvonne Loriod, Bratislava, 7 December 1987

---

[2] *Pravda Bratislava* (daily newspaper), 7/8 December 1987, translated from the Czech original.

This was also supported by my knowledge of the indigenous cultures to which Messiaen refers in *Harawi* and the congenial accompaniment of Yvonne Loriod at the piano, with whom I had identical feelings concerning tempo, dynamics and expression.

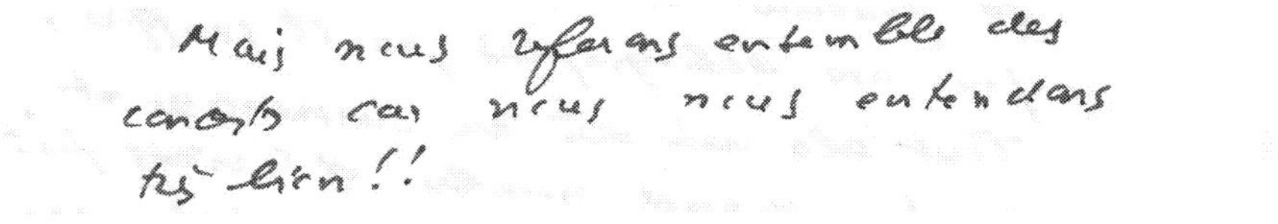
Mais nous referons ensemble des concerts car nous nous entendons très bien!!

Illustration 5.2 Letter from Yvonne Loriod to the author, 10 October 1988 (excerpt)[3]

In a way I feel that it is my duty to publish the experience I had with Olivier Messiaen and Yvonne Loriod during our rehearsals and performances and to explain which vocal sounds and interpretation came out of the detailed discussions with Messiaen in comparison with what can be found in the score, especially because Messiaen complained very frankly about most of the recordings of *Harawi* that existed at that time: 'Yes, the CDs are very bad, horrible, I don't know what it is, what I heard is very bad, very bad; the singers are very bad, they did not understand anything' [Oui, les disques sont très mauvais, horrible; je ne sais pas ce que c'est, ce que j'ai entendu est très mauvais, très mauvais; c'est de mauvaises cantatrices, elles n'ont pas compris]. I also feel that it is important for every singer (and pianist) to know that there are many demands on the voice (and the sound of the piano) that cannot be understood from the score.

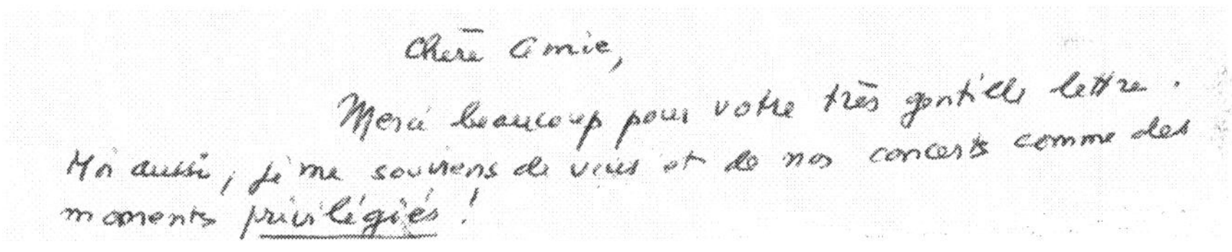
Chère amie,
Merci beaucoup pour votre très gentille lettre.
Moi aussi, je me souviens de vous et de nos concerts comme des moments privilégiés!

Illustration 5.3 Letter from Yvonne Loriod to the author, 28 May 1997 (excerpt)[4]

It is well known that *Harawi* was greatly influenced by folk cultures and music, especially that of the Inca and Maya of Peru, but also by music from India and Bali. (When Messiaen composed *Harawi* in 1945, he had read the book *La musique des Incas et ses survivances* by Marguérite Béclart d'Harcourt and her

3 'Mais nous referons ensemble des concerts car nous nous entendons très bien!!' [But we shall do other concerts as we get on very well!!]

4 'Moi aussi, je me souviens de vous et de nos concerts comme des moments privilégiés!' [I also remember you and our concerts as special moments!]

husband Raoul.[5]) The ethnic influence must be taken into consideration regarding the interpretation. When one looks at the score, the writing appears traditional – as it was in that time – and, apart from very few remarks, there are almost no special written demands on the voice.

Illustration 5.4　　Letter from Yvonne Loriod to the author, 29 December 1987 (excerpt)[6]

While I was working with Messiaen, it became obvious that he had in mind specific sounds that come more from original folk singing than from the classical *bel canto* tradition. And although Messiaen demands a great dramatic soprano, *Harawi* has nothing to do with a dramatic interpretation in the sense of Wagner's Brünnhilde (although *Harawi*'s first interpreter was Marcelle Bunlet, who also sang Brünnhilde). But at the time of the première in 1946, the vocal literature did not yet have Berio's *Sequenza*, with the twentieth century's new demands on the voice.

Illustration 5.5　　Sigune von Osten rehearsing *Harawi* with Olivier Messiaen and Yvonne Loriod, Bratislava, 7 December 1987

---

　　[5]　Marguérite and Raoul Béclart d'Harcourt, *La musique des Incas et ses survivances* (Paris: Paul Geuthner, 1925).

　　[6]　'Pour nous deux, ça sera partie remise, nous prendrons notre revanche, et les ferons souvent ensemble! nos chers *Harawi* …' [For the two of us, it will have to wait, but we will have our revenge, and often perform our beloved *Harawi* together!]

The Songs of *Harawi*

Step by step, song by song, I shall point out the specifications of the changes in the interpretation of *Harawi,* which – in my opinion – is one of the most extraordinary song cycles of the twentieth century.

'La ville qui dormait'

Messiaen explained to me the meaning of the first song – 'The city that sleeps'. It symbolizes the sleeping, immobile city and the situation in which the young man sees the young girl for the first time from a long way off; he dares not move, dares not disturb the beautiful image of the lovely young girl named *Piroutcha.* According to Messiaen's vision, the first song demands a certain kind of non-vibrato style of singing right at the beginning. The tempo, based on the semiquaver, cannot be slow enough, the *ppp* not soft enough, close to whispering, nearly inaudible, although sung on pitch and in precise rhythm. The voice should stay on the notes as long, as still and as immobile as possible – like the young man in the image – preferably non-vibrato, all the sounds sung as though from a far distance, like in a dream. Positioned at the beginning of the cycle, this first song is very important for the whole atmosphere (Example 5.1).

Example 5.1   'La ville qui dormait', opening bars 1–3

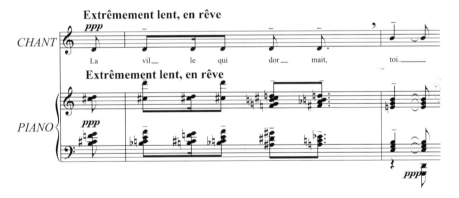

'Bonjour toi'

The second song, 'Bonjour toi', involves the salutation of the young girl by the young man. It is a song in classical style, characterized by the melodic love theme. Messiaen wanted a fresh, dynamic voice, full of joy and expectation, sung classically with normal vibrato in a good, fluent tempo. At the end of the phrases, one should never make a *diminuendo* up to the end of the piano, as they explain:

Yvonne Loriod: One should not make a *diminuendo* when you sing 'retour du ciel', the voice should remain *forte.*

Messiaen: Yes, yes, it remains always *f* [thereby creating a kind of youthful strength]. And when you have the deep C ['et d'eau'], strong and black [he demonstrated a very deep sound], chest voice.

[*Yvonne Loriod*: Il ne faut pas diminuer quand on fait 'retour du ciel', le chant doit rester *forte*.
Messiaen: Oui, oui, ça reste *forte*; et quand vous avez des *do grave*, le *do grave* fort et noir; poitrine.]

Messiaen demanded strictly pure chest voice in this and in other parts – which one cannot see from the score alone (Example 5.2).

Example 5.2   'Bonjour toi', p. 10, system 2, bar 2

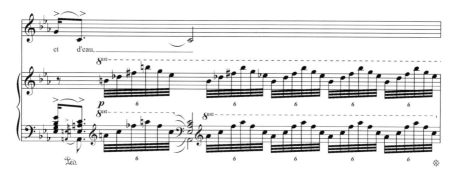

'Montagnes'

In the third song, 'Montagnes', Messiaen explained the image of 'la pierre agenouillée porte ses maîtres noirs' (Example 5.3):[7]

Messiaen: It [the atmosphere] is gloomy, these are the mountains. When you say 'The kneeling stones carry their black masters', these are the mountains and the masters are the trees.
Yvonne Loriod: It is the Andes Cordillera.
Messiaen: That is in Peru.

[*Messiaen*: C'est sombre, c'est la montagne; quand vous dites 'la pierre agenouillée porte ses maîtres noirs', c'est la montagne et les maîtres sont les arbres.
Yvonne Loriod: C'est la cordillère des Andes.

---

[7]   The kneeling stones carry their black masters.

Messiaen: Ça, c'est au Péru.]

Messiaen wanted to have a very dark voice, again the pure, so-called chest voice. The words should be practically spoken, strong, and completely equal in rhythm and duration, straight, not at all free like a recitative, the last note always long and without *diminuendo*:

> *Messiaen*: Don't rush. '*L'antique inutile rayon noir*' more spoken. ...
> The semiquavers all equal.
> *Signe von Osten*: Not like a recitative?
> *Messiaen*: No, no, no, no, no, completely equal, completely equal.

> [*Messiaen*: Ne pressez pas; 'l'antique inutile rayon noir' plus parlé. ...
> Les doubles croches égales, tout droit.
> *Signe von Osten*: Pas comme un récitatif?
> Messiaen: Non, non, non non, non, tout droit, tout droit.]

Example 5.3   'Montagnes', p. 15, system 4

This song has nothing to do with a *bel canto*, dramatically sung song, but instead requires a nearly brutally dark, strong, spoken sound that describes a rough and threatening landscape.

Messiaen principally attached great importance to the use of the chest voice also in some of the following songs to mark the darkness of the situation as well as to emphasize the idea of the connection to original folk singing, like that of non-Western cultural rituals. None of this is explained in the score, and the singer would normally have no way of knowing this information.

'Doundou tchil'

'Doundou tchil', the fourth song, is best explained by Messiaen:

> 'Doundou tchil' is an onomatopoeia. The Peruvian dancers wear small bells around their ankles. And when they dance, they move them. It makes a noise and the noise sounds like 'doundou tchil'; you can do it quasi parlando.
>
> ['Doundou tchil' c'est une onomatopée; les danseurs péruviens ont des petites cloches aux chevilles ici et en dansant ça remouit et ça fait un bruit et ce bruit c'est 'doundou tchil'; vous pouvez le faire presque parlando.]

This means that the sound should be nearly spoken, nearly on the written note, the *tchil* articulated as a very hard, sharp, bright sound, starting in a mysterious *mp* way like a ritual and ending wildly *f* (Example 5.4).

Example 5.4   'Doundou tchil', p. 19, bars 2–4

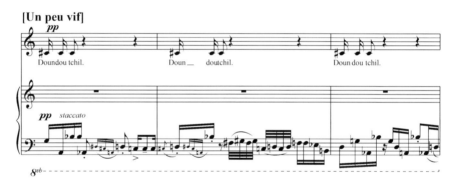

Again, this cannot be seen in the score. One would falsely assume that the C♯ should first be sung *pp* with a gradual *crescendo* up to the end.

'L'amour de Piroutcha'

Before 'L'amour de Piroutcha', Messiaen indicated:

> Here one has to make a long silence because it ['Doundou tchil'] is very exhausting and you have to take your time for this [the next song]. It ['L'amour de Piroutcha'] is very slow.'
>
> [Alors là il faut avoir une grande silence parce que c'est fatigant et il faut prendre votre temps comme ça; c'est très lent.]

'L'amour de Piroutcha' is a gentle lullaby, a dialogue between Piroutcha, the young girl, and her lover. The girl starts to sing in a delicate, soft, bright way. The young man answers in a darker and stronger voice with strange words: 'Coupe-moi la tête' (Example 5.5).[8]

Example 5.5   'L'amour de Piroutcha', p. 30, last bar

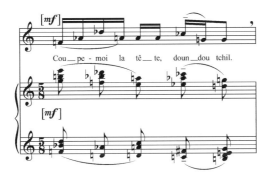

On this image, Messiaen said:

> 'Coupe-moi la tête' – I have to explain this: in the fairy tales, one has to cut-off the head of a woman who was transformed into a cat or of a man who was transformed into a sheep in order for him to turn back into a man and for her to turn back into a woman.

> ['Coupe moi-la tête' – il faut expliquer: dans les contes de fées la femme qui est métamorphosée en chat et l'homme qui est métamorphosé en mouton il faut leurs couper la tête pour qu'il redevient un homme et pour qu'elle redevient une femme.]

The sound of the voice should always be like a lullaby for a child: simple, light, bright, always in a lulling rhythm. And when the young man speaks, a little darker and stronger. The tempo for the whole song has to be very slow but always in the lulling rhythm.

'Répétition planétaire'

'Répétition planétaire', the next song, includes the following remarks in the score: 'à pleine voix, un peu faux, comme un appel en forêt',[9] and one does not exactly know what the composer had in mind. He explained:

---

8   Cut off my head.
9   In a loud voice, a little false, like a call in the forest.

Messiaen: Did you see the actor – he died already – who played Tarzan? His name was Johnny Weissmuller. He was the man who ran around in the forest.

Signe von Osten: Oh yes, he made an 'aaaaaa', not at all bel canto.

Messiaen: Exactly this, 'aaaaaaa'.

[*Messiaen*: Est-ce que vous avez vu un acteur qui est mort, qui faisait Tarzan, il s'appelait Johnny Weissmuller. C'était un homme qui courait dans la forêt.

Signe von Osten: Ah oui, il a fait 'aaaaaa', pas du tout bel canto.

Messiaen: Oui, c'est ça 'aaaaaa'.]

Messiaen produced an incredibly hoarse and wild scream. What this means is that the written coloratura notes do not have to be sung accurately, but more like a yell as in traditional cultures, and the *ahi* should have the same sense of the yell with the accent on the *I* (Example 5.6).

Example 5.6   'Répétition planétaire', p. 33, bar 1; p. 37, bars 4–5

In the middle of the same song, Messiaen imagined the evocation of a witch like in the paintings of the Spanish artist Goya:

And now to 'Mapa nama lila'. This is like a witch in front of her cauldron who recites magic spells to get it hot: 'tchil'. Have you seen the paintings of Goya? The little witches one sees, they are like the 'mapa nama'.

[Alors, 'mapa nama lila' c'est comme une sorcière qui a un chaudron et elle fait des signes pour que ça devient chaud: 'tchil'. Vous avez vu les aquatintes de Goya? On voit, les petites sorcières sont comme ça 'mapa nama'.]

Then Messiaen demonstrated a hoarse, brutal sound. And for the piano he explained: 'The left hand like a bass clarinet, the right hand, nothing, like smoke' [La main gauche c'est comme une clarinette de basse, la main droite, rien, comme une fumée] (Example 5.7).

Example 5.7   'Répétition planétaire', p. 38, bar 1

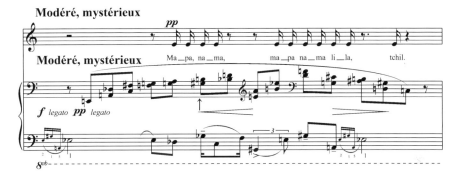

This image and its explanation changed the sound of my voice. I used the voice more in a speaking, mysterious, evocative way, less clear, darker and somewhat frightening.

Messiaen explained further:

> When you come to the words 'Étoile rouge, Planète mange en tournant': At the beginning of the earth, the earth was a hot mass, and there were hot drops that fell down from the sun. And while the earth rotated, it absorbed the drops of the sun and it took form. The earth ate parts of the sun.

> [Quand vous avez les mots 'Étoile rouge, Planète mange en tournant': au début de la terre la terre était une matière chaude et il y a des goûttes chaudes qui sont tombées du soleil et la terre en se tournant a reçu ces goûttes et c'est formée. Et elle a mangé les morceaux du soleil.]

The vocal sound changed with this image into a kind of brutal, wild colour, practically non-vibrato and sharp.

Later in the same song, Messiaen explained the correct Indian rhythm for one of the very difficult parts: 'tchil, tchil, tchil, pampahika':

> I shall explain what this is, this 'bam ba ba'. It is quaver, dotted quaver, quaver, three quavers, three dotted quavers, quaver, quaver, dotted quaver, three quavers and it is written with syncopations.

[Je vous explique que ça c'est 'bam ba ba'. Croche, croche pointée, croche, trois croches, trois croches pointées, croche, croche, croche pointée, trois croches. Et c'est écrit avec des syncopes.]

Messiaen clapped his hands and demonstrated the correct rhythm with his voice – he knew how difficult this passage was.

And he also wanted to have this part sung evocatively, based on the image of the witch in front of her cauldron. The sound of the voice changed to practically non-vibrato, very straight, as in folk singing, and the 'tchil' became sharp and bright, similar to 'doundou tchil'. The final 'Ahi' and 'o' are not to be sung; they are cries.

'Adieu'

Everything is written at the beginning of this song: 'Très lent, solennel et très soutenu'.[10] With this song, full of utmost sadness, the story of the lovers has an end in this life. The sound, in contrast to the second song, which is bright and bold and has the same melodic theme, is dark and desperate. Messiaen made some demands:

When you have the deep notes 'de jour', chest voice, darker and stronger. And don't make a diminuendo at the end of the phrases 'soleil gardien', 'aile d'amour', only for the last 'pour toujours'. Because this is a third and in the whole work the third should always be strong.

[Quand vous avez les graves 'de jour', voix de poitrine, plus noir et plus fort. Et alors, ne diminuez pas sur les fins des phrases 'soleil gardien', 'aile d'amour', seulement le dernier 'pour toujours'. Parce que c'est une tierce et dans toute l'oeuvre il faut que toujours la tierce doit être fort.]

After this song, which ends with the piano like a 'tam-tam', Messiaen wanted a long pause.

'Syllabes'

The next song, 'Syllabes', also changed a lot through my work with Messiaen and his visual explanation, which differs greatly from what one can read in the score:

The words at the beginning, 'Colombe verte', mean the young girl, and 'la violette double doublera' is a folk song. These are the flowers in full bloom. 'Très loin, tout bas' means distant separation and finally death. These are the words one repeats

---

10   Very slow, solemn, and very intense.

at the end: very far, very deep … 'Kahipipas, mahipipas', this means 'right, left, here, there', 'mahipipas, kahipipas', these are words from the Quechua language.

[Les mots au début, 'Colombe verte', c'est la jeune fille, alors, 'la violette double, doublera' c'est une chanson populaire. C'est la fleur qui se multiple. Et 'très loin, tous bas' c'est à la fois la séparation très loin et finalement la mort. Et c'est le mot que l'on reprendra à la fin: très loin, tous bas …. Ah, il y a 'kahipipas, mahipipas' ça veut dire à droite, à gauche, par ici, par là, 'mahipipas, kahipipas', c'est la langue Quetchua.]

Messiaen explained that the song refers to the petals the young girl tears off from the flower piece by piece while repeating: he loves me, he loves me not, he loves me, he loves me not, etc. (Example 5.8).

Example 5.8   'Syllabes', p. 56, bars 4–5

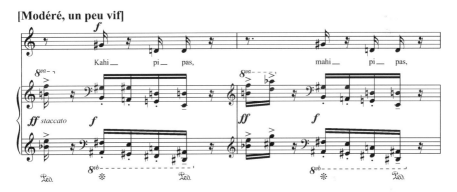

Messiaen went on to say:

It is night and the people come together. And they sing a single syllable. And everybody sings it in his own way. A hundred people are there, and each of them sings only once, but they do it so quickly that it sounds like 'pia pia pia pia pia pia pia pia pia', it is frightening. In Bali, they sing 'čac čac čac čac čac čac čac čac čac' and here 'pia pia pia pia pia pia pia pia pia', but it is the same. One has to get the impression of a crowd. But it is not so difficult because the piano does everything. And you, you practically speak, it sounds nearly spoken. The only problem is the breath. But if one ['pia'] is missing to breathe, it doesn't matter.

[C'est la nuit et les gens s'assemblent et ils chantent une syllabe. Mais ils la chantent chaque un à un autour, c'est il y a cent personnes chacun ne fait qu'une fois; mais ils font tellement vite que ça est 'pia pia pia pia pia pia pia pia pia', ça c'est terrible. Alors, á Bali ils font 'čac čac čac čac čac čac čac čac čac' et là c'est 'pia pia pia pia pia pia pia pia pia', c'est la même chose. Alors, il faut donner l'impression d'une foule. Mais ce n'est pas difficile parce que c'est le piano qui fait tout, vous parlez presque, c'est presque parlé. C'est seulement la difficulté c'est de respirer. Mais si un en manque pour respirer, tant pis.] [Example 5.9]

Example 5.9   'Syllabes', p. 68, system 3 up to 2 bars before the end of the song

I had been to Bali in 1976 and seen this incredible virtuosic 'dance of the monkeys', called *kecak*, and it was fascinating to me to translate the image with my voice. This image really changes the style of interpretation. It is not meant to be sung but is more like a word play on the pitch, practically *parlando* and as quick as possible.

'L'escalier redit, gestes du soleil'

In this song, the lovers rise in ecstasy into paradise. Messiaen wanted this song to have an extremely fast tempo such that the singer is nearly out of breath, in great ecstasy but with a certain lightness. He made a point about the words 'pour nous chercher, pour nous pleurer, pour nous rêver, pour nous trouver' (Example 5.10):[11]

> *Messiaen*: One has to understand these words, they are beautiful, one has to understand them.
> *Yvonne Loriod*: You can breathe between each [word], I think.
> *Messiaen*: Breathe between each note. Except joy.

> [*Messiaen*: Il faut qu'on entende les mots, pour nous chercher, pour nous pleurer, pour nous rêver, pour nous trouver. Ils sont beaux les mots, il faut qu'on les entende.
> *Loriod*: Vous pouvez respirer entre chaque [mot] je pense.
> *Messiaen*: Vous pouvez respirez à toutes les notes. Respirez à toutes les notes. Sauf joie.]

Example 5.10   'L'escalier redit, gestes du soleil', p. 79, bars 2–5

---

[11]   To look for each other, to weep for each other, to dream of each other, to find each other.

Yvonne Loriod and I used a very rapid tempo, which Messiaen liked very much. I even mixed some air in the vocal sound – which is usually forbidden in classical singing – to imitate somebody who is out of breath.

'Amour oiseau d'étoile'

Messiaen is known to have been influenced by a surrealistic painting by the English artist Roland Penrose for this song. Regarding the composition, Messiaen explained:

> This painting shows the face of a woman upside-down, first the hair, then the eyes, then the mouth, the neck, and then it finishes, above that the clouds and the stars. It is very slow, very slow and at a very great distance.
>
> [Ce tableau représentait un visage d'une femme à l'envers, d'abord les cheveux, puis les yeux, puis la bouche, puis le cou et puis ça s'arrête et les nuages et les étoiles. C'est très lent, très lent et très lointain.]

To make the sound of the voice nearly disembodied, I used pure head-voice for the first phrases, sang the end note practically non-vibrato, straight, very soft, and sang the whole song in a translucent, ethereal way – except the *mf* part: 'Tous les oiseaux des étoiles, loin du tableau mes mains chantent' (Example 5.11).[12]

Example 5.11   'Amour oiseau d'étoile', p. 86, bars 3–4

Messiaen went on:

> I shall also explain another part to you: 'Tous les oiseaux des étoiles'. There are, of course, no birds in the stars. But this would be my dream. I think that after my death, I shall also have birds around me in paradise because I am an ornithologist.

---

12   All the birds of the stars, far from the picture my hands sing.

[Je vous explique aussi ça ce que nous avons chanté: 'Tous les oiseaux des étoiles'. Il n y a pas des oiseaux dans les étoiles bien entendu, mais ça c'est mon rêve, je pense que après la mort quand même je rencontre des oiseaux en paradis parce que je suis ornithologue.]

This vision also influences the interpretation, requiring a simple, pure, almost insubstantial voice, with practically no vibrato and a very, very slow tempo.

'Katchikatchi les étoiles'

A song in which an image of the Inca plays an important role: A ball game existed in their culture in which the head of the winner was cut off as a sacrifice to the gods. Messiaen already spoke about this image in the earlier song 'L'amour de Piroutcha'. The lover says: 'Coupe-moi la tête', and Messiaen explained that the bewitched person is transformed by the beheading. There is a certain brutality in the vision and in the song, a wildness that should be brought out by the sound of the voice (Example 5.12).

Example 5.12   'Katchikatchi les étoiles', p. 92, bars 3–4

One can think about the image of purgatory. Chaos, everything disperses in a wild dance. The voice should not be used in the classical way. It is essential to maintain a constant *f,* somewhat brutal, rhythmically strong and wild, the deep notes with chest voice, the 'Ahi's and 'o's like cries (Example 5.13).

Example 5.13   'Katchikatchi les étoiles', p. 92, bar 5

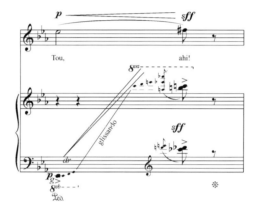

'Dans le noir'

The last song – with the love theme from the second and seventh songs – is sung in traditional classical style. Messiaen wanted the tempo to be as slow as possible and with great emphasis, a kind of ulterior joy. The lovers are together in the other world, in paradise. And at the very end, Messiaen imagined a different sound to that demanded in the score. He wrote 'bouche fermée', which means 'humming'. And when I hummed, he said that this was not what he wanted to have; rather, he

Example 5.14   'Dans le noir', end

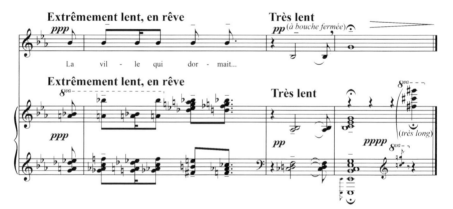

had a sound like a French horn in mind. To achieve this sound with the voice, just imagine imitating a French horn by blowing up the cheek and letting the sound come out through closed lips, *diminuendo* at the end. And for the piano part, Messiaen said the left hand ends with an imagined tam-tam (Example 5.14).

Closing Remarks

My work with Olivier Messiaen and Yvonne Loriod on *Harawi* revealed that the cycle is more experimental than the score suggests and that it is unique in the vocal compositions of this composer. Our collaboration began under a different premise to those of the singers with whom Messiaen had worked for the almost 40 years since *Harawi* had been composed. I came, so to speak, from the other side of the musical experience. The singers with whom Messiaen (and Yvonne Loriod) had worked before came from a traditional background. I came from contemporary music and was used to applying many different kinds of styles and colours to my voice. I was familiar with the *Sprechgesang* of Schoenberg, the non-vibrato of the early Cage pieces, and all kinds of experimental sounds like those in Berio's *Sequenza* (1965). In addition to *bel canto*, I was familiar with the development of the wide spectrum of vocal expression including all kinds of experimental vocal techniques. So, when I listened to Messiaen's visions and explanations, I understood them easily because in the years 1976–79 I had already travelled to the countries he spoke about: Peru, Mexico, India, Bali. I had seen the ruins of their historical cultures and listened to the ethnological music and dances he referred to. Being well acquainted with these cultures, the poetic images in the songs of *Harawi* were miraculously near to my feelings. And, having large experience with the experimental enrichment of the vocal expression beyond traditional singing, it was a pleasure for me to translate the scenes in *Harawi* by creating adequate vocal sounds.

This was one of the rare moments in the artistic life where three components were melted in a singular way into an unforgettable performance: the composer's unique creation influenced by ethnological cultures, the special personal and artistic experience of the singer and the congenial harmony between the interpreters. It brought to life an interpretation that obviously fulfilled Messiaen's expectations more vividly than even he himself may have imagined. The result was tears in his eyes (Illustrations 5.6 and 5.7).

I had no chance to make the CD with Yvonne Loriod: she had signed an exclusive contract for all the works of Messiaen and her recording of *Harawi* was already under contract at the time we met.[13] There are private live recordings of *Harawi* from

---

[13]   Yvonne Loriod, letter from 10 October 1988: 'C'eût été avec le plus grand plaisir que j'aurais enregistré avec vous les *Harawi* pour une maison de disques. Mais… Je ne le puis, car je viens de le faire avec Rachel Yakar il y a plusieurs mois pour Erato, je n'ai pas le droit de le faire avant quelques années…!' [It would have been with greatest pleasure that I would have recorded *Harawi* with you for a record company. But… I cannot, for I have

Illustration 5.6   Sigune von Osten, Olivier Messiaen and Yvonne Loriod after
performing *Harawi*, Bratislava, 7 December 1987

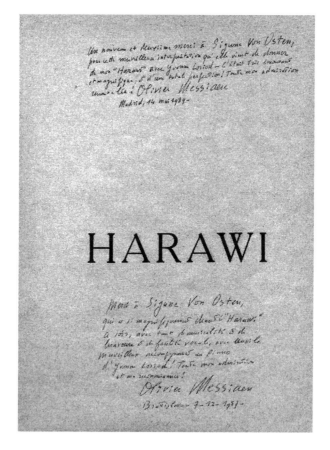

Illustration 5.7   Messiaen's dedication to the author in her score of *Harawi*,
Madrid 1988

our concerts in Bratislava in 1987 and in Madrid in 1988 as well as live recordings of the orchestral version of *Poèmes pour Mi* by Radio France in 1988 (80th anniversary concert for Messiaen at the Rencontres Internationales de Musique Contemporaine, Metz) and a live recording at Bruckner Tage in Linz by ORF – one of the last concerts to which Messiaen came and for which he rehearsed personally.

During our meetings, I could always feel that *Harawi* was especially close to the hearts and souls of Olivier Messiaen and Yvonne Loriod. After Messiaen's death, I asked Yvonne Loriod to perform *Harawi* again in several concerts. She replied that after Messiaen had departed from this life, she would never perform *Harawi* again. It was too close to her heart. And when I sent her my CD of *Harawi* with pianist Pi-hsien Chen in 1993, she replied: 'I am very touched by your friendship and will listen to this CD when I can. For now it is still too emotional for me.' (Illustration 5.8)[14]

Illustration 5.8   Letter from Yvonne Loriod to the author, 6 December 1993 (excerpt)

---

already made one several months ago with Rachel Yakar for Erato, and I have no right to make another for several years...!]

[14]   Je suis très touchée de votre amitié et vais écouter ce CD dès que je pourrai. Pour le moment cela m'est encore une trop grosse émotion.

Chapter 6
Olivier Messiaen's *Timbres-durées*

Christopher Brent Murray

The spring of 1952 is often described as a turning point in the evolution of Messiaen's musical language.[1] Creatively stimulated by his contact with the naturalist and amateur ornithologist Jacques Delamain, Messiaen shifted from composing short pieces experimenting with serial techniques to develop a new style using birdsong notations. It was during that same spring of 1952 that Messiaen wrote one last abstract rhythmic experimental work in the form of his *musique concrète* study, *Timbres-durées*, with technical help from his former student Pierre Henry. Though dismissed as a failure by Messiaen and considered a minor footnote in Henry's long career in *musique concrète*, *Timbres-durées* is worthy of consideration not only as an early example of electroacoustic music for tape, or as an early experiment in the spatialization of electroacoustic music, but also and perhaps most importantly, as Messiaen's last short experimental piece. This study analyses the rhythms, timbres and spatialization of this little-known rhythmic étude, and considers *Timbres-durées* as an episode in the development of Messiaen's musical language with as much to tell us about the composer's interests and motivations as his better-known and widely lauded works from the same period.[2]

The present research integrates information from a number of primary sources. Pierre Henry very graciously granted my consultation of his copies of the manuscript scores of *Timbres-durées*, including Messiaen's manuscript in traditional notation, as well as Henry's own versions of the scores, his notes on the spatialization of *Timbres-durées* and a document titled 'Répertoire et analyse de sons' that describes in detail the sounds chosen by Messiaen. Henry may have created this list as a pedagogical document for use in lecture-demonstrations on *musique concrète* in 1952 and 1953. I also located a second copy of the document with handwritten musical transcriptions of recorded sounds that can be found

[1] See, for example, PHNS, pp. 198–205.

[2] The findings presented here are the result of research begun in 2005 with a grant from the Florence Gould Foundation and the Council for European Studies at Columbia University, which also enabled my initial study of Messiaen and *musique concrète*, my master's thesis, *Les Timbres-durées d'Olivier Messiaen et la relation du compositeur avec la musique concrète* at the Université Lumière Lyon 2 in 2006. For a detailed study of the history of Messiaen's activity in Schaeffer's studio, see Christopher Brent Murray, 'A History of *Timbres-durées*: Understanding Olivier Messiaen's Role in Pierre Schaeffer's Studio', *Revue de musicologie*, 96/1 (2010): pp. 117–29.

in Antoine Goléa's archives at the Institut Supérieur de Musique et Pédagogie in Namur, Belgium. Goléa frequently wrote and lectured on both *musique concrète* and Messiaen's music, beginning in 1952. I also make reference to radio interviews, articles and programme notes from the archives of the Institut National de l'Audiovisuel (INA) and the archives of Pierre Schaeffer at the Institut Mémoires de l'Édition Contemporaine (IMEC). The recording of *Timbres-durées* released in 2004 was also essential to my analysis showing the permutations and symmetrical structures at work on the global and local levels of the work.[3]

Background

Messiaen was already familiar with the innovations of Schaeffer's studio when he began working with Pierre Henry in February 1952. He had heard the *Symphonie pour un homme seul* in 1950 and had attended the first concert of spatialized *musique concrète* created with magnetic tape in 1951. Messiaen was also regularly featured in radio broadcasts promoting the work of Pierre Schaeffer's studio for *musique concrète*, giving his opinion on Henry's *Musique sans titre* and participating in round table debates.[4]

Pierre Henry's notes show that work on *Timbres-durées* began during the first nine days of February 1952.[5] Henry recalled that Messiaen's first step was to choose the five families of percussive sounds or *directions sonores* that were to be used.[6] Once Messiaen had given him some initial indications of his preferences, Henry spent nearly a month recording and manipulating sounds, creating several hundred tape loops. From these loops, Messiaen made a second selection of about 20 sounds and wrote out his prescriptive six-page manuscript score in traditional notation. The top of the manuscript reads '*Timbres-durées* (musique concrète à 1 voix)', a clear reminder of Messiaen's original intention to compose a monody for tape.[7] Using Messiaen's manuscript, Henry created a *concrète* version of

[3]   *Archives GRM* (Groupe de Recherches Musicales), Vol. 1, GRM-INA 276 502 276512. A slightly different version of *Timbres-durées* is consultable in the International Digital Electroacoustic Music Archive collection, but the recording released by the GRM is cleaner and far easier to procure.

[4]   A radio broadcast of a conversation between Pierre Schaeffer, Olivier Messiaen, Roland-Manuel and Serge Moreux concerning the 1950 concert of *musique concrète* at the Théâtre de l'Empire, on the *Chaîne nationale* and produced by the Radiodiffusion française, is conserved in INA archives, as is Messiaen's critique of Henry's *Musique sans titre*, which was also recorded for the *Chaîne nationale* and broadcast 21 September 1951.

[5]   According to Pierre Henry's agenda from 1952.

[6]   Interview with Pierre Henry, 6 February 2008.

[7]   In my study I referred to a copy of Messiaen's pencil manuscript score in Pierre Henry's private collection. The original of this manuscript is now in the collection of the British Library, temporarily catalogued under Music Deposit 1998/04. I give my sincere

the score on graph paper, showing tape lengths in centimetres instead of note lengths in traditional notation.[8] This score, completed 15 April 1952, was then used as an *aide-mémoire* during the montage of the tape. Henry finished the first tape of *Timbres-durées* by early May, but Messiaen was not satisfied with the results. Messiaen made some cuts to his score and agreed to Henry's suggestion to spatialize the work, giving Henry *carte blanche* in the matter. The spatialized version of *Timbres-durées* was first performed in two concerts at the Salle de l'Ancien Conservatoire on 21 May 1952, as part of a thinly veiled propagandist festival of Western art, L'Œuvre du xxᵉ siècle, organized by Nicolas Nabokov.[9] After being played at a few concerts and demonstrations in Paris, Darmstadt and the United States in 1952 and 1953, *Timbres-durées* fell out of circulation and, except for a rare scholarly reference and its presence on Messiaen's worklist, remained more or less forgotten until its 2004 re-release.

The Timbres of *Timbres-durées*

In a little-known 1952 radio interview with Antoine Goléa, Messiaen explained that he was interested in the medium of tape because, 'It has the potential to realize extremely complicated rhythms in a rigorous, mathematical manner; rhythms that would not be possible with instruments and human performers.'[10] But Messiaen

thanks to Nicolas Bell for bringing this felicitous acquisition to my attention. A clean copy of the opening sequences of this manuscript was created by Messiaen as an insert for the May 1952 concert programmes and has been reproduced in a number of publications, most recently in PHNS, p. 198 and PHNS (Fr. edn) p. 259. A passage from a version of Henry's concrète score was also copied for the 1952 programmes and can be found in the various editions and translations of Erhard Karkoschka's *Notation in New Music* (New York: Praeger, 1966), p. 164.

[8]   This conversion was facilitated by the indicated tempo of 144 quarter notes per minute, where one quarter note lasts 5/12 of a second. On the studio's tape machines running 76 cm of tape per second, this was the equivalent of 32 centimetres of tape. As a power of two, these 32 centimetres are easily divided to create traditional note lengths from simple tape lengths of 16, 8 and 4 centimetres.

[9]   For more on the geopolitical dimensions of this CIA-funded festival, dubbed 'le festival de NATO' by Serge Lifar, see Michèle Alten, *Musiciens français dans la guerre froide* (Paris: l'Harmattan, 2000), Francis Saunders, *Who Paid the Piper, the CIA and the Cultural Cold War* (London: Granata, 2000), and Mark Carroll, *Music and Ideology in Cold War Europe* (Cambridge, Cambridge University Press, 2003).

[10]   'Depuis qu'elle est exécutée sur ruban, qu'elle est découpée sur ruban, c'est la possibilité de faire entendre d'une façon rigoureusement mathématique des durées extrêmement compliquées qui ne seraient pas exécutables avec des instruments et surtout des instrumentistes.' Messiaen interviewed by Antoine Goléa circa 1952, reused in *Acousmathèque: Musique Concrète, Musique Électroacoustique* radio broadcast presented by François Bayle on France Musique, 5 February 1985, and conserved in the INA archives

was also interested in the potential of *musique concrète*'s timbres. Like his later *Chronochromie*, the title of *Timbres-durées* refers to Messiaen's philosophy that timbre colours lengths of time that would otherwise be silent. Messiaen's approach in composing *Timbres-durées* was to render time audible with 'non-musical' noises, instead of the splashy orchestral chords he would later use to the same ends in *Chronochromie*.

Though his ideas would evolve, in 1952 Messiaen was still distinguishing between timbres he considered to be 'noise' and timbres that he considered to be 'musical'. His programme note tellingly describes *Timbres-durées* as 'a rhythmic work with no musical sounds'.[11] In his 1952 interview with Goléa, Messiaen explained how he had hoped that taped sounds would realize his rhythms more abstractly than the familiar timbres of traditional acoustic instruments: 'I tried to make only the note-lengths themselves audible, abstract note-lengths that were almost inaudible and only thinkable. I didn't accompany them with musical sounds, just noises, timbres, like the title says. The timbres were meant to bring out, to emphasize the durations.'[12] Messiaen hoped that the lengths of the sounds would be more noticeable than the sounds themselves, and imagined that noise might bring rhythms to the foreground of the listening experience differently or more successfully than the organ and piano of his previous experimental works. The restrained selection of sounds chosen by Messiaen baffled Schaeffer, who seems to have expected the *musique concrète* equivalent of *Turangalîla-Symphonie*'s orchestral kaleidoscope. As he recounted, 'We invited Messiaen to a feast where we thought everything would flatter his taste, but he didn't even open the cupboards. He clapped and murmured: "Something like that. The least sound possible."'[13]

(www.ina.fr). The English translation is my own, as are all of the English translations in this chapter when not noted otherwise. Other authors noting Messiaen's interest in *musique concrète* as a medium for rhythmic experiments include Jean Barraqué, 'Qu'est-ce que la musique concrète', *Guide du concert*, 1952, no. 18: p. 417, reprinted in Jean Barraqué, *Écrits*, ed. Laurent Feneyrou (Paris: Sorbonne, 2001), pp. 33–6, Michel Chion, *Pierre Henry* (Paris: Fayard, 2003), pp. 44–5, and Jean Boivin, *La classe de Messiaen* (Paris: Bourgois, 1995), p. 117.

[11]   Messiaen's programme note for *Timbres-durées*, cited in PHNS, p. 198.

[12]   From a 1952 interview with Antoine Goléa reused in *Acousmathèque*. 'En composant cette œuvre, j'ai essayé de faire entendre des durées seules, des durées abstraites, presque des durées qui ne sont pas audibles, mais seulement pensables. Je ne les ai pas accompagnés des sons musicaux, mais seulement des bruits, des timbres, ce comme le dit le titre. Les timbres qui étaient destinés à les faire valoir, à les mettre en valeur.'

[13]   'Messiaen, que nous avions convié à un festin de sons où tout, pensions-nous devait flatter sa gourmandise, n'ouvrait même pas les armoires, frappait dans ses mains et murmurait: quelques chose comme cela, le moins de son possible.' Schaeffer continues, 'Messiaen, restait malheureusement un peu loin du réalisateur, laissait se produire cet étonnant *Timbres-durées* qui demeurera sans doute à la fois le plus grand succès et le plus grand échec de cette période'. Pierre Schaeffer, 'Vers une musique expérimentale', *La revue musicale*, no. 236 (1957): p. 18. For Pierre Henry's reaction to *Timbres-durées*, see his

Ultimately, Messiaen was not satisfied with the sounds he had chosen. He said that his disappointment with the water sounds in particular led to his realization that fluctuations in timbre are rhythms in themselves, that rhythm and timbre are inextricably linked.[14] Messiaen had chosen gurgling water sounds for the long durations of the work's most important motive, Personnage A, but ultimately found that these sustained sounds did not give the impression of unity he wanted in a long note value. As he put it:

> I must say that I was disappointed with some of the timbres I myself had chosen. In nature there are particularly lively timbres. The streams of water disappointed me because I wrote long values for the streams. In such streams, as you know, there is a gurgling. Each little gurgle is a new event and where I expected to hear a long value, there were thousands of short values one after another and leaving no impression of a long value.[15]

At the end of the 1950s, at a time when he was preparing to incorporate transcriptions of water sounds into *Chronochromie*, Messiaen made a veiled reference to the discovery yielded by his experience with *musique concrète* in his preface to a special issue of the *Revue musicale* on *musique concrète*:

> Thus, our old companion Time reveals one of its secrets: at the interior of each expected note-length, dynamic changes create thousands of unexpected short lengths, recalling the prediction of *Macbeth*'s witches, 'until Great Birnam wood to high Dunsinane hill shall come against him....' – Yet, the miracle occurs: the forest begins to march! The once docile whole- and half-notes begin to move,

---

interview with Jean Boivin cited in *La classe de Messiaen*, pp. 117–18, or Michel Chion's *Pierre Henry*. Henry reiterated these views in our interview on 6 February 2008.

[14]   Messiaen would return to this idea in his discussion of rhythm in the first volume of his *Traité*. Although he was disappointed with *Timbres-durées*, it should be noted that, with time, he became an increasingly harsh judge of his 'experimental period' of 1949–52 in general. Seemingly concerned by persisting interest in his *Quatre Études rythmiques*, and 'Mode de valeurs et d'intensités' in particular, he began declaring them undeserving of so much attention. See, for example, the changes made to the text of his 1967 interview with Claude Samuel in its 1986 re-edition. Claude Samuel, *Conversations with Olivier Messiaen*, trans. Felix Aprahamian, (London: Stainer and Bell, 1976), pp. 47–8, and *Music and Color*, pp. 79–80.

[15]   1952 interview with Antoine Goléa. 'Je dois dire d'ailleurs que j'ai eu une déception pour certains de ces timbres, que pourtant j'avais choisi. Dans la nature [il y a] des timbres particulièrement vivants, et ceux qui m'ont déçu, c'étaient les jets d'eau, parce que j'avais décrit pour ces jets d'eau des valeurs très longues, et dans les jets d'eau comme vous savez, il y a un crépitement. Chacun de ces crépitements est un événement nouveau pour l'oreille, et là où j'attendais une très grande valeur, il y en avait un millier de petites valeurs ... dans la peinture impressionniste par exemple, où il y a des milliers de petites couleurs, les petites valeurs frappaient toutes l'oreille les unes après les autres et il n'y avait plus de grande valeur.'

much to the *rythmicien*'s dismay! There is no need to travel to the moon to learn something new – as microphysicists have already told us. *Musique concrète* confirms this.[16]

The dismayed 'rythmicien' in question here is, of course, Messiaen himself, contemplating the ambush rebellion of *Timbres-durées*'s gurgling *objets sonores*.

Messiaen uses timbre in *Timbres-durées* the way he does in some of his other serial experiments with rhythm – as a marker to guide the listener. By linking rhythm and timbre, he effectively tags individual note values and rhythmic motives, making it (theoretically) easier for the listener to distinguish between them. In *Timbres-durées*, Messiaen not only links duration to timbre, but to the morphology of a recorded event, including its attack, decay and variations of intensity. It should be noted that Messiaen had played with the idea of formally pairing parameters from the beginning of his experimental period. Yves Balmer's study of Messiaen's compositional methods indicates that even before employing these experimental pairings, Messiaen conceptualized and composed the parameters of his music separately – for example, composing a chord progression first and adding a rhythm later.[17]

Messiaen elaborates his vision of these isolated and recombined parameters in his analysis of *Chronochromie*:

> Harmony is given rhythm, rhythm is coloured with chords, the quantitative domain (durations) and the phonetic domain (attacks, timbres, colours) are thrown into relief by one another, and their marriage transforms them into a single sonorous flesh which could be referred to by the compound, variously expressive names of *harmonies-attaques, chiffres-couleurs, timbres-durées*.[18]

In a similar comment made in reference to his *Livre d'orgue*, Messiaen notes, 'I attribute so much importance to this work's rhythmic values (*durées*) that I call the sounds (*sons*) *sons-durées*. Like timbre, they are nothing more than a vulgar

---

[16]   Preface to the 1959 issue of *La Revue musicale*, 'Expériences musicales', 244: p. 5. 'Et voici que notre vieux compagnon le Temps nous livre un de ses secrets. À l'intérieur de chaque durée prévue, les changements dynamiques créent des milliers de petites durées imprévues. Rappelons-nous la prédiction des sorcières de *Macbeth*: "Tant que la forêt de Birnam ne marche pas vers Dunsinane...." – Or, le miracle se produit: la forêt se met en marche! Les sages longues et brèves qui s'agitent ici pour le plus grand désarroi du rythmicien.... Point n'est besoin d'aller dans la lune pour apprendre du nouveau: la microphysique nous l'avait déjà dit – la musique concrète le confirme.'

[17]   See Yves Balmer's work on the sketches for *Les Visions de l'Amen*, in *Edifier son œuvre: Genèse, médiation, diffusion de l'œuvre d'Olivier Messiaen*, PhD thesis (Université Charles-de-Gaulle Lille 3, 2008), particularly pp. 144–8.

[18]   *Traité III*, p. 360.

medium destined to making the rhythmic values perceivable.'[19] Still, it should be noted that in *Timbres-durées*, as with the sketches for chord progressions in the *Visions de l'Amen* described by Balmer, Messiaen chose and composed his 'vulgar medium' before imposing rhythms upon it.

The five groups of timbres chosen for *Timbres-durées* reflect Messiaen's enduring affection for metallophones and the sound of water.[20] These five groups appear at the top of the 'Répertoire et analyse de sons' compiled by Henry and include water sounds, rubbed membranophones, the homogenous white sound from a Chinese cymbal, metallic percussion and wooden percussion. In his manuscript score, Messiaen used abbreviations from Henry's system for classifying his tape loops and also referred to the sounds by their sources. The exceptions to this rule were the sounds that had been altered to such an extent that they reminded him of other sounds, like the 'squeaking pulley' and 'bleating goat'. Interestingly, this practice of describing timbre through metaphor riddles Messiaen's birdsong cahiers. In his birdsong transcriptions from Delamain's garden of June 1952, Messiaen compared a quail's call to drops of water and a woodpecker's rapping to both splashing water and a woodblock. These of course were also sounds recently employed by Messiaen in *Timbres-durées*.[21] The woodblock and its shifting use in Messiaen's music during this period points to possible changes in the composer's mode of listening. Prominently featured rapping out *deçi-tâlas* in *Turangalîla-Symphonie*, the woodblock assumes a new and subdued ornithological role in *Réveil des oiseaux*, composed shortly after the experience of creating *Timbres-durées*.

The 11 *Timbres-durées* of Personnage A

Personnage A is the first and the most important of *Timbres-durées*'s four rhythmic motives or *personnages rythmiques* (in the sense that it best represents the *timbre-durée* concept of the work's title). According to Messiaen's programme note, it:

> contains eleven prime numbers which are subject to new permutations in each sequence. ... Each duration in Personnage A has its own timbre: one hears a new

---

[19] Brigitte Massin, *Olivier Messiaen: Une poétique du merveilleux* (Aix-en-Provence: Alinéa, 1989), pp. 116–17.

[20] In a 1966 interview Messiaen linked these sounds, likening the resonance and halo of harmonics of gongs, tam-tams and bells to the 'strange and enormous sounds of nature, like waterfalls and mountain torrents'. Radio broadcast, *Musique de notre temps*, with Claude Samuel, 'Où va la musique?', 25 January 1966.

[21] Messiaen's notes from the Charente 12–14 June 1952, BnF Département de la musique, Ms. 23079. The comparison of animal calls to other timbres is of course nothing new in itself (see, for example, the literature of Jacques Delamain or Jules Renard). Messiaen's observations stand out because of their context and because they often suggest a manner of orchestrating bird timbres with particular gestures and instruments.

version of the string drum imitating a bleating goat, sounds which have been filtered or had reverberation applied to them, and recordings of droplets and streams of water.[22]

In their original order, in the first sequence of the work, the 11 sounds of Personnage A are presented from shortest to longest (Example 6.1).

Example 6.1   Personnage A

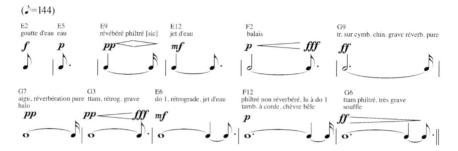

Personnage A is a series of sounds that Messiaen hoped would be heard as a series of durations, each coloured by a different timbre. As early as 1952, Messiaen's former student Jean-Étienne Marie noted a similarity between these linked parameters and John Cage's prepared piano, where the pitch and the timbre of a given preparation are always associated.[23] (Messiaen also referred to Cage as a fellow innovator in his short text for the programmes of the 1952 concerts, 'Attendre 200 ans'.) The subsequent rearrangement of the 11 *objets sonores* of Personnage A leads to the 'absence of continuity and ordered disparity' suggested by Messiaen in his early critiques of *musique concrète* as an ideal for the new art.[24]

Transcribing the *Objet Sonore*

As a model for trying to understand the sounds of *Timbres-durées*, and their notation in Messiaen's score, let us consider the third sound of Personnage A (in its position in sequence 1). The sound is labelled 'E6' in both Messiaen's and Henry's scores and was created by recording a stream of water directed into a metal bucket. On Henry's 'Répertoire et analyse des sons', all of the water sounds are labelled 'E' for *eau*, and seem to have been chosen from a far greater number of tape loops

---

[22]   Messiaen's programme note for *Timbres-durées*, cited in PHNS, p. 198.

[23]   Jean-Etienne Marie, *Musique vivante, introduction au langage musical* (Toulouse: Presses Universitaires de France, 1953), pp. 158–60.

[24]   Messiaen's analysis of *musique concrète* broadcast 21 September 1951: 'cette absence de continuité, cette disparité ordonnée'.

that were not used. Among those that survived the cuts: E2 and E5 are droplets of water, E9 is a stream of water plunged into a bucket and gradually pulled out again, and E12 is a stream of water directed against a gong.[25] In his score showing how he wanted Henry to construct *Timbres-durées*, Messiaen also noted some other information about the sound E6. 'Do 1' indicates the setting on the *phonogène à clavier*, a machine with a piano keyboard allowing the precise transposition of tape loops. Here Messiaen noted not only the original setting *phonogène* but also the setting that was used for the transposition of the final E6 tape loop. He also indicated that the sound was played in reverse, and was recorded at or amplified to a level described as *mezzo forte* in relation to the other sounds. Most strikingly, and characteristic of his focus upon traditional *écriture*, Messiaen notes the length of the note in traditional notation.

When comparing Messiaen's manuscript to Henry's *concrète* score, one remarks that Henry noted only which tape loop he would need to use (E6), and the length of centimetres of tape to be produced from the loop, since the other factors meticulously recopied by Messiaen with each occurrence of a sound were of course automatically inscribed in the tape loops themselves. Only in the first sequence of his score did Henry note dynamic levels. In later sequences the dynamics remain unchanged and were not noted.

Henry's 'Répertoire et analyse de sons' further clarifies the transformations that the original recording of sound E6 underwent. The first part of the document describes the original unaltered sound, a tape loop (*boucle*) number 227 ('B227') as 'A stream of water in an empty bucket – a continuous and homogenous sound in a medium register, recorded at the setting B2 [on the *phonogène à clavier*]'. On Henry's copy of the document there is a space on the page after which the text describes how the original recording was manipulated for use in the work: 'sound used: (B228). An excerpt from loop 227 lowered a major seventh, played in reverse with added pure reverberation, 368 centimetres in length'.

In Antoine Goléa's copy of the 'Répertoire et analyse de sons', the empty space left for examples on Henry's copy has been filled with a transcription in traditional notation of the altered sound, labelled 'example 6' alongside the equivalent length in traditional note values for the 368 centimetres of tape. The transcription of the jet of water in traditional notation (a widely spaced and trilling chord across the bass and tenor registers) is strikingly similar to Messiaen's transcriptions of natural

---

[25]   In *À la recherche d'une musique concrète*, Schaeffer sketches out a system for creating scores of *musique concrète* where letters (sound source) and numbers (versions of sounds from the same source) stand in place of complicated *objets sonores*. This was then further refined by Messiaen's former students Maurice Le Roux and Yvette Grimaud before being adopted by Henry to label the *objets sonores* and create the *concrète* score for *Timbres-durées*. See Pierre Schaeffer, *À la recherche d'une musique concrète* (Paris: Seuil, 1952), pp. 82–4.

timbres such as the wind in the trees, running water and, of course, birdsong found in his *cahier de chants d'oiseaux* from June of 1952 (Example 6.2).[26]

Example 6.2   Transcriptions of Sound E6 and 'The Wind in the Trees'

Son E6
Jet d'eau dans un seau vide (timbre métallique)

Gardépée, 12 juin 52
Le vent dans les arbres, sonorité chuchotée, veloutée et glissée

Given the contact between Messiaen and Goléa at Darmstadt in 1952 and afterwards, the notation on Goléa's copy is quite possibly Messiaen's own transcription in traditional notation of the recorded and altered sound.

The exercise of transcribing the wind, gurgling water or a cawing crow may seem futile in the context of the electroacoustic studio where tape could capture such sounds with precision. Yet it was this very manner of meticulous imaginative transcription that renewed Messiaen's musical language in his subsequent works from the 1950s, beginning with *Le Merle noir* and continuing through *Réveil des oiseaux* and *Catalogue d'oiseaux*. Recent studies have shown that Messiaen transcribed many recordings of birdsongs, both tapes and records, for use in his later works – the first known example being the American birdsong used in *Oiseaux exotiques*.[27] Messiaen's dependence upon traditional notation may have been a conceptual barrier that prevented him from fully exploiting *musique concrète*'s potential, but in a sense, he creatively took advantage of this very barrier, using musical *écriture*, his remarkable ear, and his imagination to capture natural sounds in new ways that I suggest were informed by his encounters with electroacoustic music. The transcription of the water sound E6 found in Goléa's papers is an interesting anticipation of Messiaen's development of sound transcription through traditional acoustic means during the 1950s and beyond. New charms from new impossibilities, one might say, to borrow Messiaen's parlance.

---

[26]   BnF Ms. 23079.

[27]   This was first observed by Robert Fallon in his study 'The Record of Realism in Messiaen's Bird Style', in Christopher Dingle and Nigel Simeone (eds), *Olivier Messiaen: Music, Art and Literature* (Aldershot: Ashgate, 2007), pp. 115–36. This study also links Messiaen's bird style to his work with *musique concrète*. See also Peter Hill and Nigel Simeone, *Olivier Messiaen: Oiseaux exotiques* (Aldershot: Ashgate, 2007).

The Durées of *Timbres-durées*

Timbres-durées is divided into 24 sequences resulting from all of the possible permutations of its four independently evolving rhythmic motives or *personnages rythmiques*. In his programme note for *Timbres-durées*, Messiaen labels these rhythms A, B, C, and D, corresponding to their order in the first sequence. Their 24 permutations are arranged in an elegant pattern that assures that no *personnage* is heard twice consecutively, except the repetition of Personnage B on the line of symmetry between sequences 12 and 13 (Table 6.1).

Table 6.1   Symmetrical permutations of the four *personnages* in sequences 1–24

1. ABCD	2. ABDC	3. ADBC	4. DABC	5. ACBD	6. ACDB	7. ADCB	8. DACB	9. CABD	10. CADB	11. CDAB	12. DCAB
13. BACD	14. BADC	15. BDAC	16. DBAC	17. BCAD	18. BCDA	19. BDCA	20. DBCA	21. CBAD	22. CBDA	23. CDBA	24. DCBA

As those familiar with Messiaen's music and teachings know, the composer compared his *personnage rythmiques* to actors on a stage who take the lead at different moments in the drama, alternatively speaking more or less in different scenes. We can extend Messiaen's theatrical metaphor to imagine each sequence as a scene in which certain *personnages* come to the fore while others fade into the background. Still, it should be noted that beyond their shared symmetry, there seems to be no connection between the operations governing the evolution of each *personnage*. Indeed, they are talking in turn, but not communicating – they are linked by their proximity and unfold in parallel, but were conceived separately, and are made to measure for the preconceived framework of 24 symmetrically permutated sequences.

Also of note in the composition of the four *personnages rythmiques* is the contrasting nature of their structures and development. As with the rondo-fantasy chain of sequences in *Cantéyodjayâ* and the techniques used to compose the *Quatre Études de rythme*, in *Timbres-durées*, Messiaen juxtaposes rhythms that are broken apart and treated serially (like the Personnage A of *Timbres-durées*) with traditional pulsed, dance-like rhythms, (Personnages B and C). Finally, Personnage D, with the pulsing vibrato of its transposed string-drum sounds, introduces a third and eerily vocal motive to the mix. The effect of the four *personnages* heard together reaffirms Messiaen's previous statements about expanding the notion of what rhythm means.

Personnage A

I have already pointed out how Messiaen links a series of 11 rhythmic values to a series of 11 timbres in Personnage A. Let us consider how these 'eleven prime numbers' are 'subject to new permutations in each sequence'. By 'prime numbers' Messiaen means that in his manuscript each note value is worth a prime multiple of semiquavers. Messiaen uses the first 11 prime numbers (2, 3, 5, 7, 11, 13, 17, 19, 23, 29 and 31), which he arranges from shortest to longest in the first sequence; a sort of prime number version of his concept of '*rythme chromatique*'.[28] Prime numbers held a special importance for Messiaen, and their use in Personnage A prevents the sense of a regular meter establishing itself with the entry of each *objet sonore*.

Though Messiaen links timbre to rhythmic value in the other *personnages*, it is only in Personnage A that he links specific timbres to specific note lengths to create unique '*timbres-durées*' in the sense of the work's title. As explained earlier, this is a practical measure meant to make it easier to perceive the reordering of Personnage A's 11 sounds. Unlike the augmentation or diminution of individual note values, changing the order of the composing elements of a rhythm is a serial operation that radically changes the rhythmic motive's character. The orders used by Messiaen for Personnage A are described in his *Traité* as 'reprises par interversion' and he considers them to be among the most immediately recognizable rearrangements of an already 'chromatic rhythm' such as the original order of Personnage A.[29] In the context of the *Livre d'orgue*, Messiaen imagined that such 'reprises par interversion' might render 'the colourations of the durations divided, fragmented, and scattered in an unexpected puzzle'.[30]

It is a slight exaggeration on Messiaen's part to claim that these 11 sounds are subject to a new permutation in each sequence. There are only six different permutations of Personnage A used in *Timbres-durées*, and they are heard in the first six sequences. To show these arrangements I have assigned numbers to each of the *objets sonores* of Personnage A from 1 to 11 according to their order in the first sequence (Table 6.2). As I have already observed, in sequence 1, the sounds are arranged from shortest to longest. In sequence 2, the shortest object is followed by the longest, the second shortest by the second longest, and so forth. In his *Traité* Messiaen called this particular interversion 'extrêmes au centre' or 'ciseaux fermés'. In the third sequence, he presents the alternative version of 'extrêmes au centre' starting with the longest value instead of the shortest.

Presenting yet another instance of symmetry, sequences 4–6 are the retrograde of sequences 1–3. Thus, sequence 4 is the retrograde of sequence 3, an arrangement used in his rhythmic étude *Île de feu 2* where he called it 'centre aux extrêmes' or

---

[28]   See, for example, certain passages of *Cantéyodjâya* where Messiaen labels a 'gamme chromatique des durées', rhythms composed of values of 1, 2, 3, 4, etc. 32nd notes.

[29]   *Traité III*, p. 348.

[30]   Ibid., p. 179.

Table 6.2   Permutations and symmetries in Personnage A (grey shading and italics indicate cuts made by Messiaen)

1.	1	2	3	4	5	6	7	8	9	10	11
2.	1	11	2	10	3	9	4	8	5	7	6
3.	11	1	10	2	9	3	8	4	7	5	6
					(line of symmetry)						
4.	6	5	7	4	8	3	9	2	10	1	11
5.	6	7	5	8	4	9	3	10	2	11	1
6.	11	10	9	8	7	6	5	4	3	2	1
					(line of symmetry)						
7.	*1*	*2*	3	4	5	6	7	8	9	10	11
8.	*1*	*11*	*2*	*10*	3	9	4	8	5	7	6
9.	*11*	*1*	*10*	*2*	*9*	*3*	8	4	7	5	6
					(line of symmetry)						
10.	*6*	*5*	*7*	*4*	*8*	*3*	*9*	*2*	10	1	11
11.	*6*	*7*	*5*	*8*	*4*	*9*	*3*	*10*	*2*	*11*	1
12.	*11*	*10*	*9*	*8*	*7*	*6*	*5*	*4*	*3*	*2*	*1*
					(line of symmetry)						
13.	*1*	*2*	*3*	*4*	*5*	*6*	*7*	*8*	*9*	*10*	*11*
14.	*1*	*11*	*2*	*10*	*3*	*9*	*4*	*8*	*5*	*7*	6
15.	*11*	*1*	*10*	*2*	*9*	*3*	*8*	*4*	7	5	6
					(line of symmetry)						
16.	*6*	*5*	*7*	*4*	*8*	*3*	9	2	10	1	11
17.	*6*	*7*	*5*	8	4	9	3	10	2	11	1
18.	*11*	*10*	9	8	7	6	5	4	3	2	1
					(line of symmetry)						
19.	1	2	3	4	5	6	7	8	9	10	11
20.	1	11	2	10	3	9	4	8	5	7	6
21.	11	1	10	2	9	3	8	4	7	5	6
					(line of symmetry)						
22.	6	5	7	4	8	3	9	2	10	1	11
23.	6	7	5	8	4	9	3	10	2	11	1
24.	11	10	9	8	7	6	5	4	3	2	1

'ciseaux ouverts'. Sequence 5 is the retrograde of sequence 2 and sequence 6 is the retrograde of sequence 1.

In the original versions of Messiaen's manuscript and Henry's first *concrète* score, these six permutations were repeated without variation in sequences 7–12, 13–18 and 19–24. All of the cuts made by Messiaen after hearing Henry's first tape were made to Personnage A. Table 6.2 shows these eliminated passages in italics. These eliminations preserve a certain symmetry – except in sequence 17 where Messiaen leaves 8 *objets sonores* instead of 7. The cuts mean that Personnage A disappears entirely from sequences 12 and 13.

Personnage B

In reference to Personnage B Messiaen notes, 'The Hindu rhythm *dhenkî*, is subject to diverse transformations, added dots, doubling, replacement of sounds by rests of equal value, the division of a value into thirty-second notes, and combinations of these transformations. It is entrusted to the woodblock.'[31]

The distinctive timbre of the woodblock used for this *personnage* makes it easy for the listener to pick out. The sound of the woodblock itself is not noticeably transformed and the rhythmic procedures employed here are based on techniques used by Messiaen beginning in the 1930s, as documented in his *Technique de mon langage musical*. Where Messiaen changes the order of the same eleven *timbres-durées* in Personnage A without changing their length, he maintains Personnage B's symmetrical structure while varying the length and number of its elements. The overall length of Personnage B is not subject to much fluctuation over the course of the work, qualifying it as a *personnage immobile* according to Messiaen's theory of *personnages rythmiques*.

Messiaen's explicit use of the *deçi-tâla*s described by Joanny Grosset in Albert Lavignac's *Encyclopédie* as alterable *personnages rythmiques* is yet another common point between *Timbres-durées* and other works from the experimental period.[32] In his *Traité*, Messiaen describes the *dhenkî* as 'the oldest, the simplest and the most natural of the non-retrogradable rhythms', a dubiously verifiable affirmation that nevertheless betrays the rhythm's special significance to the composer. In a work permeated with symmetry on multiple levels, it seems appropriate that Messiaen chose to use the pattern he felt to be the ancestor of his celebrated neologism, the *rythme non-rétrogradable*.

Table 6.3 describes the four transformations of Personnage B and their combinations over the course of the 24 sequences. Individual transformations include the addition of a dot, the repetition of an element, the replacement of note values with a silence of equal value and the division of a value into 32nd notes. The original three-value *dhenkî* rhythm can be heard in the first and last sequences. The 22 sequences from 2 to 23, can be grouped in pairs where each transformation or combination of transformations is first applied to alter the outer values of the rhythm, and then used to alter what Messiaen termed the *valeur centrale*. The first four pairs of sequences, 2 to 9, are the product of only one transformation. Sequences 10–19 combine two, and the last two pairs of sequences, 20 to 23, result from the two possible combinations of three different transformations. Here Messiaen systematically exhausts the possibilities of transformations and their combinations, just as he exhausted the permutations of the four *personnages* to generate the étude's form. This maximizing of potential is reminiscent of Messiaen's

---

[31]   Messiaen's programme note for *Timbres-durées*, cited in PHNS, p. 198.

[32]   Joanny Grosset, 'Inde' in Albert Lavignac (ed.), *Encyclopédie de la musique et dictionnaire du Conservatoire*, Première Partie, *Histoire de la musique, Antiquité–Moyen âge* (Paris: Delagrave, 1913), pp. 301–4.

Table 6.3   Transformations of Personnage B

1.	original dhenkî	–
2.	added dot to exterior values	**W**
3.	added dot to interior (central) value	
4.	repetition of exterior	**X**
5.	repetition of interior	
6.	exterior replaced by rests	**Y**
7.	interior replaced by rest	
8.	exterior divided into 32nd notes	**Z**
9.	interior divided into 32nd notes	
10.	added dot and repetition of exterior	**W*X**
11.	added dot and repetition of interior	
12.	exterior replaced by rest and added dot	**W*Y**
13.	interior replaced by rest and added dot	
14.	added dot and division into 32nd notes of exterior	**W*Z**
15.	added dot and division into 32nd notes of interior	
16.	exterior repeated and replaced by rests	**X*Y**
17.	interior repeated and replaced by rests	
18.	repetition and division into 32nd notes of exterior	**X*Z**
19.	repetition and division into 32nd notes of interior	
20.	repetition, added dots and division into 32nd notes of exterior	**W*X*Z**
21.	repetition, added dots and division into 32nd notes of interior	
22.	repetition, added dots and replacement by rests of exterior	**W*X*Y**
23.	repetition, added dots and replacement by rests of interior	
24.	original *dhenkî*	–

reflection upon his need to write out all possible options, a combination of his monk-like penchants for litany and *écriture*: 'I can't write out millions and millions of permutations, and yet I must write them out to able to know and love them.'[33]

Personnage C

Messiaen explains that 'Personnage C is a non-retrogradable rhythm developed through interpolation and extrapolation. It is played by a Chinese cymbal and an anvil.'[34] The original rhythm of Personnage C played by the Chinese cymbal is heard in all of the odd-numbered sequences. In the even-numbered sequences,

---

[33]   Iannis Xenakis, *Alliages* (Paris: Casterman, 1979), pp. 52–3.

[34]   Messiaen's programme note for *Timbres-durées*, cited in PHNS, p. 198.

new material in the contrasting timbre of the anvil augments the original non-retrogradable rhythm in two different ways (while always preserving its rhythmic symmetry). In sequences 2, 6, 10, 14, 18, and 22, material is inserted (or interpolated) in the centre of the original, replacing the note that once served as the *valeur centrale*.

Example 6.3 shows the first three interpolations, sequences 2, 6, and 10. The inserted rhythm grows with each occurrence, continuing to build upon what was inserted before, much like the gradual accretion of a pearl. In sequences 4, 8, 12, 16, 20, and 24, this same material is placed on either end of the original rhythm like symmetrical bookends in the process of *extrapolation*.

Example 6.3   Interpolations in Personnage C, sequences 2, 6, and 10

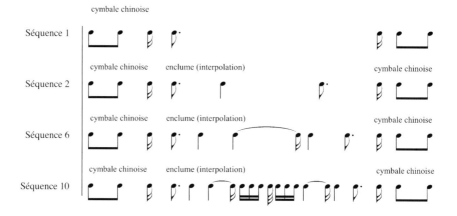

The contrasting metallophone timbres make the original rhythm easily distinguishable from its increasingly lengthy elaboration. By the end of the work, the once demure Personnage C has grown to impressive proportions, dwarfing even the 11 values of Personnage A.

Personnage D

In Personnage D, Messiaen uses a second *deçi-tâla* from the Lavignac *Encyclopédie*. He states that, 'Each duration of Personnage D (the Hindu râgavardhana) increases by a thirty-second note in each sequence. Its sound is that of a string drum transposed to three different pitches, a sound which evokes a squeaking pulley.'[35]

Like the *dhenkî*, the *râgavardhana* held a particular significance for Messiaen and is the only *deçi-tâla* extensively discussed in *Technique*, where Messiaen

---

[35]   Ibid.

understands it as the embodiment of a number of rhythmic operations.[36] In his *Traité* he observes that *râgavardhana* means 'the rhythm that most enlivens the raga', and concludes that this etymology must be related to the diverse possibilities of rhythmic transformation that the *râgavardhana* offers to the traditional Indian musician.[37] The rhythm of Personnage D itself undergoes a change that is nearly imperceptible from sequence to sequence, as each of its rhythmic values grows by a 32nd note with each iteration in sequences 1–12. In his analytical note, Messiaen neglects to mention that the values of Personnage D shrink by a 32nd note in each sequence over the course of sequences 13–24, returning to their original proportions in the final sequence. This process is perfectly symmetrical.

Some Remarks on the Spatialization of *Timbres-durées*

In both his programme note and his declaration to the SACEM, Messiaen makes it clear that Pierre Henry was entirely responsible for the spatialization of *Timbres-durées*. Henry's second version of his *concrète* score experimented with combining the two methods of spatialization being used in Schaeffer's studio in early 1952, replacing the single voice of the original monophonic version with four voices corresponding to four synchronized tapes.

The tapes of the three-track *magnétophone tripiste* were channelled directly to loudspeakers to the left, right and rear centre of the performance space, a technique known as *relief statique*. The fourth voice or the *voix cinématique* was controlled by the *pupître d'espace* (also referred to as the *pupître de relief*). Sounds on the tape for this voice could be moved back and forth from left to right by moving the magnetized reel of the *pupître d'espace*, a technique dubbed *relief cinématique*. This *cinématique* [kinetic] movement allowed the sound of a single *objet sonore* to move from one location to another while it was being played, as opposed to sounds in the other three voices that were automatically channelled to one place or another, but never heard in gradual movement between two locations. By combining these two methods of spatialization Henry could achieve precise movements in passages where the notes were too quick to be moved by physical manipulation of the *pupître d'espace*, sparingly used for the gradual movement of longer sounds.

Henry could have used spatialization to clarify and reinforce Messiaen's formal structures, but analysis of his notes and spatialized *concrète* score reveals an arrangement concerned not so much with cleaving to the mechanics of Messiaen's symmetries as with showing the capabilities and musical dimensions of the GRMC's (Groupe de Recherche de Musique Concrète) new machinery.

---

[36] *Technique*, Chapter 2.

[37] *Traité I*, pp. 297–8. It is not clear whether this is the case. To date, no study has yet verified Messiaen's observations in his *Traité* concerning the meaning and significance of Hindu rhythms described by Joanny Grosset.

Messiaen's already fragmented and constantly rearranged *personnages* were only further complicated by Henry's spatialization, which grows in complexity as the work progresses. Though Henry's spatialization reproduces non-retrogradable symmetries in places, he does not employ a generalized system for placing the sounds in space equivalent to the extreme organization and symmetry of Messiaen's constructions. Henry chose not to extend the logic of linking parameters by linking certain sounds or *personnages* to specific locations in the performance space to create a second trail of markers to help the listener distinguish between the rhythms.

Though the spatialization of the first three sequences is relatively simple and restrained (Henry does not break up the sounds of a *personnage* in multiple locations, for example), things become increasingly complicated as the piece progresses. The spatialization reaches a final paroxysm of complexity – with short 32nd-note values ricocheting back and forth across the room in sequences 21– 23. In the last sequence the spatialization returns to utter simplicity in a sort of tutti coda where the same music is projected from all three speakers at the same time.[38] Henry seems to have abandoned any hope that the listeners of May 1952 would ever manage to orient themselves in Messiaen's rhythmic labyrinth with Messiaen's terse programme note as their only guide, preferring instead to revel in the dramatic chaos of movement allowed by Schaeffer and Poullin's machines.

Conclusion

It should be emphasized that symmetry is present in *Timbres-durées* on the level of the motive, the development of the *personnages*, and in the permutations of the *personnages* themselves. These multiple symmetries, like the automatic nature of *Timbres-durées*'s generative systems, are played down in Messiaen's programme note. Yet once the carefully prepared systems of rhythmic elaboration have been set in motion, the work largely 'composes itself'. The automatic aspect of the work helped me to produce a complete score of *Timbres-durées*, reproducing Messiaen's traditional rhythmic notation by using only the 2004 GRM recording long before I was finally able to consult the scores preserved in Pierre Henry's private collection.

In a sense, *Timbres-durées* represents the unrestrained 'writing out' of permutations described by Messiaen in Xenakis's thesis defence. The serial techniques of *Timbres-durées* are related not only to those used in the *Livre d'orgue* but also to the theoretical composition exercises 'written out' by Messiaen in his *Traité*. One such passage is dedicated to '24 interversions de 4 deçi-tâlas

---

[38]   These observations are based upon the consultation and analysis of Henry's manuscript spatialized *concrète* score, not reproduced in detail out of respect for M. Henry's wishes that a restored version of his spatialization of *Timbres-durées* not be undertaken for the time being.

très caractéristiques' and is extremely similar to *Timbres-durées*. Each *deçi-tâla* is treated as a *personnage* and undergoes manipulations similar to those seen above.[39]

Attracted to Schaeffer's studio hoping that tape would be the perfect medium for serial rhythmic constructions, Messiaen found that his traditional ideas about notation and timbre conflicted with the new implications of *musique concrète*, that the timbres he had chosen defied the traditional notation inextricably linked to his ideas about rhythm. Despite his disappointment with the sounds he initially thought might be the ideal medium for 'colouring' his rhythms, Messiaen's experience led him to develop his ideas concerning the nature of rhythm and timbre. Though he would not continue to work in the medium of *musique concrète* we can posit that his experience at the GRMC contributed to new developments in Messiaen's musical language and influenced his manner of transcribing and listening to natural sounds.

It would seem that Messiaen preferred his *Livre d'orgue* and his *Quatre Études de rythme,* but not *Timbres-durées*, to stand as monuments to his rhythmic innovations. Describing the *Livre d'orgue* later in life when he had returned to a more traditionally expressive style, Messiaen insisted, 'even if one finds the music ... is long, ugly, and useless, it represents one of my greatest rhythmic victories'.[40] Given all of its common points with the *Livre d'orgue*, *Timbres-durées*, in spite of its imperfections, should also be considered as an important episode in the development of Messiaen the *rythmicien*.

---

[39] *Traité III*, pp. 337–43.
[40] Ibid., p. 204.

Chapter 7

From *Réveil des oiseaux* to *Catalogue d'oiseaux*: Messiaen's *Cahiers de notations des chants d'oiseaux*, 1952–59

Peter Hill

Messiaen's birdsong *cahiers* run to several thousand pages and form by far the largest body of surviving Messiaen manuscripts, almost all unknown.[1] As well as telling the story of Messiaen's developing understanding of birdsong, the *cahiers* enable us to trace the sources of his birdsong music. And because Messiaen was someone whose mind and imagination were in a heightened state when outdoors in the natural world, each notebook is filled not only with notations but also with spontaneous jottings of all kinds, including compositional sketches. Messiaen's *cahiers* are deposited at the Bibliothèque Nationale de France (BnF) in a private collection of the late Mme Yvonne Loriod-Messiaen. There are 203 *cahiers*, the first dating from May 1952, with the final entry coming from Messiaen's last summer, in 1991. Obvious gaps suggest there may have been many more. Many of the birdsongs in *Réveil des oiseaux* cannot be traced, and the *cahiers* contain no notations from Messiaen's extensive research in the Sologne region for the longest piece in *Catalogue d'oiseaux*, 'La Rousserolle effarvatte'.

The study of birds and birdsong consumed Messiaen's every spare moment: the weekends during the spring months when he would escape to the forests on the western edge of Paris, the summer months at his Alpine retreat at Petichet, his travels throughout France and abroad to attend concerts of his music. Even visits to his invalid wife, Claire Delbos, on Sunday afternoons were an opportunity to note down birdsong in the garden of her nursing home. The *cahiers* provide a sort

---

[1]   There are, however, numerous substantial excerpts from the *cahiers* in the two volumes of *Traité V*. See also discussions and examples in PHNS and also Peter Hill and Nigel Simeone, *Olivier Messiaen:* Oiseaux exotiques (Aldershot: Ashgate, 2007) – the latter includes excerpts from the *American Bird Songs* recording used by Messiaen in composing *Oiseaux exotiques*. These recordings were first brought to light in Robert Fallon, *Messiaen's Mimesis: The Language and Culture of the Bird Styles*, PhD diss. (University of California, Berkeley, 2005), pp. 200–20; Fallon, 'The Record of Realism in Messiaen's Bird Style', in Christopher Dingle and Nigel Simeone (eds), *Olivier Messiaen: Music, Art and Literature* (Aldershot: Ashgate, 2007), pp. 115–36; and in this article's accompanying webpage (www. oliviermessiaen.org/birdsongs), which includes excerpts from *American Bird Songs*.

of diary of Messiaen's travels, with musical notations interspersed with lengthy prose descriptions, especially in his later years on visits to Japan, the United States, Israel and Australia, together with his one experience of the tropics, the island of New Caledonia in the Pacific, where he collected much of the birdsong in *Saint François d'Assise*.

The notebooks from the 1950s have a particular importance in the absence of sketch material before the 1960s.[2] They reveal that in *Réveil des oiseaux* (1952–53), which was Messiaen's first major work based on birdsong, the notations in the *cahiers* were used as advanced compositional sketches, transferred into the score with minimal alteration. At the same time, the form of *Réveil* is dictated by the order of birdsongs in a dawn chorus, the notebooks showing the care Messiaen took to get this right. In *Oiseaux exotiques* (1955–56), Messiaen allowed himself much greater licence. Unlike *Réveil*, which had been based on birdsongs heard and collected in the countryside, Messiaen's initial researches for *Oiseaux exotiques* were from recordings, enabling him to study individual birdsongs repeatedly. The *cahiers* reveal a fascinating process as successive notations of each bird become more detailed, more refined and more imaginative. Another factor in Messiaen's new approach was the serendipitous way *Oiseaux exotiques* was composed, with 'live' notations of tropical birds heard at an exhibition in Paris incorporated at a late stage. As a result, birdsong ceased to be an end in itself, instead becoming the starting point for Messiaen's musical imagination.[3]

In *Catalogue d'oiseaux*, composed between 1956 and 1958 but based on research going back at least to 1953, Messiaen reconciled these two extremes, finding a way of being true to nature – or at least true to nature as he experienced it – while giving full rein to his imagination. The catalyst was the decision to set birds in the context of their habitats, made during a visit to the coast of Brittany in September 1956, with Messiaen's *cahier* recording the counterpoint between the cries of sea birds and sounds and swirl of the sea itself. This was the basis for 'Le Courlis cendré', placed last in the *Catalogue*'s 13 pieces, as the musical journey across France that begins in the Alps ends in the fog and darkness of the Atlantic shoreline. Throughout the *Catalogue* Messiaen found musical equivalents to the notebooks' intensely imagined prose evocations of mountains, rivers, lakes and of the passing of time as measured by the changing colours of sunrise and sunset. What is true for landscape is also true for birdsong. However passionate Messiaen was about exactitude, he always *felt* what he saw and heard, so that every notation is expressive of his emotion. It needs to be remembered that however minutely

---

[2]   Before the 1960s it seems that Messiaen's sketch material is generally limited to plans for compositions made in his diary or occasionally found in correspondence, and to fair copies of completed works, such as the full score of *Turangalîla* in the Library of Congress.

[3]   'So there's ... a certain element of composition in the "birdsong material", since I've randomly placed side by side birds of China, India, Malaysia, and North and South America, which is to say, birds that never encounter each other.' Samuel, *Music and Color*, p. 131.

observed, the natural world as it appears in the *cahiers* is a musical or literary response, not the objective record of a scientist.

The sense that every notation leaps from the page as *music* is one of the great achievements of the *cahiers*.[4] This certainly did not come easily, as the early notations show. Messiaen inaugurated the first *cahier* in May 1952, a month after a visit to the home, in the Charente, of Jacques Delamain, a producer of cognac, known also as the author of a number of books on ornithology. Reading Delamain's *Pourquoi les oiseaux chantent* [Why Birds Sing] alongside Messiaen's long, detailed, poetic prose introductions to each movement of *Catalogue d'oiseaux*, one can see that he and Messiaen experienced nature through a similar sensibility. Here is Delamain's evocative description of birds in winter:

> From the clump of blossoming, snow-sprinkled furze, the Wren's precipitated trill gushes out, so strong and vibrant that it is astonishing to see a tiny brown bird rise up, fleeing at the level of the frozen soil on little round wings. The bare hedge has its winter song, sweet and a little sad, that of the Hedge-Sparrow. The Lark drops from on high onto the field, still all white, the joyous torrent of his song, and like an inevitable and charming accompaniment, the voice of the Robin Redbreast modulates, tireless and clear. Even the icy January night has its song: the primitive, savage refrain of the great Tawny Owl, articulated now and then like a sorrowful human cry.[5]

Before the visit to Delamain, Messiaen had been notating birdsong at least since 1940. Wartime colleagues recalled his passion for birdsong,[6] and one of them – Guy Bernard-Delapierre, whose house was later used by Messiaen for private teaching of analysis and composition – remembered Messiaen filling 'any number of notebooks with the astonishing rhythmic and melodic virtuosity of birdsong'.[7] Messiaen's first public account of his researches came in a press interview in March 1948, in which

---

[4]   Indeed, many of the longer notations – especially those made during the 1960s when Messiaen's powers of transcription were at their height – would (and perhaps one day will) make superb solos or birdsong *études* for melody instruments.

[5]   Jacques Delamain, *Why Birds Sing*, trans. by Ruth and Anna Sarason (London: Victor Gollancz, 1932), pp. 47–8.

[6]   Private communication from Alex Murray, student of flute at the Paris Conservatoire and a prize-winner in 1952, the year Messiaen composed *Le Merle noir* for flute and piano as a *morceau de concours*. According to Gaston Crunelle, Murray's flute teacher, Messiaen used to volunteer for the least popular hours of sentry duty in order to be out-of-doors at the time of the dawn chorus.

[7]   PHNS, pp. 94–6. From November 1943 Messiaen held private classes in analysis and composition at Bernard-Delapierre's Paris home, 24 rue Visconti. Bernard-Delapierre's article on Messiaen, entitled 'Souvenirs sur Olivier Messiaen' appeared in the Lausanne art periodical *Formes et couleurs* in 1945.

he spoke admiringly of the Blackbird as nature's supreme melodist.[8] Messiaen gained from Delamain much-needed knowledge, as he later recalled:

> I had already, for a long time, devoted myself to noting more or less accurately the songs of birds, but without knowing which of them I was writing down. … It is [Delamain] who taught me to recognize a bird from its song, without having to see its plumage or the shape of its beak. Or its flight, so that I no longer mistook a blackcap for a chaffinch or a garden warbler![9]

What Messiaen says here about the 'accuracy' of his notations needs to be treated with caution. The early *cahiers* show that in 1952 Messiaen's notations were still comparatively elementary. Example 7.1 is the very first notation – made on 14 May 1952 – in which the Nightingale seems scarcely more advanced than that found in 'Liturgie de cristal' from the *Quatuor pour la fin du Temps*, lacking the characteristics of Messiaen's later Nightingales: the 'moonlit' long notes that explode into 'biting' tremolos, and the muffled sonority that Messiaen likens to the blending of harpsichord and gong.[10]

Example 7.1   Nightingale, Ms. 23077, p. 1

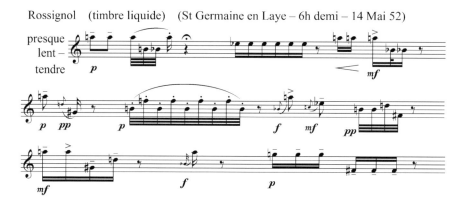

Rossignol   (timbre liquide)   (St Germaine en Laye – 6h demi – 14 Mai 52)

Progress was rapid, however. (Example 7.2). A year later Messiaen's rendering of a Nightingale is not only richer in detail, but has a musical coherence – this indeed is the passage that opens *Réveil des oiseaux*, the score being virtually identical to the notation, apart from the addition of a doubling octave, characteristic of the piano writing in *Réveil*. As with almost all the notations in the early *cahiers* this is a fair copy. The few instances of rough working use a system of dots (for pitches),

---

[8]   *France-Soir*, 28 March 1948, quoted in PHNS, pp. 176–8.

[9]   Preface by Messiaen to the 1960 edition of Jacques Delamain's *Pourquoi les oiseaux chantent*.

[10]   All these terms are found in the score of 'L'Alouette lulu'.

Example 7.2   Nightingale, Ms. 23081, p. 10

spaced according to their rhythm, and with occasional markings of articulation, making a shorthand that is surprisingly effective and expressive. From these early beginnings, this chapter outlines the nature of the riches contained in the *cahiers*, giving a detailed glimpse of Messiaen's evolving treatment of birdsong across the remainder of the decade.

The Early *Cahiers*, 1952–53

There are six *cahiers* for 1952, catalogued between Mss 23077 and 23081 (23079 comprises two notebooks, labelled by Yvonne Loriod 'Charente A' and 'Charente B').[11] At this point a word needs to be said about the catalogue numbering by the BnF. The *cahiers* run from Mss 22966 to 23165, in what I at first took to be a random order (22966 dates from 1964). The explanation is that the *cahiers* were divided by Yvonne Loriod into four types of notebook, arranged within each type in chronological order. The first is 'Petits cahiers (à spirale presque tous)', which run from 22966 to 23000, covering the years 1964 to 1982. A second type is made up of 'Grandes feuilles de papier à musique', from 1953 to 1962 (23001 to 23035). Next comes a further set of 'Grandes feuilles', this time with each *cahier* prefaced by a list of contents made by Loriod: these cover the years 1954 to 1970 (23036 to 23076). Finally, there are the 'Petits cahiers' used by Messiaen from 1952 to 1991: many of these also have lists of contents by Loriod (23077 to 23165).[12]

During the spring months of 1952 Messiaen's birdsong collecting was divided between early mornings in the garden of his home in Paris, at Villa du Danube in the 19th arrondissement, and evenings (or occasional visits for the dawn chorus)[13] at St-Germain-en-Laye, in the forests to the west of the city. A single exception in the first *cahier* (23077) is a notation in the Parc Monceau, in the 8th arrondissement.

---

[11]   Ms. 23056 also comprises two *cahiers*, hence the overall figure of 203 *cahiers*.

[12]   At the time of writing the *cahiers* in the BnF are not available for study, but I give details here in the hope that the situation may change. I wish to record my gratitude to the late Yvonne Loriod for permission to study the *cahiers* and to quote from them.

[13]   According to Yvonne Loriod, Messiaen used to stay the night at St-Germain-en-Laye at the Hôtel de l'Aigle d'or.

The most ambitious notation depicts the 'coucher d'oiseaux' (23077, p. 13), an ensemble of birdsongs featuring the Grive Musicienne, Rossignol, Fauvette à Tête Noire, Merle [noir], Pinson, Rouge-Gorge and Sitelle (Song Thrush, Nightingale, Blackcap, Blackbird, Chaffinch, Robin and Nuthatch). From this Messiaen extracted a single phrase, repeated by the Grive Musicienne in three places in *Réveil des oiseaux*: from the middle of the sixth bar before fig. 16 (oboes, clarinets and trumpet), and in the main tutti from just before fig. 22 and at fig. 37. Other fragments for the Grive Musicienne (23077, p. 19) were used in transposition: insistent motifs just before fig. 5, and the phrase on piccolo and cor anglais just before fig. 16, heard again before fig. 39. The first substantial passage for *Réveil* is a Merle [noir] ('mon jardin, 1er juin 1952, 4.15 du matin', 23077, p. 17) found at fig. 34, the piano solo that divides the central and final tuttis. Here only the tessitura is changed – an octave higher, and doubled an octave higher again; otherwise, score and *cahier* match exactly, including dynamics and articulations.

A day later (2 June 1952), Messiaen devoted two closely written pages to a Rouge-Gorge. The first six lines of the notation (23078, pp. 17–18) correspond to the piano solo at fig. 16; the remaining 14 lines become the piano part from fig. 17, where the central tutti begins to form, until fig. 22. At this point, in the middle of the tutti, Messiaen runs out of material, so he simply restarts, re-using two-thirds of the notation by the time the tutti ends (before fig. 28). Even the dynamics remain the same the second time round, despite the presence of the orchestra. In these respects, the central tutti reflects Messiaen's strategy in *Réveil*, with 'automatic' characteristics in the composing that reflect his reluctance to alter his birdsong data. At the same time, the tutti is carefully layered, with circling birdsongs of unequal lengths, of which the piano part is the longest. From the point of view of Messiaen's later developments in birdsong writing, the descending figures of the Rouge-Gorge are noteworthy (see fig. 19, bars 3 and 7–8, and fig. 21, bars 4–5).

The two *cahiers* that make up 23079 record a second visit to Delamain (12–14 June). *Cahier* 23079 ('Charente A') has the Fauvette à Tête Noire that forms the piano solo in *Réveil* at fig. 28. The details of date, time and place (even down to the location of Delamain's house) are characteristic of the systematic way in which Messiaen set about keeping his field notes, although the song itself has little in common with Messiaen's later notations of the Blackcap; indeed, the opening phrase is an unconscious echo of the main theme of 'Séquence du Verbe' from the *Trois Petites Liturgies* (1943–44). A number of short birdcalls used in *Réveil* include the Tourterelles (Turtle Doves) heard in delicious scorings for flutes or violins between figs 29 and 30, and a Bouscarle (Cetti's Warbler), played by the E♭ clarinet seven bars after fig. 3. In the notation this is 'impérieux', toned down in the score to 'un peu irrité'. Besides these, the notebook contains Messiaen's first transcription of a sound other than birdsong: 'the wind in the trees' ('sonorité chuchotée, veloutée, glissée'[14]). On the same page (p. 10) is a Bruant Ortolan (Ortolan Bunting), a primitive pre-echo of the cadences that would be used to

---

[14]   The sonority whispered, velvety, gliding.

such poetic effect in 'Le Traquet stapazin' (from *Catalogue d'oiseaux*). 'Charente B' continues the June visit to Delamain. Notations include a trio for Merle [noir], Loriot (Golden Oriole) and Pinson that starts the central tutti in *Réveil* (fig. 17), where they combine with the Rouge-Gorge on the piano that had been notated at St-Germain on 2 June; bringing together birdsongs from different locations was a minor form of cheating that Messiaen permitted himself. There are no further notations from 1952, apart from brief jottings made in July, some of them at Darmstadt where Messiaen was teaching on the summer course.

The 1953 season began on 26 April in Messiaen's garden, followed by three days of visits at dawn and sunset to St-Germain. These are recorded in 23080 and 23081, a rich harvest that includes three passages for *Réveil*: the Grive Musicienne at figs 29 and 32 (with excerpts from the notation arranged as a duet between clarinets and oboes), the Rossignol of the piano solo that opens the work, and the Merle [noir] that forms the left hand of the final piano solo (in a duet with a Rouge-Gorge, fig. 43) (Example 7.3). This last notation is preserved in the form of Messiaen's field notes as well as in the fair-copy version.

Example 7. 3   Merle [noir], Ms. 23080

(a) Page 6

(b) Page 7

The same *cahier* (23080) contains intriguing notes for another 'Concerto oiseaux', this time based on 'chants japonais', together with a musical sketch of tumbling harmonies on horns or piano with spiky interjections on woodwind or in the form of tremolos. A note in the margin reminds Messiaen to revisit Ravel's *Gaspard de la nuit* and *Miroirs*.

The most Messiaen-like of the early notations is the song of the Golden Oriole (Loriot), invariably notated in E major, inclining towards the second mode of limited transposition. Example 7.4 (a) and (b) was made at Orgeval (in the Forêt de St-Germain-en-Laye, near Paris) on 4 June 1953 (23084, p. 21) alongside that of a Blackcap, Messiaen observing that the two birdsongs seem to form a dialogue, 'le loriot intervenant dans les silences de la Fauvette à Tête Noire, comme pour donner une conclusion à ses strophes', wittily realized in the score of *Réveil* at fig. 40, with the phrases for the Golden Oriole putting the brakes on the more voluble song of the Blackcap.

Example 7.4   Notations at Orgeval and their use in *Réveil des oiseaux*

(a) Loriot, Ms. 23080, p. 21

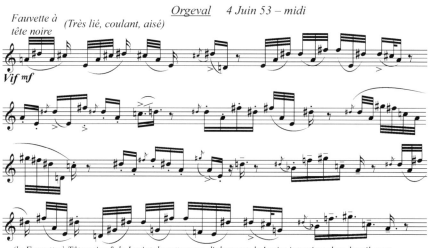

(la Fauvette à Tête noire & le Loriot de cette page dialoguent: le Loriot intervient dans les silences de la Fauvette à Tête noire, comme pour donner une conclusion à ses strophes)

(b) *Réveil des oiseaux*, fig. 40

The remaining notations from the spring and summer of 1953 are all used in the later stages of *Réveil*:

> 23083, p. 25 Verdier (Greenfinch) for the beginning of the piano solo at fig. 39.
>
> 23084, p. 23 Pouillot Fitis (Willow Warbler) for the xylophone at fig. 37.
>
> 23084, p. 26 Rouge-Queue de Muraille (Redstart) at fig. 42.
>
> 23084, p. 27 notations for the dialogue at fig. 41 between a Loriot and Fauvette à Tête Noire, with interlude for a Pigeon Ramier (Wood Pigeon) wrongly identified in the *cahier* as a Tourterelle des Bois (European Turtle Dove).
>
> 23084, p. 29 the Rouge-Gorge at figs. 43–4.
>
> 23086, p. 3: the Serin Cini (Serin) before and after fig. 40; the Sitelle (Nuthatch) 13 bars after fig. 40; the Mésange Bleue (Blue Tit) after fig. 39.
>
> 23086, p. 5: Corneille Noire (Carrion Crow), just before fig. 41; Grive Musicienne (Song Thrush) 3 bars after fig. 39.

By July 1953 Messiaen was turning his thoughts to a new work. Notes made on 12 July (23086, p. 7) show this to be a series of birdsong pieces for solo piano: 'Pour pièces piano sur oiseaux: noter les <u>rythmes</u> et les <u>silences</u> des bruits de la forêt qui font le milieu dans lequel chante l'oiseau … spécialement le soir: tombée de la nuit – grive musicienne et chouette hulotte (forêt)' [For the piano pieces on birds: note the <u>rhythms</u> and <u>silences</u> of the sounds of the forest which make the surroundings to the bird's song … especially in the evening; nightfall – song thrush and tawny owl (forest)]. During the late summer of 1953 Messiaen seems to have made no further birdsong notations. But in October, when he was in Donaueschingen attending rehearsals for *Réveil*, notes in his *cahier* show the plan for solo piano pieces growing to encyclopaedic proportions (23001, p. 9). Under a notation of the Tawny Owl (Chouette Hulotte – 'Vocifération lugubre et douloureuse'), made in the Black Forest on the evening of 6 October, we find a list that divides birds into ten categories of habitat, together with tropical and nocturnal birds. Twelve of the species were to feature in *Catalogue d'oiseaux*:

> Birds of the high mountain: Chough
> Birds of the vineyards: Linnets, Ortolan Bunting
> Night birds: Tawny Owl
> Tropical birds: Shama, Indian Minah, White-Throated Laughing Thrush
> Sea birds: Curlew
> Birds of the reeds and ponds: Great Reed Warbler
> Birds of the pine woods: Willow Warbler, Great Tit
> Birds of the cornfields and open sky: Lark
> Birds of orchards and woods: Blackbird, Robin
> Birds of the oak trees, Golden Oriole
> Birds of gardens and parks: Blackcap, Garden Warbler, Starling, Chiffchaff
> Birds of the copses: Robin
> Birds of the woods: Green Woodpecker, Great Spotted Woodpecker[15]

Birdsong from Recordings, 1954–56

Réveil was an experiment in musical ornithology, conducted under strict rules. With *Oiseaux exotiques* came a decisive move in the opposite direction. Messiaen seems to have realized that rendering birdsong in musical notation was not a matter of copying but of translation. The change becomes apparent from 1954, coinciding with the first notations from recordings to appear in the *cahiers*. These are at once recognizable because of the absence of details of time and place, punctiliously noted by Messiaen on his live notations; in their place Messiaen copies full information from the record sleeves. But the one piece of information he never

---

[15]   See also PHNS, pp. 210–11, Hill and Simeone, *Oiseaux exotiques*, p. 32; Fallon, 'The Record of Realism', pp. 116; and Fallon, *Messiaen's Mimesis*, pp. 207–8.

gives is the date on which he made the notation. Happily, there are a number of clues. One is Messiaen's fair-copy musical script, which changes markedly over quite short periods of time. Then there is the type of paper used by Messiaen and noted by Yvonne Loriod on some of the *cahiers*. Finally, there are the live notations, invariably dated, found nearby in the same notebook.

A case in point is the recording *American Bird Songs* issued by Comstock Publishing on behalf of Cornell University in 1942, a set of six 78 rpm discs containing the songs of no fewer than 72 birds found in the United States. These may well have been the first recordings notated by Messiaen, and were certainly the first to be used in a composition (*Oiseaux exotiques*). How and when Messiaen acquired the set is a matter for conjecture. Possibly, he may have come across them during one of his visits to the United States in 1949. Another possibility is that they were the 'gift of birdsong discs' from Milhaud, noted in Messiaen's diary for 2 January 1954. At all events, we can be fairly certain that he first worked on them in that year, because the same *cahier* contains notations (from a private aviary in Paris) dated May 1954.

Messiaen's notations made at Mme Billot's aviary, together with the first notations from *American Bird Songs*, give no hint that he was planning a new work based on these notations. It was only later, during the winter of 1954–55, after the request from Boulez for a new work for the Domaine Musical concerts at the Petit Théâtre Marigny, that Messiaen returned to the *cahier* and started to develop his notations by repeated listening to the *American Bird Songs* discs.

Why did Messiaen decide to fulfil Boulez's commission with a work on American rather than French birds? It may be that he wanted the piece for Boulez to be as distinct as possible from the planned *Catalogue d'oiseaux*. In keeping with this, the first intention was a scoring for small orchestra; only gradually did the piano part take on a solo role, so that the work became (in Messiaen's words) 'almost a piano concerto'.[16] Another consideration may have been that Messiaen's research for his great birdsong project was not going well. Even Loriod admits that a number of the *cahiers* for 1954 are uninspired. The contents page she added to 23089 (May–June 1954) has the explanation: 'Cahiers pas très intéressants – époque douloureuse où Olivier Messiaen allait voir Claire à la Varenne.'[17] Messiaen's wife had been showing signs of mental deterioration since as long ago as the early 1940s; in 1953 her condition worsened and after tests at the Salpetrière Hospital in Paris she was moved to a nursing home at La Varenne, on the outskirts of Paris.[18]

Material for *Oiseaux exotiques* comes from three *cahiers*. Cahier 23036 starts with brief notations of all 72 birds on the recording, making a précis of each song and its characteristics. Messiaen uses the categories on the discs – Birds of the

[16]   See 'Author's First Preface' in the score of *Oiseaux exotiques*.

[17]   Not very interesting *cahiers* – painful period when Olivier Messiaen went to see Claire at La Varenne.

[18]   PHNS, p. 209.

Example 7.5   Wood Thrush, Ms. 23036, p. 26, and appearance in *Oiseaux exotiques*

North Woods, Birds of Southern Woods and Gardens, etc. – and copies the names of birds in English, translating some into French. There are descriptions of timbre and character: 'strident', 'ironique', 'grincé' (for the Mockingbird); 'miaulé, grincé' (Catbird); 'très grave, sourd, exactement le bruit d'un moteur qui démarre' (Ruffled Grouse); 'comme si on souffleût dans un jarre' (Dusky Grouse); 'appel lugubre, genre chevêche, signal de chemin de fer, sirène de bateau' (Burrowing Owl) [Strident, ironic, grating / mewing, grating / very weighty, muffled, exactly the sound of an engine starting up / as if one were blowing into a jar / a mournful call, like a little owl, a train, a boat's foghorn].

(d)

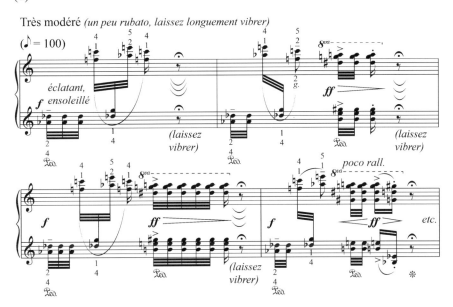

The next step was to re-notate all the birdsongs, many of them repeatedly (23036, pp. 29–42). By this point composition was clearly underway, almost all the notations having details of instrumentation. There is then a further stage of refinement and elaboration, including harmonization, a series of sketches (23036, pp. 13–23) that form what seems to be the penultimate step before the finished score. The four stages of the process can be seen in the sketches for the Wood Thrush, the last being the music in the finished score (Example 7.5 (a)–(d)).

Another instance is the Virginia Cardinal (23036, p. 26). This had achieved its final form apart from its scoring – eventually a piano solo – which a note in the margin gives as for 'glockenspiel, xylophone, piano, temple block, and perhaps piccolo and E-flat clarinet'. When playing through the passage Messiaen seems to have realized its pianistic qualities, because he started to add fingerings. This may be the moment when Messiaen decided to give the piano a solo role in *Oiseaux exotiques*.

The difference between notations is well illustrated by the Bobolink (Example 7.6). Two of the later versions were evidently considered by Messiaen to be equally good, and both were used in the long piano cadenza (score fig. 24, pp. 62–5), which becomes in this way a binary form, with the first half using the third notation, the second half (from score, p. 64) using the second; this is common practice in *Oiseaux exotiques* and accounts for the preponderance of binary forms. In one case – the American Robin – Messiaen used all his notations. These form a chain of variations (played by two clarinets, from 6 bars after fig. 11 to 3 bars after fig. 20) that make a continuity running through the central medley.

The pages at the back of the *cahier* (23036, pp. 43–50) are the notations made at Mme Billot's aviary, dated 25 May 1954. Many of the birds received rather

Example 7.6   Bobolink, Ms. 23036

(a) Page 15

(b) Page 16

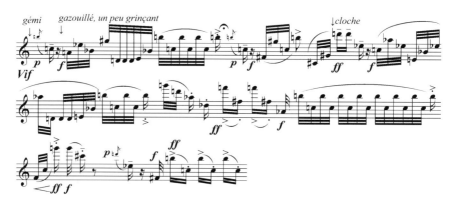

perfunctory notations, Messiaen's attention repeatedly caught by the Virginia
Cardinal, the one American bird in the aviary, that sang continuously for three
hours. The many notations of the Virginia Cardinal were joined together in a fair
copy (23088), together with Mme Billot's Indian Shama. Both birdsongs would
play leading roles in *Oiseaux exotiques*'s central medley.

The third notebook for *Oiseaux exotiques* (23039) has notations made at a
birdsong exhibition in Paris, which Messiaen visited on 11, 12 and 14 November
1955.[19] By this time composition of *Oiseaux exotiques* had been underway for

---

[19]   The bird exhibition was the VIe Salon des oiseaux, sponsored by the Ligue pour
la protection des oiseaux and the *Journal des oiseaux*. An advertisement for this event is
reproduced in Fallon, 'The Record of Realism', p. 117.

several weeks, since 5 October,[20] and in all probability was designed as a work solely about American birdsongs. But the tropical birds at the exhibition made such an impression on Messiaen that he decided to remodel the work so as to include them. In a note on the cover of the *cahier* Messiaen reminds himself to verify in his books on ornithology details of the name, colour, plumage, etc., though many of these details were in fact noted on the spot. These notations are the source for the music of the Mainate hindou (Minah), Garrulaxe à huppe blanche (Himalayan Laughing Thrush), Bulbul orphée (Red-Whiskered Bulbul), and (most of all) the Shama (Indian Shama), to which Messiaen devoted no fewer than 12 pages of notations.

Oiseaux exotiques shows how the techniques Messiaen was now using with recorded birdsongs influenced his compositional approach to live notations. Instead of lengthy passages of unedited birdsong, as in *Réveil*, with the tropical birds for *Oiseaux exotiques* he became very selective, choosing only a few promising motifs from pages of notations.

Over the winter of 1954–55 Messiaen worked on a number of other recordings (as yet unidentified) besides *American Bird Songs*. One of these was of birds from North America including Mexico (23029). Messiaen returned to this *cahier* when composing *Chronochromie* (1959–60). Mexican birds found in the score (Antistrophe 1, from p. 77) include the Solitaire Ardoise (Slate-Coloured Solitaire), the Oropendoza de Montezuma, the Moqueur des Tropiques (Tropical Mockingbird) and the Moqueur-bleue de Mexique (Mexican Blue Mockingbird). At one point in the *cahier* Messiaen sketches different patterns of 'accords tournoyants' (turning chords), as in *Chronochromie*.

The other recordings Messiaen worked on over the winter of 1954–55 were the 'Disques Angleterre': *Songs of British Birds* and *More Songs of Wild Birds*.[21] These were by Ludwig Koch, a pioneer of birdsong recording, and may have been acquired by Messiaen on a trip to London in April 1954. A notation of the Nightingale from *More Songs of Wild Birds* at the back of the *American Bird Songs* notebook (23036) suggests that Koch's recordings were studied by Messiaen at the same time or shortly after. The Nightingale was an interim fair copy and shows the care Messiaen took at arriving at definitive transcriptions; it appears in definitive form in the notebook reserved for the Koch recordings (23037, p. 25), which is a pristine fair copy throughout (Example 7.7). The notation has the explosive characteristics of Nightingales in *Catalogue d'oiseaux* that were only hinted at in earlier notations for *Réveil*.

Throughout the Ludwig Koch *cahier* the notations are minutely annotated. Here Messiaen describes the Blackbird from *More Songs of Wild Birds*:

---

[20]   Date from the 'Author's First Preface' in the score.

[21]   E.M. Nicholson and Ludwig Koch, *More Songs of Wild Birds*, rec. 1937, Parlophone E 8471/8536, E 8535/8484, E 8473/8483; Ludwig Koch, *Songs of British Birds*, rec. December 1952 and January 1953, HMV B 10473-6 (78 rpm discs).

Disque B 10473, face 1: Birds in gardens and parks (oiseaux des jardins et des parcs? [sic])

Timbre sifflé, un peu rauque, caractère mocqueur, gaieté désabusée, narquois, avec aussi de la vraie joie – c'est une voix claire, qui porte loin. Les chiffres [the figures added by Messiaen in the *cahier*] indiquent les numéros des strophes. Les 'forte' constituent le chant proprement dit – les 'pianissimo' sont du gazouillement en écho dans l'aigu ... et ne s'entendent qu'à proximité de l'oiseau.

[The timbre is whistling, somewhat raucous, with a mocking character, a disillusioned cheerfulness, sneering, but also with a real joyfulness – the voice is bright, carrying a long way. The figures [added by Messiaen in the *cahier*] indicate the numbers of the verses. The 'fortes' constitute the song itself, the 'pianissimos' a shrill, warbling echo ... only heard when near the bird.]

Koch's recordings are superior in sound quality to *American Bird Songs*, and the excerpts longer. Hearing the birds as Messiaen heard them, and comparing them with the notations, is an impressive demonstration of Messiaen's growing skill. With rapid and high-pitched songs – Skylark, Meadow Pipit, Goldfinch – Messiaen is resourceful at finding equivalents in musical notation, with sufficient detail and variety of detail to convey the structure of the song. He is equally imaginative in translating songs that have a high degree of unpitched noise, such as the water birds, in which Koch's collections are especially strong. This was Messiaen's first encounter with the Reed Warbler, Coot and Moorhen, and the notations in 23037 lay foundations for the *Catalogue*'s 'La Rousserolle effarvatte' and 'La Bouscarle'. To talk of 'accuracy' seems beside the point, however. The

Example 7.7   Nightingale, Ms. 23037, p. 25

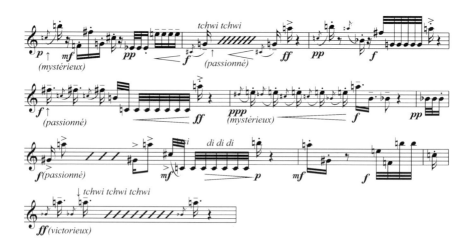

most recognizable of the notations are those of the Woodlark, which features in both recordings, thanks to a timbre that Messiaen describes as 'very pure'. The song descends chromatically, often oscillating against an upper note, in a series of varied patterns. In 'L'Alouette lulu' Messiaen selected phrases from both notations to create the developments of the Woodlark's song in the central section of the piece. These were among the earliest notations to be used in *Catalogue d'oiseaux*.

As well as allowing Messiaen to analyse more closely, the gain from recordings was the enrichment of his birdsong language. With more detail came a stronger sense of character and a clearer differentiation between one bird and another, essential ingredients in the *Catalogue*'s dramatic portrayals of nature.

The other notation from 23037 found in the *Catalogue* is of the Curlew, used in the opening pages of 'Le Courlis cendré'. The notation has three phases, clearly recognizable as the source for the music. The first of these, oscillations against a fixed upper note, are not yet 'lent et triste' – here the effect is described as 'aboiement musical, comme poulie qui grince'.[22] The other two are closer: the accelerations of the 'sauvage chant nuptial',[23] and the repeated upward figures ('dans le sentiment d'un glissando', as the score puts it) swelling and fading. Messiaen's description of the Curlew in the *cahier* encapsulates the spirit of the piece: 'cri d'appel exprimant la solitude et la désolation de la nuit qui descend sur la mer'.[24]

The other recordings used for *Catalogue d'oiseaux* were the Swiss and Swedish discs (as Messiaen called them) which he studied during the winter of 1955–56, returning to them frequently thereafter: Hans Traber's *So Singen Unsere Vogel*, and Gunnar Lekander and Sture Palmér's *Radions fågelskivor*. The Swedish radio discs were to be the most important single source for the *Catalogue*, never acknowledged by Messiaen whose accounts of the work's genesis scarcely mention recordings. No fewer than five *cahiers* are devoted largely or entirely to the Swedish discs, and excerpts were copied into other *cahiers* containing live notations. It seems likely that Messiaen began work on the two collections in the autumn of 1955, just after his first trip to the island of Ouessant, off the coast of Brittany (22–23 September). In 23040 the first four pages describe the boat trip from Brest to Ouessant, with musical studies of the waves; there follows a page at La Varenne, Claire's nursing home, on 25 September. After this, the *cahier* is divided between the Swedish and Swiss recordings. As with the 'Disques Angleterre', Messiaen returned to this notebook to quarry material for the *Catalogue* – for the alarm-call of the Pie-grièche Écorcheur (Red-backed Shrike) for 'La Buse variable' (score, p. 12), the Chardonneret for the right hand part of the duet for Goldfinches in 'Le Traquet stapazin' (score, p. 21), and the music of the Kingfisher in 'La Bouscarle' (score, pp. 1, 2 and 21), where the *cahier*'s 'bruit d'eau' becomes in the score 'le martin-pêcheur plonge'. Despite countless Blackcaps notated from nature, Messiaen returned to the Swiss discs for the important solo in 'La Bouscarle'

---

[22] A musical barking, like a creaking pulley.
[23] Wild wedding song.
[24] Cry expressing the loneliness and desolation of the night descending on the sea.

Example 7.8   Fauvette à Tête Noire notation and use in 'La Bouscarle'

(a) Ms. 23040, p. 11

(score, pp. 12–14, 23040, p. 11). Here again we see a huge change, in terms of detail and individuality, from *Réveil* (Example 7.8 (a) and (b); cf. Example 7.2).

Further research from the Swedish discs comes in four consecutively catalogued *cahiers* (23045–8). Ms. 23045 supports a dating to 1955–56, with live notations from May 1955 and April 1956. This notebook is full of details found in the *Catalogue*. Among them are the Râle d'Eau (Water Rail), which screams like a 'porcelet égorgé'[25] in 'La Rousserolle effarvatte' (score, p. 37), the 'bruitage' of the Rouge-queue Tythis (Black Redstart) – 'crépitant ou cascade de papier froissé, de verre pilé'[26] ('Le Merle de roche', p. 7), and the Bittern for 'La Rousserolle effarvatte' (score, pp. 3 and 51), here vividly described: 'Mugissement de héron butor – beuglement – aspiration d'air, puis énorme trompe – timbre gros, énorme, un peu caverneux, mélange de clarinette basse et de tuba – <u>tuba</u> surtout' [Booming of the bittern – bellowing – air inhaled, then a trumpet blast – the sound is thick, huge, somewhat cavernous, a mixture of bass clarinet and tuba – <u>tuba</u> above all]. Another fragment transformed in the *Catalogue* is the Hibou Moyen-duc (Long-eared Owl), whose cries are punctuated in the notation by the 'claquements

---

25   A piglet having its throat cut.
26   Crackling or a cascade of riffling paper, glass crushing.

(b) 'La Bouscarle', p. 12

d'ailes',[27] written as low Cs, staccato and 'très sec'. In 'La Chouette hulotte' these low Cs become the stuttering pulse labelled 'la peur'.

We also find from the Swedish discs important solos in their entirety: the Loriot (for 'Le Loriot', p. 1), another bird for which Messiaen had dozens of live notations but for which he preferred a recording, and the opening solo for the Reed Warbler ('La Rousserolle effarvatte', pp. 4–8), fully harmonized and ready to go into the score unaltered, apart from minor changes for pianistic reasons. Equally finished is the music for the Hibou Grand-duc (Eagle Owl), later incorporated into 'Le Merle de roche'; and equally striking the Goéland Argenté (Herring Gull), source of a haunting passage in 'Le Courlis cendré' (score, p. 19).

Ms. 23046, titled 'Swedish discs B' by Loriod, and dated by her to 1956,[28] is a source for 'Le Courlis cendré': the Guillemot de Troïl (Guillemot), Chevalier Gambette (Redshank), and the Huîtrier Pie (Oystercatcher), used for the climax of the central section (Example 7.9).

---

[27] Clapping/clacking of wings.
[28] Ms. 23046 predates 23045, having a Kingfisher that is obviously an earlier notation.

Example 7.9   23046, pp. 28 and 29 – motifs used for the Oystercatcher in 'Le Courlis cendré' (see score, pp. 11 and 12)

Indeed, a huge swath is patched together from these three notations. The passage in question runs from p. 8 of the score (bar 2, the Guillemot de Troïl) to the end of the top line of p. 10, and from the Huîtrier Pie on p. 11 to the end of p. 12. A coincidence is that on the Swedish recording the background to the Oystercatcher is a distant foghorn, perhaps sowing the seed in Messiaen's imagination for the mighty cluster of sound in the final section of 'Le Courlis cendré'. Ms. 23047 ('Disques Suède C') has fully harmonized versions in piano score, including revisiting the Skylark in *Songs of British Birds*. Later notations in the *cahier* suggest that it and 23048 came too late for the *Catalogue*, apart from extensive work on the Rouge-queue Tythis, useful for 'Le Merle de roche', one of the last pieces of the *Catalogue* to be composed.

Live Notations for *Catalogue d'oiseaux*, 1954–58

The first notation from the *cahiers* used in *Catalogue d'oiseaux* was a Rouge-queue (Redstart) at Orgeval (near St-Germain-en-Laye) on 22 April 1954 (23085, pp. 25 and 27). Messiaen noted that the bird sang for seven hours, from 5:30 in the morning. A few fragments from the notation were selected for 'Le Loriot', during the dawn chorus (score, pp. 2–3) and in an adaptation near the end (score, pp. 2–3 and p. 11) (Example 7.10 (a)–(b)).

Example 7.10   Rouge-queue notation and use in 'Le Loriot'

(a) 23085, p. 27

(b) 'Le Loriot', p. 11

Rouge-queue à front blanc

The first visit to the Alps to be recorded in the *cahiers* came in August 1954 (23002). Messiaen returned in May the following year, this time with Loriod, who was making her first visit to Petichet. The weather was unseasonably cold and few birds sang. But on a later visit, in June, Messiaen made the notations that lay the foundations for 'Le Chocard des Alpes'. Messiaen described a solitary Alpine Chough flying 200 metres below him in an abyss, with the timbre of its cries 'strident, cruel et émouvant, joie féroce' (see score, p. 5). There are superb descriptions of scenery, and of the circling of the Aigle Royal (Golden Eagle) (score, pp. 2–3 and p. 6), whose talons reminded Messiaen of the fingers of Balinese or Cambodian dancers.

In the spring of 1956 Messiaen resumed his researches at Orgeval. On 7 May (23049, p. 9) he notated a Loriot heard in the distance: 'timbre doré, riche en harmoniques, glissé, nonchalant' – written first as a single line, then harmonized (Example 7.11).

This points the way not only to the harmonizations of the soloist's song in 'Le Loriot' but specifically to the slow-motion version (score, pp. 9–10), the first of many such passages in the *Catalogue*, with birdsong recollected in poetic tranquillity. In the finished score Messiaen enriches the harmony further by adding (in the left hand) chords associated with the love-potion (the reference is to the Tristan legend) from *Cinq Rechants* (1949), the setting of the line: 'Tous les philtres sont bus ce soir'. This secret musical symbolism unites pianist and birdsong, Loriod and Loriot.

Example 7.11   23049, p. 9

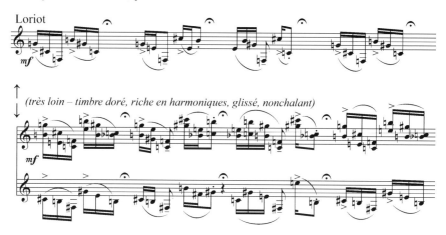

In July 1956 came one of the longest and richest of the *cahiers* from the 1950s (23043). More than any other this shows the intensity of Messiaen's researches, and the vividness of his response, as we follow his journey down France, noting birdsong, scenery and historic buildings – the Palais des Papes at Avignon, the west portal of St-Trophime at Arles, the medieval fortifications of Aigues-Mortes, and the Abbey of Montmajour. Near Montmajour Messiaen found a desert-like landscape, which would become the setting for 'L'Alouette calandrelle': 'Sous le soleil ardent, le chant simple du Cochevis huppé, d'une joie plus monotone que celle de l'Alouette des champs, peuple le ciel blanc' [Under the scorching sun, the artless song of the Skylark, more monotonous in its joyfulness than the skylark, peoples the clear sky]. Almost all the material for 'L'Alouette calandrelle' comes from just two pages (23043, pp. 6 and 8): the solos, the duet with the Cochevis Huppé, the clucking of the Quail, the whirlwind flight and song of the Skylark, and the Kestrel flying from its perch on a tower of the Abbey.

The main focus of the visit was the wetlands of the Camargue, in particular the nature reserve at Salin de Badon. In the Camargue, Messiaen found inspiration for 'La Rousserolle effarvatte', the central piece of the *Catalogue*, with all the relevant water birds, and descriptions of lakes, ponds and reed beds, vegetation and flowers, and the sunsets over the salt-water lake, Étang de Vaccarès: 'Le soleil éclatant disque d'orange et d'or, s'est enfoncé dans les nuages violets, laissant dans le ciel un souvenir d'incendie rouge et rose, et rêveur…' [The sun a brilliant disc of orange and gold, sinking through violet clouds, leaving in the sky a memory of a red and pink conflagration, dreamily…] (score, pp. 38–42). However, the lack of direct correspondences with the score suggests that Messiaen considerably reworked his notations during the process of composition, as well as indicates that notations made in the Sologne (where the piece is set) seem to be missing.

The return from the Camargue to Paris took Messiaen and Loriod through central France and a region known as the Forez, between Clermont-Ferrand and St-Étienne. At the Col du Grand Bois, on the road to St-Sauveur-en-Rue, Messiaen came across a Woodlark perched on a branch. It flew away, but an hour later its song was heard in the distance – 'doux, fluté, limpide, très lié, un peu plaintif'. The episode in the Forez formed the basis for 'L'Alouette lulu'. Comparing *cahier* and the score marks a fascinating case study in the negotiations between Messiaen's observations of nature and the workings of his musical and poetic imagination. In the score the single Woodlark becomes a flock, unseen in the depths of night, but heard through their song, with its 'descentes chromatiques et liquides' (preface to the score), as the birds peel off in pairs. Another liberty is the importing of a Nightingale for the development in the middle of the piece, taken from the Camargue *cahier* (23043). Even more artificial are the sources for the Woodlark's song. While the exposition and reprise use the notations made in the Forez,[29] the centre of the piece is a jigsaw taken from the two Woodlark excerpts in the Ludwig Koch recordings (23037) alongside another Woodlark borrowed from the Swedish discs.

There follows a hiatus in Messiaen's research over the next two months of the summer of 1956. True, Messiaen had plenty to do: there was the editing (for Ducretet-Thomson) of his recordings of the organ works, time-consuming concerns over whether Durand would publish *Oiseaux exotiques*, and the drawing up of a detailed plan for the *Traité*. Possibly, a more significant reason for the pause was uncertainty over how to turn his vast reservoir of birdsong material into music. Composing from birdsong for solo piano brought a new set of musical problems, since Messiaen would have to manage without the medleys of birdsong that had shaped *Réveil* and *Oiseaux exotiques*. Even with Loriod as the pianist, there was a limit to the number of birdsongs that could be played simultaneously by two hands on one piano.

In this respect, the next *cahier* (23044) is of key importance. The material is from a second stay on Ouessant, in September 1956. As with the visit a year earlier, much of the notebook is concerned less with birdsong than with the sounds of the environment, the ebb-and-flow of the sea and the crashing surf, and also the booming siren of the Créac'h lighthouse, which would feature memorably in the final pages of 'Le Courlis cendré'. The lighthouse obsessed Messiaen ('higher than the tower of a medieval castle'), and its keeper must have been startled by a visit from the composer at 11:30 at night. After describing the operation of the light, Messiaen cross-examined the lighthouse keeper on the movements of the tide and the formation of waves, noting his responses verbatim. Elsewhere in the *cahier* the scattering of birdsongs is outnumbered by prose descriptions, many of

---

[29] 'L'Alouette lulu': from the beginning to the end of line two on the second page, and the last two pages.

which slither into hyperbole as Messiaen's imagination gets to work. The shapes of the rocks remind him of everything from lions' teeth or dragons' tongues to processions of ghostly figures or dinosaurs. The most significant notations (*cahier*, p. 11) cover the music of the Goéland Argenté (score, pp. 6–7), under the heading 'la nuit vient'.

Even more significant are the pages at the back of this Brittany *cahier* (23044), which are filled with musical sketches side by side with speculations on the structure of the *Catalogue*. Working backwards from the end of the *cahier* (as it seems Messiaen did) we encounter first a page of developments of the Woodlark, using notations from the Forez and from Ludwig Koch's *More Songs of Wild Birds*, with a note to modulate the accompanying harmonies away from B♭ major (as they do on the second page of 'L'Alouette lulu'). Above this is a Rossignol, the one imported from the Camargue, in very untidy script but fully harmonized and exactly as it will appear in the score. Squeezed sideways into the margin is a series of general ideas. These include the use of rhythmic pedals ('avec mille variations') and Hindu and Greek rhythms. The most striking thought is that the *Catalogue* should be based on a serial plan, with one piece having a series of rhythms, another a series of pitches, and so on. 'Voir Boulez, Stockhausen', Messiaen notes.[30]

The next page back (p. 19) contains ideas for individual pieces. There are cadences (in E major) for 'Le Loriot, including the descending phrase found on the second page of the score (line 2); bass clusters for the darkness in 'La Chouette hulotte'; jottings on the birds and locations for 'Le Chocard des Alpes'; and, most intriguingly, an ending for 'Le Courlis cendré' with massive C minor chords below a descant of the Curlew's glissandi. The idea was discarded, but the minor sonorities remain, at the opening of the piece (score, pp. 1–4) and in the flashback on the last two pages. Messiaen may have had some of the earlier *cahiers* with him, especially those from recordings, because the next page continues the musical sketching for 'L'Alouette lulu', now introducing the Woodlark from the Swedish set.

Finally, these strands of thought come together on Messiaen's last sheet of manuscript paper, his handwriting getting smaller and progressively less legible in his efforts to squeeze his ideas on to the page (23044, p. 17). The untidiness suggests that Messiaen may have been working on the train back to Paris. We begin at the top of the page with the final notation on the beach at Ouessant, the splash of the surf, an alternation of black and white note clusters, as on the final page of the score, but here a roar of sound, rising to *fff*, that would be reduced in the finished music to a fragmentary whisper. Messiaen then sketches the opening chords for 'Le Loriot', reminding himself in the margin of the places he has collected the Golden Oriole's song, and then giving the first phrase of the song (from the Swedish discs), harmonized by a descant. Below this he writes: 'Forêt, la nuit pour la Lulu', followed by chains of chords. These make a working

---

[30]   For more on the bird style and serialism, including a dodecaphonic bird in *Livre d'orgue*, see Fallon, *Messiaen's Mimesis*, pp. 190–97.

blueprint for 'L'Alouette lulu'. Although the phrases are in the wrong order, a shape is beginning to emerge (the rising and falling sequence at the centre of the piece is in place), and between the phrases are notes to indicate the source of the birdsong – 'Anglais... Suédois... Forez'. Thus, in a few pages at the back of the *cahier*, Messiaen moves from an abstract serial conception to a structure founded on the interaction between birdsongs (here the Woodlark and the Nightingale) and between birds and habitat.

After the breakthrough of the Brittany *cahier*, composition of the *Catalogue* progressed at speed. By late February 1957 Messiaen had completed the five pieces sketched in 23044 – 'Le Chocard des Alpes', 'Le Loriot', 'La Chouette hulotte', 'L'Alouette lulu' and 'Le Courlis cendré' – together with 'L'Alouette calandrelle' (from the notations made near Arles the previous July). They were performed by Loriod as 'Extracts from the *Catalogue d'oiseaux*' on 30 March 1957; a first (shorter) version of 'La Rousserolle effarvatte' arrived too late for her to learn in time for the recital.

The second wave of composition commenced immediately, inspired by a trip in April to the Charente, five years after Messiaen had first visited Delamain. Ms. 23051 contains descriptions of Chartres, visited by Messiaen and Loriod on 18 April and again ten days later on the return journey. Messiaen was fascinated by the incongruity between the sculpture and stained glass of the cathedral and the chorus of Jackdaws, perched high in the asymmetrical west towers:

> L'ombre noire sous les arceaux, les clochetons, les gargouilles à têtes énormes de lion, aux yeux exorbités de grenouille, avec un immense rictus, une bouche ouverte d'une oreille à l'autre pour laisser passer l'eau de pluie, le plein ciel autour des cloches – c'est le royaume des Choucas!

> [The deep shade under the arches, the bell turrets, gargoyles with huge lion heads, bulbous frog's eyes, with a grin gaping from ear to ear as a channel for the rainwater, and the open sky around the bells – this is the kingdom of the Jackdaws!]

Notes made later that summer[31] show that Messiaen was tempted to write a piece about the Jackdaw, set at Chartres, incorporating the sound of the bells. Perhaps he was deterred by the impossibility of finding a musical expression for the architecture. Besides, he seems already to have planned a role for the Jackdaw in a piece about the Rock Thrush ('Le Merle de roche'), for which there is a sketch in piano notation at the end of the *cahier*, perhaps done in May 1957, though the piece was not composed until the late summer of 1958. Another notation that looks forward is the Grive Draine (Mistle Thrush) found in 'La Buse variable', composed later in 1957 at Petichet. In the score the rich chording reflects the

---

[31]   In 23056(2), the second of two notebooks catalogued as 23056.

many-faceted character of the song, as described in the *cahier* (23051, p. 6): 'Fort, clair et puissant – mais triste, nostalgique, et lancinant'.[32]

Within two or three miles of Gardépée, still owned (as it is today) by the Delamain family, following the death of Jacques Delamain in 1953, Messiaen found the setting for 'La Bouscarle', the narrow stream of the Charenton, encircling a large meadow adjacent to the south bank of the Charente.[33] The description in the *cahier* (23009, p. 19) matches the preface to the score: 'Le Charenton: tout petit bras de rivière, bordée de roseaux et de grands peupliers, trembles qui bénissent … feuilles agitées par le vent … de jolis saules au feuillage argenté …' [The Charenton: narrow branch of the river, fringed by reeds and tall poplars, aspens that give blessing … leaves shaken by the wind … pretty willows with silvery foliage …]. The trees form a tunnel of green, down which one can imagine the arrowing 'nuptial flight' of Messiaen's Kingfisher. The same page (23009, p. 19) contains the Grive Musicienne (score, pp. 6–7), and Cetti's Warbler, the Bouscarle itself. Other birdsongs are suffused with the lyricism found in 'La Bouscarle', with notations of the Robin, for example, distilled to its descending cascade and interrogatory cadence. A definite attribution is the Robin used at nightfall ('La nuit vient' – see score, pp. 9–10, 23009, p. 19). The notebooks also contain birdsongs copied from recordings: the Huppe (Hoopoe), Râle de Genets (Corncrake) and Poule d'Eau (Moorhen), all in 'La Bouscarle' and all from the Swedish anthology. Climbing the hillside south of the Charente Messiaen described the muted medley of birdsongs floating up from the river, the Charenton half-hidden by foliage, and above and beyond the geometric patterns of the vineyards and distant blue hills (23009, p. 30).

In late June 1957 Messiaen paid his first visit to the Mediterranean coastline around Banyuls, close to the border with Spain. By now Messiaen's notations show a marvellous virtuosity of observation and imaginative response, joining seamlessly with compositional sketches. Two *cahiers* of exceptional richness (23056 and 23057) provide material for two of the *Catalogue*'s masterpieces, 'Le Merle bleu' and 'Le Traquet stapazin' (Messiaen's own favourite). Ms. 23056 has two sections. Ms. 23056(1) begins with 12 pages of notations, almost all recognisable in the music of 'Le Traquet stapazin'. These give way to full compositional sketches (worked on in conjunction with prose plans contained in 23056(2)). First come two pages for 'La Bouscarle', including the 'strophe dominante', the swing to the dominant (and the dominant of the dominant) in the music of the river (score, pp. 12–13). The sketches for 'Le Traquet stapazin' that follow show Messiaen working on a revision of the ending. The first sketch goes straight from the chords of sunset (score, pp. 22–23) to the fragmentary birdcalls that close the piece. Messiaen then introduces a lengthy bridge (23056(1), p. 17), a sketch for the chorale (score, pp. 25–6), with its phrases interspersed with the song of the Fauvette à Lunettes (Spectacled Warbler).

---

[32]   Loud, bright, powerful – but sad, nostalgic and insistent.

[33]   The Charenton is not marked on any local maps of the area, apart from one on a public notice board in the car park at the hamlet of La Trache.

The next few pages of the *cahier* contain a full sketch of the opening, followed by work on the flight of the Kingfisher for 'La Bouscarle', and finally sketches for the middle section of 'Le Traquet stapazin' (23056(1), pp. 19–26). It would be tempting to think that Messiaen composed 'Le Traquet stapazin' on the thyme-scented clifftops, but the reality is that these sketches were worked later in the summer at Petichet (the clue is that they include a notation of a Goldfinch made at Petichet in July – see 23052, pp. 4–5).[34]

With what must have been intense work on composition, the summer months at Petichet in 1957 yielded only one notebook (23052). Here, in a week in July, Messiaen records the events of 'La Buse variable': the circling flight of the Buzzard (*cahier*, p. 1), and the central drama, the attack by a flock of Corneilles Noires (*cahier*, pp. 2 and 7, score, pp. 7–13), the alarm call of the Pie-grièche Écorcheur (Red-Backed Shrike), to add to earlier Swedish notations, and the refrains of the Yellowhammer (score, p. 8).

Two more pieces remained to be composed. 'Le Traquet rieur' stems from notations in 23057 (pp. 43–45) made at Cap Béar near Banyuls in 1958. The final piece, 'Le Merle de roche', is made up of birds that had already been extensively notated, mostly from recordings. But in late June 1958 Messiaen found the setting, at the Cirque de Mourèze, in the mountains west of Montpellier, a 'paysage Dantesque'. The rocks outlined in the gathering darkness stirred Messiaen to flights of fancy: 'Énorme palais Assyrien – masses colossales … armée de bêtes préhistoriques – armée de géants – procession de moines en cagoules' [Huge Assyrian palace – colossal masses … army of prehistoric beasts – army of giants – procession of hooded monks] (23063, p. 10). Beside this is a practical explanation of a musical realization that becomes the sequence of durations in the central part of the piece, an echo of the 'Soixante-quatre durées' from *Livre d'orgue* (1951–52).

Just possibly, it was this passage from 'Le Merle de roche' that gave Messiaen the idea for a work in which time is measured by an abstract process, inhabited and 'coloured' by birdsongs. *Chronochromie* (1959–60) began with the provisional title of 'Postlude', suggesting a pendant to the *Catalogue*, drawing on Messiaen's huge reserves of birdsongs. Meanwhile, though Messiaen had his material for the *Catalogue*, there was to be no slackening in his researches. Immediately after the account of the Cirque de Mourèze comes a *cahier* (23064) with the Cévennes, the Gorges du Tarn, the caves of the Aven Armand, a storm in the mountains, and a superb Alouette Lulu, included by Loriod in the *Traité*.[35] The summer of 1958 brought some of Messiaen's most imaginative descriptions of the Alps (23012) and foreshadows *La Fauvette des jardins* (1970) in long solos by the Garden Warbler, together with a description of the lake below Messiaen's house at dawn: 'Lac du Laffrey comme un miroir – reflet du Grand Serre dans l'eau: – un grand nuage rose, à pointe mauve, fait une merveilleuse bande rose dans l'eau au premier plan.' [Lake Laffrey like a mirror – the Grand Serre reflected in

---

[34]   The final pages of 23057 also include sketches for 'Le Traquet stapazin'.

[35]   Ms. 23064, p. 11, and in *Traité V:1*, pp. 194–7.

the water: a great pink cloud, medium mauve, makes a marvellous pink streak in the water in the foregound.] Ms. 23013 records intense research in the Jura in the early spring of 1959, and a month later a poignant last notation at Claire's nursing home at Bourg-la-Reine, ten days before her sudden death (22 April 1959). By a cruel irony Claire died exactly a week after the triumphant premiere of *Catalogue d'oiseaux*, performed by Yvonne Loriod on 15 April at the Salle Gaveau.

From the tentative beginnings of the early *cahiers* it would have been impossible to predict the musical riches that would follow. It was typical of Messiaen – never lacking in courage – to discard the work planned for Donaueschingen in 1953 and to replace it with a piano concerto on birdsongs. Perhaps in 1953 Messiaen did not realize how much he still had to learn. If he had, he might have been less insistent on *Réveil*'s authenticity.[36] The *cahiers* show how literally Messiaen incorporated his notations into the score of *Réveil*, so that at times, in the long piano solos, the music has a didactic air. What saves *Réveil* as music is the freshness of the scoring, and the way in which birds are brought together to interact, particularly (as we have seen) in the later stages, with the birdsongs collected in the summer of 1953.

   Réveil might have been an isolated experiment. Indeed, the notebooks for the following year, 1954, show Messiaen's researches running out of steam. He was at a low ebb, personally and professionally, beset by Claire's worsening condition and by a sense of artistic isolation. But the discovery of birdsong recordings reinvigorated the birdsong project. They both deepened Messiaen's ornithology, and enormously enriched his musical response – so that (to take one aspect) a world of timbre and harmony opened up, replacing the unisons of *Réveil*. *Oiseaux exotiques* is a jubilant *tour de force*, starting a new chapter, just as the freewheeling *Cantéyodjayâ* had six years earlier, in 1949.

   Another benefit of recordings was that they enabled Messiaen to prepare for the birds that he would later encounter in nature. And thanks to Loriod – who had acquired a small car – Messiaen was able to explore beyond Paris and its environs into the remoter French countryside. As a result, as the *cahiers* show, there was a new fascination with landscape. The decisive step came in the Brittany *cahier* (23044), when Messiaen considered a serial plan, which was rejected as soon as he started to sketch the chorale in B♭ major (for darkness in 'L'Alouette lulu': 23044, p. 17). But the serial idea was more than a passing whim. Eight of the 13 pieces contain it in some form, clear quasi-serial passages that follow strictly their own logic but at the same time create a counterpart to the image in nature being described. In 'La Chouette hulotte', for example, the ominous darkness is represented by a 'mode de valeurs' technique similar to that in the study of that name from *Quatre Études de rythme* (1949–50). Then there is the reflection of trees in water (in 'La Bouscarle') represented by a canon, with the durations of the pianist's left hand elongating and reflecting those of the leading voice. The idea of musical 'metaphor' became central –

---

[36]   See Messiaen's prefatory note to the score: 'Il n'y a dans cette partition que des chants d'oiseaux. Tous ont été entendus en forêt et sont parfaitement authentiques.'

Messiaen, incidentally, always spoke disparagingly of musical 'impressionism'.[37] In earlier works Messiaen had placed birdsong and abstractions together. We find this in the 'Soixante-quatre durées' (in *Livre d'orgue*) and a decade earlier in the opening movement of *Quatuor pour la fin du Temps*, 'Liturgie de cristal'. But it has no place in *Réveil*, and only a trace in *Oiseaux exotiques* (the patterning of unpitched percussion in the central medley). In this sense, Messiaen's next step, in *Chronochromie*, was a return to unfinished business.

---

[37] In conversation with the author.

Appendix
Inventory of the 'Cahiers de notations des chants d'oiseaux' for the 1950s

Manuscripts found in the Bibliothèque Nationale de France, Département de la Musique. The two numbers given for each *cahier* are for the Ms. (manuscript) and the *Bobine* (microfilm).

Grandes feuilles de papier à musique

23001/Bob. 17784: May 1953, St-Germain-en-Laye and October, Baden-Baden. Contains list of birds for great birdsong project.

23002/Bob. 17785: June 1954, Orgeval and August 1954, Petichet.

23003/Bob. 17786: April–July 1954, Paris region and London.

23004/Bob. 17787: June 1955, Paris region.

23005/Bob. 17797: 1954–5, La Varenne and Marne.

23006/Bob. 17798: April–May 1955, Paris region.

23007/Bob. 17799: May 1955 and March 1957.

23008/Bob. 17800: April 1957, Charente ('La Bouscarle').

23009/Bob. 17801: April 1957, Charente.

23010/Bob. 17802: March–May 1957, Paris region.

23011/Bob. 17803: March–April 1958, Karlsruhe and Paris region.

23012/Bob. 17804: July–August 1958, Petichet.

23013/Bob. 17805: March 1959, Jura.

23014/Bob. 17806: April–May 1959, Orgeval.

23015/Bob. 17807: May 1959, Jura.

23016/Bob. 17808: June 1959, Orgeval and L'Île-Adam.

23017/Bob. 18966: June 1959, Paris.

23018/Bob. 18967: July 1959, Petichet.

23028/Bob. 18977: 1950s, Swedish and Swiss discs.

23029/Bob. 18978: 1954–5: Discs of North America and Mexico.

Grandes feuilles de papier à musique (with lists of contents by Yvonne Loriod)

23036/Bob. 18985: 1954–5, *American Bird Songs* (for *Oiseaux exotiques*).

23037/Bob. 18986: 1954–5, Disques Angleterre.

23038/Bob. 18987: April 1955, Orgeval.

23039/Bob. 18988: November 1955, Paris. *Oiseaux exotiques* notations made at the Exposition.

23040/Bob. 18989: September 1955, Brittany and Swedish discs.

23041/Bob. 18990: Late 1950s, Oiseaux des côtes marines (discs).

23042/Bob. 18991: July 1956, Forez (for 'L'Alouette lulu').

23043/Bob. 18992: July 1956, Arles and Camargue.

23044/Bob. 18993: September 1956, Brittany.

23045/Bob. 18994: Swedish discs A.

23046/Bob. 18995: Swedish discs B.

23047/Bob. 18996: Swedish discs C and Swiss discs.

23048/Bob. 18997: Swedish discs D.

23049/Bob. 18998: April 1956, Orgeval.

23050/Bob. 18999: March 1957, Zurich.

23051/Bob. 19000: March–April 1957, Chartres and Orgeval.

23052/Bob. 19001: July 1957 Dauphiné (material for 'La Buse variable') and 1959, Dauphiné.

23053/Bob. 19002: March–April 1957, Orgeval.

23054/Bob. 19003: April 1957, Orgeval.

23055/Bob. 19004: June 1957, Roussillon.

23056(1)/Bob. 19005: June 1957, Banyuls (for 'Le Traquet stapazin').

23056(2)/Bob. 19005: Plans for 'Le Traquet stapazin' and 'La Bouscarle'.

23057/Bob. 19006: May–June 1957, Banyuls, Orange and Cap Béar.

23058/Bob. 19007: May 1958, Banyuls.

23059(1)/Bob. 19008: March–May 1958, Banyuls, Cantal and Gorges du Tarn.

23059(2)/Bob. 19008: May 1958, Banyuls.

23060/Bob. 19009: 1958, Swedish discs and live notations.

23061/Bob. 19010: 1958 – just a title page (Dictionaire de l'Hérault), which Messiaen planned with François Huë.

23062/Bob. 19011: 1958, Orgeval.

23063/Bob. 19012: 1958, Hérault (for 'Le Merle de roche').

23064/Bob. 19013: June 1958, Cévennes.

23065/Bob. 19014: 1955, Dauphiné ('Le Chocard des Alpes') and 1959.

23066/Bob. 19015: 1959, Forêt de St-Germain-en-Laye.

Petits cahiers

23077/Bob. 19026: May 1952, St-Germain-en-Laye.

23078/Bob. 19027: May 1952, St-Germain-en-Laye.

23079/Bob. 19028 ('Charente A'): June 1952, Charente, Branderie de Gardépée.

23079/Bob. 19028 ('Charente B').

23080/Bob. 19029: July 1952, St-Germain-en-Laye and Darmstadt.

23081/Bob. 19030: 1952 (Darmstadt) and April 1953 (Forêt de St-Germain-en-Laye).

23082/Bob. 19031: March 1953, St-Germain-en-Laye, Paris and Stuttgart.

23083/Bob. 19032: May–June 1953, St-Germain-en-Laye and Buttes Chaumont.

23084/Bob.19033: June 1953, Fontainebleau and Orgeval.

23085/Bob. 19034: April 1954, Orgeval.

23086/Bob. 19035: July 1953, Versailles, 'Mon jardin' and June 1954, Orgeval.

23087/Bob. 19036: May 1954, La Varenne, the Var, 'Mon jardin' and Toulon.

23088/Bob. 19037: May 1954, St-Cloud (chez Mme Billot).

23089/Bob. 19038: May–June 1954, Paris.
23090/Bob. 19039: April 1954, La Varenne and Marne.
23091/Bob. 19040: May 1954, Buttes-Chaumont and October, La Varenne.
23092/Bob. 19041: May 1954 – October 1955, Paris and La Varenne.

Chapter 8

In the Beginning Was The Word?
An Exploration of the Origins of
Méditations sur le mystère de la Sainte Trinité

Anne Mary Keeley

Completed in 1969, Olivier Messiaen's *Méditations sur le mystère de la Sainte Trinité* is an organ work of monumental proportions. Although the title of the work suggests a commonality between its nine pieces, a cohesive musical structure does not immediately reveal itself: the pieces vary considerably in their individual structures and lengths, while certain clearly identifiable musical features are common to some pieces, but not to all.[1] In exploring whether and how these nine meditations on the Holy Trinity might function as a coherent whole, it is profitable to take account of Robert Sherlaw Johnson's seminal study of Messiaen's music wherein, in the course of his analysis of Messiaen's *Réveil des oiseaux*, he observes that 'The form of the piece depends entirely on the programme underlying the work.'[2] Adopting Sherlaw Johnson's approach seems appropriate in the case of the *Méditations*, because the composer's intention to convey a theological programme is unambiguously declared in the title of the work.

There are two ways in which Messiaen incorporates theological elements into his *Méditations*. Most notably, by means of his *langage communicable* Messiaen integrates three precise theological statements into the actual music.[3] More usually, however, Messiaen includes in the score a written quotation or title at the beginning of a piece, section or theme that functions as a kind of theological

---

[1]   An example of this is Paul Griffiths's statement that 'the piecemeal presentation of the material encourages a view of the movements not as independent entities but as simply different selections from a common store of elements'. Paul Griffiths, *Olivier Messiaen and the Music of Time* (London: Faber and Faber, 1985), p. 223.

[2]   Robert Sherlaw Johnson, *Messiaen*, 2nd paperback edn, updated and additional text by Caroline Rae (London: Omnibus Press, 2008), p. 188. Pagination is identical in the 1st (1989) paperback edition up to p. 195.

[3]   The principles of Messiaen's *langage communicable* are well-known. Quotations from St Thomas Aquinas are incorporated into the music by way of monophonic themes assigned to key words and a complex musical alphabet that actually spells the remaining words. Messiaen's own explanation of the *langage communicable* can be found in a preface to the score of the *Méditations*.

epigraph. There are 24 of these epigraphs in the score, many of which are repeated, always in accordance with repetitions in the music.

The three theological statements concern the Holy Trinity and are taken from St Thomas Aquinas's *Summa Theologiæ*.[4] Messiaen's appropriation of Aquinas's words has meant that his organ cycle is usually – and perhaps perfunctorily – associated almost exclusively with Aquinas's theology. In the course of this colossal organ work, however, there are but three brief quotations from Aquinas's even more colossal work of theology.

An exegesis of Messiaen's score suggests that the inspiration for the work derives from a theology that diverges significantly from that of Aquinas. In order to test this hypothesis, this chapter explores the origins of *Méditations sur le mystère de la Sainte Trinité*, focusing on the event in 1967 that gave birth to the work. Arising from this exploration, certain theological doctrines and concepts are indentified as being important in the theological programme of the work. These doctrines and concepts – ranging from well-known (for example, Holy Trinity, Holy Spirit, divine persons) to more specialized (for example, economic Trinity, breath of the spirit, *filioque*, consubstantiality) – are scrutinized to determine how they may have influenced Messiaen's choice and arrangement of musical materials and, therefore, the structure of the work. The question of how these doctrines and concepts may be related to the music is also addressed.

From time to time, the origins of the *Méditations* have been linked to organist Almut Rößler's request that Messiaen compose another large-scale organ work.[5] However, a musical work does not simply materialize on request. In their 2005 biography of Messiaen, Peter Hill and Nigel Simeone presented a more precise identification of the work's origins:

> On 23 November 1967 the Trinité celebrated its centenary with a special event billed as *Le Mystère de Dieu*. Monsignor Charles, famous for his sermons at the Sacré-Coeur, was invited to preach, and Messiaen provided a series of improvisations, which he had planned with even greater care than usual, so much so that some of his sketched outlines for these improvisations were to be developed to form part of his next great organ cycle.[6]

A publicity poster for the event supplied the information shown in Figure 8.1.

---

[4]   The statements appear in the first, third and seventh meditations and are taken respectively from the following three questions in the *Summa Theologiae*: Ia q.33, 4, reply; Ia q.28, 2, reply; Ia q.37, 2, reply.

[5]   Almut Rößler, *Contributions to the Spiritual World of Olivier Messiaen*, trans. Babara Dagg and Nancy Poland (Duisburg: Gilles und Francke, 1986), p. 20.

[6]   PHNS, p. 275.

Centenaire de l'Église de la Sainte Trinité et Inauguration de Grand Orgue
Sous la Présidence de S. Exc. Monseigneur BERTOLI, Nonce Apostolique en France
Le MYSTÈRE de DIEU
Évocation alternée
meditations par
Mgr. CHARLES
improvisations à l'orgue par
OLIVIER MESSIAEN

Figure 8.1   Information supplied in the publicity poster for the event at the Trinité[7]

The poster, together with an amusing anecdote recounted by Yvonne Loriod to Hill and Simeone, indicates a significant level of collaboration between Messiaen and the man who had been invited to preach.[8] This raises the question of whether or not there might be a relationship between the musical composition that evolved from Messiaen's improvisations on 23 November 1967 and the words that were spoken on that occasion.

That this was a high-profile event is witnessed by the fact that the Apostolic Nuncio presided over the proceedings. Furthermore, the event took place in the period immediately following the Second Vatican Council, a time when theology was high on the agenda of intellectual discourse, not only in France but throughout the world.[9] All the signs are that the event required a high-octane performance on the theological front. But who exactly was the man chosen to fulfil this role and whose name, moreover, deserved to rank ahead of that of Olivier Messiaen, who by this time was already an establishment figure in France?

Maxime Marcel Charles was an exact contemporary of Messiaen, outliving him only by a few months. He was born in Ribérac, in the Dordogne region in 1908 and died in Paris in 1993. Ordained for the Archdiocese of Paris in 1935,

---

[7]   Hill and Simeone provide a photograph of the poster. PHNS, p. 274.

[8]   'Yvonne Loriod recounts a snatch of conversation between Messiaen and the Monsignor about a practical matter: 'Mgr Charles: How will I know when your improvisations are finished? Messiaen: My wife can switch a light on and off, or even better, I will finish each improvisation with the song of the yellowhammer: seven repeated notes, followed by a long held note, which you'll recognize easily.' PHNS, pp. 275–6.

[9]   The Second Vatican Council, held between October 1962 and December 1965, was an event of global significance, about which American historian John W. O'Malley has observed: 'Although commentators assess the council's ultimate importance differently, many would agree that it was the most important religious event of the twentieth century.' John W. O'Malley, *What Happened at Vatican II* (Cambridge, MA: Belknap-Harvard, 2008), p. 1. For more on Messiaen and Vatican II, see Christopher Dingle, 'La statue reste sur son piédestal: Messiaen's *La Transfiguration* and Vatican II', *Tempo*, 212 (April, 2000): pp. 8–11, and Robert Fallon, 'Two Paths to Paradise: Reform in Messiaen's *Saint François d'Assise*' in Robert Sholl (ed.), *Messiaen Studies* (Cambridge: Cambridge University Press, 2007).

he became chaplain to the Catholic students at the Sorbonne in 1944. Over the course of his career as *aumônier* at the Sorbonne, Père Charles – as he was then – became famous in Paris and throughout France, owing to the intellectual and physical energy, and the highly effective organizational approach with which he undertook his mission to the students.[10] He brought this dynamism to his next post, rector of the Basilica of Sacré-Coeur de Montmartre, which he held from 1959 to 1985, after which time he was emeritus rector at the basilica. A lifelong friend of, and collaborator with, Jean Cardinal Lustiger, and publicly commended by Jean Cardinal Daniélou[11] for his dynamic approach to theology, Maxime Charles was most definitely one of the movers and shakers in the French Catholic Church establishment of the mid-twentieth century, and one, moreover, who was held in deep and genuine affection by the French public at large.

Hill and Simeone say only that Charles 'was invited to preach', thus echoing Messiaen's terse explanation to Claude Samuel.[12] However, Messiaen has left us a more detailed account of the background to this invitation in his contribution to a collection of essays published in 1984 as an *hommage* to the Parisian priest.[13] For a two-year period prior to 1967, during which the organ at the Trinité was undergoing restoration, Messiaen was free to attend religious services in other churches. He chose to attend Sacré-Coeur de Montmatre for a variety of reasons, but principally, it seems, to listen to the sermons of Mgr Charles, which he describes in truly glowing terms:

> Sublime, the word is not too strong, because I have never heard such beautiful sermons elsewhere. … The text, without doubt meditated on at length … seemed to come naturally. It was always classically divided into three points. But what robust and unshakeable faith, what theological depth, and what admirable French! And all that without effort. A divine depth passed through the words with a disconcerting sublimity. This did not prevent good sense, irony and humour, so much so that the divine came to meet the human as in a prolonged incarnation.[14]

Messiaen tells us that when the organ restoration at the Trinité was completed, he (i.e. Messiaen) was invited to organize a public inauguration of the restored organ

---

[10]   A detailed account of Charles's impressive career at the Sorbonne can be read in Samuel Pruvot, *Monseigneur Charles: Aumônier de la Sorbonne, 1944–1959* (Paris: Éditions du Cerf, 2002).

[11]   Daniélou was one of the main protagonists in the *ressourcement* movement, which is discussed later in this essay.

[12]   *Music and Color*, p. 125.

[13]   Olivier Messiaen, 'Grand jeu pour la Trinité', in *La politique de la mystique: Hommage à Mgr Maxime Charles*, editor unacknowledged (Limoges: Criterion, 1984), pp. 121–3. All translations from Messiaen's essay are mine.

[14]   Ibid., pp. 121–2.

in what was anticipated as 'an important ceremony'. He immediately seized the opportunity to ask Charles to preach and the two men met for a detailed discussion about the event: 'My visit lasted more than an hour, the time it took to focus on the various aspects of the ceremony, and the meticulous noting of the principal ideas of the sermon, on which I would make many improvisations on the organ.'[15] Messiaen's account of the background to the centenary event at the Trinité makes clear two things. First, the extraordinary personal impact of Charles's preaching on him was the decisive factor in the composer's decision to invite him to preach at the event. Second, there was a significant level of collaboration between preacher and composer, and a mutual understanding about the substance of the spoken elements on the mystery of God.

When it came to the event, Messiaen was not disappointed by Charles's efforts: 'Of course, the sermon was truly inspiring. It surpassed all my expectations. It was comprised of deep theology, worthy of St Augustine and of St Thomas Aquinas.'[16] It is worth emphasizing that Messiaen does not say the sermon was comprised *of* the theology of Augustine and Aquinas, rather that it was comprised of theology *worthy* of the two.

A transcript of the sermon preached by Mgr Charles at the event at the Trinité on Thursday 23 November 1967[17] discloses information that adds significantly to our understanding of that event and 'the programme underlying the work' that emerged from it (to borrow Sherlaw Johnson's phrase). While there is much that could be said about the sermon, it is sufficient for the present purposes to draw attention to a few observations only.

The transcript suggests that Charles was not reading from a fully worked-out text. Rather, the sermon appears to have been an extemporization, possibly based on some notes; a stream of consciousness delivered in a high rhetorical style which, although perhaps somewhat dated, nevertheless exemplifies a long tradition of French oratory.[18] This corroborates Messiaen's remarks about Charles's sermons at Sacré-Coeur. More importantly, however, it points to a symmetry of approach by preacher and organist to the event at the Trinité, since we know that Messiaen also improvised with the assistance of preparatory sketches.[19]

The sermon comprises an introduction and three parts. The introduction defines God as a Trinity. Part 1 deals with the manner in which the mystery of the Trinity has been revealed to the faithful in the history of salvation. Part 2 concerns

---

[15]   Ibid.

[16]   Ibid.

[17]   The sermon is unpublished, but a transcript was made available to me by Les Archives Historiques de l'Archevêché de Paris.

[18]   For example, Jean-Baptiste Lacordaire OP (1802–70) was famous for his outstanding preaching and oratory, while in the political sphere, two famous exponents of this high rhetorical style of oratory were Alexis de Tocqueville (1805–59) and Charles de Montalembert (1810–70).

[19]   PHNS, p. 275.

the nature of the Trinity – which is explained as a phenomenon of love – and emphasizes the role of the Holy Spirit. Part 3 considers the effect of this Trinitarian mystery in the lives of the faithful, through the role of the Holy Spirit.

In part 2 of his three-part sermon, in which he explains the Holy Trinity as a phenomenon of love, Charles makes specific reference to the work of only one theologian, the twelfth-century Paris-based Richard of St Victor.[20] St Thomas Aquinas is mentioned only in passing. Overall, the theological orientation of the sermon suggests a man in step with the modern Catholic Church. Frequent references to sacred scripture bespeak an endorsement of *ressourcement*, a twentieth-century French Catholic movement advocating a return to the sources of Christian faith, away from Scholasticism.[21] Charles's endorsement of *ressourcement* is underscored by his theological approach to the mystery of God: his focus is on the 'economic' Trinity, that is, the gradual revelation of God as Father, Son and Spirit, as set forth in the Bible.[22] This approach follows theological developments arising from the Second Vatican Council, since, as Karl Rahner observed in his groundbreaking treatment of the doctrine of the Trinity first published in 1967, 'In the theology of the Second Vatican Council the Trinity is mentioned within the context of salvation history.'[23]

---

[20]   Richard of St-Victor (d. 1173) was a theologian of the medieval school of the monastery of St Victor in Paris. In his *De Trinitate*, Richard identified supreme goodness with supreme and most perfect love. Rejecting Boethius's generally accepted definition of divine personality, Richard used his own unique approach to develop an idea of the personal distinctions in God. This singular Trinitarian doctrine differs from the work of contemporaneous theologians and was not taken up by later theologians. 'According to Richard, the most perfect love, which is God, cannot remain in itself but must direct itself outward toward some other person of equal value and dignity. This *proprium amoris* equally demands that the two persons in their mutual love have a third person as object of their common love. These persons are perfectly one in essence but still to be distinguished as persons (*existentia incommunicabilis*). The Father is without beginning and is the principle of the other persons as well; the Son is from a principle and is himself, together with the Father, the principle of the Holy Spirit; the Holy Spirit is not the principle of another person.' H. C. Van Elswijk, 'Richard of Saint-Victor', *New Catholic Encyclopaedia*, Vol. 12 (New York: McGraw Hill, 1967), p. 483.

[21]   'On the eve of Vatican II, the call to return to the sources, now explicitly under the name *ressourcement*, drove much of the theological ferment in France. ... Just as Erasmus had wanted to displace medieval Scholasticism with a biblical/patristic theology, the twentieth-century *ressourcement* wanted to do essentially the same.' O'Malley, *What Happened at Vatican II*, p. 41.

[22]   The term 'economic Trinity' arises from the distinction between terms that developed in the Patristic age: *theologia*, meaning a consideration of God in God's essence as one in nature and three in persons, and *oikonomia*, meaning a consideration of God in God's saving activity in human history through creation and redemption.

[23]   Karl Rahner, *The Trinity*, trans. Joseph Donceel (New York: Crossroad, 2010), p. 10. The question arises as to whether Charles may have been aware of Rahner's work. The

Such an approach runs contrary to the scholastic method, which begins with the immanent nature of the one God, proceeding only later to a consideration of God as Trinity. This is the methodology followed by Aquinas in his classical exposition of the mystery of God in Part I of the *Summa Theologiæ*.[24] Over time, the primary issue in Part I of the *Summa*, between what pertains to the divine essence and what pertains to the distinction of the divine persons, attracted much criticism, as summarized here by Brian Shanley:

> Critics have objected that such an approach relegates the Trinity to a kind of afterthought; according to this view, Aquinas is taken to be the most eminent practitioner of Western Latin 'essentialism' that conceives of God in static metaphysical categories divorced from God's self-disclosure in the history of salvation as Father, Son, and Holy Spirit.[25]

Modern dissatisfaction with the scholastic approach to the mystery of God is reflected in the modern preference for the 'economic' approach, which can be identified clearly in Charles's introduction: 'First I shall share some reflections on the manner in which this mystery was revealed to us throughout the history of our salvation. Then … I shall try to lead you in some reflections on the understanding of this mystery.'

Thus, it is clear that the content of the sermon is representative of late twentieth-century, post-Vatican II theology, rather than scholasticism. In order to assess the relevance of these findings to Messiaen's completed organ work, let us first consider the overall structure of the *Méditations* and then examine in greater detail some musical elements of the particular meditation that was described by Messiaen as 'the most important piece in the cycle'.[26]

Published in 1973, the work comprises nine numbered but untitled meditations. Although initially resistant to naming the movements, Messiaen later assigned

---

enormity of Rahner's international profile in the fields of philosophy and theology strongly suggests that Charles could not have been unaware of his work.

[24]   Part I of the *Summa Theologiæ* is structured as follows. Question 1: Sacred Doctrine; Questions 2–26: God's Essence; Questions 27–43: The divine persons; Questions 44–119: The procession of creatures from God. Referring to Part I of the *Summa*, Nicholas Healy observes, 'These questions consider the existence and knowledge of God, first as One, then as the Trinity. They conclude (at ST 1.43) with a treatment of the mission of the Son and the Holy Spirit outwards, so to speak, to creation. This reflects a shift from what is often called the "immanent Trinity" to the "economic Trinity"'. Nicholas M. Healy, *Thomas Aquinas: Theologian of the Christian Life* (Aldershot: Ashgate, 2003), p. 49.

[25]   Brian Shanley OP, *The Treatise on the Divine Nature: Summa Theologiæ I, 1–13* (Indianapolis: Hackett, 2006), p. 178. (It should be noted, however, that Shanley challenges this criticism of Aquinas's approach.) Rahner also levels the criticism that textbook theology had led to 'the isolation of Trinitarian doctrine'. Rahner, *The Trinity*, p. 10. Rahner devotes an entire section of his essay to this point.

[26]   *Music and Color*, p. 126.

titles to each of them. A written introductory section is devoted to explaining the *langage communicable*. This is followed immediately by the meditations, each of which begins with a brief written commentary on the music. These terse commentaries announce what is about to happen musically and often include brief theological statements and/or scriptural quotations that can be linked to the annotations accompanying the music. From this material it is possible to assemble a great deal of information on the theological programme of the work. As with Mgr Charles's sermon, Messiaen's frequent recourse to scripture suggests the influence of *ressourcement*.[27] Also in keeping with Charles's approach is Messiaen's particular choice of scriptural quotations and theological statements which, over the totality of the work, presents us with the 'economic' Trinity. The theological programme put forward over the course of the nine meditations can be condensed into the essential elements set out in Figure 8.2.

Meditation	Principal theological idea
I	God the Father: the principle without principle ●
II	Divine holiness
III	Relationality in God ●
IV	The glory of the Father
V	God is infinite, eternal & immutable; God is Father, Son & Spirit; God is Love
VI	The glory of the Son
VII	Relationality in God ●
VIII	Divine simplicity
IX	'I Am Who I Am': the principle without principle

● = The idea centres on a quotation from Aquinas's *Summa Theologia*

Figure 8.2   A summary of the theological elements in the *Méditations*

This summary of theological elements discloses a chiastic structure. A chiasmus, or chiasm, is a rhetorical or literary figure in which words, grammatical constructions or concepts are repeated in reverse order, in the same or a modified form. In the *Méditations*, the theological elements identifiable over the course of the nine meditations give rise to a chiastic structure in which the first four meditations

---

[27]   Messiaen's choice of Exodus 3:14 ('I am who I am') for the final meditation is particularly interesting, as it suggests that his reception of St Thomas Aquinas may be via the medievalist Étienne Gilson, one of those scholars who is considered to be a precursor in the development of the *ressourcement* movement. 'It was one of the characteristic themes of Étienne Gilson to assert that Aquinas's entire metaphysics was inspired by [Exodus 3:14] such that there is a kind of "metaphysics of Exodus" in Aquinas.' Shanley, *The Treatise on the Divine Nature*, p. 192.

lead to the fifth – the central piece in the work – and the last four meditations lead away from it. The main theological idea in each of the first four meditations has a parallel in each of the last four meditations, as illustrated in Figure 8.3.

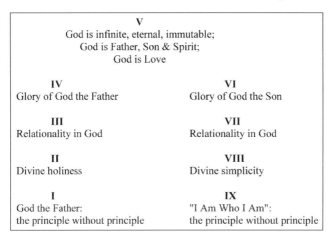

	V God is infinite, eternal, immutable; God is Father, Son & Spirit; God is Love
IV Glory of God the Father	**VI** Glory of God the Son
III Relationality in God	**VII** Relationality in God
II Divine holiness	**VIII** Divine simplicity
I God the Father: the principle without principle	**IX** "I Am Who I Am": the principle without principle

Figure 8.3   Chiastic structure of the *Méditations*

In the biblical-theological context in which Messiaen composed his *Méditations*, a chiastic structure is entirely plausible, since 'chiasm … is common in biblical narrative'.[28] Furthermore, precedents for the use of chiastic structure in musical composition already existed, most notably in religious works by J. S. Bach. The theological context and strongly didactic nature of many of the works in which Bach employed chiastic structure bear close comparison with Messiaen's *Méditations*.[29]

---

[28]   Richard J. Clifford SJ, and Roland E. Murphy O. Carm, 'Genesis', in Raymond E. Brown et al. (eds), *The New Jerome Biblical Commentary* (London: Chapman, 1997), p. 15. Clifford and Murphy discuss the chiastic arrangement of the story of the great flood.

[29]   'The use of chiastic structures is a marked feature of Bach's mature vocal works, such as the passions, which portray the death of Christ, the Christmas Oratorio, which celebrates the birth of Christ, and the B minor Mass'. Robin A. Leaver, 'The Mature Vocal Works', in John Butt (ed.), *The Cambridge Companion to Bach*, (Cambridge: Cambridge University Press, 1997), p. 101. Leaver suggests the reason for Bach's use of chiastic structure is due to the provenance of the word *chiasmus*, which comes from the Greek letter *chi*, X, and to the fact that *chi* is the first letter of the word *Christos*. These explanations notwithstanding, the possibility that Bach's use of chiastic structure may have been influenced by his remarkable familiarity with the Bible and biblical scholarship also deserves consideration. (Modern biblical interpretation had begun *c.* 1650 and Bach had a 'substantial theological library' in which 'of particular importance [were] Bible commentaries'. See Christoph Wolff, *Johann Sebastian Bach: The Learned Musician* (Oxford: Oxford University Press, 2000), p. 334).

When this chiastic theological structure is superimposed with the principal musical features of the individual meditations, a number of cross-related textural and thematic relationships can be identified, as set out in Figure 8.4.[30]

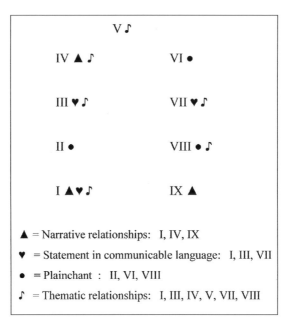

V ♪

IV ▲ ♪   VI ●

III ♥ ♪   VII ♥ ♪

II ●   VIII ● ♪

I ▲ ♥ ♪   IX ▲

▲ = Narrative relationships: I, IV, IX
♥ = Statement in communicable language: I, III, VII
● = Plainchant : II, VI, VIII
♪ = Thematic relationships: I, III, IV, V, VII, VIII

Figure 8.4   Textural and thematic relationships in the *Méditations*

Chiastic structure calls attention to the word or concept at the centre of a figure; in the case of Messiaen's *Méditations* the central meditation is obviously the fifth movement. From a musical perspective, the argument in favour of the fifth meditation being of central significance can be advanced on two fronts. First, as a summary of the work's overall musical structure demonstrates (Figure 8.5), there is a density of musical activity in the fifth meditation that surpasses anything that occurs elsewhere in the work.

Second, thematic relationships between the fifth meditation and five of the remaining eight meditations can be identified. These thematic relationships reside in Messiaen's use of particular themes from his *langage communicable*. Obviously, these themes appear as part of the *langage communicable* in the first,

---

[30]   Similar patterns of relationships between movements have been identified in other works by Messiaen. Early examples of this are Sherlaw Johnson's analyses of *Les Corps glorieux* and *Quatuor pour la fin du Temps*, Sherlaw Johnson, *Messiaen*, pp. 51 and 63. A more recent example is Cheong's proposed structure for *Sept Haïkaï*, 'Buddhist temple, Shinto shrine and the invisible God of Sept Haïkaï', in Andrew Shenton (ed.), *Messiaen the Theologian* (Farnham: Ashgate, 2010), p. 260.

MÉDITATION I

A	B	C	B
Le Père des étoiles (fragments of Père theme)	Statement in communicable language	Les étoiles tournent	Statement in communicable language

MÉDITATION II

A	A¹		
Plainchant opening / Vous êtes le Seul Saint / Birdsong Theme	Modified repeat of A	Coda	Truncated plainchant theme / Le Saint Nom / Birdsong (bruant jaune)

MÉDITATION III

A	A	C	A
Statement in communicable language (using *Dieu* theme)	Birdsong	Toccata Passage: *'Je suis! Je suis!''*	Birdsong / Coda

MÉDITATION IV

A	B	A
3 Themes: *Dieu est immense* / *Dieu est éternel* / *Dieu est immuable*	Toccata Passage: *Le souffle de l'Esprit*	3 Themes: repeated transposed / transposed

A	B	C	A
Birdsong Opening	Trio: *Père* / *Fils* / *Esprit*	Toccata Passage: *'Je suis! Je suis!''*	Birdsong / Coda

MÉDITATION V

B	C	A+B	A+C	D
Toccata Passage (transposed)	2 new themes: *Le P. tout puissant* / *Notre Père*	Toccata Passage +*Dieu est immense* as pedal ostinato	*Dieu est éternel* / *Le P. tout immense* / *Notre Père*) x 2	*Dieu est Amour*

MÉDITATION VI

A	A¹
Plainchant: *Offertoire de l'Epiphanie* / *Graduel de l'Epiphanie* / *Alleluia de l'Epiphanie*	Modified repeat of A

MÉDITATION VII

A	B	A¹
Introductory passage + Birdsong	Statement in communicable language (using *Père*, *Fils*, *Saint Esprit* themes)	Modified repeat of A

MÉDITATION VIII

A	A¹	A²	B	
Plainchant opening / *Les Trois sont Un* / *Père+Fils+Esprit* / *Ô profondeur…*	Modified repeat of A	P'chant (acc.)	*Mon jong est suave…* / *Qui me donnera…*	B'song coda

MÉDITATION IX

A	A¹	B	A²
Dieu / Birdsong	Modified repeat of A	Toccata Passage: *le souffle de l'Esprit*	Modified repeat of A

Figure 8.5   Summary of overall musical structure of the *Méditations*

third and seventh meditations. But they also appear in different musical contexts in the fourth, fifth and eighth meditations. Thus, Messiaen uses the *langage communicable* not simply as a vehicle for Aquinas's words, but as the fabric that gives considerable musical cohesion to the work overall. Finally, and conclusively, by describing the fifth meditation as 'the most important in the cycle', Messiaen himself has confirmed its central role.[31]

In the score, Messiaen divides the fifth meditation into six sections:

1. The meditation opens with three consecutive musical statements representing the concepts of divine infinity ('Dieu est immense'), divine eternity ('Dieu est éternel') and divine immutability ('Dieu est immuable').
2. These are followed by a passage called 'le Souffle de l'Esprit' (the breath of the Spirit).
3. All of this material is then repeated in slightly varied forms.
4. A pair of motives – 'le Père puissant' and 'Notre Père' (the Almighty Father and Our Father) – interrupts the end of the second version of 'le Souffle de l'Esprit', which then develops into a lengthy toccata passage with a pedal based on the opening theme.
5. This is followed by another version of the themes 'Dieu est éternel', 'le Père puissant' and 'Notre Père'.
6. The meditation culminates in a theme not previously heard in the work ('Dieu est amour') and concludes with brief birdsong (the call of the Yellowhammer).

Although there is no statement in communicable language in the fifth meditation, three of its monophonic themes are integral to the musical structure of the meditation. The principal themes of the communicable language are set out in Example 8.1.

The opening theme of this fifth meditation, 'Dieu est immense', is a variation of the 'Dieu' theme from the third and ninth meditations. Example 8.2 shows how the 'Dieu' theme has been transposed and rhythmically varied.

This new theme is heard twice in the fifth meditation: at the outset and then in a further transposed form, following which it becomes the raw material for the pedal part in the long toccata section called 'le Souffle de l'Esprit', which is the central musical feature of this meditation (Example 8.3). In this pedal part, the theme is rhythmically varied, then transposed, then subjected to rhythmic elimination, before finally developing into something else.

In its first two versions, the opening of 'le Souffle de l'Esprit' combines transposed versions of the 'Père' and 'Fils' themes from the first and seventh meditations (Example 8.4). This composite theme is then repeated a couple of times and finally develops into something else.

---

[31]   *Music and Color*, p. 126.

Example 8.1   The principal themes of the communicable language in the *Méditations*

Example 8.2   'Dieu est immense' is a variation of the 'Dieu' theme

This use of themes from the communicable language supports the theological programme of the meditation. At the outset of the meditation, the three musical statements representing attributes of the divine nature can be said to represent the One God. Following these statements, the toccata passage called 'le Souffle de l'Esprit' begins with a combination of the 'Père' and 'Fils' themes. This passage,

Example 8.3   The pedal part in 'le Souffle de l'Esprit' is based on the 'Dieu est immense' theme

Example 8.4   The opening of 'le Souffle de l'Esprit' is a composite of transposed versions of 'Père' and 'Fils' from the first and seventh meditations

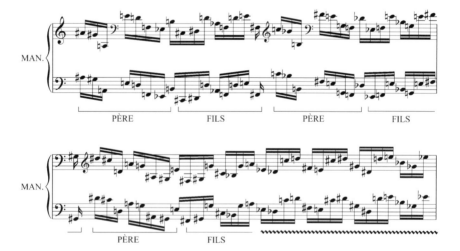

which represents the Third Person of the Trinity, grows out of alternating iterations of the themes representing the First and Second Persons of the Trinity. Thus, this theme may be interpreted as representing the theological concept of three divine persons of one substance. Both the title and the construction of the theme reflect important theological points. First, in relation to the theme's title, Messiaen states: 'It is known that, in Scripture, the word Spirit is linked to the notions of wind and breath'. Although he provides no specific reference, Messiaen's statement can be linked to numerous biblical references. The Hebrew word for wind is *rûah*, which also means 'breath' or 'spirit'.[32] While the contexts in which this word appears in the early books of the Old Testament show that it may have meant simply 'wind' or 'divine wind', the fully-developed idea of wind and breath as theophanies of the Spirit is clear in the Greek of the New Testament, the accounts of the apostles' Pentecost experience in Acts 2:1–4 and the post-Resurrection Jesus breathing the Spirit on the apostles in John 20:19–23 being, respectively, the examples *par excellence*. This idea was adopted by the fourth-century theologian St Basil of Cæserea, who was instrumental in the development of the Christian doctrine of the Holy Spirit. Basil said that the Holy Spirit 'comes forth as a breath from the mouth of the Father'.[33] (A later development of this doctrine holds that 'the Holy Spirit is eternally from the Father *and* Son' [emphasis added]. This is commonly referred to as the *filioque* doctrine.)[34]

Second, Messiaen's understanding of Trinitarian theology appears to be further reflected in his construction of the 'Père' and 'Fils' themes that comprise 'le Souffle de l'Esprit'. He states in the score that the themes are in contrary motion 'like two crossing glances': 'Père (thème du Père), Fils (la même thème en mouvement contraire, comme deux regards qui se croisent)'. This may be a reference to a very popular genre of images in Christian iconography. For many centuries, artists have used images like the one in Illustration 8.1 to attempt to convey the theological concept of consubstantiality, that is, that God the Son is at the same time distinctive from and 'of one being with' God the Father.[35]

Despite Messiaen's assertion, however, the 'Père' and 'Fils' themes are not in strict contrary motion. Example 8.5 shows how, when the themes are superimposed, their central notes move in parallel motion.

---

[32]   Clifford and Murphy, 'Genesis', p. 10.

[33]   Cited in Andrew Ryder SCJ, *The Spirituality of the Trinity* (Dublin: Carmelite Press, 1982), p. 86.

[34]   The doctrine takes its name from the words of the Niceno-Constantinopolitan Creed: 'Et in Spiritum Sanctum, Dominum, et vivificantem: qui ex Patre Filioque procedit'. The official translation is: 'I believe in the Holy Spirit, the Lord, the giver of life, who proceeds from the Father and the Son'. *CTS New Daily Missal Standard Edition* (London: Catholic Truth Society, 2012), pp. 962–3.

[35]   'The consubstantiality defined by Nicaea I ... affirms essentially that the Son is equal to the Father, as divine as the Father, being from His substance and of the same substance with Him.' T.E. Clarke, 'Consubstantiality', in *New Catholic Encyclopaedia*, Vol. 4 (New York: McGraw Hill, 1967), pp. 251–2.

Illustration 8.1   Illumination on parchment, unknown Netherlandish artist, from
the well-known early fifteenth-century illuminated manuscript
Très Belles Heures de Notre Dame de Jean de Berry. This type
of image may have inspired Messiaen's use of contrary motion
themes to represent God the Father and God the Son[36]

That Messiaen may have made a mistake cannot be ruled out. However, as the
likelihood of an error on Messiaen's part is somewhat implausible, perhaps the
solution to this anomaly lies in a theological explanation:

> The Holy Spirit is eternally from Father and Son; ... He proceeds eternally from
> both as from one principle. ... And, since the Father has through generation

---

[36]   Folio 87 *recto*. The manuscript is conserved at Museo Civico d'Arte Antica,
Palazzo Madama, Turin, Italy. Reproduced by permission from Fondazione Torino Musei
Biblioteca d'Arte e Archivio Fotagrafico.

Example 8.5   The 'Père' and 'Fils' themes move in contrary motion, except that
their central notes move in parallel motion

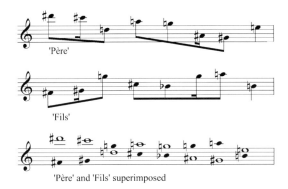

given to the only-begotten Son everything that belongs to the Father, except
being Father, the Son has also eternally from the Father ... that the Holy Spirit
proceeds from the Son.[37]

Thus, the contrary motion of the two themes – their mirror-imaging – may be
said to convey the doctrine of consubstantiality, the simultaneous one-ness and
distinctiveness of God the Father and God the Son, while the parallel movement
may be said to depict the one instance in which God the Father and God the Son
are considered to act together, in the spiration of the Holy Spirit. This passage, in
other words, musically symbolizes the *filioque* doctrine. Richard of St Victor's
unique and distinctive contribution to this theology is the idea that this Spirit is
actually the mutual love of God the Father and God the Son.

The manner in which Messiaen has used and developed the musical materials
discussed above, and his introduction and naming of subsequent themes in the
fifth meditation, all point to a theological programme that ultimately conforms
not to the Trinitarian theology of St Thomas of Aquinas, but to that of Richard
of St Victor, the theologian who features in Maxime Charles's sermon, as shown
below. It is Messiaen's emphasis on God as love that drives this argument. As
explained by William Hill in his acclaimed theological study, *The Three-Personed
God*, Richard of St Victor presents the Trinity as a community of love:

> Richard's *De Trinitate* begins with God in the oneness of his nature, but stresses
> love as the most distinctive and identifying trait of that nature. Uppermost, almost
> surely, is the inspiration of St John's 'God is love'. But, with some originality,
> Richard notes that love is a tending to the other; by its very nature it demands
> the other, and in God this can only be the infinitely lovable other. ... The Divine

---

[37]   *The Catechism of the Catholic Church*, article 246.

Society terminates at Three, since anything more would be superfluous. But this opens the way to further created societies.[38]

Figure 8.6 further summarizes this outline of Richard of St Victor's Trinitarian theology and links it to the different sections of the fifth meditation to demonstrate how Messiaen has followed the Trinitarian doctrine specifically cited by Mgr Charles in the central section of his sermon.

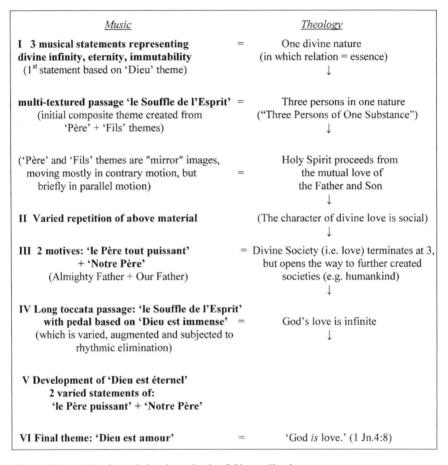

Music		*Theology*
I 3 musical statements representing divine infinity, eternity, immutability (1st statement based on 'Dieu' theme)	=	One divine nature (in which relation = essence) ↓
multi-textured passage 'le Souffle de l'Esprit' (initial composite theme created from 'Père' + 'Fils' themes)	=	Three persons in one nature ("Three Persons of One Substance") ↓
('Père' and 'Fils' themes are "mirror" images, moving mostly in contrary motion, but briefly in parallel motion)	=	Holy Spirit proceeds from the mutual love of the Father and Son ↓
II Varied repetition of above material		(The character of divine love is social) ↓
III 2 motives: 'le Père tout puissant' **+ 'Notre Père'** (Almighty Father + Our Father)	=	Divine Society (i.e. love) terminates at 3, but opens the way to further created societies (e.g. humankind) ↓
IV Long toccata passage: 'le Souffle de l'Esprit' **with pedal based on 'Dieu est immense'** (which is varied, augmented and subjected to rhythmic elimination)	=	God's love is infinite ↓
V Development of 'Dieu est éternel' **2 varied statements of:** **'le Père puissant' + 'Notre Père'**		
VI Final theme: 'Dieu est amour'	=	'God *is* love.' (1 Jn.4:8)

Figure 8.6   Music and theology in the fifth meditation

───────────

38   William J. Hill, *The Three-Personed God* (Washington, DC: Catholic University of America Press, 1982), pp. 78–9.

In Charles's own words:

> God is incomparable, is transcendent, is that about whom nothing exact or
> exhaustive can be said, is not only the principal cause of all that exists, but is
> also love; love that is an internal movement, that is an experience of giving, love
> that is joy, happiness, life. Yes, to us, our God is not an immobile God, is not a
> supreme cause ... our God is Father, Son and Holy Spirit who love one another
> and who want to lead us in their love.

In the theology of both Richard of St Victor and St Thomas Aquinas, relationality
was the key concept in their Trinitarian doctrines. However, the principal difference
between those doctrines is that St Thomas's concept of relationality is rooted in the
metaphysical concept of being, while Richard's concept of relationality is rooted in
the mystical concept of love.[39] Although Messiaen's *Méditations sur le mystère de
la Sainte Trinité* certainly contain elements of Aquinas's theology, the theological
message presented at the culmination of the most important meditation – and
surely, therefore, the overarching message of the entire work – is 'God is love'.
This is a direct quotation from scripture, rather than a quotation from a systematic
theologian.[40] In terms of systematic theology, however, the emphasis on the three-
personed God as love ultimately depends on the Trinitarian doctrine of Richard of
St Victor, as set forth in Mgr Charles's sermon at the Trinité in 1967.[41]

Speaking to Claude Samuel about the *Méditations* and the event at the Trinité in
November 1967, Messiaen said, 'It was from that sermon and those improvisations
that the work we're speaking of was born'.[42] The findings in this chapter serve to
support the composer's statement and so it can be said of the origins of Messiaen's
Méditations that 'in the beginning was the Word'.[43]

---

[39]   For detailed discussion of the Trinitarian doctrines of both theologians, see ibid.

[40]   1 John 4:8.

[41]   Richard of St Victor's Trinitarian doctrine influenced the Franciscan tradition
through the writings of St Bonaventure (1217–74). (I. C. Brady, 'St. Bonaventure', in
New Catholic Encyclopaedia, Vol.2 (New York: McGraw Hill, 1967), p 661.) As anyone
familiar with Messiaen's life and music will know, the composer was deeply influenced by
Franciscan spirituality.

[42]   *Music and Color*, p. 125.

[43]   John 1:1.

Intermède

Chapter 9

Yvonne Loriod as Source and Influence

Christopher Dingle

Friday 28 June 1957 is unlikely to feature prominently in history books. It is not going to go down in infamy, either politically or musically. Britain was nearing the end of a heat-wave, which may explain in part the pitifully small audience of two to three dozen that attended a concert in St Michael-le-Belfrey, a small church that nestles in the shadow of York Minster. There was just one piece on the programme, Messiaen's *Vingt Regards*, and the pianist, as in all of the early performances, was Yvonne Loriod. As Colin Mason noted in the *Manchester Guardian*, Hans Hess, the director of the York Festival, 'needed not merely courage but a very cool nerve indeed to put this before a festival audience'.[1] While the meagre audience may not have done much for festival finances, the concert still reaped a significant dividend for it marked a key moment in the reception of Messiaen's music in Britain. Until this point, reaction in the mainstream press tended to be hostile or, at best, a grudging acknowledgement of Messiaen's technical skills strongly tempered by overt distaste for the results. A significant portion of the small audience at the York performance of *Vingt Regards* numbered critics, one or two doubtless begrudging missing the evening sunshine in order to fulfil their duties. And yet, this little known event was the first in Britain where Messiaen's music received broadly positive, even enthusiastic coverage.

Two things are striking about the York concert; it happened far from the London bubble and Messiaen did not attend the concert. It may be that the first of these was actually advantageous, a break from the ordinary making the critics more open to the extraordinary. Messiaen's absence, though, deprived the concert of the added frisson that a living, breathing composer brings to an event, whether an established figure or one still forging a reputation. Moreover, given that Messiaen was the kind of composer for whom there were no unimportant performances, and this appears to have been the first complete performance of the *Vingt Regards* in the UK, it might be thought surprising that he was not in York to ensure that all went well. However, on the latter point, he would have been entirely confident for, as he later put it:

> I have an extraordinary, marvellous, inspired interpreter whose technical brilliance and playing – by turns powerful, light, moving and coloured – suit my

---

[1] Colin Mason, 'Messiaen's "Vingt Regards Sur L'enfant Jesus" [sic]: Yvonne Loriod at York Festival', *Manchester Guardian* (1 July 1957): p. 7.

works exactly, an exceptional pianist who understands and knows my music as though she had written it, and who plays it like no one else plays it or ever will play it: Yvonne Loriod.[2]

Loriod was neither the first to perform Messiaen's music regularly nor to inspire him, but she rapidly became his greatest evangelist. Aside from the composer himself, no-one knew his music better; the York concert could not have been in safer hands.

Even before her death in 2010, it was intended that there should be some consideration in this book of Yvonne Loriod's role. She is an essential point of reference for the study of Messiaen by performers and scholars alike. With her passing, it is possible to take stock of the totality of her contribution. Nonetheless, while there may be an inevitable undercurrent of tribute, this is neither an extended obituary nor a comprehensive examination of Yvonne Loriod's life and activities either as a pianist or as companion of the composer. Rather, the intention is to consider some of the ways in which she was important both for Messiaen himself and for those studying him, to view her specifically through the lens of this book and explore her role as a profound influence upon Messiaen, and a source of insight and information about him. As a consequence, what follows falls into two broad sections, first exploring Loriod's profound influence upon Messiaen, then her position as a source of insight and information about him. In terms of influence it starts with Loriod's pianism and the way it opened out Messiaen's compositional thought, before going on to consider the love between them, its implications, ways in which it is manifest in his works and the ways in which she supported him. As a source, Loriod is considered as a teacher, then as the first custodian of her husband's legacy, becoming an invaluable source of materials and memories. If some of what follows comes across as a defence of Loriod, it is a reaction to the rather narrow picture that is often given of her, and an attempt to understand better the woman who is an essential part of understanding the composer. Messiaen and Loriod formed one of the supreme musical partnerships, arguably running even deeper and bearing more substantial fruit than the oft-made comparison with Robert and Clara Schumann. It may seem odd, then, but the first point that needs to be made – and possibly the most essential – is Loriod's pedigree in music other than Messiaen's, for this is vital for understanding her artistic importance to him.

Given that in later years Messiaen and Loriod were constant companions at events, increasingly so as his health became less secure, it is easy to forget that this was not always the case. At the time of her York performance of *Vingt Regards*, Messiaen was nearly a thousand miles to the south, exploring the Cirque de Mourèze, setting of 'Le Merle de roche' from *Catalogue d'oiseaux*.[3] It is true that Messiaen attended many of Loriod's performances, and they spent much time together by the late 1950s, but, especially before their marriage in 1961, her career

---

[2]   *Music and Color*, p. 202. Translation emended.

[3]   PHNS, p. 223.

was not inextricably linked to his. She did not appear as a fully formed Messiaen specialist who occasionally played other music. Rather, it was her performances of a wide range of repertoire allied to her exceptional, unflappable advocacy for the most complex avant-garde scores that inspired Messiaen to write for her.

It is worth emphasizing the range of Loriod's repertoire and the high regard in which her performances of it were held. By the age of 14, a few years before she met Messiaen, her repertoire included the 48 Preludes and Fugues of Bach's *Well-Tempered Clavier*, the 32 Beethoven sonatas and many of Mozart's works, and she soon added the major works of Chopin, Schumann, Debussy and Ravel. This repertoire came thanks to Loriod's regular performances at the Parisian salon, on the rue Blanche, of her Austrian godmother and first teacher, Nelly Eminger-Sivade. As Loriod's parents, Gaston and Simone, had little money, Mme Sivade gave Yvonne free lessons, and subsequently paid for her lessons with Lazare-Lévy. The discography that forms the appendix to this book provides a limited insight into this. While it is increasingly dominated by Messiaen's music, there is also Bach, Mozart, Beethoven, Chopin, Liszt, Mendelssohn, Schumann, Albéniz, Falla, Debussy, Stravinsky, Schoenberg, Berg, Webern, Barraqué, Boulez and Chaynes. Nor are these incidental pieces. Beethoven's 'Hammerklavier' Sonata (op. 106), Liszt's B Minor Sonata, the Debussy Études and Albéniz's *Ibéria* are significant undertakings, and that is before even considering Boulez's Second Sonata. It is well-known that Loriod gave the first performance of the Boulez and also continued to play it, but it is less appreciated that, along with Messiaen, she played a significant part in ensuring the riches of *Ibéria* were brought to the attention of the post-war generation of French musicians. As for her Beethoven pedigree, on her death Rob Cowan observed that Loriod 'recorded one of the truly great "Hammerklaviers"'.[4]

Nonetheless, the recordings only provide a glimpse of her range, which extended back to Scarlatti and also took in figures such as Prokofiev, Bartók, Tcherepnin and Gilbert Amy. In Charles Timbrell's book on French pianism, Pierre Réach recalls that:

> one of her most extraordinary recitals consisted of music featuring fugues: some Bach and Mozart, the Beethoven 'Hammerklavier' Sonata, Franck's *Prélude, choral et fugue* and two fugues from Messiaen's *Vingt Regards sur l'Enfant-Jésus*. … Certainly her playing of Schumann's Fantasy was different from that of other pianists, especially of the old school.[5]

She may be regarded as the benchmark in Messiaen, but in the earlier part of her career, she was a point of reference for other composers, so that a critic for *The Times* noted in a 1966 recital by Francoise Thinat that 'one was reminded

---

[4]   Personal communication.

[5]   Charles Timbrell, *French Pianism: A Historical Perspective*, 2nd edn (London: Kahn and Averill, 1999), p. 168.

of Yvonne Loriod's playing of Schumann'.[6] The French première of Bartók's Second Piano Concerto, widely regarded as one of the most challenging pieces in the repertoire, underlines why she was in demand by numerous composers aside from Messiaen. First Monique Haas then Samson François withdrew from the performance, protesting that the work was too difficult to learn in the available time. The 21-year-old Loriod stepped in and mastered the concerto in just eight days.[7] As she later recalled: 'I was very young and, well, obviously it hurts the fingers, the second concerto, so I put the little things for calluses on my thumbs and I played it anyway.'[8] Such an approach was clearly something of a leitmotif. After the first British performance of *Turangalîla*, there was a gathering at the house of Felix Aprahamian at which Loriod played the entirety of Boulez's Second Sonata. As Alexander Goehr has recalled, the performance was, 'in the confines of the drawing-room, a stupendous noise. I was, for the second time that evening, completely overwhelmed, not least because when she had finished playing, the piano was covered with blood.'[9]

Loriod strove to maintain her non-Messiaen repertoire throughout her career in concert, for instance performing a Mozart concerto (K. 503) alongside *Oiseaux exotiques* in a concert with Musica Aeterna in New York in October 1970. While Boulez at one point demanded that Loriod stop playing Chopin (she refused),[10] her philosophy, conveyed to generations of students (see below), was:

> Do not deprive yourself. Because when you play Schumann well, you learn to play Mozart, too. When you play Boulez well, you find fingerings to play Schumann. Everything fits together. The role of an interpreter is not to specialize. But you must deliver works to the public. The public chooses afterwards.[11]

Despite this, it was inevitable that, as her name became increasingly associated with that of Messiaen, as the number of pieces he wrote for her grew in number and as performances of his music increased in frequency, Loriod's position as his most authoritative interpreter would crowd out opportunities to perform other repertoire. There is a strong case for saying that Loriod's love for, and devotion to, Messiaen undermined her broader career and distorted perceptions of her as a pianist. That is not to suggest that Messiaen's music held anything other than the central, most important place in her career. Rather, in as much as it implies

---

[6]   [Unsigned], 'Japanese Baritone's Lieder Recital', *The Times* (28 November 1966): p. 6.

[7]   PHNS, p. 94, n. 38.

[8]   Bruno Serrou (dir.), 'Yvonne Loriod-Messiaen', interview (video), INA Musique Mémoires series, rec. 12–13 September 2002, Paris, INA, INA video stream, available at www.ina.fr/grands-entretiens/video/Musique/Loriod.

[9]   Alexander Goehr, *Finding the Key: Selected Writings*, ed. Derek Puffett (London: Faber and Faber, 1998), p. 44.

[10]   Serrou, 'Yvonne Loriod-Messiaen', video stream.

[11]   Ibid.

an exclusion of other repertoire, Loriod saw herself as a specialist neither of Messiaen nor of contemporary music in general. This is clear from the fact that, as well as Messiaen, the repertoire explored in the master classes in François Manceaux's film *Yvonne Loriod: Pianist and Teacher* includes Mozart, Beethoven and Chopin.[12]

The initial, and perhaps the most profound, influence that Loriod had on Messiaen's music was the removal of technical barriers and, hence, conceptual limitations. Some composers need tight restrictions, Stravinsky being an obvious example. While Messiaen was not averse to such creative spurs – hence the modes of limited transpositions and non-retrogradable rhythms – he thrived on the blank canvass in a way few of his contemporaries did. Koussevitsky's commission for *Turangalîla* – 'choose as many instruments as you desire, write a work as long as you wish, and in the style you want'[13] – is the best-known example of this, but few of Messiaen's major compositions had significant parameters imposed on them from without. Even when they did, as with *Couleurs de la Cité céleste* or *Vingt Regards*, Messiaen went beyond the stated instrumentation or required number of pieces. Yvonne Loriod provided Messiaen with an instrumental blank canvass. As Peter Hill recalled in conversation with Loriod:

> Messiaen more than once apologized to me for the fact that his piano music was so difficult to play, but he said that no matter how difficult a passage was that he placed in front of you [Loriod], you always seemed to master it immediately and without any problems, and that he'd therefore never had to worry about the difficulty of his music for piano.[14]

It is worth remembering that the piano was Messiaen's first instrument, and he was more than proficient, having *Gaspard de la nuit* in his repertoire. Whether in the *Préludes* or in the accompaniments to chamber works and the song cycles, Messiaen's piano writing before he began writing for Loriod in 1943 is challenging, but there is the sense of it inhabiting the realm of his own pianistic abilities. It is tempting to say that it was Loriod's facility with difficult repertoire that made the difference, but numerous students have testified to Messiaen's own facility in such pieces. Rather, it appears to have been Loriod's easy mastery of the most demanding works. Messiaen outlined the difference in relation to *Ibéria*: 'I've often played and replayed the twelve pieces contained in its four books – especially "Almería", "El Polo", and "Lavapies" – without attaining perfection, for they're so terribly difficult: I'll never be able to play them like Yvonne Loriod.'[15]

---

[12]   François Manceaux, *Yvonne Loriod: Pianist & Teacher – A Film by François Manceaux*, TV programme filmed 1990–91, Harmonia Mundi DVD HMD 9909032.

[13]   *Music and Color*, p. 156.

[14]   Peter Hill, 'Interview with Yvonne Loriod', in Peter Hill (ed.), *The Messiaen Companion* (London: Faber and Faber, 1995), p. 288.

[15]   *Music and Color*, p. 114.

The piano works written for Loriod break through that barrier of the romantic piano tradition in which Messiaen's fingers were immersed (and which is discussed by Caroline Rae later in this volume) and ruthlessly take compositional ideas to their logical imperatives. These traits can be seen throughout *Visions de l'Amen*, and especially in the fifth movement where Messiaen's part (piano II) carries the musical line, while Loriod's part (piano I) flits irregularly, with birdsong that refuses to be caged, seemingly indifferent to any compositional or pianistic niceties. As Peter Hill has observed:

> The writing for piano 1 [of *Visions de l'Amen*] – Loriod's part – tells us what first caused Messiaen to be dazzled by her playing. Her passage work must have been sparkling, she was adept at juggling complexities (rhythmic canons in three layers, for example) and – a particular trademark – she had a remarkable capacity to fire off streams of rapid chords.[16]

Disregard for the physical logic of the piano is taken further in the *Vingt Regards*, with techniques such as *agrandissement asymétrique*. In 'L'Échange' it is awkward, but manageable, for the tempo is moderate. The coda to 'Les Anges' is far more challenging, while in 'Par Lui tout à été fait', awkward leaps and contortions are required at speed and in a manner that leaves little room manoeuvre.[17] By the time that he came to write 'Le Loriot', Messiaen relishes Loriod's skills in the two Fauvettes des jardins singing at the centre of the movement. The individual lines of this duet are challenging in themselves, but putting them together creates a punishing, disjunct counterpoint in two distinct voices.

Allied to Loriod's supreme technique was her absence of fear. That might appear to be a given for someone with her abilities, but as many composers will testify, there are numerous performers who are great technicians, yet struggle when faced with new ways of writing. It can take a certain kind of openness and daring to embark on new works. Then again, as a teenager in occupied Paris, Loriod inserted a Mendelssohn *Song Without Words* 'as a prank' into a Bach concert packed with German officers.[18] After his death, Loriod identified 12 ways in which Messiaen enriched piano writing. Some of these are specifically related to purely technical matters, such as the use of the thumb, but others are at least as much to do with mindset (typically, she neglects to mention that she made them possible).[19] That technique alone is not enough was demonstrated when Loriod was preparing for the first performance of *Réveil des oiseaux*. Faced with

---

[16]   PHNS, p. 123.

[17]   Arguably Loriod's abilities similarly enabled Boulez to write for the piano with complete technical freedom.

[18]   Bruno Serrou, 'Yvonne Loriod-Messiaen', video stream.

[19]   Yvonne Loriod-Messiaen, 'Étude sur l'Œuvre Pianistique d'Olivier Messiaen', in Catherine Massip (ed.), *Portrait(s) d'Olivier Messiaen* (Paris: Bibliothèque Nationale de France, 1996), pp. 75–158.

a work that so fundamentally reinvented the notion of what constituted a piece of orchestral music, even she, despite having already performed numerous new works by a remarkable diversity of composers, struggled at first to grasp what Messiaen was trying to achieve. She later recalled:

> I wasn't familiar with birds, so I invited Messiaen to my little studio. ... So he comes. He takes the score and I play it, very proud to have gotten through it without fault. Then I look at him holding his score. He starts to frown. He says, 'I'm sorry that's not it at all'. 'What do you mean? I didn't make a single mistake. Where did I make a mistake?' 'No, the notes are correct but the timbre is all wrong.' He said, 'To play this really well you have to go into nature'. I go to my mum's and say, 'Mum this man's a real pain. Can you pick me up at 6 am and drive me out to St-Germain [-en-Laye] or Orgeval or wherever the birds are? I want to play it well, but I'm way off track, I'm completely lost'. So my mother took me to Orgeval and I understood.[20]

When next she played to Messiaen, he was in raptures.

The conceptual openness of a performer like Loriod is invaluable for new music, while her zeal for all manner of music would have heartened the pedagogue in Messiaen who similarly taught repertoire from a wide range of periods, places and species. Such enthusiasm was central to her strength as an advocate for composers in general, and Messiaen in particular. Faced with a dishearteningly small audience at the York performance of *Vingt Regards*, Loriod clearly did not simply go through the motions. As Colin Mason put it in the *Manchester Guardian*, 'if anybody could make us enjoy it all it would be Mme Loriod'.[21] Similarly, Ernest Bradbury, writing in *Musical Times*, commented that Loriod's real achievement 'was to persuade us of the worth of this piano writing as music ... the devotion and insight of the interpreter on this occasion were surely obvious to all'.[22]

Nonetheless, if it were simply a matter of being an outstanding pianist, Loriod's influence would not be so clearly imprinted on Messiaen's output. There is also the matter of the love that flourished between them. It would be foolhardy to try to be too specific in terms of dates in trying to chart their personal development of love, for it was never simply Messiaen and Loriod, but also, of course, Claire Delbos, his first wife. It is doubtful that they could recall with any certainty what was implicit or explicit themselves even if they were around and inclined to discuss such matters. Loriod's presence clearly energized Messiaen, but the complexity of emotions felt by him in the midst of what can only be viewed as a relentlessly

---

[20]   Olivier Mille (dir.), 'Birds, Nature', filmed in 1997 and included as a DVD extra in Olivier Mille (dir.), *Olivier Messiaen: La Liturgie de Cristal*, DVD, Ideale Audience International DVD9DS44.

[21]   Mason, 'Messiaen's "Vingt Regards Sur L'enfant Jesus"': p. 7.

[22]   Ernest Bradbury, 'The York Festival 1957', *Musical Times* 98/1375 (August 1957): p. 445.

tragic period of his life must remain a matter of conjecture. Moreover, it should never be forgotten that, until Claire's death, which was not expected, there was no end in sight to this double separation between Messiaen and the two women that he loved.

Loriod clearly added a moral complication for Messiaen, the implications of which will be parsed probably for as long as his music is discussed. It is only possible to speculate, though, whether Messiaen would have been as receptive to – in need of – Loriod's talents had Claire remained healthy. The tendency is to dwell on the difficulties Messiaen's forbidden desire for Loriod brought, and their reflection in the works of the mid-1940s to the late-1950s. However, what would Messiaen have written in these years had he not encountered Loriod? Would the exuberance of *Turangalîla* have replaced the dark intensity of *Harawi* without Loriod? Might the *Catalogue d'oiseaux* have been an organ cycle or even an orchestral work? Conversely, would some of the pieces in *Catalogue d'oiseaux* have been written without Loriod being on hand to drive Messiaen to remote parts of the French countryside? Crucially, would Messiaen simply have composed less music without the positive creative spur of Loriod's pianism?

In terms of the last question, it is worth noting that between 1943 and his death Messiaen wrote 34 works. Nine of these are dedicated to Loriod (those with an asterisk have additional dedicatees):

> *Visions de l'Amen*
> *Vingt Regards sur l'Enfant-Jésus*
> *Réveil des oiseaux**
> *Oiseaux exotiques*
> *Catalogue d'oiseaux**
> *Sept Haïkaï**
> *La Fauvette des jardins*
> *Petites Esquisses d'oiseaux*
> *Concert à quatre**

To this litany should be added a further eight works that, though not explicitly dedicated to Loriod, include a solo piano part written for her:

> *Trois Petites Liturgies de la Présence Divine*
> *Turangalîla-Symphonie*
> *Couleurs de la Cité céleste*
> *La Transfiguration de Notre-Seigneur Jésus-Christ*
> *Des Canyons aux étoiles...*
> *Un Vitrail et des oiseaux*
> *La Ville d'En-Haut*
> *Pièce (pour piano et quatuor à cordes)*

This substantial body of solo and concertante works stands as a testimony not just for Loriod's remarkable pianism, but also for the love Messiaen felt for her. Some may have wished that there was not quite so much piano in his output. For instance, Heinrich Strobel was insistent that there should be no piano (and no ondes) when he commissioned *Chronochromie*. The piano is also striking by its absence in *Un Sourire* and *Éclairs*, and this has a significant impact on the perception of these works, not least in the oft-noted affinity with the spirit of Messiaen's early (pre-Loriod) orchestral works. Nonetheless, in the compositional malaise he felt in 1985, it is doubtful anyone other than Loriod could have prompted him to set pen to manuscript paper. The resulting *Petites Esquisses d'oiseaux* are not only charming works in their own right, but set the tone for Messiaen's last creative burst.

The influence is directly musical in some of the works from the late 1940s and 1950s. Fragments from *Turangalîla* turn up in *Cinq Rechants*, a work with no explicit connection to Loriod, yet suffused with implicit reference to Messiaen's hidden feelings for his beloved (though it should be remembered that the object of his desire is ambiguous). Some of these fragments, with others, turn up in *Cantéyodjayâ* and return, rather more explicitly, in 'Le Loriot', in which the song of the bird is transformed into a love song in the closing pages.

For Messiaen, that Loriod's name was a homonym for Loriot was a sign of providence. For several years after they first met, his diaries refer to 'Mlle Loriot' and Messiaen was keen that she should retain her bird name after they married:

> She's called Madame Messiaen, but I was the one who wanted her to keep the name of Loriod because it's a name I like and it's a bird. For me she is Yvonne Loriod, she isn't Yvonne Messiaen. I got to know her as Yvonne Loriod, with her bird name, and for me she remains Yvonne Loriod.[23]

Unsurprisingly, Loriots always get special treatment in Messiaen's works. The large bird concert in 'Le Prêche aux oiseaux' is a notable example. Deep within the most complex part of this marathon opera, Messiaen pays tribute to his wife by posing the performers a particular challenge with the song of the Loriot. It is one of the *hors tempo* birds and is scored for three horns, crotales, glockenspiel and vibraphone. In other words, this idiosyncratic sextet has to fly free of the barlines, playing independently of the conductor's beat, yet remain together. Even when no piano was involved, Loriod was the catalyst for Messiaen to push techniques further.

Aside from her pianism, perhaps Loriod's greatest influence was that she enabled Messiaen simply to be. The use of the word 'devotion' in the *Musical Times* review of the York concert is apt, for Loriod essentially placed herself at the service of Messiaen's music. She provided practical support for an impractical man, created a stable and orderly bedrock so that he could concentrate on composing. It is only necessary to read Berlioz's memoirs to understand the importance of this. From housekeeping to booking train and plane tickets, there were numerous

---

[23] Manceaux, *Yvonne Loriod: Pianist & Teacher,* DVD.

small ways in which Loriod cleared the path for Messiaen. In addition to driving Messiaen to his birdsong trips, she made the tape recordings that would later be compared with the live transcriptions. It was invaluable that she fully understood the imperatives and demands of a professional musical life. As time went on, while Messiaen maintained his compositional secrecy, Loriod was able to assist with proofreading and, notably, preparing the vocal scores for *Saint François*. She had studied composition with Milhaud, and Messiaen encouraged her to carry on composing, though the demands of her performing career made it difficult to complete pieces; unlike him, she evidently did not feel compelled to compose. Nor should the emotional support provided by Loriod be overlooked. There must have been numerous undocumented times when this was vital, but few could have been as significant as when Messiaen fell into a depression while trying to complete *Saint François d'Assise*. It is doubtful the opera would have been completed if Loriod had not been there for Messiaen.

Now that the notion of 'the great man' is treated with scepticism, her devotion to his career may seem rather subservient, and it is true that there remained an echo of the initial student and master relationship between Loriod and Messiaen. However, there was also an aspect of Loriod mothering Messiaen, attempting, for instance, to ensure that he ate properly, trying to temper his delight in cakes and other treats.[24] In reality, they were a formidable team, each supporting and enhancing the other's professional activities. In modern parlance they might be termed a power couple were it not so patently absurd a concept in their case. They simply enjoyed being together and increasingly arranged their lives so that their concert and pedagogical activities complemented each other. As such, Loriod's influence endured until the day Messiaen died.

While he was still alive, the composer was naturally regarded as the prime source on his music, and it was easy to view him as the only authoritative one. However, for decades, Loriod's extensive teaching had provided a significant additional vein of insight. This is not to overlook her extensive recordings; these are invaluable, and become even more so as time passes. However, the more ephemeral direct source of Loriod's teaching and playing will have been of far greater import for the pianists involved. Nicholas Angelich has noted her matter-of-fact, enabling approach:

> Madame Loriod has a pragmatic, down-to-earth approach as a teacher, and her positive, encouraging attitude benefited me very much …. Her comments were always expressed in simple, clear, straightforward terms. She had a demystifying approach to teaching, unlike some professors. She gave me confidence, but she also instilled in me the need to have a clear idea about the concept of the piece and the right sound.[25]

---

[24]   See, for instance, note 2 of Anne-Sylvie Barthel-Calvet's chapter 'The Messiaen-Xenakis Conjunction' in *Messiaen Perspectives 2*.

[25]   Timbrell, *French Pianism*, p. 169.

In the case of Paul Crossley, it was not contemporary music, but his playing of Mozart in a chance encounter that brought him to Loriod's attention. Crossley was in Oxford and, needing a piano to prepare for a concerto performance with the Northern Sinfonia, found a decent instrument in the Playhouse Theatre: 'Here am I, practising this Mozart when suddenly the orchestral accompaniment sets off on another piano from behind the safety curtain. It's Yvonne Loriod and she says "Will you come to Paris to study with me?"'[26] Like Messiaen, Loriod was interested in talented individuals and would chivvy and chide the necessary authorities to remove obstacles standing in their way. So, for Crossley, the French government found themselves providing one more scholarship than expected.

While Messiaen coached numerous pianists on various of his works, Loriod ensured that his music was a natural part of the extensive and inclusive approach to repertoire that she preached. Once again, her authority in Messiaen's music was reinforced for pianists by her achievements in other music. Just like his teaching, she would draw attention to the links between apparently disparate works. Pierre Réach recalls that:

> She didn't take time to play much at our lessons, although she demonstrated passages and talked a lot about different concepts. She taught the widest possible repertoire, from Bach through the whole nineteenth century, to Russian music and the most modern works. There were no barriers for her. She expressed her ideas very logically and simply, and she communicated warmth and friendliness at lessons.[27]

Similarly, in conversation with Loriod in François Manceaux's film, Roger Muraro fondly remembered her range of reference:

> Muraro: Then you discussed that famous passage in [Chopin's] Barcarolle where the right-hand melody keeps returning to the same notes harmonized in a different way ... and you had an extraordinary term to describe it, you called it 'musical litanies'.

> Loriod: But that's Messiaen's term, 'harmonic litanies', just as you say 'St Francis, pray for us, St Damien, pray for us, St Jacques, pray for us'. It's a really lovely term of Messiaen's, because the melody is the same, but the harmonies change ....

> Muraro: There's one thing that's always struck me, it's the references you make to support the opinions you express. I think of Pelléas for Debussy's Études. I think of Bach for that famous prelude [plays the opening of the E♭ Minor Prelude, BWV 853] ... which was so terribly hard to get right. I still remember

---

[26]   Paul Crossley, unpublished interview with the author, London, 4 September 1996.

[27]   Timbrell, *French Pianism*, p. 168.

the allusions to the Récit of Nicolas de Grigny you told me about. Of course, I rushed out to buy Grigny's Organ Book to get some idea of what you meant.

Loriod: But that comes from Messiaen's class. When I was his harmony pupil, he always quoted Debussy to us, saying 'Listen, go and see Signac, go to the Louvre, otherwise you can't understand these harmonies'.[28]

Equally striking, and typical, is the way that Loriod's response to Muraro's attempts to compliment her is always to pass the credit to Messiaen. This playing down of her own contribution was a persistent leitmotif. For instance, asked by Peter Hill to say something about her own background, she replied: 'Well, I'll keep it short because it's not very interesting.'[29]

This selflessness also characterized her approach after Messiaen's death. She evidently felt a deep responsibility to do the best for his music and his memory. To start with, there were significant loose ends, notably the preparations for the first performances of *Éclairs sur l'Au-Delà...*, completing the *Concert à quatre*, shepherding the scores of works from *Un Vitrail et des oiseaux* onwards through the publication process and the herculean task of gathering together the material for the *Traité*. Amidst all this, she was still performing and making recordings, giving master classes and dealing with an ever-increasing postbag.

There are some clear instances where Loriod was poorly advised or, at least, that advice was lacking where it was clearly needed. This is most apparent in editions of certain works. The Durand edition of *Pièce (pour le Tombeau de Paul Dukas)* is a case in point. It contains differences of dynamics, performance markings and ties from the original edition that appeared in *Revue musicale*, all of which are eminently sensible and may have been conveyed by Messiaen himself to Loriod. She was not an academic and she had no training as an editor (or, if she did, it was many decades out of date), so was doubtless unaware of the conventions in place by the early 1990s. That being the case, Durand should have provided assistance so that proper editorial notes could be provided. Similarly, her account of the completion of the *Concert à quatre* in the preface to the score is commendably open and straightforward. Nonetheless, Leduc should have provided editorial assistance for a full critical edition. Ideally, where the more significant interventions needed to be made, an indication of the source materials would have been given (in the manner of Deryck Cooke's performing edition of Mahler's Tenth Symphony), or facsimiles could have been included.[30] As for the *Feuillets inédits*, Loriod clearly was trying to find a useful way to make these bits and pieces available, but it is overstating the case to give Messiaen as the composer without any qualification.

---

28   Manceaux, *Yvonne Loriod: Pianist & Teacher*, DVD.

29   Hill, 'Interview with Yvonne Loriod', p. 288.

30   For details of some of the key alterations made in completing the *Concert à quatre* from Messiaen's short score, see Chapter 24 of Christopher Dingle, *Messiaen's Final Works* (Farnham: Ashgate, 2013).

Again, Loriod was open about how the pieces were put together, and, as ever, she doubtless did not want to take any credit when the harmonies, melodies and rhythms are entirely Messiaen's. However, Durand should have insisted that the work be described as 'Messiaen, arranged by Yvonne Loriod-Messiaen'. Beyond such omissions, it is a pity that neither publisher grabbed the opportunity to create a 'Loriod edition' of Messiaen's piano works.

For scholars, Loriod became the primary oral and written source. Her prefaces for the posthumously published scores of *Éclairs*, the *Concert à quatre* and *Le Tombeau resplendissant* are invaluable. Similarly, interviews, such as the one with Peter Hill in *The Messiaen Companion*,[31] filled in substantial blanks in the knowledge of numerous events, while Hill and Simeone's seminal *Messiaen* repeatedly notes that key pieces of information were conveyed by Loriod. In this role, she shared many traits with Messiaen. Like him, she was happy to provide much information, telling the story as best she could. Like him, there were certain favoured anecdotes. Like him, and any witness, different accounts of the same event did not always match, and she sometimes misremembered. Like him, some of her stories seemed to have grown in the re-telling, conveying the essence of what happened rather than the reality. While such traits might occasionally be frustrating for scholars, they merely reflect the fact that Messiaen was her hero; why should or would she be anything other than entirely subjective?

It is clear, too, that some areas of Messiaen's life had remained essentially a closed book to her. Uncovering his activities in the 1930s was as much an exploration for Loriod as it was for scholars, and the same could be said of the various compositional drafts and sketches. She donated some material to the Bibliothèque National de France relatively soon after Messiaen's death, and slowly began making steps towards making other things available. This culminated in providing access to Messiaen's personal archive for Peter Hill and Nigel Simeone, leading to their seminal book on the composer. Loriod made available photographs, letters, draft scores, Messiaen's birdsong *cahiers* and his pocket diaries. The generosity of this step was remarkable and should be underlined, for there were those who insinuated, before her death, that Loriod was an obstacle to research. Almost inevitably, as scholars, we tend to dwell on what has been held back, for there is always the desire for more documentation, for further evidence. It is true, also, that she refused some requests that might have seemed reasonable. Nonetheless, it is easy to forget that she had a personal and private life with Messiaen as well as the publicly visible one, that the rue Marcadet was her home, that its contents also related to her life, that she was managing everything without the support of the man she loved. With myriad enquiries and demands from countless strangers, trying to parse what was significant from what was superficial must have been near impossible at times. Furthermore, given that, sadly, there are those who are less than scrupulous, discerning who to trust could not have been easy. At times she must have felt very alone. That Loriod threw open the doors far more than might

---

[31]   Hill, 'Interview with Yvonne Loriod', pp. 283–303.

have been expected or hoped was truly remarkable. It may have been a difficult step, but it would benefit the cause of Messiaen's music, and what was right for him was right for her. That was her yardstick throughout and, ultimately, it is why she was, is and will remain of paramount importance. He was everything to her, and on this she was absolutely emphatic:

> I've always loved Messiaen, and everyone feels it in my way of playing Messiaen, in my way of playing Mozart. Let me tell you that Yvonne Loriod does not exist without Messiaen. I was entirely shaped by the teaching of Messiaen, the music of Messiaen, the love of Messiaen, with a large M, period. That's Loriod. Steeped in Messiaen, like you put a special sauce on a beautiful roast. I tell you, Loriod doesn't exist without Messiaen. Is that clear?[32]

---

[32] Serrou, 'Yvonne Loriod-Messiaen', video stream.

PART II
Influences

Perspectives on Influences

Christopher Dingle and Robert Fallon

Discussing the influences on any artist is a tricky business. Establishing musical influence is especially so, for it can be like trying to capture fog, the hard evidence melting away the closer it is examined. Moreover it takes myriad, unpredictable forms. Parsing what derives and does not derive from one composer or another is hard to do with any certainty, for although the analogy of fingerprints is often used, the reality is often less specific and closer to sharing eye or hair colour. Identifying a composer's use of models, or even quotations, is one reasonably clear form of establishing influence, but even here the presence of a model or quotation does not of itself provide an indication of its function or meaning in relation to its source. While such direct allusions are natural and vital pieces of evidence, they do not tend to address broader notions of influence, a deeper entrenchment of an aspect of one artist's aesthetic in that of another.

For these and other reasons, there are critics who are extremely sceptical of such discussions or who even prefer to dismiss notions of influence from the equation altogether, as outlined in the introduction to Robert Fallon's commentary on the tombeaux of Messiaen. The view tends to be that, as influence is difficult to prove decisively and cannot be resolutely pinned down in a causal path of 'a' influencing 'b' on this basis in a clear-cut, exclusive manner, then it is too dangerous to allow into the mix at all. This is the sterile laboratory approach to music. However, just as *texttreue* fundamentalism in performance has increasingly come to be seen as providing an unnecessarily partial view of the interpretative act, this parsimonious view of the quest for musical understanding should be challenged if it is preached as the one true way. While concentrating on one or two lines of influence does not give a full view of the creative act, ignoring them can be equally partial. The fact is that creative acts are messy, complex things with numerous elements feeding into them. While care and rigour are needed, it is not merely taking the easy option, but can also be actively misleading to stick to what is neat and tidy. There is immense value to viewing a composer or a piece of music through the magnifying glass of carefully controlled intellectual enquiry, like butterflies pinned in the glass cases of museums. However, full understanding of those butterflies comes from combining such scrutiny with observation of them interacting with their far-from-sterile environment, and the same can be said of creative acts. It may be difficult to follow and hard to describe, but a seasoned observer can learn and convey much from sifting through the chaotic melee, sometimes even making an informed hypothesis for the catalyst that marked the otherwise bemusing transformation from caterpillar into butterfly.

The relationship of sources to influence maps onto that of art to artist. Sources feed the artwork as influences feed the artist; sources tend to be local and specific while influences tend to involve entire composers or broader cultural movements affecting part of the artist's aesthetic identity. Such relationships are, perhaps, the messiest, but the most interesting of all for scholars wishing to get their hands dirty.

When it comes to Messiaen, ignoring influence would be especially absurd, for he openly discussed it, both in terms of his own music and as the foundation of his pedagogical approach. The major influences upon Messiaen have long been known as he happily acknowledged them in interviews and in *Technique*. For that reason, discussion of Messiaen's influence goes back some way.[1] However, it is

---

[1]   Some notable examinations of Messiaen's influences include: Julian Anderson, 'Messiaen and the Notion of Influence', *Tempo*, 63/247 (2009): pp. 2–18; Yves Balmer, 'Religious Literature in Messiaen's Personal Library', in Andrew Shenton (ed.), *Messiaen the Theologian* (Farnham: Ashgate, 2010); Siglind Bruhn, 'Traces of a Thomistic *De musica* in the Compositions of Olivier Messiaen', *Logos: A Journal of Catholic Thought and Culture*, 11/4 (2008): pp. 16–56; Jonathan Cross, *The Stravinsky Legacy* (Cambridge: Cambridge University Press, 1998); Christopher Dingle, 'La statue reste sur son piédestal: Messiaen's *La Transfiguration* and Vatican II', *Tempo*, 212 (April 2000): pp. 8–11; Robert Fallon, 'Two Paths to Paradise: Reform in Messiaen's *Saint François d'Assise*', in Robert Sholl (ed.), *Messiaen Studies* (Cambridge: Cambridge University Press, 2007); Robert Fallon, 'Birds, Beasts, and Bombs in Messiaen's Cold War Mass', *Journal of Musicology*, 26/2 (Spring 2009): pp. 175–204; Robert Fallon, 'La spiritualité gothique de Messiaen et le renouveau catholique', in Sylvain Caron and Michel Duchesneau (eds), *Musique, Art et Religion dans l'Entre-deux-guerres* (Lyon: Symétrie, 2009); Robert Fallon, 'Dante as Guide to Messiaen's Gothic Spirituality', in Andrew Shenton (ed.), *Messiaen the Theologian* (Farnham: Ashgate, 2010); Jane Fulcher, 'The Politics of Transcendence: Ideology in the Music of Messiaen in the 1930s', *The Musical Quarterly*, 86/3 (2002): pp. 449–71; Gareth Healy, 'Messiaen: Bibliophile', in Christopher Dingle and Nigel Simeone (eds), *Olivier Messiaen: Music, Art and Literature* (Aldershot: Ashgate, 2007); Karin Heller, 'Olivier Messiaen and Cardinal Jean-Marie Lustiger: Two Views of the Liturgical Reform according to the Second Vatican Council', in Andrew Shenton (ed.), *Messiaen the Theologian* (Farnham: Ashgate, 2010); Madeleine Hsu, *Olivier Messiaen, the Musical Mediator: A Study of the Influence of Liszt, Debussy, and Bartók* (Madison, NJ: Fairleigh Dickinson University Press, 1996); Matthew Schellhorn, '*Les Noces* and *Trois petites Liturgies*: An Assessment of Stravinsky's Influence on Messiaen', in Christopher Dingle and Nigel Simeone (eds), *Olivier Messiaen: Music, Art and Literature* (Aldershot: Ashgate, 2007); Stephen Schloesser, 'The Charm of Impossibilities: Mystic Surrealism as Contemplative Voluptuousness', in Andrew Shenton (ed.), *Messiaen the Theologian* (Farnham: Ashgate, 2010); Douglas Shadle, 'Messiaen's Relationship to Jacques Maritain's Musical Circle and Neo-Thomism', in Andrew Shenton (ed.), *Messiaen the Theologian* (Farnham: Ashgate, 2010); Robert Sholl, 'Love, Mad Love and the "*point sublime*": The Surrealist Poetics of Messiaen's *Harawi*', in Robert Sholl (ed.), *Messiaen Studies* (Cambridge: Cambridge University Press, 2007); Roger Smalley, 'Debussy and Messiaen', *Musical Times* 109/1500 (February 1968): pp. 128–31; Arnold Whittall, 'Messiaen and Twentieth-century Music', in Robert Sholl (ed.), *Messiaen Studies* (Cambridge: Cambridge University Press, 2007).

only in recent years that scholars have begun getting to grips with the extent of the influences, finding much deeper evidence for those mentioned by him, and also starting to look beyond his canonic frame of reference. There is much still to explore, with the impact of figures he identified, such as Villa-Lobos, Milhaud or Massenet, remaining essentially uncharted, and that is only keeping with the musical influences, for there are those from poetry, literature and the visual arts as well.

The following chapters explore a variety of notions of influence. Christopher Dingle makes the case for treating Mozart as having a position of pre-eminence among Messiaen's musical sources, while Caroline Rae draws upon performing as well as musicological experience to outline his inheritance from the Romantic piano tradition. Julian Anderson explores Messiaen's need for something to express, for the music to portray, in order for his imagination to catch fire. Stephen Broad examines the impact of the *art sacré* movement on Messiaen, and vice versa, while Philip Weller explores the complex web of influence, allusion and meaning in the *Cinq Rechants*. Finally, Hugh Macdonald takes a step back for a broad-brush essayistic view of how Messiaen fits into the cultural melting pot of his age. In an artist as broadly cultured as Messiaen, it is easy to become mired in the disconcerting range of influences; these perspectives begin to clear a path through the fog.

Chapter 10

Messiaen and Mozart:
A Love without Influence?

Christopher Dingle

Why is so little written about Messiaen and Mozart? It is a question that might be posed about Messiaen's relationship with a number of composers he cited as in some way having an impact upon his musical thought. For Messiaen, though, Mozart was not just any composer. Mozart was the key figure in Messiaen's pantheon. And yet, while he is acknowledged as a great love, Mozart is treated as an influence on the specifics of Messiaen's musical technique rarely, if at all. What follows is not a definitive exposition of ways in which Mozart's style and technique found resonances within Messiaen's music. Rather, this chapter first makes the case for the quasi-divine pre-eminence of Mozart among Messiaen's influences, outlining the evidence as it currently stands. Beyond that, the chapter draws attention to, and attempts to explain, the lack of such a discourse thus far in Messiaen studies. It suggests that the Mozartean influence may run far deeper than the adaptation of specific phrases, and considers some of the reasons that make exploring the extent of its reach especially challenging. It is essentially a call to arms for this elusive task, a plea for the highly talented new generation of scholars interested in Messiaen to cast their nets wide, far beyond the usual frame of reference for progressive twentieth-century music.

The Pre-eminence of Mozart

Messiaen had a deep love for the music of Mozart throughout his life. The vocal scores of *Don Giovanni* and *The Magic Flute* figure prominently in the well-worn anecdotes about his early life, being the first two scores to feature on his Christmas lists.[1] In his 1931 interview with José Bruyr, the earliest that Messiaen is known to have given, it is against Mozart that the neoclassical composers are tested and found wanting:

> I think there is a misconception on the part of many young musicians of my time. What they borrow from classics is the flow, the counterpoint, the chord progressions, which you have to admit are usually similar. But there is nothing

---

[1] See, among others, *Music and Color*, p. 109.

of the melodic vein which courses at full flood through Mozart – and for good reason.[2]

In his class at the Conservatoire, Messiaen not only analysed Mozart's operas and the late symphonies, but also the piano concertos, something that, as he stressed to Samuel, was a radical departure at the time.[3] His 1987 book *Les 22 concertos pour piano de Mozart* was based upon programme notes written in 1964 for a complete cycle given by Yvonne Loriod, with Pierre Boulez, Bruno Maderna and Louis Martin conducting.[4] These 'analyses' were then incorporated into the *Traité* alongside other observations about Mozart's music.[5] The only composers afforded comparable prominence in the *Traité*, aside from Messiaen himself, are Debussy, Le Jeune (*Le Printemps*), Stravinsky (*Le Sacre du Printemps*) and, of course, the birds.

In Messiaen's final years Mozart almost became a leitmotif. Asked to provide a piece for the Conservatoire harmony exam in 1986, Messiaen wrote the pastiche *Chant donné dans le style Mozart* rather than (in his terms) an original work. Marek Janowski's request for a piece 'for small orchestra in the spirit of Mozart' prompted Messiaen to break off work on *Éclairs* at the end of 1988. Within a week he had decided upon a title: *Un Sourire* (A Smile).[6] Then there is the *Concert à quatre*, in which, according to Loriod's analysis in the preface to the score ('taken from notes by the composer himself'), the opening theme of the first movement, 'Entrée', has a 'shape inspired by Susanna's aria from *The Marriage of Figaro* by Mozart'. That Mozart was very much in Messiaen's thoughts is confirmed by the fact that he had been perusing *The Marriage of Figaro* when Peter Hill had lunch with him in April 1991.[7]

What makes Mozart special, though, is not merely the longevity of Messiaen's adoration but its nature. The piano concertos, for instance, are at the heart of a decidedly chauvinistic declaration about the genre from Messiaen:

> I don't believe in the 'concerto form'; most of the time it's supremely boring, and, personally, as far as masterpieces are concerned, I know only the twenty-two concertos of Mozart. All others seem to me failures, except for two or three very beautiful passages in the Schumann Concerto and a few moments in the Franck *Symphonic Variations* or Prokofiev's Concertos.[8]

---

[2]   Interview (October 1931) in José Bruyr, *L'écran des musiciens, seconde série* (Paris: José Corti, 1933), pp. 124–31, cited in Nigel Simeone, 'Offrandes oubliées 2' in *Musical Times*, 142 (Spring 2001): p. 21.

[3]   *Music and Color*, p. 178.

[4]   As was standard in his time, Messiaen is referring to the mature works and does not count either youthful pieces or various fragments and recent discoveries.

[5]   *Traité IV*, pp. 191–200.

[6]   PHNS, p. 370.

[7]   Private communication.

[8]   *Music and Color*, pp. 116–17.

Aside from the idiosyncratic list of honourable mentions, this statement is striking not so much for the supremacy accorded to Mozart as the indiscriminate inclusion of the entirety of each concerto, when the best that others can achieve are 'a few moments'. It is the sense that Mozart can do no wrong and is beyond criticism. Nor is this the only instance of this lack of moderation: 'As for Mozart, he was surrounded by mediocre composers who were botching their minuets. Mozart was the only great composer of his time.'[9]

It is true that Messiaen asserted that he 'remained loyal to [his] childhood loves: Debussy, Mozart, Berlioz, Wagner'.[10] However, the way that Messiaen discussed Mozart is qualitatively different from his comments about other composers. Whereas he was passionate about Debussy, Berlioz and Wagner for their immense musical and aesthetic contributions, Mozart was treated in a way that took the discussion beyond the musical canon to canonization. This difference of tone is clear in the half of *Traité IV* devoted to Mozart. The opening credo entitled 'Why I love Mozart' begins with a series of unequivocal statements:

> Music pure and perfect. Mozart is the musician's musician. One looks in vain for an error in his music. ... The accent is always in the proper place. ... Melodic lines, so personal, so poetic. ... [Mozart's harmony is] always light, always heard, always true. ... [Mozart's form] is always perfect and constantly renewed.[11]

These sentiments are echoed at the end of the first part of the chapter 'Mozart and accentuation', subtitled 'Theory of accentuation', where Messiaen draws a contrast with the 'masculine rhythms' of Beethoven:

> Mozart, more intimate, more touching, between the melancholy of the past and the serene expectation of the future, Mozart, who is neither a child, nor an androgyne nor an angel, but a little of all these, Mozart, always loving, always confident, Mozart smiled, even before death: he primarily uses feminine rhythms and groups.[12]

Messiaen may have been referring to his faith when he told Claude Samuel that he'd 'never had doubts',[13] but his statements suggest the same applies to his perception of Mozart. The sweeping, unquestioning terms that Messiaen used when talking about Mozart echo the language he used about saints or characters from scripture, accentuating the other-worldly and not countenancing usual human frailties or foibles: 'Joy is a great deal more difficult to express than pain. ... Mozart was able

---

[9] Ibid., p. 112.

[10] Ibid., p. 112. N.B. Wagner was not mentioned at the equivalent point in the 1967 conversations with Samuel.

[11] *Traité IV*, p. 129.

[12] Ibid., p. 141.

[13] *Music and Color*, p. 17.

to do it, since he was an ecstatic person himself. No matter what befell him, he was cheerful.'[14] It is a sentiment echoed in Messiaen's preface to *Un Sourire*: 'Mozart always had many enemies. He was hungry, cold, almost all his children died, his wife was ill, he knew only tragedy. ... And he always smiled. In his music and in his life.' Whether or not this perceived refusal by Mozart to be cowed by suffering, to transfigure it into joy, bears historical scrutiny matters less here than that much of what Messiaen says could equally apply to himself. However, with Mozart he goes even further.

Messiaen repeatedly uses sacred language and imagery in describing Mozart's music. These may be passing metaphors, such as when he states that the masked trio in Act 1 of Don Giovanni 'sings with all the nobility, the gravity, the purity of a celestial trio'.[15] However, their persistence and tone in his programme notes on the piano concertos suggest a correspondence for Messiaen between Mozart's music and the preoccupations of his own works. According to Messiaen, the 'Andantino' of the E♭ major Piano Concerto (KV. 271) 'is certainly a meditation on death – faithful companion of Mozartean evenings – that Mozart soon accepts as the initiation to true Life...'.[16] Death as a prelude to the afterlife is a recurrent theme. In the slow movement of the A major Concerto (KV. 488) 'the soul leaves its old companion of flesh', before the 'Resurrection of the finale!'.[17] The G major Concerto (KV. 453) 'without doubt reveals to us the most secret part of the soul of the musician, his charm, his delights, his sorrows, his disappointments, his alternations of despair and wild gaiety, all dominated by the profound serenity of those who await death as a passage to a superior life...',[18] while the coda of the 'Andante' from the same concerto 'prepares us to leave earthly suffering, for the Divine Praise [Louange] which is stronger than passing Time...'.[19] Similarly, in the slow movement of the B♭ major Concerto (KV. 456) 'the acceptance of the Cross brings for a time the celestial consolations and the marvellous healing of a fourth variation in the major', yet at the close 'the lights from on high have faded, and the Angels support a poor body broken by suffering...'.[20] The mention of comforting angels is far from rare, the E♭ major Concerto (KV. 482) providing another prime example. In the second couplet of the 'Andante', Messiaen exclaims that 'the sky opens, the Angels descend towards the suffering soul'. Later on, 'the piano speaks like the Angels ... as if it can finally articulate the first words of the Truth. ... But the Light blinds us again, and it is entirely dazzled, staggering, that we climb towards it, supported

---

[14]   Almut Rößler, *Contributions to the Spiritual World of Olivier Messiaen with original texts by the composer*, trans. Babara Dagg and Nancy Poland (Duisberg: Gilles und Francke Verlag, 1986), p. 91.

[15]   *Traité IV*, p. 144.

[16]   Ibid., p. 176.

[17]   Ibid., p. 194.

[18]   Ibid., p. 184.

[19]   Ibid., p. 184.

[20]   Ibid., p. 186.

by the Angels...'.[21] The concerto ends with 'celestial insouciance'.[22] Elsewhere he evokes traits of the heavenly creatures, as in the 'Andante' of the C major Concerto (KV. 415), described by Messiaen as having a 'certain smile ... which hides so many angelically repressed tears'.[23] Likewise, the theme of the 'Larghetto' from the D major Concerto (KV. 537) has 'an angelic courtesy, the politeness of the Beyond. ... almost Franciscan...'.[24] This leads to two especially intriguing instances that (remembering that Messiaen's notes on the concertos were written long before his opera) presage 'L'Ange musicien' from *Saint François d'Assise*. In the later stages of the 'Larghetto' of the F major Piano Concerto KV. 413, Messiaen states that 'all combines to give each melodic movement an angelic smile and the sweetness of another world...',[25] while the F major episode in the final 'Allegretto' of the C major Concerto (KV. 503) is even more explicit: 'It is perhaps like the melody of the angel who transported Saint Francis of Assisi into regions forbidden to man...'.[26] Messiaen's comments above that Mozart was able to write music of joy are especially pertinent here, for joy is central to Franciscan spirituality and is (literally) the last word in Messiaen's opera.

While this litany, which is not exhaustive, gives a flavour of Messiaen's sacralized view of Mozart's music it is equally important to note that Messiaen does not use such language about other composers and music unless prompted by its inherent subject matter. The evidence indicates that Mozart was not merely a favourite composer of Messiaen, but that he was *the* composer *par excellence*. Indeed, for Messiaen, Mozart was the epitome of the composer and his works represented a kind of Ur-music. Such a statement does not belittle the importance of other favoured composers. It is simply that Mozart was placed in a different category by Messiaen. While Gluck, Berlioz, Debussy, Wagner and Stravinsky were great composers, Mozart was, if not Messiaen's musical god, then certainly a higher order of angel. It is surely no accident that discussion of Mozart shares *Traité IV*, the numerical centrepiece of the treatise, with plainchant, the latter described by Messiaen as probably the 'only one truly religious music'.[27]

The sacralized, angelic perspective is underlined by the fact that 'Why I love Mozart' is headed by a quotation from the first poem of Rilke's *Duino Elegies* – 'For beauty is nothing but the beginning of terror, which we still are just able to endure, and we are so awed because it serenely disdains to annihilate us' – and closes with Rilke's next line: 'Every Angel is terrifying'.[28] Before the latter, Messiaen

---

21   Ibid., p. 192.
22   Ibid., p. 193.
23   Ibid., p. 180.
24   Ibid., p. 198.
25   Ibid., p. 176.
26   Ibid., p. 197.
27   *Music and Color*, p. 29.
28   *Traité IV*, pp. 129 and 130. The English text of Rilke's poem comes from *The Selected Poetry of Rainer Maria Rilke (1975–1926)*, trans. and ed. Stephen Mitchell

explains why angelic is a suitable description for Mozart, first suggesting that many traditional views of Mozart, from boy playing to beautiful ladies, via respectful son of his father, womanizer and insulter of authority to genius dying of hunger, cold and fatigue are 'at the same time true and false'. Having essentially dismissed the historical biography, the human story, Messiaen goes on explicitly to associate Mozart with the divine: 'The adjective "angelic" is perhaps the least disproportionate. Angelic, yes, and because of that, very difficult to understand, very difficult to interpret. His apparent charm hides a deep mystery'.[29] In quoting Rilke, Messiaen is linking Mozart with the sense of divine awe he describes in movements such as 'Terribilis locus iste' [How awesome is this place], the twelfth movement of *La Transfiguration* and the fifth movement of *Des Canyons aux étoiles...*, 'Cedar Breaks et le don de crainte' [Cedar Breaks and the gift of awe].[30] Mozart's music arouses in Messiaen the sense of being in the presence of the divine. He uses the same angelic quotation from Rilke in discussing communication in the preface to the score of the *Méditations sur le mystère de la Sainte Trinité*: 'Only the angels have the privilege of communicating among themselves without language, conversation, and, still more marvellously, without any consideration of time and place. Therein is a power that surpasses us completely, a faculty of transmission almost frightening. Rilke is justified in saying "Every angel is terrifying".' It may be inferred, therefore, that Messiaen viewed Mozart as the ultimate musical communicator.

Another common feature of his references to Mozart is the way that Messiaen repeatedly highlights the progressive nature of his hero. When he talks about other specific composers, Messiaen notes musical associations as part of a larger web of connections with the evolution of compositional thought. By contrast, he is repeatedly at pains to point out that his trinity of divinely inspired musics, Mozart, plainchant and birdsong, got there first. In Mozart's case, the piano writing in the concertos is variously prophetic of Chopin, Debussy and the modern piano,[31] while the orchestral writing presages 'Nuages' and *Pelléas*.[32] Elsewhere he emphasizes that Mozart 'had a sense of specific timbre' before Berlioz,[33] and the coda of the 'Andante' from the B♭ major Piano Concerto (KV. 450) is preceded by 'an

---

(London: Picador, 1987), p. 151. Messiaen's text in the *Traité*, which does not specify the *Duino Elegies*, reads as follows (omitting the bracketed text): 'Le beau n'est qu'un degré du terrible [qu'encore nous supportons et] nous [ne] l'admirons [tant que], car il reste impassible, et dédaigne de nous détruire' and 'Tout Ange est terrible...'. Rainer Maria Rilke, *Poésie*, nouvelle édition, trans. Maurice Betz (Paris: Émile Paul: 1941), p. 199.

[29]   *Traité IV*, p. 130.

[30]   For further discussion of Messiaen's treatment of awe in his music, see Christopher Dingle, 'Sacred Machines: Fear, Mystery and Transfiguration in Messiaen's Mechanical Procedures' in *Messiaen Perspectives 2*.

[31]   See, among others, *Traité IV*, pp. 176 and 178.

[32]   Ibid., p. 194.

[33]   Ibid., p. 129.

extraordinary echo effect, a canon of intensities, which is prophetic of Berliozian instrumentation and twentieth-century stereophonies'.[34] In the Statue scene of *Don Giovanni* can be found 'two sonorities dear to Debussy'[35] and one 'dear to Ravel',[36] while the Ball scene superimposes four layers of music 'before Darius Milhaud'.[37] It is almost as if Messiaen is musically applying the prologue of John's Gospel to Mozart: 'All things came into being by him'.

Mozart's Influence?

It is clear, then, that Mozart was not merely an enduring and supreme musical love, but also represented a kind of musical perfection for Messiaen. That being the case, why is precious little said about Mozart and his influence in the literature on Messiaen? Yes, Messiaen's childhood anecdotes are noted about the delivery of vocal scores for *Don Giovanni* and *The Magic Flute* by Père Noël and discussion of *Un Sourire* naturally mentions that it was written for the Mozart bicentenary, but why is Mozart largely absent from the examination of Messiaen's music? A pioneering and valuable contribution was made by Raffaele Pozzi in 1992, comparing Messiaen's view of Mozart with those of other rhythmic analysts, such as Grosvenor Cooper and Leonard B. Meyer, and, more recently, Po-Yi (Nelson) Wu has also discussed Messiaen's attitude to accentuation in Mozart.[38] However, neither Pozzi or Wu explore any influence upon the Frenchman's own music. Mozart generally eludes the frame of reference both for broader observations and, especially, specific technique. *Le Nozze di Figaro*, *Don Giovanni* and *Die Zauberflöte* find a passing mention in Nils Holger Petersen's examination of historical precedents for *Saint François*.[39] Nearly a decade later, Messiaen's opera provoked a conjunction of (independent) observations by the editors of the present volume. In the conclusion to his essay on *Saint François* in Robert Sholl's *Messiaen Studies*, Robert Fallon suggests that the work could be regarded as 'the

---

[34]   Ibid., p. 182.

[35]   Ibid., p. 129.

[36]   Ibid., p. 164.

[37]   Ibid., p. 130.

[38]   Raffaele Pozzi, '"Le rythme chez Mozart": Alcune osservazioni analitiche di Olivier Messiaen sull'accentuazione ritmica in Mozart', in Rudolph Angermüller, Dietrich Berke, Ulrike Hofmann and Wolfgang Rehm (eds), *Bericht über den Internationalen Mozart-Kongreß Salzburg 1991* (Kassel: Bärenreiter, 1992): pp. 613–24; Po-Yi (Nelson) Wu, 'Messiaen's Dynamic Mozart', in Judith Crispin (ed.) *Olivier Messiaen: The Centenary Papers* (Newcastle upon Tyne: Cambridge Scholars Publishing, 2010), pp. 281–300.

[39]   Nils Holger Petersen, 'Saint François and Franciscan Sprituality', in Siglind Bruhn (ed.), *Messiaen's Language of Mystical Love* (New York: Garland, 1998), pp. 182–3.

negative image of Messiaen's favourite opera, *Don Giovanni*'.[40] Although my own examination of *Saint François*, published the same year as Fallon's, suggests Dukas's *Ariane et Barbe-bleue* as photographic negative, it goes on to observe, 'Given Messiaen's love of, and long acquaintance with, *Don Giovanni*, specifically the Commendatore scene with its interaction of the natural and supernatural, it is not so surprising that the climax of his opera should involve pounding *tutti* chords, of which there is an earlier premonition.'[41] The point here is not the merit of such comments, but their rarity. It is striking that all three relate to Messiaen's *Saint François*, a work that invites examinations of precedents and cultural resonances, the composer feeling the need to position it within operatic tradition.

This might be regarded as inevitable, reflecting the extent to which Messiaen abandons the conventions of the genre. However, he makes equally radical departures in other works. Would applying the same exercise produce parallels with Mozart's symphonies in *L'Ascension* or *Turangalîla*, or with the piano concertos for any of Messiaen's orchestral works involving solo piano? It is easier to make the case for parallels in opera thanks to the combination of the broad characteristics of the plots supported by the more significant musical gestures. Fleshing out equivalences and echoes elsewhere may require a deeper analysis of technique and gesture in order to be convincing, but, thus far, this has been distinctly lacking in the literature. Where are the studies examining whether Mozart's approach to melodic shape and phrasing is used as a model in any of Messiaen's scores? There are plenty of mentions of Çarngadeva or Greek rhythms in analyses of Messiaen's music, often making no more sophisticated a musical point than that they are there, but are there any resonances of Mozart's approach to rhythm and accentuation?

One reason for the dearth of research on the lessons Messiaen learnt from Mozart is that the two composers' sound worlds are far removed from each other. Whereas Poulenc's love of Mozart resulted in clear allusions, even almost direct quotations in explicit *hommage*, few passages in Messiaen sound even loosely Mozartean. This not only makes it difficult to see past the differences, but it also makes it less likely that scholars will have the requisite skills to do justice to the subject. Few, if any, specialists in Messiaen's music are equally attuned to the nuances of Mozart's music. This is not to suggest that Messiaen scholars understand nothing about Mozart. Peter Hill, for one, has given exquisite performances of several of the concertos conducting from the piano, quite apart from the fact that most, if not all, musicologists working on Messiaen would have studied Mozart

---

[40]   Robert Fallon, 'Two paths to paradise: reform in Messiaen's *Saint François d'Assise*', in Robert Sholl (ed.), *Messiaen Studies* (Cambridge: Cambridge University Press, 2007), p. 230.

[41]   Christopher Dingle, 'Frescoes and Legends: The Sources and Background of *Saint François d'Assise*', in Christopher Dingle and Nigel Simeone (eds), *Olivier Messiaen: Music, Art and Literature* (Aldershot: Ashgate, 2007), p. 321.

and written pastiches in their student years. However, what is needed surely goes far beyond knowledge of rounded binary form or of classical harmonic practice.

Nonetheless, it is striking that, while Mozart has acquired the status of a love without influence, plainchant, a musical resource that is even further removed from Messiaen chronologically, is tackled with gusto. Messiaen's music attracts the attention of a relatively high number of specialists in sacred music, so it is possible that there is greater confidence in traversing the stylistic gulf. Or maybe we have fewer qualms about, or are less aware of, our ignorance regarding plainchant. There are also plenty of explicit quotations of plainchant in Messiaen. It is clear where the plainchant occurs so the nature of the problem is qualitatively different from any deep-rooted Mozartean influence. Or is it?

One of the most prevalent errors in perceptions of Messiaen's music is noting an element on the musical surface and, as a consequence, assuming that its influence upon the piece extends no further. We know that Messiaen's interest in plainchant was musical as well as spiritual. In the *Traité* melodic shapes are discussed in terms of plainchant neumes, and his teaching repeatedly drew attention to this melodic resource, as Alexander Goehr has made clear:

> He showed us continually how his own way of composing was based on the study of Gregorian chant and the imitation of it. Admittedly with octave displacements and rhythmic lengthenings and shortenings and all the rest. Every student I've ever had I've pushed onto the Gregorian chant and I make everybody here [at Cambridge] study Gregorian chant and that's because it seems to me the most fertile influence. Messiaen said to me 'You're not a Catholic, but the Graduale is the cheapest book you can buy and the most useful book any composer can have'. I've had my copy for forty-five years and I paid at that time four, five pounds for it and it's the best pattern book. I still use it all the time because it's full of basic ideas. Messiaen influenced a lot of people in that way. That's why I think all the students, certainly the earlier ones, you can always tell they're students of his from the way they push the notes melodically. A certain way of doing it which is not like Webern or any of the other big influences.[42]

His adaptation of these clumps of notes was explicit in *Neumes rythmique*, but it is implicit throughout his music and far more extensive than the various instances labelled in the score or mentioned in Messiaen's prefaces. There is clearly scope for an extensive examination of Messiaen's melodic construction. Eventually this may uncover both the adaptation of neumes in forming melodic patterns, and, lest he had been forgotten, the influence of Mozart.

---

[42]   Alexander Goehr, unpublished interview with the present author, Cambridge, 4 July 1996. For more on Messiaen's use of plainchant neumes in the analysis of melody, see Jean Boivin, 'Musical Analysis According to Messiaen: A Critical View of a Most Original Approach', in Christopher Dingle and Nigel Simeone (eds), *Olivier Messiaen: Music, Art and Literature* (Aldershot: Ashgate, 2007), pp. 146–8.

That Messiaen was open to, and conscious of, direct melodic influence from Mozart is clear from two instances where the relationship was acknowledged; 'Amen du Désir' from *Visions de l'Amen*, and the 'Entrée' of the *Concert à quatre*. In both cases, the melodic source of certain phrases is music sung by Susannah in *The Marriage of Figaro*.

In his examination of *Visions de l'Amen* in the *Traité*, Messiaen provides an example of the opening two bars of the 'thème extatique' of the 'Amen du Désir', stating that it 'brings to mind Mozart (Susanna's aria, *Noces de Figaro*)', giving two bars from 'Deh vieni, non tardar' beneath it:[43]

Example 10.1   First examples from 'Amen du Désir' and Mozart's 'Deh vieni, non tardar' (*Marriage of Figaro*) as quoted in *Traité III*, p. 249

He goes on to observe that the fifth bar of 'Amen du Désir' resembles another contour of the same aria:

Example 10.2   Second examples from 'Amen du Désir' and Mozart's 'Deh vieni, non tardar' (*Marriage of Figaro*) as quoted in *Traité III*, p. 249

While Messiaen usually divorces his sources from their original context and inferred meaning, the text and sentiment of 'Deh vieni non tardar' is far from inappropriate for the 'Amen du Désir', especially the opening lines: 'Come, do not delay, oh bliss, Come where love calls thee to joy.' Regardless, Messiaen makes clear his admiration for the phrase when discussing it in *Traité IV*: 'One of the most exquisite and most typical melodic contours of Mozart.'[44]

The *Concert à quatre* contains a similar use of a Mozartean model. Yvonne Messiaen-Loriod's preface to the score, based on Messiaen's notes, states that the opening theme of the first movement, 'Entrée', has a 'shape inspired by Susanna's

---

[43]   *Traité III*, p. 249.
[44]   *Traité IV*, pp. 142–3.

Aria from the *Marriage of Figaro* by Mozart'. However, while it may seem to have a certain similarity of spirit with 'Deh vieni, non tardar' and 'Amen du Désir', the source on this occasion is the more impish 'Venite, inginocchiatevi' from Act 2:

Example 10.3   Opening of 'Entrée' from *Concert à quatre* and Mozart's 'Venite, inginocchiatevi' (*Marriage of Figaro*)

This phrase comes at the climax of Susanna's affectionate taunts of Cherubino, as she teaches him how to act like a girl. Messiaen quotes the aria only in passing during a litany of 'several brief examples of masculine and feminine groups' in the chapter on Mozart and accentuation in the *Traité*, referring to this as 'Susannah's little aria' (*petit air de Suzanne*).[45]

This all raises the question of whether there are other prominent passages in Messiaen's music that are inspired by similar models. His adaptations of fragments from Mussorgsky (the 'Boris' motif) and Grieg are well-known because Messiaen revealed them himself, and the same is true of 'Deh vieni, non tardar' in Amen du Désir'. Julian Anderson has drawn attention to passages that use Jolivet, Berg, Tournemire and Skryabin as models, in the case of the first two, creating harmonic sequences that appear prominently in several works.[46] Loriod's identification of 'Suzannah's Aria' in the 'Entrée' of the *Concert à quatre* stems from Messiaen's tendency to write comments on music, his own or that of others, noting the provenance of the material. However, as so often, the phrase in question is a fragment buried in the middle of the aria. It may be that much of Messiaen's melodic material is based upon models drawn from diverse musical ancestors in much the same way as certain harmonies. Christopher Brent Murray has drawn attention to a list of 71 melodic fragments from diverse composers that Messiaen referred to at least from his student days to his early teaching.[47] An example of Debussy's influence appears in the chapter on Messiaen and the Prix de Rome by Murray and Laura Hamer that

[45]   Ibid., p. 152.

[46]   See Julian Anderson, 'Messiaen and the Notion of Influence', *Tempo*, 63/247 (January 2009): pp. 2–18.

[47]   Christopher Brent Murray, *Le développement du langage musical d'Olivier Messiaen: traditions, emprunts, expériences*, PhD thesis (Université-Lumière Lyon 2, 2010).

opens this volume,[48] while Yves Balmer, Thomas Lacôte and Murray are working on a book examining Messiaen's thematic borrowing.[49] However, the general lack of access thus far to the early sketch materials for most Messiaen works, rather than one of the various stages of fair copy, means that identifying sources beyond those named directly or indirectly by Messiaen is unlikely to occur with any certainty. It is improbable that anyone would have made the connection with Mozart for any of the passages mentioned above had it not been pointed out. Nonetheless, even if other such direct links were established, this is still at the level of thematic models. It deepens our understanding of Messiaen's tendency (like that of numerous other composers) to take off-the-peg melodic and harmonic patterns and tailor them to his own needs. It is possible, though, that there is a deeper embedding of Mozart's melodic syntax within Messiaen's music. Rather than the wearing of melodic garments, this would be the Mozartean influence that is in his blood and bones, the fabric of his musical being.

Rhythm is a much trickier prospect than melody, not least since Messiaen was so revolutionary, and Mozart's use of rhythm seems relatively simple by comparison. However, this was not a view to which Messiaen himself subscribed. He referred to Mozart as being 'an extraordinary rhythmician', indeed 'the greatest rhythmician in Classical music', going on to explain his thinking:

> Mozartean rhythm has a kinematic quality, but it mainly belongs to the field of accent, deriving from the spoken and written word. In Mozart, one distinguishes masculine and feminine groups. The first comprises a single burst and a dead stop, exactly like the male body and character. The feminine groups (more supple, like the female character and body) are the more important and more characteristic. They include a preparatory period, the *anacrusis*; a relatively intense apex that is the accent; and a relatively weak falling-back, the mute or inflectional ending, formed of one or several notes, of one or several beats. Mozart used these rhythmic groups constantly; they figure so greatly in his work that if the exact placement of the accents is not observed, Mozartean music is completely destroyed. That's the reason one hears so many bad interpretations of Mozart, for most musicians are not sufficiently educated in rhythm to discern the true placement of accents. ... If he makes a mistake, he commits a crime against Mozart by completely destroying the rhythmic movement of the work.[50]

Not surprisingly, the operas that were beloved of Messiaen from his boyhood days are identified by him as the wellspring for this rhythmic variety:

---

[48]   Laura Hamer and Christopher Brent Murray, 'Olivier Messiaen and the Prix de Rome as Rite of Passage' in this volume.

[49]   Yves Balmer, Thomas Lacôte, and Christopher Brent Murray, working title *Les techniques du langage musical d'Olivier Messiaen* (Lyon: Symétrie, forthcoming).

[50]   *Music and Color*, pp. 68–9.

There is a rhythmic language with powerful and varied accentuations in his music. That's a result of his having composed for libretti in German and Italian. In his music, then, there's a constant variation of stressed and unstressed beats and that produces an enormous rhythmic energy. Mozart is merry, enchanting, playful, but, in reality, rhythmically very powerful'.[51]

The influence of various languages is certainly a plausible candidate for explaining Mozart's rhythmic approach, but it is striking that Messiaen, a composer renowned for revolutionizing our understanding of rhythm, should identify language as a crucial element when he claimed to speak barely a word of anything other than French.

Messiaen cites Mozart as an early proponent of polytempos, the simultaneous use of different metres or tempi:

> We'll say 'polytempos', which exist in nature, but which are very difficult to realize in the orchestra. The Classical composers did not risk it, except for Mozart, in the ballroom scene in the first-act finale of *Don Giovanni*, when three little onstage orchestras play in different metres. But the result is less obvious since all the musicians are playing in G major. Unfortunately the tonal effect absorbs the rhythmic combinations. Still, Mozart had a brilliant idea.[52]

This is intriguing, but the correlation between such isolated experiments and specific rhythmic techniques used by Messiaen may ultimately prove to be of less interest than the more subtle resonances of what he identifies as the kinematic, word-inspired rhythm of Mozart. Is this the source of the fluidity of passages such as the opening of *Les Offrandes oubliées* or the 'Louanges' from the *Quatuor* or any number of passages from the song cycles? Is it to Mozart we should look rather than Debussy in trying to understand the vocal writing in *Saint François*?

Messiaen's continual desire to brandish Mozart's radical credentials is not limited to rhythm and melody, for his hero is also identified as a great colourist, a position that apparently throws him into sharp relief with his contemporaries: 'that's exactly what makes him different from the other classical composers. Mozart is not always tonal. He's often chromatic. He is always coloured'.[53] As so often, *Don Giovanni* is the touchstone, underlining Mozart's dramatic skills and instinct for musical colour:

> The case is similar with Mozart, who was an exceptional man of the theatre. Whenever unusual things are happening on stage, the colours of his orchestration and harmonies change. So, for example, in the scene with the Commendatore at the end of *Don Giovanni*, there appears a different Mozart; it's an extraordinary

---

[51]   Rößler, *Contributions*, p. 123.

[52]   *Music and Color*, p. 81.

[53]   Ibid., p. 63.

and terrifying style which matches the walking statue well, and there's an unusual orchestration with trombones and tied notes in the inner parts and chromatic chords. The colours are produced by the harmonies and the timbres of the instruments.[54]

Messiaen elaborated on this in conversation with Claude Samuel:

> You'll notice in regard to musical theatre that, for a long time, composers had little concern for lighting that was supposed to accompany the unfolding of their music. It's with Mozart that we begin to see a premeditated relationship. Certainly the entrance of the Commendatore's statue in *Don Giovanni* produces a complete change in tone, absolutely brilliant for the period, not only because the character is frightening and the subject terrifying, but because at that moment night falls over the scene, enhanced by supernatural lighting; all this is conveyed by the orchestration and also by the chord-colouring. In this statue scene there's a certain inversion of diminished seventh and diminished fifth chords with an altered third, which would be taken up by Chopin as colour and used by Debussy under the name of 'whole-tone scale'.[55]

In fact, Messiaen stresses time and again that the strength of Mozart's music is not the use of the common triad, but his divergence from it:

> Let's take the example of Mozart again: he is said to be tonal? Marvellous passages like the Andante of the Concerto in E♭, K. 482, the statue scene in *Don Giovanni*, the defeat of all the nocturnal characters (the Queen of the Night and her cohorts) in *The Magic Flute* are not tonal, but chromatic.[56]

Mozart is in the pantheon of favoured composer because his music is colourful, literally so from Messiaen's perspective. While Messiaen's enthusiasm for describing his harmony in terms of colour from the early 1960s onwards provided a neutral set of terms for discussing music – a deft semantic side-step of the aesthetic debates regarding what musical material was permissible or legitimate – colour also became the trump card in explaining the worth of a piece of music. Mozart is better than Haydn because his music is more coloured. Berlioz and Wagner are preferred to Mendelssohn and Brahms for the same reasons.

In talking about coloured music, it is these childhood loves of Mozart, Berlioz and Wagner that are the constant leitmotifs in Messiaen's conversations. These composers are the great innovators of musical colour, but they are also the composers that he discovered first, quite some time before the bombshell of Debussy's *Pelléas*, or the teenage discovery of Stravinsky's early works. Mozart

---

[54] Rößler, *Contributions*, p. 77.
[55] *Music and Color*, pp. 41–2.
[56] Ibid., p. 52.

was the first of these childhood loves and it stands to reason that the influence runs very deep indeed.

In Tome VII of the *Traité*, Mozart is not only cited in relation to sound-colour, but also makes repeated surprise appearances during the sections outlining the 'etymology' of Messiaen's most characteristic chords. In the process, he demonstrates that he was certainly open to the notion that Mozart's music infiltrated his own at the most fundamental levels. Towards the end of the passage on the chords of Transposed Inversions on the same bass note, Messiaen reveals 'the final surprise' with an example from *Don Giovanni*:

Example 10.4   Passage from Commendatore scene of *Don Giovanni* as quoted by Messiaen in *Traité VII*, p. 139

I read the entirety of Mozart's *Don Giovanni* as a child: I sight-read it at the piano, though poorly, singing all the roles with a horrible voice, in Grenoble, when nearly 8 years old. It was the first opera that I knew. Now, I noticed myself, nearly sixty years later, that the scene of the Commendatore strung together these strange sounds. One finds there all of the notes of the 'accord à renversements transposés',[57] in its most beautiful form, in its best transposition, and one of its most characteristic colours.[58]

Example 10.5   Accord à Renversements Transposés, chord B, 5th transposition

It is possible to sense the stupefaction and glee that Messiaen evidently felt on making this discovery. Moreover, it adds substantive weight to the parallel noted above between *Don Giovanni* and *Saint François*. It was suggested that the pounding chords that mark the Angel's knocking on the monastery door and return for the infliction of the stigmata are an equivalence of those from the Commendatore scene. In fact, the pounding chords in *Saint François* are

[57]   Transposed Inversion Chord.

[58]   *Traité VII*, pp. 139–40.

underpinned by Transposed Inversion chords. Messiaen's dating places his self-discovery of the source of these chords in the Commendatore scene before the composition of *Saint François*, so it is possible that the hammering chords are a deliberate private tribute to Mozart.

Messiaen's 'discovery' of the Transposed Inversion chords in *Don Giovanni* was not the end of the matter. In the following chapter, on the etymology of the Contracted Resonance chords, Messiaen recalls a later revelation. He first invites a closer look at chord B (transposition 1):

Example 10.6   First accord à Resonance Contractée, transposition 1, chord B

We have already noted, for the 'accord à renversements transposés', that one could find it in the Commendatore scene of Mozart's *Don Giovanni*. To my great astonishment, I myself noticed once more (thirty five years later!) that the first 'accord à resonance contractée' derived from – this also! – this same passage of *Don Giovanni*.

We have there all the notes of chord B above: from top to bottom – F♮, D♭ (or C♯), A♭ (or G♯), E♭, B♭, E♮, D♮. Even chord A (the quintuple appoggiatura) can, at a pinch, find its source in the Commendatore scene of *Don Giovanni*. In effect, the two bars that precede the example from Mozart above are in G minor and contain the G♮, the A♮ and the G♭ (F♯). Of course, I never thought of all that![59]

Example 10.7   Passage from Commendatore scene of *Don Giovanni* as quoted by Messiaen in *Traité VII*, p. 151

Leaving aside the mismatch in timescale between these two passages from the *Traité*, what emerges from these self-analytical anecdotes is the extent to which Messiaen continued throughout his life to revisit both Mozart's music and his own techniques; he did not leave Mozart as a thing of his childhood. It is, of course, impossible to say whether these discoveries are musical coincidences or signify a deep-rooted influence, but Messiaen, to his relish, clearly believed them to be the latter. Although Messiaen did not use these terms, this is Mozart using angelic

---

[59]   Ibid., pp. 151–2.

forms of communication so that the influence goes into the heart of Messiaen's musical thought without conscious use of language. The observations about the influence of *Don Giovanni* would be dismissed as wishful thinking if made by anyone other than the composer, and even he is not immune to such charges. Nevertheless, while it may not be possible, or remotely advisable, for anyone else to emulate this kind of identification, it does underline the fundamental importance that Mozart held for Messiaen in purely musical terms.

Messiaen's proselytizing zeal on behalf of Mozart admits neither limitation nor moderation. Moreover, it remained unashamed. It is worth remembering that he started analysing the piano concertos in his Conservatoire class in the 1949–50 academic year, a time when the *maître* was harried by his progressive students and in the midst of composing *Mode de valeurs et d'intensités* and *Neumes rythmiques*. Mozart was certainly not what his radical protégés expected, but this music was also regarded as too lightweight to be worthy of serious consideration by his more traditionally minded colleagues.

Times had changed by 1986 when Claude Samuel recorded his conversations with Messiaen. He made comments about Mozart not found in the 1967 conversations that could be attributed to his being an old man nostalgic for things past. However, they also captured a more general sentiment that has now become almost orthodox, but that was unusual in progressive circles at the time: 'I think we need to get back to charm, to sweetness, or just simply to what sounds good. The music of Mozart is simple, frank, very elaborate in its accentuation, but the result is beautiful, and no one dreams of criticizing him for it'[60]. This certainly seems to have been Messiaen's approach in his own later music, not least *Un Sourire*, the piece written for the bicentenary of Mozart's death. At the work's British première in 1992, Kent Nagano related how, the afternoon before the first performance of *Un Sourire*, in Paris the previous December, Messiaen had told him:

> It's a very special piece because I've always written works and I've been really scared what people would think about [them] after they've heard the piece. I've always wondered if they would really be able to accept the pieces. This is a piece that I just wrote for myself. It's a piece where I really wanted to do something particularly beautiful, something particularly personal, and I felt so determined to make it a piece for myself that I called it *Sourire*.[61]

It is fitting that this was the last of his pieces for which Messiaen attended the première. He ended where he had begun, with Mozart, his alpha and omega. His comments to Kent Nagano encapsulate how deeply personal was his love of Mozart's music, and they underline just why this composer above all others should matter to anyone interested in Messiaen's music.

---

[60]   *Music and Color*, p. 169.

[61]   Platform speech by Kent Nagano during the Hallé Orchestra concert on 20 September 1992 at the Free Trade Hall, Manchester.

Chapter 11

Messiaen and the Romantic Gesture: Contemplations on his Piano Music and Pianism

Caroline Rae

'I'm not ashamed of being a romantic', declared Messiaen in his conversations with Claude Samuel.[1] 'The romantics were magnificent craftsmen .... The romantics were aware of the beauties of nature, they were aware of the glory of divinity; they were grandiose, and many of our contemporaries would be better off if they "romanticized" themselves'.[2] While Messiaen made these statements in the context of his organ music, pointing out that accusations of romanticism had been levied against his works as a negative criticism, much of his music for piano bears witness to these traits. Revealing his own meticulous craftsmanship through a wide range of innovative compositional procedures, the gargantuan piano cycles *Visions de l'Amen*, *Vingt Regards sur l'Enfant-Jésus* and *Catalogue d'oiseaux* pronounce his affirmation of faith while celebrating awe of the divine through God's presence in nature and the cosmos. The keyboard was central to Messiaen's creative thinking, the piano being represented in his major solo works for the instrument as well as functioning as a featured soloist in many of his works for orchestra and ensemble. Among the most substantial and significant contributions to the literature by any composer of the twentieth century, Messiaen's works for, and including, piano span his entire compositional œuvre from the early *Préludes* to the *Concert à quatre*. They explore new sonorities and compositional techniques while making colossal musical, technical and intellectual demands on even the most accomplished virtuoso performer. Yet, these works also reveal indebtedness to the past.

Messiaen's writing for piano was built on a pianistic foundation inspired not only by the outstanding abilities of Yvonne Loriod, for whom most of his mature piano works were composed, but also by a deep appreciation of a virtuoso tradition he described as stemming from Rameau and Domenico Scarlatti, extending to Chopin (via Mozart) and culminating in Debussy, Ravel and Albéniz.[3] These were Messiaen's preferred keyboard composers. They also provided the core

---

[1] *Music and Color*, p. 120.

[2] Ibid.

[3] Ibid, p. 114.

repertory for his analysis classes at the Paris Conservatoire and were those to whom he felt closest in developing his own approach to the piano: 'After them, I see no "good" piano music; there are perhaps some very beautiful pages but they have no particular pianistic importance.'[4] While Messiaen avoids mentioning Liszt no doubt for reasons of aesthetic and national alignment (his own flag was otherwise nailed firmly to the Berlioz mast, not least through his association with La Jeune France),[5] this giant of nineteenth-century pianism was a great admirer of Chopin as well as an important influence on the pianistic language of Ravel and Albéniz, and to some extent Debussy. Despite Liszt's conspicuous absence from Messiaen's preferred tradition, his influence was nevertheless an important one, stimulating certain pianistic textures as well as a highly orchestral approach to the instrument, especially in the construction of powerful climaxes. Both composers demonstrated a predilection for writing pianistic tone poems and drew on a range of theologically inspired ideas.

Underlining the interconnectedness of these sources, this pantheon of keyboard composers represents a tradition in which Yvonne Loriod herself was immersed, as evidenced by her teaching, recital programmes and recordings of works by composers other than Messiaen, and upon which her own substantial technique was founded as a product of her performer's training at the Paris Conservatoire.[6] A student of Marcel Ciampi and Lazare-Lévy, she was part of the distinguished school of twentieth-century French pianists that descended from Louis Diémer, a pupil of Debussy's teacher Antoine-François Marmontel.[7] She inherited the Chopin tradition through her studies with Isidor Philipp who had been a student of the renowned Chopin pupil Georges Mathias.[8] Considering aesthetic alignments together with aspects of pianistic genealogy and exploring the physicality of Messiaen's pianism as a tactile reference to his predecessors, this chapter investigates the ways in which Messiaen acknowledged romantic

---

[4]   Ibid., p. 115.

[5]   The importance of Berlioz for Messiaen is not only reflected in the name of the compositional group La Jeune France, founded in 1936 around a hundred years after the similarly named group attributed to Berlioz (see Hugh Macdonald's chapter in this volume), but also in his celebrating of a Mass at the Trinité in March 1969 to commemorate the composer's centenary (PHNS, p. 280). Berlioz's years of struggle for recognition in France resulted in him becoming a figure around whom many French composers of later generations rallied in the assertion of their own sense of Frenchness.

[6]   Yvonne Loriod's many recordings of works by composers other than Messiaen include the Chopin Études and Liszt Sonata in B Minor Sonata (see Appendix).

[7]   The piano pupils of Louis Diémer (1843–1919) at the Paris Conservatoire included Alfred Cortot, Marcel Ciampi, Marius-François Gaillard (notable for being the first pianist to perform Debussy's complete piano music in 1920), Lazare-Lévy, Yves Nat and Robert Casadesus.

[8]   Isidor Philipp also studied with Henri Fissot who had been a student of Antoine-François Marmontel, see Charles Timbrell, *French Pianism: A Historical Perspective*, 2nd edn (London: Kahn and Averill, 1999) p. 79.

tradition through incorporating pianistic gestures and figurations developed from Chopin, Albéniz and Liszt in his writing for piano.

That Messiaen began his virtuoso tradition with reference to his seventeenth- and eighteenth-century harpsichordist predecessors has a compositional as well as pianistic significance. Like Messiaen, Rameau was one of the great harmonic theorists of his age, his music featuring bold harmonies, modal and even chromatic innovations as well as unusually colourful orchestrations. Rameau's fondness for imitating birdsong, which abounds in the keyboard works as well as in his operas (also much admired by Messiaen), must have provided some additional appeal, although Messiaen was careful to assert his own pre-eminence as the 'first to have made a truly scientific and … accurate notation of bird songs'.[9] While Messiaen acknowledges the charm of Rameau's music, as well as that of Couperin, particularly the latter's *Le rossignol en amour* (from the *Ordre* no. 14 of 1722), he suggests that, given what they wrote, these composers seem never to have heard real nightingales.[10] The use of stylized bird calls in French keyboard music, almost a tradition in Rameau and Couperin 'le grand', as well as famously occurring in Daquin's *Le coucou*, was revitalized by Chabrier and Ravel before Messiaen began his more extensive ornithologically informed incorporations.[11]

In acknowledging Rameau, as well as Couperin, Messiaen asserted a distinctly French lineage that connects not only with the golden age of Louis XIV and the repertoire's revival in late nineteenth-century France (notably advanced through the editions and performances of Louis Diémer[12]), but also with Debussy and Ravel whose admiration for the French *clavecinistes* inspired elements of their own piano writing while affirming their respective sense of Frenchness.[13] Writing in 1878, Antoine-François Marmontel described the works of the French *clavecinistes* as having paved the way for 'modern' pianism.[14] The evocation of

---

[9]   *Music and Color*, p. 97.

[10]   Ibid.

[11]   See, for example, Chabrier's *Aubade* (1883), Ravel's 'Oiseaux tristes' from *Miroirs* (1904–05) and *Ma mère l'Oye* (1908–10). The first of Liszt's *Deux légendes*, 'St François d'Assise: La prédication aux oiseaux' (1862), and Schumann's 'Vogel als Prophet', *Waldszenen* op.84 (1848–49) are earlier (non-French) examples of is an earlier (non-French) example of stylized evocations of birdsong-like twittering. The same subject yields opportunities for more elaborate actual birdsong in the sixth tableau of Messiaen's opera *Saint François d'Assise*.

[12]   Louis Diémer published many editions of the music of Rameau and Couperin from the 1880s onwards, performed their music on period instruments and founded the Société des Instruments Anciens in 1895. He was professor of piano at the Paris Conservatoire from 1888, succeeding his own teacher Antoine-François Marmontel with whom Debussy also studied.

[13]   For more on the influence of the French *clavecinistes* in French piano music, see Roy Howat, *The Art of French Piano Music* (New Haven and London: Yale, 2009), pp. 145–58.

[14]   Antoine Marmontel, *Les pianistes célèbres* (Paris: Heugel, 1878) available via Project Gutenberg download, www.gutenberg.org, E-Book no. 37654.

Rameau is a particularly resonant one for any French composer and connects with a web of references to the composer reaching back through both World Wars (his music was frequently programmed in 'non-official' Parisian concerts during the Occupation) to the period after the Franco-Prussian war when the revival of his music was associated with assertions of French national identity.[15]

Stepping away from French tradition, Messiaen's reference to Domenico Scarlatti acknowledges the importance of the composer's keyboard sonatas as foundation stones in the training and performance repertoire of the twentieth-century virtuoso pianist. These works were notably championed by pianists such as Vladimir Horowitz and Nina Milkina as well as by those trained at the Paris Conservatoire including Nikita Magaloff (a pupil of Isidor Philipp) and Clara Haskil (whose teachers included Lazare-Lévy). In addition to their wealth of musical inventiveness and explorations with new approaches to form, Scarlatti's sonatas represent a catalogue of innovative keyboard techniques that remain a test of dexterity for pianists today with their rapid passagework, repeated notes, hand-crossing, athletic leaps, chains of thirds (a perennial problem for keyboard players) and imaginative juxtapositions of register for colouristic effect. The technicality of Scarlatti's keyboard writing prepared the way for later pianistic developments, a feature recognized by Bartók, another composer of compositional significance for Messiaen as well as other French composers of his generation including Jolivet, Ohana and Dutilleux. Bartók is known to have performed Scarlatti sonatas together with works by Couperin, Rameau and Mozart, in his recital programmes of the 1930s.[16] Messiaen's admiration for Scarlatti, Rameau and Mozart came together at the very end of his life in the *Concert à quatre*, which includes the piano as one of its four soloists (the others being flute, oboe and cello). Unfinished at the time of Messiaen's death (and completed by Yvonne Loriod with George Benjamin and Heinz Holliger), the work was intended as a 'révérence admirative' for the three composers. Although far from being a pastiche, the *Concert*'s overall subtlety of instrumental colouring (the full ensemble plays only in the exuberant conclusion) creates a sense of classical intimacy indicative of Messiaen's admiration for the grace, elegance and directness of Enlightenment composers that characterized his final years.

En route to exploring Messiaen's indebtedness to Chopin, something must be said of his admiration of Mozart, a composer whose music epitomizes the principles of terseness, simplicity, clarity and logic that have long been prized

[15] See Caroline Rae, *The Music of Maurice Ohana* (Aldershot: Ashgate, 2000), p. 20; Nigel Simeone 'Messiaen and the Concerts de la Pléiade: "A kind of clandestine resistance against the Occupation"', *Music and Letters*, 81/4 (November 2000) p. 555; and Barbara L. Kelly (ed.), *French Music, Culture and National Identity, 1870–1939* (Rochester NY: University of Rochester Press, 2008).

[16] Bartók also performed Mozart's D Major Sonata K. 448 for two pianos with Ernst von Dohnányi in April 1936. See Malcolm Gillies (ed.), *The Bartók Companion* (Faber and Faber: London, 1993), pp. 66, 68 and 333.

Example 11.1   Messiaen *Visions de l'Amen*, 'Amen du Désir', bars 1–4

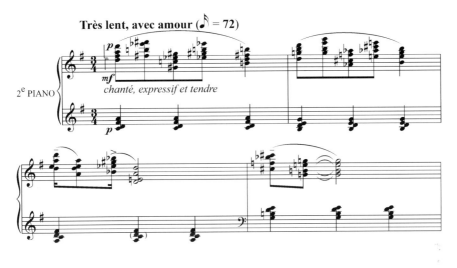

by the French, not least Debussy.[17] Mozart was also a composer receiving the unqualified praise of Chopin, who performed his music both in his youth and adulthood.[18] Messiaen connected the two composers in terms of their respective harmonic evolution of particular chord structures, which he proposed reached fulfilment in Wagner and Debussy.[19] Commenting on the Mozartian clarity of Debussy and his ability, like Mozart, to write an apparently 'lighthearted tune with an almost tragic significance', Constant Lambert also suggested that Debussy's predecessor Chabrier shared similar qualities as 'the first composer since Mozart to show that seriousness is not the same as solemnity', a feature that finds resonance in Messiaen's late works.[20] While Messiaen felt particularly close to Mozart during his last years and paid notable homage in his orchestral miniature *Un Sourire* (for which he acknowledged the operas, especially *The Marriage of Figaro*, as being important influences on his approach to melodic gesture), he had long been immersed in the study of Mozart's music. He makes several references to Mozart in *Technique de mon langage musical* and suggests that the principal melodic idea opening the fourth movement of *Visions de l'Amen*, 'Amen du Désir', has a Mozartian quality (Example 11.1).[21] There is a similar reference to this theme in

---

[17]   Caroline Rae, 'The Works of Messiaen's Final Years', in Robert Sherlaw Johnson, *Messiaen*, , updated and additional text by Caroline Rae (London: Omnibus Press, 2008), p. 198.

[18]   See Jim Samson, *The Music of Chopin* (London: Routledge & Kegan Paul, 1985) p. 6.

[19]   *Music and Color*, p. 42.

[20]   Constant Lambert, *Music Ho!* (Faber and Faber: London, 1934) pp. 34 and 195.

[21]   *Technique*, example 370.

the *Traité de rythme, de couleur, et d'ornithologie* that specifies the influence of 'Suzanna's aria' in *The Marriage of Figaro*.[22]

Although pure Messiaen, this highly expressive manifestation of lyrical pianism is as vocal in its inspiration as any of the operatic-inspired melodies in the slow movements of Mozart's piano concertos. The arc-shaped sighing phrases are features that can also be found in the melodic designs of Chopin. As in both Mozart and Chopin, much of Messiaen's melodic idiom absorbed elements from the vocal style of opera, all three composers achieving a directness of personal expression that is intimate as well as beguiling, the end result in each case converting to an entirely idiomatic pianism. Mozart's piano concertos formed an important part of Messiaen's teaching at the Paris Conservatoire, his detailed analyses of these works, together with his essay 'Pourquoi j'aime Mozart', being reproduced in the fourth volume of the *Traité*.[23] As Yvonne Loriod performed the complete Mozart piano concertos in a series of seven concerts during the autumn of 1964, it is tempting to ponder whether there may have been a mutual flow of ideas between husband and wife; Messiaen's analyses influencing Loriod's interpretations and perhaps vice versa.[24]

Messiaen and Chopin

Messiaen was a highly accomplished pianist and performer (not just at the organ console) who belonged to the great historical tradition of composer-pianists. Although characteristically modest about his piano playing, he remarked: 'I'll never have the transcendental virtuosity and the absolutely amazing technical facility of Yvonne Loriod. But I'm a decent pianist all the same, and I sight-read easily.'[25] He considered much of his early technique self-acquired, a view that Chopin, according to Jim Samson, is reputed also to have shared and that may have fostered a strong sense of individuality in both composers.[26] While Messiaen's encounters with the music of Ravel and Debussy, notably *Estampes* and *Gaspard de la nuit*, represented important early discoveries that indicated a prodigious

---

[22] *Traité III*, p. 249. For more on this, see Christopher Dingle's chapter in this volume, 'Messiaen and Mozart: A Love without Influence?'

[23] *Traité IV*, pp. 127–71.

[24] Yvonne Loriod's performances of the complete Mozart piano concertos were given with the Orchestre Lamoureux at the Paris Conservatoire on successive Saturdays from November to December 1964, and were directed by three conductors: Pierre Boulez, Bruno Maderna and Louis Martin. Loriod also composed her own cadenzas for several of these concertos (PHNS, p. 259.). During the early 1960s, Loriod recorded the four early Mozart piano concertos with Boulez and the Orchestre du Domaine Musical (see Appendix).

[25] *Music and Color*, p. 113.

[26] Samson, *The Music of Chopin*, p. 15.

pianistic ability, his main attraction to the piano during his boyhood was as a means of deciphering operatic scores by Mozart, Gluck, Berlioz, Wagner and of course Debussy.[27] Nevertheless, he achieved a standard of proficiency that was sufficiently high to be accepted into the piano class of Georges Falkenberg when he entered the Paris Conservatoire in 1919 at the tender age of 11.[28] Falkenberg was known at the time for his influential treatise on piano pedalling, *Les pédales du piano* (1892), which discusses pedalling techniques and notation, including in relation to Chabrier, one of the key, if sometimes neglected, figures of late nineteenth-century French pianism and an important influence on Debussy.[29] According to Lockspeiser, Falkenberg's treatise informed Debussy's approach to pedalling and, in 1909, both Falkenberg and Debussy published short pieces in Théodore Lack's *Méthode de piano*.[30] Both Debussy and Lack had been piano students of Antoine-François Marmontel, who had known and revered Chopin's playing (although he had not studied with him).[31]

The pianistic genealogy goes deeper still. Falkenberg had been a student of Georges Mathias, who studied with Chopin from around 1838–39 for a period of between five and seven years, the longest of all Chopin's known pupils.[32] Mathias taught at the Paris Conservatoire for more than 30 years (from 1862 to 1893) and was largely responsible for embedding Chopin's music and pedagogical philosophies into French pianistic tradition. Living until 1910, Mathias is reputed to have been on friendly terms with Debussy whose piano music he may have performed. Another of Mathias's notable students was Paul Dukas, who later taught Messiaen composition and who was a strong supporter, as well as teacher,

[27]   PHNS, p. 13.

[28]   Falkenberg was also one of the teachers of the pianist and composer Claude Delvincourt (1888–1954) who won the Prix de Rome in 1913, and became Director of the Paris Conservatoire in 1940. Although Messiaen was encouraged by Falkenberg to develop a concert career, he soon realized that he wished to devote his energies primarily to composition (see Christopher Dingle, *The Life of Messiaen* (Cambridge: Cambridge University Press, 2007), p. 13). Messiaen remained with Falkenberg for several years but then moved to the piano accompaniment class of César Abel Estyle, with whom Yvonne Loriod later also studied.

[29]   See Roy Howat, *The Art of French Piano Music*, pp. 83–94.

[30]   Edward Lockspeiser, *Debussy: His Life and Mind* (London: Casell, 1962) pp. 46–7. Debussy's contribution to Théodore Lack's collection was *Le petit Nègre*, a piece recalling 'Golliwog's Cake-walk' from *Children's Corner*.

[31]   Ravel's teacher Émile Descombes had been another member of Chopin's circle in Paris. See Roy Howat, *The Art of French Piano Music*, p. 63. Ravel progressed to the piano class of Charles-Wilfrid de Bériot (a pupil of Thalberg) after winning the Conservatoire's Concours de Piano of 1891.

[32]   Jean-Jacques Eigeldinger, *Chopin Pianist and Teacher*, ed. Roy Howat, trans. Naomi Shohet, Krysia Osostowicz and Roy Howat (Cambridge: Cambridge University Press, 1986), p. 170. See also Charles Timbrell, *French Pianism: A Historical Perspective*, pp. 43–4.

of Albéniz, and a close friend of Debussy. Messiaen was thus placed in a direct line of pianistic succession that embraced Debussy, Albéniz and Chopin. Together with Chopin's 'grand-pupil' Paul Dukas (and his pianistic muse Yvonne Loriod), Messiaen belonged to a distinguished line of French composer-pianists, including Chabrier, Fauré, Debussy and Ravel, who inherited the Chopin tradition.[33]

The tracing of genealogy is revealing, but more significant is the way in which Messiaen acknowledged and explored his inheritance in developing his own approach to the piano. He expressed unreserved praise for Chopin:

> I adore Chopin, the ballades as well as the preludes and études, the scherzos as well as the Barcarolle, the Berceuse, and the 'Funeral March' Sonata; I love all Chopin, who is the greatest composer for the piano. He discovered the most extraordinary passagework, fingerings and combinations.[34]

Completed in 1929, Messiaen's eight *Préludes* were composed as he came to the end of his student days at the Paris Conservatoire; that they were published so rapidly was due in no small part to the support of Paul Dukas.[35] The set already sounds like quintessential Messiaen due to the assiduous use of his modes of limited transposition, yet, while they demonstrate a confident and distinctive musical language that is astounding for such a young composer, they also bear witness to the influences he absorbed during his studies, or to be more precise, the influences that stimulated the development of his own compositional thinking.

Although Messiaen's *Préludes* are often compared to Debussy's as a result of certain conceptual and textural similarities – the descriptive titles (albeit with a surrealist tinge) and the propensity for impressionistic sweeps of sound bathed in pedal – Chopin's Preludes also served as meaningful models. Like Chopin's Preludes op. 28, Messiaen's explore similarly focused musical ideas. Some are condensed, some are more elaborated, and they are constructed in a clear progression of contrasting mood and texture from piece to piece leading to a dramatic concluding climax, suggesting that Messiaen may have intended his own to be played as a set. Both works also end emphatically on the same pitch: the D at the very bottom of the piano that in both Messiaen, at the end of 'Un reflet dans le vent…', and Chopin, in the last three bars of the 24th Prelude, is an accented triple *fortissimo* (Example 11.2). The parallel goes even further. While Chopin's Prelude is in D minor and Messiaen's is ostensibly oriented towards D major, the final 12 bars of 'Un reflet dans le vent…' present similar D minor harmonic colourings as in the last 13 bars of Chopin's Prelude, including with the emphasis of B♭; an F♯ appears only very briefly in the final chordal flourish, a gesture derived from Chopin's descending arpeggio, and is immediately overpowered by the forceful bottom D. The final bars of both

---

[33]   For more on Chopin's legacy in French pianism from Fauré to Ravel, see Roy Howat, *The Art of French Piano Music*, pp. 63–82.

[34]   *Music and Color*, p. 114.

[35]   Dingle, *The Life of Messiaen*, p. 14.

Preludes also span six octaves from the uppermost D in the treble to the bottom D, the maximum possible from this pitch. Such a dramatic pianistic gesture constructed around the same harmonic outline is unlikely to be mere coincidence, especially as the 24th Prelude presents one of Chopin's boldest and most ominous endings and is a work Messiaen acknowledges in his *Traité*.[36]

Example 11.2   Concluding gestures of the Messiaen and Chopin sets of Preludes

(a) Messiaen 'Un reflet dans le vent…', bars 199–202

(b) Chopin Prelude no. 24, bars 73–77

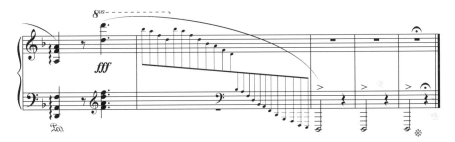

Close inspection of 'Un reflet dans le vent…' yields further pianistic similarity to Chopin. While the chromatic double note patterns (for example, bars 11–13 and 25–28) are close to those found in Ravel (notably 'Scarbo' from *Gaspard de la nuit*) due to Messiaen's requirement for the thumb to be used laterally to play two notes simultaneously, they also relate closely to the passages in chromatic thirds in Chopin's Prelude op. 28, no. 24, and the more extended exploration of the pianistic problem in Chopin's Étude op. 25, no. 6, which, like Messiaen's fingering in 'Un reflet dans le vent…', requires inner fingers (especially the third) to extend over (and sometimes under) the fourth and fifth fingers to achieve a

---

[36]   *Traité II*, p. 468.

rapid legato.[37] This is itself an extension of principles based on older Baroque keyboard fingerings alluded to by Chopin in the Étude op. 10, no. 2. The rapid triplet patterns such as occur in bars 49–50 of Messiaen's prelude involve hand-shapes that are very similar to those in Chopin's Étude op. 10, no. 5 (particularly the central section), while the right-hand octave ostinato pattern (bars 91–92, and bars 97–98) involving the substitution of fourth or fifth finger and thumb on a repeated note (to ascend the octave) is identical to that featured in similarly climatic passages in Chopin, such as in the development section of the A♭ Major Ballade, op. 47 (right hand, bars 165–172). The appearance of the melodic chordal idea in the left hand underpinning Messiaen's octave ostinati maintains the continuity of the tactile borrowing from Chopin. Other left-hand patterns are also suggestive of Chopin; in the 'Toujours très lent' section of 'Cloches d'angoisse et larmes d'adieu', the ascending accompanimental double notes (for example, bar 39) both fill in the harmony and maintain forward momentum. Similar left-hand patterns can be found in the coda of Chopin's A♭ Major Ballade. Messiaen extends this type of crab-like ascending (and descending) patterning to accompanimental figures played by the right hand, as in the decorative added-resonance passages in the same prelude (for instance, the upper stave of bar 39).

Messiaen's link with Ravel in 'Un reflet dans le vent...' owes much to a common musical ancestry descending from Chopin, yet the mood and musical substance of this prelude remain what might be considered Messiaen's response to 'Scarbo', a piece he knew well from his boyhood. Like 'Scarbo', Messiaen's prelude is highly virtuosic and exploits many abrupt alternations of material as well as the dramatic use of silence. Certain pianistic effects, however, are more reminiscent of Liszt, most notably the use of rapid, tremolando hand-alternation (bars 105–108), although these are also features that Messiaen could have derived from Albéniz. The other strongly Ravelian connection among Messiaen's *Préludes* occurs in 'Cloches d'angoisse et larmes d'adieu', the opening of which, with its tolling bell and melodic chordal idea, closely resembles 'Le gibet' from *Gaspard de la nuit*.

Like Chopin's Preludes, those of Messiaen fulfil the role of pianistic, interpretative and compositional studies. Messiaen's consistently explore pianistic problems found in Chopin (and explored most extensively in the études): rapid successions of chords (in both hands simultaneously as well as individually), passagework, varied articulations of similar material, legato playing, trills, contrary motion, athletic leaps (single notes and chords), double notes (thirds, sixths and other interval combinations), octaves, wide stretches of the hand, cross-rhythms between hands, and part-playing requiring hierarchical definition between voices (played within and between the hands). Messiaen also focuses individual sections on tone production, often in very quiet passages requiring a Chopinesque veiled

---

[37]   In his conversations with Claude Samuel, Messiaen also mentions use of the slanted thumb in relation to Prokofiev (see *Music and Color*, p. 115). Ravel's use of the slanted thumb in *Gaspard de la nuit* predates that of Prokofiev.

pianissimo, and uses the full range of the instrument, but extends his technical explorations to include toccata-like hand-alternation and specific effects of pedalling.

Not surprisingly, Chopin's own études provide a useful point of pianistic reference for Messiaen, the importance of these works in the formation of his piano writing being acknowledged in his *Traité*.[38] Madeleine Hsu [Forte] has already pointed out that the chromatic passages in contrary motion in 'Le Nombre léger' (bar 11) bear a startling resemblance to those in the central section of Chopin's Étude op. 10, no. 3 (bar 38),[39] but it is not merely the shape and chromatic harmony that are reminiscent of Chopin; Messiaen's passage requires a smooth lateral movement of the hand, one of the main technical problems in the central section of Chopin's study. Connections with Chopin's op. 10, no. 3, also occur in 'La colombe', notably the 'pleading' semiquaver couplets (bars 9 and 19) that echo the articulation and character of similar pairings in the central chromatic section of Chopin's study, although Messiaen compacts the melodic line and thickens the texture to three notes per hand rather than two. Op. 10, no. 3, is further evoked in 'Chant d'extase dans un paysage triste'; like Chopin's study, a long-breathed melody is juxtaposed with chromatic movement, and the central section incorporates a similar combination of melodic material with syncopated accompaniment (bar 33). Although the contemplative mood of this prelude is more akin to a Chopin nocturne or the *Berceuse* with which it partially shares its tonality; the F♯ major section presages the serene calm of 'Le Baiser de l'Enfant-Jésus' in *Vingt Regards* (also in F♯ major) and certain figurations recall passages in other Chopin studies including op. 10, no. 4 (arpeggiated descents) and op. 10, no. 11 (spread chords). The curling chromaticism within the initial theme also relates to the chromatic semiquaver accompanimental figure at the opening of op. 10, no. 6, which is itself a melodic idea.

While the scherzo-like 'Les sons impalpables du rêve...' is pure Messiaen in terms of its juxtaposition of different modes of limited transposition, cascading chords and use of rhythmic canon, some of its chordal patterns, particularly those in contrary motion such as at bar 16, connect with the chromatic passages of the central section in Chopin's op. 10, no. 3. The final cadence with its filigree glissando followed by a chord with a resonant tonic note at the bottom of the keyboard also develops similar gestures found in Chopin, such as at the end of the F♯ Minor Nocturne op. 48, no. 2 (see Example 11.3). Like Chopin, Messiaen juxtaposes extremes of register, leaving the main harmonic resonance to sound in the central part of the piano. The pedal notation in both the Chopin and Messiaen underlines the colourism of this effect. A similar gesture appears at the end of Chopin's Étude op. 25, no. 5, while the chordal leaps in contrary motion to the top

---

[38] *Traité II*, p. 480.

[39] Madeleine Hsu, *Olivier Messiaen, the Musical Mediator: A Study of the Influence of Liszt, Debussy, and Bartók* (Madison, NJ and London: Associated University Presses, 1996), p. 43.

Example 11.3　Resonant effects in concluding cadences of Messiaen and Chopin

(a) Messiaen 'Les sons impalpables du rêve…', bars 67–68

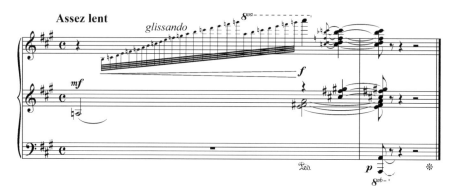

(b) Chopin Nocturne op. 48, no. 2, bars 136–137

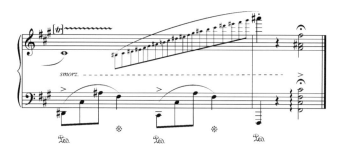

and bottom registers of the piano appearing a few bars earlier (bars 124, 126 and 128) presage Messiaen's concept of added resonance.

It is worth commenting briefly on Messiaen's pedal notation in the *Préludes* as indications tend to be reserved for special effects, suggesting a Chopin-like economy of use. Indeed, pedal notation of any kind is not used until the fifth prelude, 'Les sons impalpables du rêve…', Messiaen leaving use of the sustaining pedal to the discretion of the player. Notation, where it does appear, is designed either to clarify resonance where ambiguities may arise, such as long combinations of chords where the pianist might otherwise clear the sound, or to specify changes to ensure particular combinations of sounds and avoid unintentional blurring. Curiously, for a composer writing in the twentieth century, Messiaen provides no indications for either the 'una corda' or the 'sostenuto' (third) pedal. Such indications would have been useful in 'Cloches d'angoisse et larmes d'adieu', notably for the passages where added-resonance chords in the piano's upper register sound against the principal, chordal melody (for example at bar 10). While Yvonne Loriod suggested that the 'sostenuto' pedal could be used for these passages, she advocated the very

French technique of 'half-pedalling' to thin the sound progressively without losing the resonance of the main chord.[40] In *Vingt Regards*, however, Loriod insisted that the 'sostenuto' pedal should be used, particularly in 'Le Baiser de l'Enfant-Jésus', even though it is not indicated in the score.[41]

All of this suggests a studied approach to Chopin's pianism. In these early works, Messiaen proved himself to be a great melodist but one, like Chopin, who was also concerned with exploiting, and extending, the colouristic possibilities of the instrument; he considered Chopin 'a very great colorist'.[42] Messiaen's closeness to Chopin's music persisted well into his later years. At the time of writing his opera *Saint François d'Assise*, Messiaen considered composing a work taking the recitative-type structure of Chopin's Prelude no. 18 in F Minor as his point of departure, while his *cahier* of 1984, which records plans for his projected (but abandoned) *Le Vitrail de l'Assomption*, notes that he should consult Chopin's études for the piano parts.[43]

While Messiaen's *Préludes* are essentially miniatures, essays of pianistic and compositional discovery with a clarity and intimacy akin to both Chopin and Mozart, they laid the foundation stone for the subsequent development of his pianism. Having absorbed the lessons of Chopin's music, Messiaen moved towards composing on a much larger scale and adopted a more orchestral approach in his great cycles of the 1940s, not only *Visions de l'Amen* and *Vingt Regards*, but also *Harawi*, in which the gargantuan piano part is just as much a tour de force as in the works for solo piano. Although written for Yvonne Loriod, either in partnership or as soloist, these works acknowledge Messiaen's own approach to the piano as a player: 'I play the piano as though I were conducting an orchestra, which is to say by turning the piano into a mock orchestra with a large palette of timbres and accents.'[44] With the works of the 1940s, Messiaen significantly expanded his pianistic as well as compositional canvas, the sheer power, volume of sound and stamina required of the pianist indicating a pianism that has more in common with Liszt, or even at times Rachmaninov, not least in terms of the latter's predilection for cascading chords imitating pealing bells. Messiaen's pathway to this approach was informed by his contact with the piano music of Albéniz.

Messiaen and Albéniz

Although Albéniz is reputed to have studied the piano privately in Paris with Antoine-François Marmontel for a short period during his boyhood, his most

---

[40]   Caroline Rae in conversation with Yvonne Loriod during piano lessons with her in Paris in 1983.

[41]   Ibid.

[42]   *Music and Color*, p. 114.

[43]   PHNS, pp. 333 and 351.

[44]   *Music and Color*, p. 113.

important pianistic formation was in Spain and Brussels, where his teachers included the then highly renowned Belgian pianist Louis Brassin, who had been a pupil of Moscheles in Leipzig.[45] Albéniz's pianistic training thus stands largely outside the French tradition, although his later years in Paris brought him into contact with Debussy, Ravel, Fauré and Paul Dukas, the latter with whom he formed a close friendship and took lessons in orchestration.[46] The four books of his piano work *Ibéria* (1905–09) were premièred in France by the French pianist Blanche Selva in four recitals from 1906 to 1909. By the time Messiaen began to discover this collection of 12 pieces around 1927 they had been performed by many pianists including Alfred Cortot and Arthur Rubinstein, although it is possible that Dukas may have played a role in drawing Messiaen's attention to Albéniz's music.[47] Messiaen encountered *Ibéria* before completing his *Préludes*, the discovery by his own account being a significant one:

> Finally, I'll mention a work that has played a great role in my knowledge of the piano: Albéniz's *Ibéria* which I discovered around the age of nineteen! I've often played and replayed the twelve pieces contained in its four books – especially 'Almeira' [sic, 'Almería'], 'El Polo', and 'Lavapies' – without attaining perfection, for they're so terribly difficult: I'll never be able to play them like Yvonne Loriod.[48]

Traits of Albéniz's pianism can be found in Messiaen's *Préludes*. The toccata-like hand-alternation in 'Le Nombre léger' is close to the figuration that characterizes 'El Albaicin' (Debussy's preferred piece from *Ibéria*) which eventually builds into an alternating chordal pattern (as in Messiaen) after the initial single notes; both necessitate a lightness of touch to achieve the required ethereal *pianissimo*. This delicate figuration also occurs in 'El polo'. In 'Le Nombre léger', Messiaen goes the extra step of embedding a melodic line that requires subtle dashes of pedal to give the effect of a legato. The usual precedent for this type of patterning where the hands are in alternation is often taken to be Liszt but the texture in Messiaen's prelude is quite different; Liszt's rapid hand-alternation patterns are usually in octaves and generally occur at points of intense *fortissimo* climaxes where maximum resonance is sought, as in *Wilde Jagd*, the 'Presto tempestuoso' section of *Vallée d'Obermann* and *Après une lecture de Dante*. Messiaen's texture

---

[45]   Louis Brassin (1840–84) left Belgium in 1878 to take over Theodor Leschetizky's piano class at the St Petersburg Conservatoire.

[46]   Walter Aaron Clark, *Isaac Albéniz: Portrait of a Romantic* (Oxford: Oxford University Press, 1999) p. 197. Clark also explains that it is now known that Albéniz did not study with Liszt, despite having travelled to Budapest with that objective.

[47]   The première of Albéniz's opera *Pepita Jiménez* at the Opéra-Comique in 1923 was due in no small part to the support of Dukas as well as Fauré.

[48]   *Music and Color*, p. 114. Yvonne Loriod often performed Albéniz's *Ibéria* and made a recording of the complete work in 1955 (see Appendix).

also differs from the repeated-note patterning that opens Mussorgsky's 'Limoges Market' in *Pictures at an Exhibition* – the hands move in unison rather than in alternation – as well as from the final 'meno mosso' section of the same piece where the *fortissimo* hand-alternation creates a strident climax as in comparable passages in the Lisztian 'Baba Yaga'.[49] While the couplet hand-alternation pattern found at bar 14 of 'Le Nombre léger' bears a fleeting resemblance to a similar articulation occurring at the beginning of bar 8 in Mussorgsky's 'Limoges Market', the mood and sound-colour of Messiaen's figuration is more Debussian despite the phrase being followed by a scherzo-like staccato as in the Mussorgsky. Although Messiaen makes use of tremolando and rapid chordal hand-alternations in both *Visions de l'Amen* and *Vingt Regards*, especially for tumultuous crescendos, he distinguishes this extrovert pianistic technique from the more delicate figuration derived from Albéniz, such as occurs in the ethereal final section of 'Regard du silence'.

Sections of 'Instants défunts' suggest different aspects of Albéniz's writing. In the 'Modéré' section (for instance, bars 9–11), the delineation of parts, left-hand harmonic resonances and partial use of octaves for the melodic line recall similar textures in 'Almería'. Like Albéniz, Messiaen also begins to make use of multiple staves in the *Préludes*, although there are additional precedents for this practice in Debussy and Ravel as well as in Liszt. The three-stave notation that dominates 'Cloches d'angoisse et larmes d'adieu' recalls Albéniz in terms of its dense part-writing and complex organization of the hands, notably at the appearance of the thematic canon (bars 14–17) and in the 'Toujours très lent' section from bar 39. While the music itself is slow, the physical movements of the pianist's hands are fast as swift leaps are required particularly in the right hand, which, in the 'Toujours très lent', has to negotiate both the principal melodic line and the added-resonance chords above. This complexity is combined with an additional problem; each strand of material has to be played at a different dynamic level. The intricate crossing and interweaving of the hands that is required in the thematic canon section is also characteristic of Albéniz's piano writing throughout *Ibéria*, as is the construction of climaxes via contrary motion and (in 'Lavapies' particularly) cascades of chords. These features characterize much of Messiaen's pianism, not only in *Visions de l'Amen* and *Vingt Regards* but also in the birdsong-inspired works of the 1950s and beyond.

Another feature connecting Messiaen's piano writing with that of Albéniz is their approach to dynamic markings. While both composers make use of dynamic extremes ranging from *pppp* to *ffff* (Messiaen even extends to *fffff* at the end of *Visions de l'Amen* – Albéniz to *ppppp* in 'El Albaicin'), precedents for Messiaen's careful delineation of separate strands of musical material with individual dynamic markings, such as at the opening of 'La Colombe' and 'Chant d'extase dans un paysage triste' (for example bar 12), can also be found in Albéniz, not least in 'Almería' and 'El Albaicin'. As in Albéniz, Messiaen often assigns principal melodic lines to a lower, or inside, part. These practices are indicative of orchestral

---

[49] See Dingle, *The Life of Messiaen*, p. 23.

thinking. It is likely that Albéniz composed *Ibéria* with specific orchestrations in mind; he completed his own orchestration of 'El puerto' only one year after the work's première in 1906, before assigning his friend and colleague Enrique Arbós to orchestrate other pieces from three of the four books comprising the complete set.[50]

Messiaen's concept of added resonance also has precedents in Albéniz, a notable example occurring in 'Almería' (bars 144–145) where *pianissimo* triplets in the piano's upper register provide harmonic resonance over the *forte* principal melodic line below. In the later sections of 'El Albaicín', the opening hand-alternation pattern appears as a similarly quiet resonance over a louder sustained double octave (for example, bars 249–252), while at bars 273–274 a *fortissimo* chord is decorated with *pppp* chordal resonances held within the sustaining pedal. Other examples of innovative effects of resonance can be found in 'Fête-Dieu à Seville', particularly the final section, as well as in 'Evocación' and 'El puerto'.

In addition to experimentation with resonance, dynamic extremes and other colouristic effects, Albéniz's approach to harmony and rhythm must have attracted Messiaen. Although operating within a conventional diatonic framework, the pieces comprising *Ibéria* are characterized by a rich harmonic colourism in which individual chords (and sometimes successions of chords) are amplified by numerous piquant added dissonances, some of which fall conveniently under the hand, others of which are notoriously awkward to play due to the sheer profusion of notes, but all of which serve to enhance the Spanish characterizations. Certainly, Messiaen was not looking to compose Spanish-inspired music but the concept of these colouristic added notes contributed to the development of his own harmonic thinking, particularly as he cited 'Lavapies', which contains some of Albéniz's most startling dissonances, among his preferred works.[51] *Ibéria* is also remarkable for its rhythmic ingenuity. Albéniz's exploitation of metric ambiguity, superimposed rhythms, cross-rhythms, displaced accentuation and the use rhythm for percussive effect must have appealed to Messiaen as early examples of an innovative language that could combine flexibility with rhythmic precision. Again, Messiaen's favoured pieces 'El Polo' and 'Lavapies' are both notable for their particular rhythmic complexity. Yet, most of all *Ibéria* demonstrated how far pianistic boundaries could be pushed in terms of combining a transcendental virtuosity with an innovative approach to rhythm and instrumental colour while still achieving clarity and even delicacy within a relatively large-scale work. To underline his enduring admiration for these works, Messiaen wrote the sleeve notes for Yvonne Loriod's complete recording of *Ibéria* released in 1955, while his kinship with Albéniz was underlined by Loriod's combining of extracts from *Ibéria* and *Vingt Regards* in her concert programmes.[52]

---

[50]   Arbós orchestrated four pieces from *Ibéria*: 'Evocación', 'Triana', 'El Albaicín' and 'Fête-Dieu à Seville'. Carlos Surinach later orchestrated several additional pieces including 'Almería'.

[51]   *Music and Color*, p. 114.

[52]   See, for example PHNS, p. 207.

Visions de l'Amen and *Vingt Regards sur l'Enfant-Jésus*

By the time Messiaen came to compose *Visions de l'Amen*, written for himself and Yvonne Loriod to perform, and *Vingt Regards*, his pianistic and compositional language of the period were fully formed. These were the first works he dedicated to Yvonne Loriod, the grandeur of the pianism acknowledging her extraordinarily prodigious virtuosity as well as her ability to absorb and understand complex new musical ideas rapidly, a remarkable feat for such a young performer; Loriod was 19 when she first performed *Visions de l'Amen* with Messiaen in May 1943, and still only 21 when she premièred *Vingt Regards* in March 1945. As Peter Hill has observed, 'the inspiring influence of Loriod, whose unquenchable powers enabled new complexities of thought, liberated Messiaen's imagination (as he many times testified) from practical limitations'.[53] While distinctive and original in their approach to the piano, these works nevertheless reveal indebtedness to Messiaen's romantic forebears.

In *Visions de l'Amen*, the clearest example occurs in the extended solo of the fourth movement 'Amen du Désir'. Despite Messiaen's assertion of a Mozartian quality to the shape of the introductory theme, the contrasting second theme is as grandiose as the most impassioned and declamatory statements of Liszt in his B Minor Sonata or *Après une lecture de Dante*. In the main climaxes of the second theme, Messiaen, like Liszt, opens up the full resonance of the instrument with emphatically repeated chordal structures in surging crescendos of an orchestral dimension leading to successions of accented chords in which multiple registers are sounded to prolong the extended *fff* (Example 11.4). He further indicates that the sustaining pedal should be held throughout the four bars of each climax. The approach to these climaxes is also redolent of Liszt; ascending triplets, combined with intermediate patterns in contrary motion, climb to the upper registers of the piano with the climax itself sounded by octaves in the lowest register reinforced with a widely spaced chord between the hands. The moment of white heat when the climax occurs spans the full seven octaves of the piano. This highly physical gesture where the hands move outwards to the extremes of the keyboard is also dramatic visually and is common throughout Liszt's virtuoso piano music, although Messiaen presents the idea in its most extreme form.

The theme is later repeated with an accompaniment on Piano I, which initially superimposes a succession of rhythmic canons in the bass register of the instrument (a percussive texture strongly reminiscent of the 'Princesse de Bali' movement from Jolivet's *Mana*, completed eight years earlier in 1935). As the theme in Piano II approaches its successive climaxes, the first piano supports the crescendos with Lisztian figurations, rapidly ascending hand-alternations in octaves and tremolandos. Like Liszt, Messiaen juxtaposes impassioned outbursts with moments of great tenderness, framing the two solo sections with decorated

---

[53]   Peter Hill, 'Piano Music I', in Peter Hill (ed.), *The Messiaen Companion* (London: Faber and Faber, 1995), p. 88.

Example 11.4   Climactic chordal resonances in Messiaen and Liszt

(a) Messiaen *Visions de l'Amen* 'Amen du Désir', bars 48–52

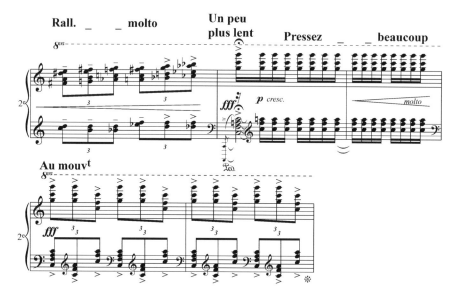

(b) Liszt *Après une lecture de Dante*, bars 102–103

(c) Liszt *Après une lecture de Dante*, bars 308–309

restatements of the intimate opening theme. The descant melodic material in the first piano's upper register that characterizes these 'Très lent' sections recalls the crystalline quaver motifs in Liszt's 'Bénédiction de Dieu dans la solitude', the third of his *Harmonies poétiques et réligieuses*, particularly those that appear in the piano's upper register after the impassioned climax in the first section. (A similar texture, although less extensive, appears in the final bars of the Largo movement of Rachmaninov's G Minor Cello Sonata.) The serene calm of these passages suggests the evocation of Paradise to which Messiaen refers in his preface to the score of *Visions de l'Amen*, an allusion that is also highly appropriate for Liszt's 'Bénédiction de Dieu dans la solitude'; both Messiaen and Liszt combine intense yearning in the preceding climactic sections with a peace and serenity that suggests a shaft of religious illumination descending from the heavens.

While *Visions de l'Amen* as a whole demonstrates Messiaen's fully fledged orchestral pianism in the sheer power of sound produced from the two pianos, the density of his writing and his simultaneous use of the extreme treble and bass registers of the keyboard, certain figurations bear witness to his study of Chopin's études. These include the semiquaver couplets in 'Amen des étoiles, de la planète à l'anneau', which recur more prominently in 'Amen de la Consommation', and the successions of chords in contrary motion that presage each repeat of the theme in the final movement. The manic virtuosity of 'Amen de la Consommation', however, extends far beyond that of Chopin or even Liszt, the athletic agility and rapid finger dexterity required in the first piano part (performed by Loriod) approaching that of Rachmaninov. The descending bell-chords that introduce the final thrust of the last movement may also have Russian precedents, as may those of 'Regard de l'Esprit de joie' and 'Regard de l'Église d'amour' in *Vingt Regards*; peals of bells feature prominently in 'The Great Gate of Kiev' from Mussorgsky's *Pictures at an Exhibition* and also occur in Rachmaninov's Second Piano Sonata, the latter being expanded to chordal structures (as opposed to Mussorgsky's octaves) that anticipate Messiaen. The chimes of 'Regard de l'Église d'amour' are particularly reminiscent of the clanging bells in Mussorgsky.

Vingt Regards takes Messiaen's pianism to an epic level. While the abundant innovations of texture and figuration are Messiaen's own, other aspects of his writing connect with practices of his romantic predecessors to provide tactile points of pianistic reference: the use of pounding repeated chords to swell the resonance; rapid chordal hand-alternation; tremolandi (in a single hand as well as between the hands); chains of trills; chains of octaves; athletic leaps (of single notes as well as chords, and to extremes of register in contrary motion); leaps to bass notes (or octaves) that provide foundation harmonic resonances; chordal figurations in contrary motion leading to climaxes, sometimes combined with long *rallentandi*; extended sections of arpeggiated chords; rapidly repeated notes; and a finger dexterity in passage-work (often in triplets) that is built from the most demanding passages in both Chopin and Liszt. In addition, Messiaen uses *pianissimo tremolandi* and arpeggiated chordal figurations bathed in pedal that recall Liszt's 'Les Jeux d'eaux à la villa d'Este' from *Années de pèlerinage, troisième année*, as well as decorative filigree figurations and gently pulsating octaves evocative of those in 'St François d'Assise: La prédication aux oiseaux', the first of his *Deux légendes*, and 'Bénédiction de Dieu dans la solitude'. Like Liszt, Chopin and Rachmaninov, Messiaen also does not eschew expansive, expressive melodies.

The connections with 'Les Jeux d'eaux à la villa d'Este', 'St François d'Assise: La prédication aux oiseaux' and 'Bénédiction de Dieu dans la solitude' are particularly interesting as all these works are in sharp keys. Like 'Le Baiser de l'Enfant-Jésus', 'Les Jeux d'eaux à la villa d'Este' and 'Bénédiction de Dieu dans la solitude' are also in F♯ major, Messiaen's preferred key for love and communion with the divine.[54] While the contemplative mood and religious associations link these works together, the key is significant from a pianistic point of view as the preponderance of black notes facilitates execution of the delicate figurations, a feature also appreciated by Ravel in *Jeux d'eau* (although the latter is in E major rather than F♯).[55] In 'Les Jeux d'eaux à la villa d'Este', Liszt even adds a very Messiaen-like annotation to the score quoting from the Gospel According to Saint John: 'But whosoever drinketh of the water that I shall give him, shall never thirst. But the water that I shall give him shall be in him a well of water springing up to everlasting life.'[56] Messiaen refers to this same text from John 4:14 in his account of *Fêtes des belles eaux*, a work for the unusual combination of six ondes Martenot written to accompany the Festival of Sound, Water and Light (a sort of *son et lumière*) organised by the City of Paris that took place over the river Seine as part of the 1937 Exposition Internationale des Arts et des Techniques appliqués à la vie moderne. Explaining that the jets of water in the display accompanying his music engendered a predominantly 'dream-like and contemplative' mood, Messiaen described the long slow melody of his piece as a prayer, the water becoming 'a symbol of Grace and Eternity'.[57] This same melody was subsequently reworked as the 'Louange à l'Éternité de Jésus' in the *Quatuor pour la fin du Temps* (in the sharp key of E major), the gently pulsating chords of the accompanying piano part in this movement and the final 'Louange à l'immortalité de Jésus', creating a sense of timelessness that enhances the prayer-like quality of these supremely expressive statements. The three Liszt pieces mentioned above are also prayer-like contemplations, while their shimmering figurations in the upper registers of

---

[54]   Liszt's 'St François d'Assise: La prédication aux oiseaux' is in A major.

[55]   I am grateful to my brother Charles Bodman Rae for reminding me about the connection with Liszt's 'Bénédiction de Dieu dans la solitude'.

[56]   John 4:14. Liszt cites the text in Latin: 'Sed aqua quam ego dabo ei, fiet in eo fons aquae salientis in vitam aeternam.' I am grateful to The Reverend Peter Crocker for sourcing this quotation.

[57]   Olivier Messiaen, 'Commentary' [for *Fêtes des belles eaux*], reproduced in Nigel Simeone, *Olivier Messiaen: Catalogue of Works* (Tutzing: Schneider, 1998), p. 194. See also Vincent P. Benitez, *Olivier Messiaen: A Research and Information Guide* (New York and London: Routledge, 2008) p. 54.

the piano equate with the delicately cascading melodic descants of 'Le Baiser de l'Enfant-Jésus' and the final section of the 'Amen du Désir' in *Visions de l'Amen*. Whether in Liszt's fountains in the garden at Tivoli, Messiaen's mystical embrace in 'Le Baiser' or his expression of Paradise in 'Amen du Désir', these textures suggest an eternal peace: 'all that remains is the harmonious silence of Heaven...'.[58]

An entirely different pianism is evoked in the tumultuous movements of *Vingt Regards*, 'Par Lui tout a été fait', 'Regard de l'Esprit de joie' and 'Regard de l'Onction terrible'. In these pieces Messiaen releases the full force of a ferocious virtuosity, as well as a considerable musical complexity, that makes *Vingt Regards*, as Peter Hill has remarked, 'an Everest among pianistic challenges'.[59] (With 'Par Lui tout a été fait' and 'Regard de l'Esprit de joie' both appearing in the first half of the cycle, the pianist earns a well-deserved interval break!) Messiaen's orchestral treatment of the piano in these movements has precedents in Liszt as well as in Albéniz, although it is developed significantly further. Many of his figurations originate in these composers, albeit in a more compact form, while the pounding chords, dramatic crescendi in contrary motion and extended climactic *rallentandi* additionally suggest a Lisztian ancestry. (Yvonne Loriod advised that Messiaen's climactic *rallentando* should be as dramatic as possible, and even start slightly earlier than notated.)[60] Liszt also incorporated and paraphrased plainchant in a number of his late piano works, although Messiaen's approach in the raucous percussiveness of his parody in the 'Thème de danse orientale et plain-chantesque' at the opening of 'Regard de l'Esprit de joie' is entirely new. Following the final statement of the 'Thème de joie' towards the end of the same movement, Messiaen uses an intricate rotational figuration played by the right hand in the upper register, a fingering pattern in which the hand pivots about the thumb.[61] Although this figuration in itself is new, it combines complex lateral movements with principles of expansion and contraction of the hand that were explored by Chopin in many of his études. Finally, Messiaen's unusual notational device in 'Regard de l'Esprit de joie', in which arrow-headed diagonal lines are used to signify moments where particularly rapid leaps of the hands are required to ensure rhythmic precision, can also be found in 'Lavapies' from Albéniz's *Ibéria*.

---

[58] 'il n'y a plus que le silence harmonieux du Ciel...'. Messiaen's preface to the score of *Visions de l'Amen*. This echoes the preface to the *Quatuor pour la fin du Temps*, which also mentions 'the harmonious silence of heaven' in relation to 'Liturgie de cristal', while the text introducing the 'Louange à l'Éternité de Jésus' incorporates a reference to Saint John's Gospel 1:1, 'In the beginning was the Word, and the Word was with God, and the Word was God.'

[59] Peter Hill, 'Piano Music I', p. 88.

[60] Caroline Rae in conversation with Yvonne Loriod during piano lessons with her on *Vingt Regards* in Paris in 1983.

[61] See also Peter Hill, 'Piano Music I', p. 99.

Conclusion

With *Cantéyodjayâ*, Messiaen's pianism began to move in a radically different direction, although even here there are vestiges of romantic figurations embedded within the musical fabric: delicate Albéniz-inspired hand-alternations, *tremolando* and chromatic contrary motion recalling the patterns learned from Chopin's op. 10, no. 3, which are used to climactic effect in the work's closing gesture. With the arrival of Messiaen's birdsong period of the 1950s his recourse to romantic gesture becomes less prevalent, the pianism being refracted into the multiple textures and sonorities resulting from shape and design of his birdsong transcriptions. Birdsong inspired Messiaen to find a new approach not only to musical content but also to invent new types of pianistic timbre, gesture, figuration and even pedalling, although the mood of some works, 'Le Traquet stapazin' in particular (based in an ethereal E major) has a spirituality redolent of Liszt. In *Catalogue d'oiseaux*, Messiaen's pedal indications are far more numerous than in his previous piano works, and he carefully specifies the use of the 'una corda' (sourdine) for particular effects. His approach to orchestral colouration at the piano also begins to change, reflecting the percussive colours of his instrumental ensembles of the period: the scores of *Catalogue d'oiseaux* include evocative sound-descriptors such as 'clear like a glockenspiel', 'ecstatic and melancholic flute', and 'harpsichord mixed with gong'.

Yet, even in the birdsong works there are momentary glimmers of tactile references to romantic gesture: arpeggiated filigree figurations blurred with the sustaining pedal and long sections of intensely complex passagework that are as austere and abstracted as the ominous final movement of Chopin's B♭ Minor Sonata. In *Oiseaux exotiques*, the contrary motion opening-out of registers at the approach to the climax of virtuoso cadenza between the Catbird and Bobolink is also a distinctly romantic gesture in terms of the physical movements of the pianist and juxtaposition of registers. While Messiaen's invention was his own, the composer-pianist's own hands influenced his compositional discovery, his romantic precursors remaining among his most enduring 'maîtres'.

Chapter 12

Messiaen and the Problem of Communication

Julian Anderson

For a composer who was the most publicly fêted of the past 50 years, Olivier Messiaen remains strikingly enigmatic. Exceptionally natural in his total and thorough musicality, Messiaen's output contains paradoxically little in the way of absolute music. Even composers strongly inclined towards depiction such as Smetana or Richard Strauss wrote more abstract music than Messiaen. This has often been put down to Messiaen's intense Catholicism, a convenient explanation that ignores the fact that devout Catholics throughout musical history (Machaut, Haydn, Bruckner, Stockhausen) experienced no special difficulty in composing masterpieces of pure music.

In Messiaen's case, the motive would appear to be somewhat different: it is not merely that each of his mature works is to some extent programmatic, but rather that he appears to have experienced a compulsion to make each musical sound a vivid illustration of something else. The urge is not one to explore pattern and design in sound as ends in themselves (as in, say, the *Well-Tempered Clavier* or most of Brahms's instrumental and orchestral works) – indeed this urge appears to have been nearly absent (unless the primary motive were illustrative or symbolic) from Messiaen's musical personality. Rather, the music exudes an obsessive need to communicate with the outside world in the most direct and concrete manner possible through outright depiction or symbolic encoding in sound. Communication is indeed at the centre of all Messiaen's finest works, whether in the fascination with the language of birds or in the construction of the composer's own personal musical code – the sonic alphabet he termed the *language communicable*, which he devised for the *Méditations* and used in many subsequent works. Any alert listener, even if unaware of the composer's detailed intentions, will not fail to register in Messiaen's most characteristic pieces the repeated impression of vivid musical signals being given forth as declaimed utterances one after the other, usually grouped into the distinct juxtaposed blocks so typical of his mature work. This unusual aspect of his style has received curiously little positive scrutiny to date (as opposed to criticism), and indeed it separates him from almost every other twentieth-century composer, save Leoš Janáček – another composer obsessed with both language and animal communication. The correspondence of interests between these two isolated figures is surely no coincidence: in Janáček as in Messiaen, music for music's sake plays little role. The task of the composer, in

Janáček's eyes, was to embody in sound 'a living being'.[1] Abstract pieces, if such there truly were in his output, Janáček wrote merely as 'playthings',[2] though that would hardly be most people's impression of, say, the *Sinfonietta* or the *Capriccio*. In a letter to Brod from 1924, Janáček had put this sentiment even stronger where he said that in his view music 'means nothing unless it is thrust into life, into blood, into an environment. Otherwise it's a worthless toy.'[3]

Mutatis mutandis, it seems to me that Messiaen shared this view. The abstract works in his catalogue are not only few but conspicuously unsuccessful, whether in the stiff manipulations of a single pitch cell in the *Pièce* for piano quintet (1990) or in the forced lightness of the *Fantaisie burlesque* and the formulaic *Rondeau*. The largest such work is the *Fête des belles eaux* for six ondes Martenot, composed as incidental music for a light and water display in the Paris Exposition of 1937. Despite its origins as functional music, it is the longest attempt at abstract music in his whole output, and as such a monumental flop. *Fête* is an unsettlingly awkward potpourri of scherzos, interludes and fugatos, most of whose movements barely rise above the level of genre composition (and in the case of the fugatos, not even that). At the other extreme is the *Mode de valeurs et d'intensités*, which explores its chosen material with determined, even unvarying thoroughness. Messiaen admitted to actively disliking most such works in his œuvre, later describing the *Mode de valeurs* as '*musicalement trois fois rien*',[4] whilst disparaging many other such works as simply 'failures'.[5] Many, including the *Fête*, remained unpublished in his lifetime, and that was surely no accident. The posthumous publishing of such music not only does nothing for Messiaen's reputation, but contradicts the composer's well-founded and carefully considered judgment on what was superfluous and what was genuine to his whole creative enterprise.[6]

---

[1]   As quoted in John Tyrrell, *Janáček: Years of a Life, Volume 2, 1914–1928: Tsar of the Forests* (London: Faber and Faber, 2007), p. 826, in Tyrrell's translation of the conclusion of Janáček's late article on the creative process, entitled 'Dusk is Falling', penned in early 1928.

[2]   See quotation in ibid., p. 593, Tyrrell's translation of a letter from Janáček to Rosa Newmarch, dated 18 February 1928. The full quoted sentence, concerning the composition of Janáček's *Sinfonietta* (which he dedicated to Newmarch) is: 'I wrote it as if it were a plaything.'

[3]   Quoted in ibid., p. 914 (in Tyrrell's translation). The letter was dated 2 August.

[4]   Translated as 'musically next to nothing' in *Music and Color*, p. 47.

[5]   George Benjamin, personal communication.

[6]   For example, Hill and Simeone note that in 1974 Messiaen made a note to himself in his diary to 'correct' *Fête des belles eaux* and get Durand to publish it. But he never did so (see PHNS, p. 303). Whatever may be meant by the word 'correct' in this context, it presumably indicated Messiaen's awareness that the piece in its existing form did not fully meet his exacting standards, and would need some reworking. Surely this was due to the low quality of invention of every part save the fine music later rearranged as the fifth movement of the *Quatuor*. See following paragraph for details of this last assertion. In any case, though Messiaen had nearly 20 further years of active life in which to 'correct' and publish *Fête*, the work remained unpublished.

Crucial evidence confirming Messiaen's particular attitude towards music as an essentially communicative utterance is provided by the later history of musical ideas first embodied in both the *Fête* and the *Modes de valeurs*. As is well known, Messiaen salvaged slow music used twice in the *Fête*, arranging it as the cello and piano fifth movement of the *Quatuor pour la fin du Temps*. The reason behind this may simply have been to make better use of the only passages in the *Fête* to sound like real Messiaen. But in his programme note for the work, Messiaen suggests another, more characteristic reason:

> In the most worthwhile [*valables*] passages of *Fête des belles eaux*, that is to say when the water twice reaches its greatest height, we hear a long slow melody – almost a prayer – which makes of the water a symbol of Grace and Eternity, as according to this phrase in St. John's Gospel: 'The water that I shall give him shall be in him a well of water springing up into everlasting life'.[7]

Notice here the linking of the music with a direct quotation from the Gospel of St John, and also Messiaen's employment of the word 'valable' to describe these sections of the work – implying that he found the rest of the work, dominated by purely abstract academic pattern-making, 'inutile', another favourite word of his.[8] The spiritual communication employed here to embody in sound a sentiment from Messiaen's favourite Gospel[9] suddenly raises the music onto an entirely different plane from the platitudes of the remaining movements, both in Messiaen's ears and in our own. As soon as the music embodies a religious or emotional message about which he cares deeply, Messiaen's purely musical technique soars to unexpected heights (quite literally, in this case!), in sharp contrast to the 'playthings' surrounding it, however academically correct they might be. In this sense, it would be fascinating to see more of the student exercises Messiaen composed whilst at the Conservatoire: the one example made publicly available, a fugue on a theme of Georges Hüe, suggests an able, hard-working but not especially inspired counterpoint student.[10] (That Messiaen nevertheless went on to win a *premier prix* in Counterpoint, whilst only gaining a *deuxième prix* for Harmony (at which he was clearly outstanding throughout his life) may say more about the oddities of the Conservatoire marking criteria at this period than about Messiaen himself.)

---

[7]   My translation of the French programme note by Messiaen as reproduced in the 1983 Adès recording (ADES 14.035 – vinyl). The biblical quotation is from John 4:14.

[8]   Messiaen used this very term when asked by Claude Samuel if he had ever considered writing an opera on a non-religious topic. He answered in the negative, unsurprisingly. See Samuel's recorded interview in French included as CD 17 of *Olivier Messiaen*, Erato's 1988 Messiaen anthology: *Entretien avec Claude Samuel*, rec. rue Marcadet, Paris, October 1988; Erato ECD 75505; Warner 256462162-2 (18 discs).

[9]   See his letter dated 16 May 1933 to Claude Arrieu, PHNS, p. 46.

[10]   See Alain Perrier, *Messiaen* (Paris: Seuil, 1979) pp. 22–3, on which the manuscript of this fugue is photographically reproduced.

In any event, the above evidence may also go a considerable way to explaining why Messiaen failed at each of his attempts to win the Prix de Rome. At the time it was suggested that Messiaen's lack of innate dramatic instincts caused the problem.[11] Yet it seems curious to accuse the author of *Les Offrandes oubliées*, *Turangalîla*, *Catalogue d'oiseaux* or *Chronochromie* – all pieces that feature the strongest and most vivid contrasts imaginable – of lacking in dramatic instincts. Surely the cause of Messiaen's failure lay in his lack of engagement with the texts he was obliged to set in composing cantatas for this prize. Messiaen simply could not compose to order. If the *Fête de belles eaux* or the *Rondeau* are anything to go by, such circumstances will have produced workmanlike but uninteresting inventions from Messiaen, square production-line music that effectively ticks all the correct boxes but with barely a hint of his real personality.

As counter-argument to this, Christopher Dingle has pointed out to me that the fifth song of *Harawi*, 'L'amour de Piroutcha', also existed as a Conservatoire test piece for oboe and piano. According to Hill and Simeone, Messiaen noted in his diary on 15 May 1945 the need to reply to the Conservatoire request for such a piece. To Hill and Simeone, Loriod asserted that the oboe piece 'was reworked almost at once as "L'Amour de Piroutcha"', that is, that it had its origins not as a song in *Harawi*, but rather as an abstract piece of functional *concours* music.[12] One wonders how Loriod knew of this creative chronology, as at this period (1945) Messiaen was still living with his first wife Claire Delbos, not Loriod herself, and Messiaen was notoriously secretive about his works-in-progress. Until further concrete evidence is provided, I for one strongly suspect from the music itself that Messiaen transcribed the song into the oboe test piece.[13] For example, the text setting at the words 'bleu et or' features a blatantly dramatic harmonic change that does correspond, in Messiaen's quasi-synesthesia, to one possible musical realization of the colours blue and gold – a harmonic type that, moreover, is not found elsewhere in this song. Furthermore the tenderness and intimacy of the whole musical setting is on a quite different level of musico-emotional intensity from the much more predictable and conventional harmonic style of all Messiaen's other functional pieces. It would therefore be very surprising if Messiaen had not at least first sketched this music as a song setting these words and then perhaps adapted it for oboe and piano (a version now apparently lost). Before leaving this question, the list of Messiaen's functional abstract works should be expanded by mentioning the charming but slight 1937 *Vocalise* (which Messiaen later transcribed for oboe) and the lightheartedly functional but only slightly more characteristic trio 'Intermède' (movement 4), the sole abstract movement in the *Quatuor pour la fin du Temps* of

---

[11] Hill and Simeone reproduce a newspaper article showing this opinion (PHNS, p. 33).

[12] PHNS, p. 154.

[13] Christopher Dingle points out that the composition of the two versions could have been concurrent: he cites the repeated low B♭s on the cry 'Ahi!' as evidence – this pitch is the lowest available on the oboe, and makes a suitably resonant sound at these points in the music if the piece is played on oboe (personal communication with the author).

1940–41. Interestingly from the perspective of the present chapter, the only really typically Messiaen parts of this latter movement, with its somewhat four-square yet curiously klezmer-like main theme, are in reality quotations from characteristic and vivid themes of other movements, which raises serious questions about the compositional history of the 'Intermède' and indeed about the rest of the work.[14]

The case of the *Mode de valeurs* is still more curious. It is hard to see how such an elaborate technical exercise could have been composed without serious engagement on the composer's part, though it takes a remarkable performance to raise this music to a level of aesthetic interest equal to his other work from this period.[15] Messiaen's own recording of the work, made within months of its completion, does suggest in its coloured playfulness that at the time of composition he saw the piece as something more spontaneously musical than he later admitted.[16] It may be that Messiaen's own attitude towards the work changed

---

[14]   It was by all accounts one of the very earliest movements of the *Quatuor* to be composed, so its quotations from several other movements in its final published form are surprising. Were these quotations – notably alluding to the 'Danse de la fureur' – inserted into the earlier version after the other movements had been finished? It is now known that the first movement to be composed was (a version of) the clarinet solo 'Abîme des oiseaux', with the 'Intermède' seemingly composed second (see Anthony Pople, *Messiaen: Quatuor pour la fin du Temps* (Cambridge: Cambridge University Press, 1998), pp. 8–9). Given that the 'Abîme des oiseaux' itself suspiciously incorporates a repeated clarinet flourish together with other material from the opening of the second movement, 'Vocalise', one also wonders if Messiaen did not insert these quotations later on in the finalizing of the composition prior to its première (although it could possibly be the other way around). If these were a later addition to the first draft of 'Abîme', the implication would be that the 'Intermède' insertions from other movements were also all made at the later stages of the finalizing of the work before its première in January 1941. For quite other reasons, Pople already suggested that 'the music Akoka sight read in a field [at Nancy in 1940] simply formed the basis for a more developed piece that Messiaen finalized in Stalag VIIIA at a later date'. (See Pople, *Messiaen: Quatuor*, p. 9.) That such a practice would not be out of character for Messiaen is shown by the final published form of the 'Appel Interstellaire' for horn solo from *Des Canyons aux étoiles…*. In origin, this piece was a piece written very fast in memory of Messiaen's pupil Jean-Pierre Guézec (it was premièred under a month following his death) for the Royan Festival in April 1971. At that time, Messiaen had no idea of it becoming part of *Des Canyons* (indeed he did not decide to put it into that larger work until early 1972, as shown by the fact that his publisher Leduc went ahead and had it provisionally engraved, though never printed, in this earlier form – see PHNS pp. 286–7 and p. 289). In its final form, the piece notably incorporates the birdcall of the Canyon Wren, which Messiaen did not hear until visiting Bryce Canyon in May 1972, and which he then made a cyclic theme for the horn in *Des Canyons*. Therefore, the quotation of this theme must perforce have been a later insertion into the 'Appel' as finally published. The parallel with the apparent insertions of cyclic material into the 'Abîme' and the 'Intermède' in the *Quatuor* is very clear.

[15]   One of the few modern performances to manage it is Peter Hill's on REGIS RRC2056.

[16]   See *Les rarissimes de Olivier Messiaen*, EMI 385275 (2007).

as his view on serialism as a whole hardened in later years into one of implacable opposition, as witnessed not only by the above quotation, but by innumerable public and private statements in which he made his hostility to both the theory and practice of serial music amply clear. Whatever the case, in most performances since then the work has tended to sound both overextended and notably devoid of spontaneous musicality.

These problems recur in exaggerated form in one of his very next uses of a similar technique, his sole work of *musique concrète, Timbres-durées*. The chosen recorded sounds of this work (water drops, tam-tams, rushing streams)[17] might have been expected to produce the very best from its composer, given how often and splendidly they are evoked in his purely instrumental music from *Le Banquet céleste* (water drops) to *Chronochromie* (torrents) and beyond. Yet Messiaen's insistence in *Timbres-Durées* on employing an alarmingly rigid and extended permutation scheme results in a vastly monotonous and ludicrously long work that he himself openly ridiculed.[18] The two movements of the *Livre d'orgue* using analogous techniques (the opening 'Reprises par interversion' and the very lengthy 'Deuxième pièce en trio'), though partially saved by the amazing timbres of Messiaen's organ registration, are similarly notable for their void of personality.[19]

Messiaen's subsequent uses of such techniques were not only conspicuously more evocative but lack most of the problems associated with them in the strictly abstract pieces just cited. Significantly, the best instances are highly programmatic, and in one case overtly dramatic. The first is a passage that occurs twice in 'La Chouette hulotte' from the *Catalogue d'oiseaux*, at its opening and again in the middle. In both cases a new, bass-dominated *Mode de valeurs et d'intensités* is deployed with alarming skill and flair to depict what the score terms 'the terror of night'. In his programme note, Messiaen typically mixes the observer's personal

---

[17]   The 'streams' were in prosaic reality recordings of the toilet being flushed at the Club d'Essai where the piece was realized by Messiaen and Pierre Henry (George Benjamin, personal communication). This cannot have strengthened Messiaen's affection for the work!

[18]   See, for example, Samuel's scripted and recorded interview with Messiaen that accompanied the first recording of *Turangalîla-Symphonie*, where he says the work 'is so bad and such a failure that I'd rather not speak of it'. Claude Samuel, *Interview d'Olivier Messiaen*, rec. Paris, October 1961, 10-inch disc (VAL 027); Vega 30 BVG 1364; C35X340; Accord 472 031-2 (1964). See also Claude Samuel, *Entretiens avec Oliver Messiaen* (Paris: Éditions Pierre Belfond, 1967), p. 211.

[19]   The final movement, 'Soixante-quatre durées', ameliorates the mysterious number crunching underpinning the music with stylized or actual birdsong decoration. However, even the birdsong fragments used in this movement sound curiously vacant for once. As Gillian Weir has pointed out, 'the charm of the *Chant d'oiseaux* movement is wholly absent from this bizarre and chilling landscape'. Gillian Weir, spoken introductions to broadcasts of the complete organ music of Messiaen, performed by Weir at the organ of the National Shrine of the Immaculate Conception, Washington, USA, broadcast by BBC Radio 3 over several weeks in winter 1980–81.

reactions to the forest night with the night itself, mentioning in excited succession 'shadows, fear, one's heart beating too quickly'.[20] The mode used here is largely tenor and bass in register, and is anything but random-sounding, with each new pitch or combination of pitches appearing to be felt and heard harmonically in itself and as a progression from bar to bar. If we recall that Messiaen liked nothing more as a child than to be frightened[21] – 'je préfère tout ce qui fait peur!' he told his mother[22] – the mystery and vividness with which these passages are imbued is less surprising. Once the technique corresponds to, or can be heard as embodying, an emotional experience from real life, the composer applies it with a degree of invention hitherto lacking. One of Messiaen's most apt later uses of it occurs (again, twice) early in the seventh scene, 'Les stigmates', of his opera *Saint François d'Assise*. Again, the scene is nocturnal and natural as St Francis prays outside on Mount Verna to experience Christ's suffering. Again, too, the cries of the Tawny Owl feature here. In this scene the serial mode employed extends the technique to cover fixed alignments of pitch, duration, dynamics, articulation and timbres, somewhat analogous to the serialization of timbres in *Timbres-durées*. Here, however, there is none of the sense of routine that kills the *concrète* work stone dead quite early on in its more than 17 minutes.[23] The mode Messiaen gives St Francis to depict his nocturnal terror is intensely expressive (especially on its extended second appearance), remarkably beautiful and again clearly totally heard as both vertical sonorities and as horizontal progressions. It is quite unlike anything else in the opera and makes precisely the dramatic impact intended at this point. It also makes one regret that Messiaen did not find more uses of this technique in his subsequent instrumental works. Once again, a personal imprint is evident at every turn – to quote Janáček, the music is transformed from mere technical exercise into a 'living being'.

The religious explanations hitherto offered for this extreme bias towards symbolic utterance in Messiaen's compositional personality are surely not completely in error. However, recent discoveries regarding Messiaen's childhood

---

[20] My translation of Messiaen's French programme notes to 'La Chouette hulotte', as reproduced for Loriod's second recording of it on Erato, originally issued in 1973, later reissued as part of the large box set of Messiaen's music on Warner Classics 256462162-2. The programme note is reprinted in French in the large booklet of liner notes accompanying this 18-CD set, on p. 185.

[21] See Béatrice Marchal, *Les chants du silence: Olivier Messiaen, fils de Cécile Sauvage ou la musique face à l'impossible parole* (Paris: Editions Delatour, 2008), p. 48.

[22] See Cécile Sauvage, *Œuvres* (Paris: Mercure de France, 1929), p. 317. This is an edition of her poems edited posthumously and anonymously by Pierre Messiaen, with a preface by Jean Tenant.

[23] It would have lasted even longer according to Messiaen's original schemes. Random cuts were applied to shorten the work once Messiaen heard an initial version in the studio: see Christopher Brent Murray's chapter, 'Olivier Messiaen's *Timbres-durées*' in this volume.

and in particular his troubled relationships with his parents suggest that his obsession with music as *langage communicable* and his aversion to art for art's sake may have had other roots. It is a cliché of Messiaen's life story that he was far closer to his poet mother than to his equally literary father, whose international authority as translator of Messiaen's beloved Shakespeare into French might otherwise have been expected to endear him to the composer.[24] The literary scholar Béatrice Marchal, in a vitally important book on this topic which has so far remained not merely untranslated but also apparently hitherto unreviewed in English, has shown that the marriage of Messiaen's parents was deeply unsuccessful for most of its duration, being scarred by both the father's absence during the First World War and above all by Cécile Messiaen's illicit affair with the writer Jean de Gourmont.[25] From the surviving documentation, admittedly somewhat laconic, it is clear that this intense but clandestine affair destroyed Cécile's perhaps already delicate mental balance, resulting in what we would now term a sequence of severe and lasting depressions that rendered her not only unable to look after her own children but at times unable to communicate at all (this is why Messiaen and his brother were brought up mainly by their aunts or grandparents at this time).[26] Cécile, deeply affectionate towards her eldest son yet prone to locking him and the rest of her family out of her darkened bedroom, or else given to unaccountable fits of hysterical weeping in his presence, placed the young Messiaen in the unenviable position of her guardian, or as he termed it at the time, her 'knight in shining armour'.[27] Whilst this may have been an understandable bit of role-play during the father's absence at war, it appears to have continued intermittently long after the father's return, to the extent that she would accept no one but Messiaen to look after her during her final tubercular illness (as a result of which he caught it himself).[28]

All this would not be of any interest beyond the purely documentary in the normal run of things. Affairs happen all the time, and the surviving documentation from this one does not appear that exceptional in its literary manifestations, save

---

[24]   This may also explain Messiaen's curious lifelong aversion to admitting he was able to read and even write in English, his father's special area of expertise. Hill and Simeone reproduce a single letter, one of a series of four from Messiaen to a Malaysian ornithologist that is in decent, if not error-free, English, including such idiomatic phrases as 'what's the change' and correctly using a subjunctive (see PHNS, p. 371). George Benjamin reports that Messiaen appeared able to read and comprehend English reviews of his (Messiaen's) music that Benjamin would show him from time to time (private communication).

[25]   His brother was the chief editor at Mercure de France, Cécile Sauvage's publisher. Jean worked in the same offices, which is where he and Cécile first met: see Marchal, *Les chants du silence*, p. 61.

[26]   See ibid., p. 69.

[27]   'Mon chevalier de rose': see Sauvage, *Œuvres*, p. 315.

[28]   Pierre Messiaen and the youngest son Alain were away until the day of Cécile's death. See PHNS, p. 20.

perhaps in the unusual intensity of their expression. To a sensitive child such as the young Messiaen, however, the inexplicable[29] outward effects of the affair must have been profoundly traumatic, causing as they did the incessant rupturing of an unusually close mother–son relationship that was already embodied in memorable poetic terms in Sauvage's *L'Âme en bourgeon*. Indeed, as Marchal points out, the intimate language of this poetic celebration of her firstborn is curiously close to the expressions of love found in the surviving poetry relating to Sauvage's doomed affair.

Marchal also gives innumerable instances over many years of dysfunctional communication between Pierre Messiaen and his wife, resulting in frequent, even violent arguments between them. The details Marchal gives from the evidence of archive letters of the cruel living circumstances forced upon the family by their father on the occasion of his move to teach in Paris are truly horrifying – parents and children sharing the same bedroom, with the nearly 18-year-old Messiaen still obliged after several years to share a bed with his now 14-year-old brother. His mother – a published author of distinction, unlike her husband – stopped writing under these impossible circumstances. As his father spent as much time out as possible and showed no interest in rectifying the situation, Messiaen was eventually forced to write begging letters on his mother's behalf to wealthier family members requesting a loan to enable a change of apartment. Her death appears to have prevented this.[30] It may be surmised that music may have saved Messiaen's sanity in these circumstances. His writer-brother Alain, an eccentric and unbalanced character in adult life, may never have recovered.[31]

---

[29] According to Marchal, Messiaen did not discover the truth of his mother's illicit love for Jean de Gourmont until he inherited papers relating to it from his aunt Germaine Sauvage on her death in 1972. Marchal guesses that Messiaen had suspected something of the sort long before – despite which he never talked to Yvonne Loriod about the matter (see Marchal, *Les chants du silence*, p. 107). Pierre Messiaen did not discover the affair till after Cécile's death, then not only hiding this from his children (which is understandable) but also either destroying quantities of the relevant love poetry (which is less so), or else publishing it as if it had been addressed to him. In the case of the seemingly thus adapted Cécile Sauvage cycle published as *Primevère* (original title *Prière*), Marchal accuses Pierre Messiaen of a 'real work of falsification' ('un vrai travail de faussaire'): Marchal, *Les chants du silence*, pp. 106–7.

[30] See ibid., pp. 88–9.

[31] It is sad but perhaps not entirely irrelevant to the present chapter to mention that Messiaen's awkward relationship with his father was apparently reproduced in his own relations with his son Pascal, in spite of the assertion in Pierette Mari's biography that the latter was and would remain 'his best friend' (see Pierrette Mari, *Olivier Messiaen* (Paris: Éditions Seghers, 1965), p. 22 – presumably a quotation from the composer himself, although not in quotation marks there). Messiaen's own father had hardly provided the ideal role model of fatherhood. For more on this topic, see PHNS, p. 226 and p. 309; also Dingle, *The Life of Messiaen* (Cambridge: Cambridge University Press), pp. 141–2. Hill and Simeone also reproduce part of a 1987 letter from Pascal to his father in which, whilst

Thus out of a prolonged and deeply dysfunctional family experience of non-communication, Messiaen, who later asserted that his mother's spirit followed him throughout his life like 'a guardian angel',[32] deliberately forged his music into a directly communicable language that would never more than passingly admit the absence of communicative utterance as an acceptable creative option.[33]

If one can (perhaps crudely) polarize composers into the twin categories of formalists excited by sonic construction as substance and realists for whom all musical expression must be a reflection of outward existence or experiences, Messiaen was undoubtedly a committed realist, as indeed was Janáček himself, for analogous, though different, personal reasons.[34] The matter becomes more serious when one adds to Messiaen's disturbed upbringing the second prolonged tragedy of his life, namely that of his first wife Claire Delbos who, as will be recalled, gradually lost all her ability to communicate with the outside world through a progressive degeneration of her brain. The need to communicate on Messiaen's part was thus not a matter of trivial self-indulgence. It was a daily urgency, often brutally thwarted by the tragic vicissitudes of his personal life. This overwhelming communicative impulse could only find its fullest realization in his own music, which accordingly remains some of the most demonstratively, even (to some) embarrassingly expressive in history.

For Messiaen, if music lacked this communicative purpose, it became 'inutile',[35] an empty sign, 'meaningless' in the most literal sense of the word. The *Mode de valeurs* was 'rien' in his eyes precisely because it embodied no external emotion or experience, and its musical details were therefore not driven by the communicative urge. Significantly, the superficially formalist fresco of

---

thanking him for the present of the newly republished Sauvage *L'Âme en Bourgeon*, he comments that on reading Messiaen's preface to this volume he had learnt more about his grandmother (Messiaen's mother) in the 10 minutes' reading of this preface than from his father in the previous 50 years. See PHNS, p. 361.

[32]   PHNS, p. 22.

[33]   Marchal, in a paragraph not free from Hollywoodish sentimentality, even suggests a relationship of cause and effect between this upsetting family background and the later great public success of Messiaen's music. Nevertheless this implies that she too sees, if perhaps rather too simplistically, the communicative intensity of his most typical works as some kind of compensation for the family tragedies. See Marchal, *Les chants du silence*, p. 103.

[34]   By this I mean Janáček's tense and difficult marriage. I employ the terms 'formalist' and 'realist' not to evoke any Soviet-style, Marxist-inspired social categorization (with all its hideous overtones) but rather in their strictly literal and technical meaning here. Messiaen's pupil Alexander Goehr employed the term 'realist' in connection with Messiaen in his article on Messiaen's composition class (see Goehr, *Finding the Key: Selected Writings* (London: Faber and Faber, 1998), p. 49). Goehr draws a comparison in this regard with Mussorgsky – surely the single influence common to both Messiaen and Janáček, aside from birdsong.

[35]   See Samuel, *Entretien avec Claude Samuel*, Warner 256462162-2.

Chronochomie is in truth saturated with *personnages* from real life – mostly birds (though sometimes torrents or mountains or gusts of wind) – which excited the composer's poetic and aural imagination. Hence the vivid success of this work that is in truth rarely purely formalist or abstract, save in two passages of five-part, ultra-chromatic woodwind counterpoint in the outer movements.[36] It is particularly significant that when publicly analysing *Chronochromie* towards the end of his life, Messiaen singled out these two passages for uniquely harsh criticism in a work of which he was otherwise very proud: he disparaged them as 'passages of neo-serial counterpoint' that he found 'regrettable'.[37] Again, their lack of external illustration or emotion rendered them meaningless to him. Otherwise, images and symbols (to borrow Eliade's expression)[38] keep breaking through to the surface of this piece, right from the dancing birdcall at its opening. Indeed to the listener, these vivid *personnages* with their Janáček-like signalling are the dominating feature of the work, not the symmetrical permutations of 32 durations that are its technical basis but that recede into the aural background of the music as it is realized. Torrents, mountains, gusts of wind, giant Swedish eagles and many other birds from France to Japan invade the scene more and more, culminating in the Epôde's vehemently manic dawn chorus on 18 solo strings, which significantly silences the permutated durations on which *Chronochromie* is supposedly built for more than four minutes – more than a fifth of the duration of the whole.[39] It is surely no accident that this totally informal, image-ridden, ultra-realistic movement depicting animal communication at its most frenzied remained

[36]   These occur at fig. 14, pp. 25–6 in the 'Introduction' and at fig. 120, p. 210 in the 'Coda' of the full score of *Chronochromie*.

[37]   First seminar on *Chronochromie* at the Centre Acanthes, Avignon, France, July 1987. Messiaen's love of *Chronochromie* generally was very evident throughout his vivid descriptions and dissections of each chord in the two seminars he gave on this work in Avignon. However, just before starting his detailed survey of each movement, he shocked us by remarking that *Chronochromie* was 'perhaps more interesting as analysis than it is as music'. This more general reservation, too, seems significant in the context of the present chapter.

[38]   See Mircea Eliade, *Images et symboles: Essais sur le symbolism magico-religieux* (Paris: Gallimard, 1952). There are many parallels between Messiaen's handling of Catholic and other symbols in his work and Eliade's approaches to comparative mythology and its symbols in this and other books of his.

[39]   This huge incursion into *Chronochromie*'s mathematical pre-planning offers an interesting parallel to Stockhausen's use of spontaneous 'inserts' in his most pre-determined works, notably *Gruppen*, in which some of the most memorable music (such as the brass and percussion climax) are precisely in these added passages. In connection with Messiaen, it is amusing to note that Stockhausen later said the decision to include these unplanned inserts in his music at first made him feel 'like a Catholic who has sinned terribly': see Stockhausen interview in Andrew Ford, *Composer to Composer* (London: Quartet Books Ltd., 1993), p. 145.

Messiaen's favourite part in *Chronochromie*: as he said after the 'Epôde' provoked a riot at the Parisian première, 'they booed the nicest passage in the whole work!'[40]

I have attempted to show throughout this chapter that the lack of any external images or symbolism in a composing project usually caused in Messiaen a serious failure of musical imagination and even a consequent drop in compositional technique. It reduced him to a situation where he was just left with music itself. And for all Messiaen's formidable musicianship, music on its own was never enough.

---

[40]   Quoted in Neil Tierney, *The Unknown Country: A Biography of Igor Stravinsky* (London: Hale, 1977), p. 64, source not given. The quotation seems eminently typical so I have regarded it as authentic.

Chapter 13
Messiaen and *Art Sacré*

Stephen Broad

Living music. Living through its subject, living through its language. The word 'life' recurs constantly in the Gospels. … The language of the musician-believer will thus try to express life. This life – inexhaustible and ever fresh for those who seek it – calls for powerfully original and varied means of expression.[1]

[*La vivante*. Vivante par son sujet, vivante par son langage. Le mot 'vie' revient constamment dans L'Evangile. … La langue du musicien-croyant cherchera donc à exprimer la vie. Cette vie – inépuisable et toujours nouvelle à ceux qui la cherchent – appelle des moyens d'expression puissamment originaux et variés.]

It is perhaps odd that the mid-twentieth century *art sacré* movement is not better known, given the great fame of some of the artistic and architectural achievements associated with it. They include the church of Notre-Dame-de-Toute-Grace at Assy, with its windows by Georges Rouault, sculpture by Jacques Lipchitz, tapestries by Jean Lurçat and decoration by Marc Chagall. The Chapel of the Rosary at Vence (on which Henri Matisse worked) is another; as is the ecclesiastical architecture of Le Corbusier at La Tourette and, perhaps most famously, at the chapel of Notre Dame du Haut, Ronchamp.

There is, in fact, a common element to all of these high-profile projects: Père Marie-Alain Couturier, a Dominican priest and stained glass artist who believed passionately in turning the best of new art to the service of the Catholic church. Acting as a sort of ecclesiastic impresario, Couturier called for '"A living art" – which must necessarily be modern', and made it his life's work to encourage the acceptance of challenging modern art in the church.[2]

The notion that new art – with its radical forms and increased abstraction – should be placed at the service of the Catholic faith was not an uncontroversial one because at its heart was the rejection of the popular religious art of the day – known, especially to its detractors, as *l'art Saint-Sulpice* (this because of the profusion of religious art producers on the Parisian Left Bank in the parish of the same name). *L'art Saint-Sulpice* remains familiar today, being typified by realistically

---

[1]   Olivier Messiaen, 'Musique réligieuse', *La page musicale* (19 February 1937): p. 1. Original emphases.

[2]   Père Marie-Alain Couturier, *Dieu et l'art dans une vie* (Paris: Cerf, 1965), p. 181.

painted, mass-produced plaster statues of the saints in suitably supplicatory poses – appropriate religious art to some, decadent kitsch to others.

L'art Saint-Sulpice had held sway over Catholic decoration in France from about the 1840s, and by the end of the nineteenth century it had, according to Colleen McDannel, become 'the international style of Catholic church art'.[3] It was subject to the occasional pot-shot for its production-line approach and perceived poor taste, but it was not until the early twentieth century that a more concerted effort to challenge it was made. The challenge came from individual artists (such as Kandinsky, in his 'Concerning the Spiritual in Art'[4]) and thinkers (such as Jacques Maritain and Léon Bloy) and then later, and with growing momentum, from clusters of artists and clerics, such as those who called themselves L'Arche (who included the sculptor Fernand Py).

The movement gained momentum with the founding of the journal *L'Art sacré* in 1935 by Joseph Pichard. Père Couturier took over the editorship shortly thereafter, and under his direction, the journal became a focal-point for the movement, bringing what had been a minority interest to a far wider audience.

In this chapter, I examine some connections between Messiaen and the *art sacré* movement, showing how the various features of the movement, and the controversy it provoked in the early 1950s, may provide some new insights for our understanding of Messiaen, his stylistic predilections, compositional trajectory and relationship with the aesthetic and theological debates of his time.[5]

The quotation that heads this chapter sums up well Messiaen's position on religious music, a position that is discernible throughout his early writing. Elsewhere, for example, he pinpoints Charles Tournemire's *L'Orgue mystique* as a work that succeeds on his criteria:

> A truly religious music must be an expression of Life. ... This Tournemire has understood – and translated into a language that is as new as it is inspired.[6]

---

[3]   Colleen McDannell, *Material Christianity: Religion and Popular Culture in America* (New Haven and London: Yale University Press, 1995), p. 170.

[4]   Wassily Kandinsky, *Über das Geistige in der Kunst* (Munich: R. Piper, 1912); English edition, *Concerning the Spiritual in Art*, trans. M.T.H. Sadler (New York: Dover Publications, 1977).

[5]   As a context for understanding Messiaen, the *art sacré* movement is relatively uncharted territory, although Robert Fallon has drawn attention to it, in connection with Messiaen's attitude to representation. See Robert Fallon, 'The Record of Realism in Messiaen's Bird Style', in Christopher Dingle and Nigel Simeone (eds), *Olivier Messiaen: Music, Art and Literature* (Aldershot: Ashgate, 2007), pp. 115–36.

[6]   Olivier Messiaen, 'Derrière ou devant la porte?... (Lettre ouverte à M. Eugène Berteaux)', *La Page musicale* (26 February 1937): p. 1.

[La vraie musique religieuse doit être l'expression de la Vie. ... Cela, Tournemire
l'a compris – et traduit dans une langue aussi neuve que géniale.]

The language here – as in the opening quotation – makes it clear that Messiaen's
position is doctrinaire: he is not suggesting that the religious or sacred *might*
be expressed by contemporary musical techniques, but rather that it *must* be:
'Religious music *must* be an expression of Life', he says: 'This life ... *calls for*
powerfully original and varied means of expression' [my emphases]. In an article
for *Carrefour*, in 1939, Messiaen expands on this belief:

> Let us promote 'true' music at last, sacred music, which is firstly and above all
> an act of faith. Is this to say that this music must necessarily be circumspect,
> limited to certain subjects, of a style and language more or less out of date?
> No, a thousand times no! ... It must always be contemporary and original to an
> epoch and personality. Without erasing the past, one must examine the present
> and investigate the future. ... The fake Bach partisans can never write a lasting
> and 'true' work.[7]

> [Faisons entendre enfin de la musique 'vraie', de la musique sacrée, qui soit
> d'abord et avant tout un acte de foi. Est-ce à dire que cette musique doive être
> obligatoirement compassée, limitée à certains sujets, d'un style, d'un langage
> plus ou moins périmés? Non, non, mille fois non! ... Il doit rester l'expression
> actuelle et originale d'une époque et d'une personnalité. Sans faire table rase du
> passé, il faut voir le présent et scruter l'avenir. ... Jamais les partisans du faux
> Bach ne feront œuvre durable et 'vraie'.]

The reference to 'fake Bach partisans' is a sideswipe at one of Messiaen's *bêtes
noires* – neoclassicism – a vexation that recurs throughout the early writing.[8] Here,
however, he is not just attacking that aesthetic on musical grounds, but also trying
to undermine the sacred status of religious works in that style. He claims that they
cannot be truly sacred because they are inauthentic:

> Why do Hindemith and Stravinsky feel obliged to write counterpoint in 4/4 in
> their religious works? Who pushes them towards the style of these fake cantatas?[9]

---

[7]　Olivier Messiaen, 'De la Musique sacrée', *Carrefour* (June–July 1939 [double
issue]): p. 75.

[8]　See, for example, Stephen Broad, 'Messiaen and Cocteau', in Christopher Dingle
and Nigel Simeone (eds), *Olivier Messiaen: Music, Art and Literature* (Aldershot: Ashgate,
2007), pp. 1–12.

[9]　Messiaen, 'De la Musique sacrée', p. 75.

[Pourquoi Strawinsky, Hindemith, se croient-ils obligés de faire du contrepoint à quatre temps dans leurs œuvres religieuses? Qui les pousse à ces allures de fausses cantates?]

While *L'Orgue mystique* is 'as new as it is inspired', Hindemith and Stravinsky are said to dutifully regurgitate a superannuated style – a 'style and language more or less out of date', to use Messiaen's words.[10]

The call for contemporaneity in sacred art, and the attack on other styles by reference to their supposed decadence, is common to Messiaen and the proponents of *art sacré*. (Recall the comment from Couturier that was quoted earlier – '"A living art" – which must necessarily be modern'.[11]) From elsewhere in Messiaen's journalism, we learn that he had read Léon Bloy, whose ideas prefigured *art sacré*, and that he was an admirer of Lipchitz and had read Roger Vitrac's book on the sculptor.[12] Of course, none of this on its own necessarily confirms that Messiaen and his like-minded contemporaries saw their music as a part of the wider *art sacré* project, but there is further evidence we can draw on: a review of Messiaen's *Hymne au Saint-Sacrement* of 1933 by Paul Le Flem (who was later to become Messiaen's colleague at the Schola Cantorum) gives us a striking indication that this may indeed have been the case:

[Messiaen] shows himself rightly preoccupied with using a new language to translate a mysticism that one feels intensely. No convention, no musical *saint-sulpicisme*.[13]

[[Messiaen] se montre justement préoccupé d'user d'un langage neuf pour traduire un mysticisme que l'on sent intense. Nulle convention, nul saint-sulpicisme musical.]

---

[10]   It is worth noting that this is really an attack on the *Symphony of Psalms*, since Stravinsky's only other religious output at the time was a number of less well-known Slavonic songs for *A cappella* SATB; oddly, Hindemith does not seem to have written any religious music so it is unclear why he should be singled out for criticism by Messiaen.

[11]   Couturier, *Dieu et l'art dans une vie*, p. 181.

[12]   For reference to Bloy, see Olivier Messiaen, 'Charles Tournemire: *Précis d'exécution de registration et d'improvisation à l'orgue*', *Le Monde musical* (30 June 1936): p. 186; For Lipchitz, see Olivier Messiaen, 'Billet Parisien: Le *Mana* de Jolivet', *La Sirène* (December 1937): pp. 8–10. For a later reference by Messiaen to an *art sacré* proponent, see Olivier Messiaen, 'The Life and Works of Jean Lurçat (1892–1966)', in Christopher Dingle and Nigel Simeone (eds), *Olivier Messiaen: Music, Art and Literature* (Aldershot: Ashgate, 2007), pp. 279–88.

[13]   Paul Le Flem, [review of *Hymne au Saint-Sacrement*], *Comœdia* (27 March 1933).

In the duality of the debate, 'musical *saint-sulpicisme*' must stand as a contrast to 'musical *art sacré*', and Le Flem makes it clear on which side he considers Messiaen to be.

In 1939 comes a more concrete link between Messiaen and the *art sacré* movement: an article by Messiaen in Couturier's journal itself, entitled 'Around a work for organ'. In this article, he explains his music in terms that seem calculated to make it appear to be an integral part of the *art sacré* programme. At the outset, Messiaen rehearses one of the movement's premises:

> Religious art, if it is 'one' is also essentially 'many'. Why? Because it expresses the search for a single thing, which is God, but a single thing that is everywhere, that may be found in everything, above and below everything.[14]

> [L'art religieux, s'il est essentiellement un, est aussi essentiellement divers. Pourquoi? Parce qu'il exprime la recherche d'un seul, qui est Dieu, mais d'un seul présent partout, et trouvable en tout, au-dessus et au-dessous de tout.]

Compare this with Maritain on the same topic:

> Everything, sacred and profane, belongs to [Christian art]. It is at home in the whole range of man's industry and joy. Symphony or ballet, film or novel, landscape or still life, vaudeville or opera, it can be as apparent in them all as in the stained-glass windows and statues of churches.[15]

Messiaen then discusses his 'sources of inspiration' for the organ work in question, *La Nativité du Seigneur*, among which he cites a nativity by Fernand Py that had 'long adorned' his study. The reference to Py (a member of L'Arche – one of the *art sacré* movement's antecedents) would, I suggest, have marked Messiaen out to the readers of *L'Art sacré* as 'one of them'.

To close, Messiaen returns to another principle that is key to the *art sacré* movement: deliberately turning the shock of the new to proselytizing ends:

> The work is written in a very new language that initially caused a scandal. … *La Nativité du Seigneur* has pleased some and displeased others. But, do you think that if it were expressed in the already 'acknowledged' language of Father Bach, or simply in formulas familiar to the man in the street, my act of faith would have stirred them up?[16]

---

[14]   Olivier Messiaen, 'Autour d'une Œuvre d'orgue', *L'Art sacré* (April 1939): p. 123.

[15]   Jacques Maritain, *Art and Scholasticism with Other Essays*, trans. J. F. Scanlan (London, 1930), p. 68.

[16]   Messiaen, 'Autour d'une Œuvre d'orgue', p. 123.

[L'Œuvre est écrite dans un langage très neuf qui, tout d'abord, fit scandale. ...
La Nativité du Seigneur a pu plaire aux uns déplaire aux autres. Mais croyez-
vous qu'exprimé dans le langage déjà classé du père Bach ou simplement avec
les formules de Monsieur tout-le-monde, mon acte de foi en eût suscité d'autres?]

Here Messiaen is portraying *La Nativité du Seigneur* as an evangelical instrument
– elsewhere, indeed, he mentions the conversion of a young man to Catholicism
on hearing the first performance of this cycle in 1936.[17]

He was clearly happy to see his music as a means of agitation. But whether
such agitation was welcome is another issue altogether: In his 1961 monograph on
Notre-Dame-de-Toute-Grace at Assy, William S. Rubin comments on this aspect
of the debate:

> The apparent advantage of kitsch and sulpician art, as far as the Church is
> concerned, would appear to be its innocuousness, its lack of the power to move
> or to challenge. It is an art that can be looked at without being seen. And it can
> never arouse sentiments which the Church might find questionable. The average
> churchgoer does not appear to desire emotional engagement by religious arts,
> and thus the imagery of Saint-Sulpice fully satisfies his taste – or lack of it.[18]

If *sulpician* art is 'innocuous', lacking 'power to move or challenge', then Rubin
implicitly argues that *art sacré*, on the other side of the duality, will be demanding,
even dangerous; like Messiaen's organ music, it will 'stir them up'.

These connections between Messiaen and the *art sacré* movement in the 1930s
provide an additional lens through which his particular view of religious art can
be viewed and contextualized. But the later history of the *art sacré* movement
suggests a further, and perhaps more influential, role that may have helped to
shape Messiaen's compositional trajectory.

So far, we have focussed on Messiaen's identification with *art sacré* in the
1930s, but it was only after the Second World War, and in particular with the
completion and consecration of the church at Assy, that *art sacré*'s critique of
taste in religious art developed into a fierce confrontation between different
factions within the church. In the *art sacré* corner, the Dominicans and a range of
liberal (especially Gallican) others; opposing them, though usually avoiding any
forthright defence of *sulpician* art, Integrists and other conservatives.

---

[17]   Olivier Messiaen, '*La Nativité du Seigneur*, neuf méditations pour orgue, d'Olivier
Messiaen', *Tablettes de la Schola Cantorum* (January–February 1936).

[18]   William S. Rubin, *Modern Sacred Art and the Church Of Assy* (New York and
London, 1961), p. 12. Compare 'It is an art that can be looked at without being seen' with
Maritain, *Art and Scholasticism*, p. 141. Rubin's monograph finds its origins in his doctoral
thesis and is a splendidly partisan and entertainingly dusty defence of *art sacré*, written
only a few years after the controversy of the early 1950s.

Initially, the Vatican stood aloof from this dispute, but after only a few months, Pius XII came down squarely on the side of the conservatives, issuing a strong condemnation of new art in which the Pontiff attacked 'works which astonishingly deform art and yet pretend to be Christian'.[19]

By June 1951, the Vatican had elaborated its denunciation. Celso Cardinal Costantini attacked what he called the 'so called modern movement in art', calling for artworks that 'retain the sacred character and the good rules of grammar and syntax of artistic speech' and avoid 'barbaric novelties, which do not respect decency or form and which arouse horror in the faithful'. 'The supreme authorities of the Church', he went on, 'have an absolute and exclusive competence in judging all that which refers to the Catholic cult.'[20]

This was a significant schism and, fascinatingly, it coincides precisely with the central transition in Messiaen's compositional career.

In the summer of 1949, at the height of the debate but before Vatican intervention, Messiaen began his *Messe de la Pentecôte*, the only liturgical work in his output, and completed it before the papal denunciation of what was termed the 'mania of novelty'. It was first performed, however, on Pentecost 1951 – 13 May 1951 – after the Pontiff's censure and just a few weeks before Cardinal Costantini's more detailed condemnation of the 'so called modern movement in art'. Intriguingly, this first performance was introduced to the parishioners of *La Trinité* by Messiaen in the parish magazine:

> For the Midday mass, reserved for modern music, I have composed two pieces specially: an offertoire and a sortie. The offertoire comments on the words 'Les choses visibles et invisibles' ('All things visible and invisible') which we recite each Sunday in the Creed, and which are applied perfectly to the kingdom of the Holy Spirit, an inner kingdom of invisible grace. The sombre colours of the registration, the construction with 'rhythmic characters'; the alternation of the 16-foot bassoon which growls in the extreme bass, with the piccolo and tierce making the sounds of distant bells in an extremely high register, depicts the workings of grace. The sortie, entitled 'Le vent de l'Esprit' ['The wind of the Spirit'], uses a text from the Acts of the Apostles: 'A powerful wind from heaven filled the entire house' (taken from the Epistle of the day). A fortissimo, at first very violent, rises up in rapid swirls, like a chorus of larks as a symbol of joy.[21]

Of course, a descriptive commentary like this is nothing especially unusual for Messiaen, but notice how he takes great care to link his new techniques to their

---

[19] From a citation in Mezzana, 'Rome 1950', *Arte Cristiana*, 38/7–10 (July–October 1951): pp. 110–12, trans. Rubin and quoted in William S. Rubin, *Modern Sacred Art*, pp. 47–8.

[20] Celso Costantini, 'Dell'Arte sacra deformatrice', *Osservatore Romano* (10 June 1951): p. 1, trans. Rubin and quoted in William S. Rubin, *Modern Sacred Art*, p. 55.

[21] Quoted in PHNS, pp. 194–5.

theological inspiration, in this his most radical organ composition to date. It is as if he feels compelled to justify his musical decisions in the face of the ongoing debate.

That summer, Messiaen composed the *Livre d'orgue* (in which, though not for direct liturgical use, most of the pieces are associated with a particular feast) before apparently turning away from overtly religious music for the next nine years. Initially, he seems to have refocused the explorations of the *Livre* in *Timbre-durées* – as far from the church as it is possible to get? – but immediately after, he changes trajectory abruptly to focus on birdsong. When Messiaen did return to religious themes, they were generally to be conveyed by instrumental forces that removed them physically from the church (and so, to some extent, from the debate) – as in *Couleurs de la Cité céleste*, *Et exspecto ressurectionem mortuorum* and *La Transfiguration*. It was nearly 20 years before Messiaen attempted an organ cycle comparable to the *Messe de la Pentecôte* (contemporary with the Vatican showdown), or the earlier cycles *Les Corps glorieux* or *La Nativité* (contemporary with the articles by Messiaen that were quoted earlier). Perhaps we might conclude, then, that the Papal verdict on the use of new art in the Catholic church – the climax of the debate on *art sacré* – was a factor in shaping the trajectory of Messiaen's output.

This hypothesis would be strengthened if it were known to what extent music was a part of the debate in the post-war period, and if we understood whether and how Messiaen featured in that debate. Music's place in this *querelle* is confirmed in a later encyclical given out in 1955:

> [The] rules and laws of religious arts apply even more strictly and completely
> to sacred music, because it is more intimately connected with divine worship
> than are the other arts. ... For this reason the Church must take the greatest care
> in rigorously excluding from her music anything not suited to divine worship
> or that could prevent the worshippers from raising their minds to God. Music's
> relation to worship is almost that of a server to a priest.[22]

Incidentally, a footnote helpfully explains that *sacred music* is a generic term, with *liturgical* and *non-liturgical music* used elsewhere for more precise reference. So, this text refers to both liturgical and non-liturgical music.

Elsewhere, the encyclical states:

> We are well aware that in recent years some artists have greatly offended Christian
> feelings. They have dared to introduce into Christian worship compositions
> of theirs that are completely devoid of religious inspiration. Moreover these
> compositions offend against the appropriate laws of art. These people attempt to

---

[22]   *Sacred Music: A Translation of the Encyclical 'Musicae Sacrae Disciplina'* (London: Challoner, 1957), p. 26.

find plausible reasons for this deplorable procedure in what they insist is the real nature and character of art.[23]

It is difficult to conceive of a stronger condemnation. While we can clearly perceive Messiaen's sympathy with the *art sacré* project in the 1930s, we might expect that any response to the controversy would be more strongly determined by the extent to which he was viewed as a proponent of *art sacré* in the later 1940s, in the time immediately preceding the Vatican denunciation.

Although *L'Art sacré* was not published during the war years, in 1946 a series of 10 *Cahiers d'art sacré* were published in anticipation of its returning to regular publication. These were on a range of important *art sacré* issues – and number 6 deals exclusively with what it calls 'Problèmes de la musique sacrée'. In its pages, we discover the extent to which Messiaen had been adopted as an emblem of musical *art sacré*. The editorial, by Père François Florand, includes a stinging criticism of the Church's relation to new music in which Messiaen seems to stand in for all modern sacred music:

> We believe that the true tradition of sacred music is its perpetual contemporaneity and that, without it, we would never have come by the least of the masterpieces that now constitute tradition. … We were happy to smile when we recently heard a venerable cleric recommend an organist with the words 'He is good: he plays *the* Fugue by Bach…'. We are less happy that, for some years, both before and during the recent war, there was, without exception, but *one* man of the cloth at concerts featuring Messiaen's music – and it was always the same one.[24]

> [Nous croyons que ce qui est vraiment traditionnel, c'est la perpétuelle *actualité* de la musique religieuse, et que, sans elle, nous n'aurions jamais acquis le moindre des chefs-d'œuvre qui, maintenant, constituent la tradition. … Nous nous contentions de sourire quand nous entendions naguère un vénérable religieux assurer d'un organiste: 'Il est très fort: il joue *la* Fugue de Bach…'. Il nous paraît moins réjouissant que, pendant plusieurs années, avant et pendant cette guerre, il n'y ait eu, en tout et pour tout, aux concerts où l'on jouait du Messiaen, qu'*un* ecclésiastique, toujours le même.]

Throughout the remainder of the volume, he is name-checked regularly: in various themed articles; in a discussion between Yves Baudrier, Daniel-Lesur, Roland-Manuel and Père Florand; and in an extensive article on Messiaen's *Trois Petites*

---

[23]   Ibid., p. 19.

[24]   François Florand, [editorial] No. 6 'Problèmes de musique sacré', *Les Cahiers de L'Art sacré* (1946).

Liturgies de la Présence Divine. In fact, in this entire volume on sacred music, only 'Father' Bach is mentioned more often – with 31 citations to Messiaen's 30.[25]

It is not, of course, possible to prove that the tumult of the *art sacré* debate in the early 1950s had a direct effect on Messiaen: these are conjectures based on significant, but circumstantial, evidence. The story of *art sacré* does, however, provide an additional perspective on the unfolding of Messiaen's compositional style – a factor to add to the musical and personal issues that we know had reached a head at the same time. Perhaps the *art sacré* debacle provided an extra impetus for Messiaen's turning away from more experimental and explicitly religious music towards the uninhibited and liturgically uncontroversial world of birdsong.

---

[25]   Interestingly, we know from Nigel Simeone's work that the editor of this special *cahier*, Père Florand, appeared in Messiaen's 1942 address book – thus, he had been known to Messiaen personally for some time when the volume was published in 1946. See Nigel Simeone, 'Messiaen in 1942: A Working Musician in Occupied Paris', in Robert Sholl (ed.), *Messiaen Studies* (Cambridge: Cambridge University Press, 2007), p. 32.

Chapter 14

Messiaen, the *Cinq Rechants* and 'Spiritual Violence'

Philip Weller

Introduction

There can be no doubt that the *Cinq Rechants* represents a brilliant and (in the strongest sense of the word) original compositional achievement, but the work exists against a dark background. Biographically and psychologically, it expresses – symbolically articulates – the composer's need for strength in the face of the dark, often disturbing realities of human and divine love. Artistically, it shows an exhilarating creative response to what was for Messiaen a very particular technical challenge, one that drew results from him that were radical and, in their individual way, astonishing. Aesthetically, *Cinq Rechants* displays a modernist assertiveness and energy, as well as an expressive tension, that are challenging yet infinitely compelling. Taking our ears as if by storm, the piece forces us to engage intensively with the poetic world projected through its textual elements and its strongly imagined musical idiom. This world makes in part a very direct impact, as the music itself does, and is in part elusive and obscure, given the often bewildering mixture of images and the unpredictable combination of fragmentary French text (in a riddling surrealist mode) with purely phonetic syllables (the pseudo-Sanskrit 'langue inventée'). The result is fantastically vivid and exciting, doubly so in a good live performance, yet it is also mysterious and disturbing. Vocal and musical immediacy are balanced by something darker and more enigmatic – our present day (relative) familiarity with the imagery and sound-world of the *Rechants* should not allow us to forget this.

In a strict sense no doubt all masterpieces are unpredictable. Or, to put it another way, nothing is foreseeable about masterpieces, least of all when or where, or even whether, there will be any. Moreover, they may come in such unusual or unexpected guise as to seem (at first sight) almost uncharacteristic. In this latter sense *Cinq Rechants* is arguably one of the composer's least predictable compositions. It contains no hint, no glimmer of birdsong; its performing ensemble is frankly unexpected; it offers no reassuring sustained organ or piano textures to give body to the harmony; and its perspective on the Tristan idea is an oblique and, to that extent, hardly a straightforward one (less so, by a clear margin, than what we have in *Turangalîla* and particularly in *Harawi*). The specifically instrumental effects of resonance and colour so typical of Messiaen's *écriture* are absent, and as a result, his chords and melodic lines have to be stretched across the available vocal forces – an ensemble of 12 solo voices – in a way that recreates in wholly new fashion the harmonic textures and sonorities familiar to us otherwise almost exclusively in instrumental form. The music is nevertheless coloured just as effectively, in its own very different terms, by the grain and human immediacy of vocal timbre and gesture.

In terms of vocal idiom, too, *Cinq Rechants* makes a forceful impact, stretching the composer's ingenuity and the singers' technical and interpretive resources to the limit. It is part of the vividness and excitement of the work that it exploits the potentialities of the human voice as differently as could be imagined from the song cycles that hitherto had been Messiaen's chief contribution to vocal music.[1] The *écriture* and the types of vocalism it demands are unashamedly modernist in character and push the technical exigencies of ensemble singing to new levels of difficulty. Such a radical new departure in overtly difficult choral writing, once undertaken, offered in turn the chance to extend the resources of the musical language available to the composer in writing for an unaccompanied chamber choir formation (in this case, the Ensemble Vocal Marcel Couraud).[2] As a result, there is an uncompromising modernist edge to be found in every dimension of Messiaen's composition. This was not just unexpected but (in a positive sense) shocking in 1948, and it set the tone for a new post-war type of virtuoso *a cappella* showpiece written in an explicitly modern and demanding idiom. This tradition began, precisely, with the great series of works premièred over the years by Marcel Couraud himself, including pieces by Daniel-Lesur, Petrassi, Jolivet, and later also by Xenakis and Ohana, in addition to Messiaen.[3]

Cinq Rechants was first in line of these new commissions, and forms in this sense an important demonstration of the composer's modernity, more specifically of his experimentalism, as it was evolving in the later 1940s and early 1950s.

---

[1] *Trois Mélodies*; *Poèmes pour Mi*; motet *O sacrum convivium!*; *Chants de terre et de ciel*; *Harawi*. My thanks to Christopher Dingle and to all those whose lively musical discussion at the 2002 Sheffield conference first set me off along a road that led, via the 2008 conference, to the present chapter and indeed to a wider project, on Messiaen and the creative use of the human voice.

[2] Marcel Couraud (1912–86) founded and directed his own professional vocal ensemble (from 1945), and then conducted in Stuttgart before becoming director of the choirs of Radio-France (ORTF) in 1967. He was later founder-director of the Groupe Vocal de France (1976–78). Among a number of other recordings of considerable historical and musical interest, Couraud conducted an important performance of Messiaen's *Trois Petites Liturgies*.

[3] Daniel-Lesur, *Le Cantique des cantiques* (1953); Goffredo Petrassi, *Nonsense* [to Italian versions of Edward Lear] (1952–53); André Jolivet, *Épithalame* (1952–56, perf. Venice, 1956); Xenakis's *Nuits* (1967, perf. 1968) and Ohana's *Cris* (1968–69) were written and premièred at a later period, when Couraud was director of the choirs of French Radio. Stockhausen's *Chöre für Doris*, composed in 1950, were performed by Couraud in Paris in 1971.

It shows in brilliant clarity how Messiaen responded, technically and creatively, to the very particular discipline of writing for a chamber choir of 12 solo voices. He achieved this in a way so utterly distinct from the choral style adopted in the motet *O sacrum convivium!* of 1937 as to make the *Rechants* inhabit an entirely different world. Not only (most obviously) the subject matter and expressive tone, but the harmonic texture, rhythmic articulation and expressive vocabulary are all radically different. Partly in response to the constraints imposed by the medium and the nature of the piece, as a prism through which the 'Messiaen style' of *circa* 1948 was to be refracted, the level of sustained dissonance marked a clear new step not just for *a cappella* writing in general, but also, more specifically, for the exploitation of more astringent, dissonant groupings in both linear and textural formations within Messiaen's own stylistic production. The intervallic and chordal sonorities of his musical language were given a new and distinct character, and brought to a new level of focus, as a result of having to be carefully distributed among the voices of the ensemble. It is in large part the very productive tension between the (given) medium and the (exploratory) idiom that goes to make up the brilliantly poetic and suggestive sonic character of these pieces. The result is a type of *merveilleux* quite distinct from Messiaen's usual practice. Here we discover a very different kind of vividness and exuberance in his music, as well as many quieter moments of a strange and haunting tranquillity. We also (re)discover the darker, less obvious world – an expressionistic world, essentially, though pointedly surrealist in its rhetoric – of ambiguous and disturbing emotion for which I have adopted the phrase 'spiritual violence'.

The Story of the *Rechants*: History, Biography, Origins

The song cycle *Harawi* and the *Cinq Rechants* frame, chronologically speaking, the enormous and very brilliant orchestral machine (a showpiece, many would call it) that is the *Turangalila-Symphonie*. Both pieces are much less familiar, and less often performed, than the symphony (which along with the *Quatuor* is by a long way Messiaen's best-known music for the concert hall). Both are notable, moreover, for their striking lack of an explanatory preface. Messiaen was not usually reticent in coming forward when it came to explaining, or simply discoursing upon, his own music. And this was especially true in the case of new (or relatively new) pieces. His verbal presentations ('illuminations'), both written and oral, were very much a part of his *modus operandi* when he came into direct contact with his audience, that is, as a way of interfacing with his musical public. And yet the *Rechants* are described simply, and surely more than a little disingenuously, as just a 'song of love'. This, in the composer's submission, is all that it is necessary for the performers (and by extension critics and listeners) to know. But is it? The complexity of the musical writing and the enigmatic nature of the verbal text hardly invite an appreciation of the work as a 'mere' *chant d'amour*. Even if we allow for the surrealist idiom, and the kinds of surface dislocation such an idiom entails, the text presents a disturbing (as well as exciting) quality and a kind of enveloping obscurity that challenge us to face up to the full reality, both conscious and unconscious, of its erotic world, and also to explore – actively search out – its range of meanings. That is well within the remit of the surrealist approach, with its strong belief in the possibility of being able to draw opposites and incongruities into a kind of deeper perceptual fusion. It also corresponds to Messiaen's own very personal reading of surrealist thought and art as operating at a nodal point where the temporal and the eternal, the seen and the unseen, the known and the as-yet-unknown, could be intuited as coexisting within a larger continuum ('un point de l'esprit où les choses visibles naturelles et les choses invisibles surnaturelles ne s'opposent plus, et cessent d'être perçues contradictoirement').

The need not just to respond musically to the *Rechants* but to search for meaning in them is generated in part by the dislocations themselves, between the images and fragments of text as they emerge, collide and eventually disappear again; in part by the forcefulness and immediacy of the writing for voices; but also by the challenge of the extreme (modernist) intensity of the expressive idiom (again, this is partly the result of the direct communicative force intrinsic to the sonority of the human voice, here stretched to its limits by the demands of Messiaen's experimental vocal writing). These 'chants d'amour' refer to a range of emotion far beyond the usual or conventional. It is Messiaen's complicated experience of love and his need to be reconciled to it, as well as his purely musical experimentation (extended techniques for *a cappella* vocal ensemble), that together give the *Rechants* their expressive reach, energy and mystery.

Commentators have always assumed, with plausibility, that the Tristan pieces refer in some oblique and coded way to the terrible personal dilemma for the composer that ran through the 1940s and 1950s: the acutely felt, cruelly prolonged loss of his beloved Mi(e), in parallel with the irruption into his life of the young Yvonne Loriod.[4] The shadowy story of the long, tragic illness of Claire Delbos will doubtless never be known in full; nor perhaps should it be. But the extreme tension it brought into Messiaen's life can be easily imagined. The loss of a woman with whom he had enjoyed a great and consuming passion (for all their seeming other-worldliness) and a marriage experience of evident completeness, was not to be easily outbalanced or compensated by any new love. Claire's frail yet continuing presence, however tenuous and psychologically fragile, and however absorbed into a beyond of distracted suffering, was not to be simply eclipsed by the phenomenon of Loriod, the initially unwitting agent (as she was soon to become) of Messiaen's artistic and psychological (self-)renewal.

No doubt it was in part the increasing unavoidability of this dilemma that gave rise to his reflection on the archetypal experiences of human longing, in all their diversity, that we find in the 'Tristan trilogy'. But the composer's situation vis à vis his musical audience must have been a factor, too. The resistance (and in some cases clear hostility) shown by a few fellow-musicians, as well as by certain self-

---

4   PHNS, pp. 157–9, and later references.

appointed guardian-critics of Parisian taste, to his presentations of his new works in the early 1940s (the *Trois Petites Liturgies* and the *Vingt Regards* especially),[5] must surely have helped to initiate, or perhaps accelerate, a move away from explicitly religious subjects in concert works. However this may be, the angle taken by Messiaen in his view of the experience of love in its erotic dimension is, precisely, that it is (or can be) transcendent. His famous positioning of human erotic love as a subgenre, or more exactly as a uniquely powerful reflection, of the immensity of divine love may or may not accord with our own understanding.[6] But it gives a larger sense, and a kind of higher dimensionality, to the paradoxical combination of spiritual ennoblement and extreme suffering inherent in the experience of Eros at this level of intensity.[7]

It offers a *telos* of all-embracing love that is able to do justice, in a mythic and universalizing (or indeed theological) sense, to the largeness of the experience, and at the same time to counterbalance the fragmented, often opposing and contradictory demands of human emotion and desire – especially when faced with the difficulty of impossible, or mutually antithetical, situations. Another way of putting this is to say that the horizons of absolute and transcendent love, as adumbrated in such stories as the Tristan myth and Messiaen's very personal and idiosyncratic adaptation of the Peruvian-Andean *harawi*, offered a larger experiential space within which the conflicted and necessarily less complete realities of human love could be accommodated, and in some sense resolved. This experiential space was potentially an opening onto the transcendent, and a link to the eternal. By this means, too, the categorical extremes of impossibility ('l'amour impossible') and death ('chant d'amour et de mort') could be fully encompassed within the mythic – and perhaps at times mystic – vision of Eros.

The tacit (or more accurately, softly spoken) assumption that *Harawi* expresses Messiaen's secret and illicit love for Loriod was neatly, and perspicaciously, turned upside down by Hill and Simeone, who instead saw this 'song of love and death' as a great leave-taking from Claire of the most poignant and impassioned kind.[8] The union of the lovers, quiet and tender at the outset, then expressed passionately in songs 3 to 6, is gradually broken down, or at any rate loosened, through the course of songs 7 to 9.[9] The first allusions to death, to the painful sense of the Beloved's

---

[5] Ibid., pp. 144–7, 150–54.

[6] See for instance Messiaen's commentary on '*Turangalîla* [qui] est un hymne à la Joie – la Joie superterrestre de l'amour unique et immortel qui est un reflet de l'autre Amour' ['*Turangalîla* is a hymn to Joy – to the transcendent, supernatural Joy of a unique, everlasting love which is itself a reflection of that other Love'], *Traité II*, p. 153.

[7] Viewed in this light, moreover, and with the necessary degree of complexity and nuance, the wider sphere of love – and under the right conditions its artistic representation, as well – has the capacity not only to mediate between, but to fully embrace and so unify the apparent divergence between the contingent and the absolute.

[8] PHNS, pp. 157–9.

[9] See also below, Appendix 1 of this chapter, 'Comparison with *Harawi*'.

distant silence and remoteness, occur within these songs, coming just after the halfway point of the cycle: 'Lointain d'amour ... Adieu toi ... Pour toujours' (7); 'Très loin, tout bas' (8); 'Ma petite cendre, tu es là ... La mort est là ... sur du ciel. Comme la mort ... La mort est là' (9). This internal balance of events, with the threat of separation, loss and death intervening so early on, emphasizes the tone of sustained lament, with its searing elegiac quality, that runs through the cycle. While song 1 sets a strangely peaceful scene as if communicated to us through the intimate, suspended gaze of the lover ('La ville qui dormait, toi'), song 2 voices the words of recognition and greeting to the Beloved ('Bonjour toi, colombe verte'), set to the mode 2/E♭ major 'thème d'amour' of February 1945, which first saw the light as part of the largely improvised (but obviously very carefully planned) incidental music to a Tristan play by Lucien Fabre.[10] These words are then achingly echoed in song 7, at the moment of first leave-taking ('Adieu toi, colombe verte'). With this phrase we also hear the associated return of the music of song 2 (again in mode 2/E♭ major), in a not so much reworked as transformed state. This gives us, in a subtle yet unmistakable way, the measure of the change in relationship to the Beloved: from possession and communion to loss, separation, distance. Threaded through the serenity of the calm greeting music of the great cyclic 'theme of love', with its atmosphere of tender eulogy, we sense a new and dark emotion.

Messiaen himself referred to this 'Adieu' (7) as the lovers' first fateful separation, and to 'L'escalier redit' (9) as representing their (temporary) joyful reunion, something that the music largely confirms (its performance indication is *Vif, joyeux et passionné*). Yet these events embody an experience that already invokes, and foresees, the unavoidability of death. It is as if the very idea of physical and spiritual union already carried within it, immanently, the fact of death, not in the form of an external intervention or a premonition, but as an intrinsic part of the experience itself. Only then was real transcendence possible, in the true, existential sense rather than simply as a conceit or an idea. 'Amour oiseau d'étoile' (10), written in a highly characteristic modal F♯ major (Messiaen's key of divine perfection), is then set to accomplish a kind of spiritual transfiguration, one with the power to resolve, or rise above, the very human anguish of loss and separation, while 'Dans le noir' (12) returns once more to the mode 2/E♭ music of songs 2 and 7 in yet another striking transformation, this time final and valedictory in nature.

In the radiant F♯ major of song 10 we are made to hear a new transformative move. The soul is finally liberated ('chaînes tombantes, vers les étoiles') and pursues its now lighter existence in a world beyond the physical ('plus court chemin de l'ombre au ciel') where silence, like music itself (and indeed, perhaps suffused with latent music), has the power to enlarge the very range and scope of what exists ('silence augmenté du ciel'). The broad narrative of *Harawi* thus inscribes the passage from life to death, from union to dissolution, with moments of extreme anguish and, yes, violence along the way – not least the agitated nightmare of

---

[10]   PHNS, pp. 143, 156.

'Katchikatchi les étoiles' (11), coming as it does between the intimation, brief but intense, of the 'divine serenity' of spiritual union (10) and the final sleep of death (12). If there are suggestions of a love and a life beyond death, that should not be taken to imply any lessening of the burden of emotion that accompanies this painful succession of human psychological 'events'.

Going through the reality of such states of the soul is precisely the point. The possibility of spiritual consolation that for Messiaen was a vital sustaining element within the travail of existence, and in which all human experience (of whatever kind) was grounded, comes not through external moralizing or religious commentary but rather internally, through the cathartic process itself. This larger vision of a possible catharsis is what underlies the Tristan pieces as a group and it is why the surrealist idiom is so important to it. In evoking a higher 'world beyond' (*au-delà*) – a poetic rather than a theological world in this instance, formed of music and the archetypal imagery it conveys – the artist sets up a space in which the limitations of the everyday fall away and transcendence becomes possible. Here, the true purposes of love could be made present in newly refracted form, hypostasized through art – this, then, is the sphere in which the seemingly irresolvable conflicts surrounding Messiaen's bond with Claire might, just might, be resolved: above the everyday, and beyond time.

The view that the *Rechants* then inscribed an erotically charged 'surreal world' around the new (and for Messiaen by now unavoidable) aura of Loriod has always been there, tactfully alluded to but rarely addressed directly. The evidence of the thematic ideas borrowed from *Turangalila*, and the presence of the 'tous les philtres' theme in the coda of 'Rechant III' (which significantly reappears eight years later, in 'Le Loriot' in the *Catalogue d'oiseaux*) make this all but certain. Yet even more intriguing than the psychological and biographical roots of these Tristanesque motifs and gestures, I suggest, are the mythic-poetic modes of thought that gave rise to them and made possible their connection with the theological and spiritual world, while at the same time allowing them to remain intensely human. Messiaen's way of transcending the particular, with all its attendant difficulties, was to aim, through art, for the absolute and the universal. It is as if the bewildering – powerful and inspiring, yet ambiguous and deeply conflicted – experience of human love had driven him to create a figural world (or better: three distinct representations of such a world) in which the various facets, embracing many of the contradictions, of Tristanesque erotic love could be explored and expressed in an essentially positive light.

Why should he have chosen this path? We might say that the creation of a *figura*, representing a symbolically enlarged and transformed world of Eros, served as a place where his own conflicted experience could be, if not finally resolved, then at least contemplated and worked through afresh. His need to present – to himself, as well as to others – the modalities of human desire as existing within a larger frame, and on a larger scale of values, required bringing these modalities into alignment with a wider sense of the inscrutable purposes (including specifically the cosmic and divine purposes) of love. Here again, as so often in Messiaen, human psychology and spiritual aspiration are made to seem closely allied, and the hidden ways of the spiritual path thereby made to seem closer at hand than they might otherwise appear. This is done, nevertheless, without distorting or denying the intrinsically human and secular character of the poetic material, and the emotions it expresses. The experiential world of the Tristan pieces is human, all too human; and it needs to be fully recognized and entered into in these terms. Yet the mythic-surrealist approach, made possible finally by a musical idiom that is powerfully adequate to the task, gives it a reach and a largeness of conception that intensify and ennoble (as other poetic and philosophical traditions have done) the humane, spiritually transforming character of Eros.

The power of his experience of such a love with Claire, and its severe testing over the long course of her illness, was one thing. But it was tried even further through the initially unsought experience of Loriod. Messiaen's 'solution' – his only possible solution, we might think: necessary, and to that extent, in some unfathomable way, providential – was to see the whole complicated skein of human interrelationships within the larger picture of a dynamic, cosmic love that was one and unchanging, yet varied and unpredictable (thus potentially complex and conflictual) in its mode of operation. It is within the bounds – what we might more positively call the range of possibilities – of such a world that emotions of violent intensity could (and maybe should) have their place, not being denied, sidestepped or suppressed. Even the sacred texts themselves ought to have their proper kind and degree of 'measured violence', which a composer attuned to such things might seek to bring out and intensify musically, as Messiaen confirmed to Claude Samuel in their conversations of 1967:

> [CS] Your [musical] approach consists in discovering within the sacred texts a contained violence…
>
> [OM] I haven't 'discovered' it at all: it exists, and I have expressed it exactly as it is.[11]

The sacred texts bring a spiritual message, the strength and intensity of which may be inspiring, but are by the same token unsettling, destabilizing, anything but comfortable: hence violent, with respect to human wishes and expectation – just as extreme intensity and passion may in themselves be anything but comfortable. The position of humanity within the created order made it certain and inevitable that any reform of life, any attempt at spiritual renewal, any striving to approach the divine, would inevitably meet with resistance, and hence go through vital and necessary phases of more or less acute struggle. The whole sphere of love at its highest level of intensity included, therefore, the violent intensity of a truly reforming, and transforming, experience. The force of resistance (to be overcome)

---

[11]   Samuel, *Entretiens avec Olivier Messiaen* (Paris: Pierre Belfond, 1967), p. 20 (present author's translation).

might in this sense be seen as correlative with the positive force of desire and spiritual aspiration (to be followed through). By this means the themes of suffering, conflict, impossibility, fatality and death could be woven into the *Harawi* tapestry with an intimation, at least, of the enduring force of love in the body's absence or demise, and of the metaphysical assurances associated with such survival. The even more vigorous world of the *Rechants*, with its very different mixture of exaltation and mystery, could then stand for a whole realm of experience on a level at which the erotic and sacred dimensions could be seen as conjoined, and entered into as such.

The world conveyed so vividly in the *Rechants* is manifestly an exuberant, secular, intrinsically human one. Its suffering, its passion, its anguish and its tumultuous joy are all quintessentially human emotions. After all, the composer referred somewhat cryptically to the 'tendresse mystérieuse' of the *Rechants*, as contrasted with the 'nostalgie [et] fatalité' of *Harawi*.[12] The sense of tension and anxiety, as well as of joy and release, are both part of this world. So too is the 'mystery' alluded to by Messiaen himself. But the lure of the metaphysical is there too, in the very centre of the experience, above all in the overwhelming power of the contrast between the quieter, reflective, at times enigmatic passages and the big climactic moments that stretch the 12 voices to the very limits of human expressivity:

> One might say the [Tristan] legend is the symbol [= symbolic archetype] of all great loves and for all the great love poems .... I've preserved only the idea of a fatal and irresistible love, which, as a rule, leads to death and which, to some extent, invokes death, for it is a love that transcends the body, transcends even the limitations of the mind, and grows to a cosmic scale.[13]

Dates, Conception, Making

The genesis of *Cinq Rechants* must on any estimate have been rapid; certainly, the rate of work on it would perforce have been quick and intensive. We have only one or two chronological pointers to go on, and cannot be precise, but the room for manoeuvre is severely limited. If the main part of 1948, from mid-February (when the *Trois Tâla* were premièred at the Théâtre des Champs-Elysées) to the beginning of December, was given over to the immense mental and physical labour of finishing and copying the entire *Turangalîla-Symphonie*, then the printed date of the *Rechants* seems impossibly close. This is nevertheless given very clearly as December 1948, not discreetly in small print at the end of the score but prominently on the title page, on information very obviously stemming directly from the composer himself. Either Messiaen had the idea for the piece earlier on

---

[12]   *Traité II*, p. 153. All translations from the *Traité* are my own.

[13]   *Music and Color*, p. 30.

(say) in the autumn of 1948, and then worked on it simultaneously with the later stages of work on *Turangalîla* (possible, but on the face of it unlikely); or else he had something like an extended initial moment of creative inspiration that was significant enough for him to want to anchor the work securely in December, while allowing the process of elaborating and finishing it to extend into the new year. Or else the dating might conceivably refer to some other event, real or imagined, of which we are ignorant but which was in some way significant to him. In any event, the piece must have been completed by early February 1949, when he was paid by the publishers.[14]

However this may be, the printed marking 'Paris, décembre 1948' in any case seems distinctly odd – not just because of the degree of precision, perhaps, nor even because of the compressed timeframe, but because it specifies Paris, whereas most of his other pieces were written at Petichet, in the Isère, during the months of the long summer vacation (the first piece to be composed in this way was *Poèmes pour Mi*, written in celebration of Claire, in the summer of 1936).[15] Perhaps the need to specify December was (part of) Messiaen's point to himself, as much as to anybody else, that the composition of this piece was very much *not* part of the usual routine. In addition, we might note (i) that December is always a very busy month for musicians working in a liturgical context, and that Messiaen in some sense needed to reassure Couraud that it had in fact been ready all along, at least *in potentia* if not in its fully written-out state; and (ii) that Messiaen may well have sketched all kinds of material, even if not (at that stage) specifically for a vocal work of the *Rechants* type, during the later stages of finishing *Turangalîla*. At any rate, *Cinq Rechants* looks very much like a piece that exploded inside the composer's mind, with an elemental musical force. Its originality and radicality are perhaps, in this sense, bound up with the quickness of its gestation and elaboration, as if Messiaen had no time for lengthy reflection or second thoughts, and no time to change his mind. (Something similar, in a very different compositional and expressive register, might be said of the equally brilliant *Cantéyodjayâ* as well, written if anything even more quickly a few months later in the summer of 1949, in spare moments at Tanglewood kept free and private for composition, and then

---

[14]   PHNS, pp. 179–80. The edition was by Rouart-Lerolle, sold through Salabert ('vente exclusive'). Marcel Couraud remarked that once Rouart had engraved the score, he (Couraud) was able to work from this clean copy with his singers in preparing the first performance (see below).

[15]   The engraved score of *Poèmes pour Mi*, published in 1937 in two fascicles as 'Livre Ier' and 'Livre IIème', carries no mention of place, even though the summer of 1936 spent in Petichet must have meant a great deal to him. In the published score of *Harawi*, by contrast, he writes very specifically: 'écrit à Petichet, Isère, du 15 juin au 15 septembre 1945' on an explanatory flyleaf that also describes what vocal demands the piece makes on the 'grand soprano dramatique'. It is quite extraordinary, to say the least, that in the case of the *Rechants* the mention 'Paris, Décembre 1948' should not just be there publicly, in print, but should appear *on the title page*.

put away in a drawer for three years – although the composer remained ambivalent about this particular piece all his life, in stark contrast to the *Rechants*.)[16]

What is also clear, when we read Marcel Couraud's short but very striking account of the early days of the *Cinq Rechants,* is that its radical modernism and degree of difficulty came straight from Messiaen himself.[17] We might say that Couraud provided the medium, the virtuoso ensemble, whose skill and performing resources allowed Messiaen to compose as he did, but gave no direct impulse towards the 'ultramodern' stamp of the piece as it finally emerged. The musical initiative stemmed from the composer, explosively so (like Char-Boulez's 'L'artisanat furieux', or as near as someone of Messiaen's nature and temperament could come to it). And it was the technical and interpretive force of the challenge he posed to the singers (implicitly likened by Couraud to that posed to orchestras by the *Rite of Spring* a generation earlier) that in effect set a new standard for *a cappella* performance in a virtuosic, modernist vein.[18] We learn, for example, about the initial, no doubt somewhat fragmented, play-through for Couraud's benefit (given no doubt in late 1948), when:

> Yvonne Loriod and Messiaen brought me the work in its raw state: four hands intertwined at the keyboard brought to life the twelve voices that I was trying to decipher from the thousands of sketches littering the music desk. A work was born from the genius of this amazing composer who, at a stroke, turned choral writing on its head and put everything back in the melting pot: [this was] a moment of history, like *Pelléas* or the *Sacre* .... [And] it was on me that the responsibility would fall of bringing this terrifying work to life![19]

We are told, too, of the 'draft performance' given much later on, after dozens of rehearsals of the different voices in every conceivable combination, at which Couraud and his singers finally performed the whole work for Messiaen, though in

---

[16]   Messiaen got around to preparing a fair copy of *Cantéyodjayâ* only in 1952. The work was then printed in 1953 and premièred by Loriod at the second of the new Domaine Musical concerts on 23 February 1954. PHNS, p. 190.

[17]   Couraud's article entitled 'Première audition' was dated Paris, December 1953 and appeared in the *Cahiers Madeleine Renaud–Jean-Louis Barrault,* II/3 (1954): pp. 104–6. Eng. trans. in PHNS, pp. 183–4.

[18]   Couraud's article refers, explicitly and at length, to the technical and expressive difficulty of the *Rechants' écriture.* And he finishes by saying what he had pointedly *not* said in response to the anxious Messiaen's questions about the feasibility of this or that passage: 'Either the work would be performed as Messiaen had written it, or else it would never be heard in a concert hall, because this was not music that could be tinkered with' (ibid., p. 183). Once Rouart-Lerolle had engraved the score, Couraud worked from the clean printed copy, which must have come as a great relief and may well have marked a step change in the complicated and very demanding rehearsal process.

[19]   PHNS, p. 183.

a very unexpected rehearsal venue: 'I shall never forget the day when we sang the *Cinq Rechants* to their composer – in the museum of the Conservatoire, because we could not find a [rehearsal] studio! Messiaen listened, reassured and, I think, even surprised.'[20]

If we cannot fully account – psychologically, technically, aesthetically – for the frankly astonishing genesis, or even for the details of the practical making, of this 'terrifying work' (Couraud), then such tantalizing glimpses as we have here ought to make us pause to consider the immensity of the creative effort and the mental exertion required for even so relatively compact a piece (by Messiaen's rather than by Webern's standards, that is) as the *Cinq Rechants*. The title may be distinctly sober, *sachlich*, almost deliberately self-effacing ('Five Refrains'); but the poetic world the music conveys is breathtaking. Not for nothing did so acute a musical mind as Dutilleux consider it one of the ten most important compositions of the twentieth century.[21]

Technique, Structure, Style

The homage to Claude Le Jeune implied in the very title, as well as in the formal layout, of the *Rechants* represents a fascinating intersection between old and new. The extreme preoccupation with metre and rhythm on Le Jeune's part was of course the key to Messiaen's abiding interest and admiration. Knowledge of Le Jeune's rhythmic innovations, and of the bigger historical-cultural project of which his work formed part (Messiaen knew and studied only the choruses of *Le Printemps*, published in 1603),[22] must have come to him initially via the teaching

---

[20]   Ibid., p. 184. *Cinq Rechants* was eventually premièred ('première audition publique'), in a concert that also included Poulenc's Lenten motets, Milhaud's *Cantate de la guerre* and two of Dallapiccola's Michelangelo choruses, on 15 June 1950 in the Salle Richelieu (Sorbonne), under the ægis of the Cercle Culturel du Conservatoire.

[21]   Caroline Potter, *Henri Dutilleux: His Life and Works* (Aldershot: Ashgate, 1997), p. 183. Dutilleux's view was expressed in response to an enquiry (in questionnaire form) organized by the Société Philharmonique de Bruxelles in 1965, cited in Pierrette Mari, *Henri Dutilleux* (Paris: Editions Zurfluh, 1988), p. 192. My thanks to Caroline Rae for discussion of this point.

[22]   The edition used by Messiaen (from which facsimile pages are reproduced in the *Traité)* is Claude le Jeune, *Le Printemps*, 3 Vols, ed. Henry Expert, Les Maîtres Musiciens de la Renaissance Française, 12–14 (Paris: Leduc, 1900–01; New York: Broude Bros, 1963). Le Jeune's published volumes include a number of important collections, many of them posthumously printed: *Livre de mélanges* (1585), *Meslanges de la musique* (1586), *Airs mis en musique* (1594), *Le Printemps* (1603) *Octonaires* (1606), *Airs* (1608) and *Airs* 2 = *Second livre des Airs* (1608). There are also several volumes of polyphonic psalm settings of different kinds, some of them set, like the *Printemps* choruses, in quantitative metres (*Pseaumes en vers mesurez*, 1606).

of Maurice Emmanuel at the Conservatoire.[23] The larger cultural project was the radical, even revolutionary practice of *musique mesurée à l'antique* associated with the poetic and musical academy of Jean-Antoine de Baïf, founded in late 1570, the governing principle of which was to apply the quantitative (durational) verse structures of classical antiquity to French verse, underpinning these newly minted metric-rhythmic (linear and strophic) patterns by means of a compositional system of strictly chordal music. Baïf was one of the members of the rather loosely associated La Pléiade, the major grouping of French Renaissance poets writing in the vernacular from the mid-sixteenth century. The Académie, holding a royal charter from the music-loving Charles IX, functioned in practice as a strongly integrated collaboration between Baïf and his musicians, notably Jacques Mauduit (1557–1627) and the older, more experienced Le Jeune (1528/30–1600). The aim was to restore the status, and above all the artistic power, of rhythm (i) as the fundamental constructive and expressive resource available to the verse-writer or composer; and (ii) as the most effective way of coordinating poetic text and musical continuity – what we might think of as a structural middle ground, a common level of intersection, between word and sound.

Over and above the happy example of a fellow musician who had consciously and deliberately pursued a goal of intellectual *recherche* into metre and rhythm, it was the creative and forward-looking side of Le Jeune's approach that Messiaen valued most. Wanting above all to arrive at something audibly new and characteristic that would be strong and effective in the music of the present (potentially *his* music, therefore), he viewed the Baïfian project not as a piece of musical antiquarianism but as a powerful catalyst to his own invention. In this as in other things, Messiaen was a strong reader. He explicitly underlined the point that the Baïf–Le Jeune choruses were not in any way archeological reconstructions of Greek metrical practice, but creative reinterpretations of that practice in a modern context – drawing on the power of example in order to produce new work, extending and enriching the historical model in the spirit of the original, but along contemporary lines and in a fully modern sense:

> In analysing [the choruses of *Le Printemps*], it must never be forgotten that this is not in any way a restoration of Greek rhythm [and metrics], but a 'Renaissance' – which is to say, that Baïf and Le Jeune made use of these Greek rhythms not in

---

[23]   Emmanuel had a lifelong preoccupation with metrics and rhythm, as well as with mode and modality in all its manifestations. He was a figure who combined detailed scholarship and a wide-ranging musical curiosity with creative energy and aspiration, something which helped to enrich the friendship and the (aesthetic *and* technical) preoccupations he shared with Messiaen. His vision of the potential of mode and of metrics clearly worked on the young composer's creative mind and sensibility in the profoundest way. His Paris dissertation, defended and published in 1895, was specifically on Greek choral metrics: *Essai sur l'orchestrique grecque: Étude de ses mouvements d'après les monuments figurés* (Paris: Hachette, 1895), Eng trans. 1916.

order to copy or to reconstruct retrospectively, but to construct afresh a new and original work [by implication, a timely and in that sense *modern* work].[24]

So far as Le Jeune's compositional procedures were concerned, Messiaen specifically observed on the changing voice-combinations within the basic *chant–rechant* repetitions and the sonic variety this engendered; and on the rhythmic subdivisions *(monnayages)* available for creating additional elaboration within the basically homorhythmic textures:

> These choruses in classical quantitative metres are 'songs with refrains': each section [or piece] consists of [the basic elements of] refrain and verse; ... and the various elements can be arranged in different ways, sometimes being doubled up, as for example: refrain à 3, reprise of the refrain à 5, verse à 3 ... or else: refrain à 3, verse à 3, verse à 5 ... [and so on]. The music of these choruses is 'homorhythmic' ... and is thus a type of music with a strong harmonic dimension [that is, fundamentally chordal]. Le Jeune allowed himself many types of rhythmic 'coinages' or diminutions *(monnayages)*, resolving breves into semibreves (i.e. for us, crotchets into quavers), extending this process to include semiquavers, and moreover mixing the different diminutions, not forgetting also the use of dotted notes. But at no point does he go so far as to *superimpose* these Greek rhythms one upon another.[25]

He thereby emphasized the – to him very congenial – notion of freedom of detail, hence also freedom of internal structure and elaboration, within the relative strictness of the larger form. The combination of strongly articulated strophic layout and durational patterns with a myriad of internal changes and asymmetries of detail, and above all the special rhythmic extensions and developments which he added to the scheme himself, is absolutely characteristic of Messiaen. It is fascinating to be able to trace the genetic source of such a combination in this particular case, growing as it does through his direct engagement with, and creative manipulation of, a known historical model.

Other striking musical features that Messiaen used, very much in his own way, at various points in the *Rechants* are:

1. the idea of the medieval *alba* (the dawn song sung to warn the lovers of the approach of day, famously employed to sublime poetic effect by Wagner in Act 2 of *Tristan)*, as for example in 'Rechant I' (Introduction and Coda);

---

24   *Traité I*, p. 184.

25   *Traite I*, p. 183. On the next page Messiaen quotes in full what he terms Le Jeune's 'extraordinary Preface' to *Le Printemps*, precisely because it places rhythm above harmony: 'en comparant l'Harmonie au corps et le rythme à l'âme, cette Préface est tellement an accord avec mon propre sentiment sur la musique et le rythme en général, elle est d'une telle actualité, et ... elle est si juste, si vraie, que je la cite *in extenso...*' (ibid., p. 184).

2. the large-scale elaboration of a non-retrogradable rhythm as a means of forceful expansion and intensification in the central part of 'Rechant III' (*couplets* 1–3);[26]
3. the use of canon and 'disjunct repeating' rhythms in layered polyphonic arrangement (e.g. 'Rechant I': score, pp. 3–4, 5–7); and
4. a passage of 'accords à renversements transposés' again in 'Rechant III', placed in a key position at the end of the Introduction (p. 16; see below, Appendix 3 of this chapter).

Such technical features combine with the great range and diversity of the vocal writing to give a mesmeric, yet extraordinarily focused, richness and vividness to the sound-world of the piece as a whole. Messiaen was well aware that such variety was needed, provided that it was judiciously arrived at, in a piece written for voices alone:[27] 'Without any instrumental participation, simply with the resources of the human voice, this work achieves a true "orchestration" through its musical *écriture*, its rhythms, its articulations.'[28] And, as the end of the last sentence indicates, a further (to Messiaen indispensable) means of ensuring such variety was to use the sounds of the 'langue inventée' not so much for any vague impressionistic quality they might have, as specifically to enrich and reinforce ('colour') the rhythm and articulation:

> These are syllables chosen for their softness or violence of attack, for their suitability to enhance and project the musical rhythms – and they enable a fluent coordination of the four orders of rhythm: 1. phonetic (timbres), 2. dynamic (intensities), 3. kinetic (accentuation, accentual contour), 4. quantitative (durations).[29]

This kind of commentary (typically for Messiaen) underlines the technical and constructive side (and *a fortiori* the experimental and 'recherche' dimension) of a work which nevertheless remains formidably expressive – in its every gesture

---

[26] Messiaen referred to this great passage of rhythmic development on several occasions. It was obviously a key instance for him, as well as a favourite piece of expression. For a fairly full discussion, see *Traité II*, pp. 37–40.

[27] This 'orchestral' dimension of the *écriture* (which we might prefer to think of, in a more neutral way, as 'vocal instrumentation') was hugely important to Messiaen, just as it was important to Jolivet when he began work on his *Épithalame* (1952–56, published 1958), also written for the same Ensemble Vocal Marcel Couraud.

[28] Olivier Messiaen, 'Note de l'auteur', written for performances of *Cinq Rechants* and the Erato recording, conducted by Marcel Couraud.

[29] Messiaen, 'Note de l'auteur': A more intensive and sustained analysis of the Le Jeune dimension, as also of Messiaen's compositional ends and means, will be found in the present author's *Messiaen and the Voice* (in progress).

and detail, explosively or poetically as needed. It is to the further reaches and consequences of this expressivity that we now turn.

The *Rechants* and 'Spiritual Violence'

The *Cinq Rechants* reach their close in a state of ambiguity. Far from offering a blazing or a serene conclusion, the sort of finish Messiaen generally worked towards, they end mysteriously on a note of anxiety, in a moment of veiled darkness. There is no celebration, no final clarity. Any sense of achievement or catharsis comes, if anywhere, in the middle of the work, not at the end. The Introduction to 'Rechant V' ends with the words 'Tes yeux voyagent, dans le passé / mélodie solaire...', while the end-framing Coda has only the questioning, riddling 'dans l'avenir', standing all alone and cadencing on the same open tritone, as in the Introduction (Example 14.1).

Example 14.1   *Rechant V*, end of Coda with the text 'dans l'avenir', showing also the parallel instance from the end of the Introduction ('dans le passé')

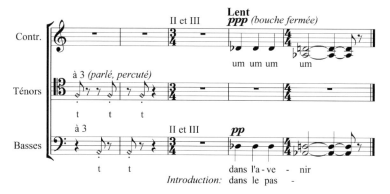

This is a moment of strange, uneasy quietness, one that hints at the underlying anxieties and tensions present within the work, at its 'mystery'. The words 'tes yeux' must come from the mouth of the lover and refer to his Beloved. But where does her searching gaze alight: does it really look back on the past (what could this mean?), and, if so, with what spirit or intent? And does she hazard an uncertain glance into the future, as well? What is implied at the end? Part of the point is that we are not meant to know. This wonderful, haunting ending (which is in one sense not an ending at all) is by no stretch of the imagination typical of Messiaen, yet it is a characteristically brilliant, poetic invention. The riddle casts a shadow against which the burning light and warmth of the central part of the work are measured. The fierce intensity and accumulated rhythmic momentum of 'Rechant III', with its extended climax and gentle coda (score, pp. 26–9) are at this end-point an emotion recollected, but no longer present. The fierceness and strength of expression within 'Rechant V' are of a quite different character and order. Perhaps, at the end, we are left in a state of 'possible hope': a place where there is (or may be) everything still to play for, where even the condition of hope and aspiration is provisional and uncertain. It is only in 'Rechant V', after all, that the figure of Perseus, the mythological slayer of Medusa, appears as a symbol in the work's narrative. His name comes at the very end of a *couplet* which begins by invoking symbols of love's harmony and delight, with allusions to Yseult and her potion; to 'fée Viviane'; to the lover's *chant d'amour* and the arching span or sphere of day ('cercle du jour'). Meanwhile, the refrain contains clear hints of danger and death, paradoxically associated with the beauty of flowers, bees and other motifs of the garden of love:

COUPLET	losangé ma fleur toujours *(berceur et tendre)*
Bien modéré	philtre Yseult rameur d'amour
	fée Viviane à mon chant d'amour
	cercle du jour.
	Hayo hayo foule rose hayo bras tendu
	pieuvre aux tentacules d'or
	Persée Méduse l'abeille l'alphabet majeur.
RECHANT	Fleur du bourdon tourne tourne tourne à mort
Un peu vif	quatre lézards la grotte pieuvre et la mort:
	corolle qui mord deuxième garde à manger d'abord
	Ha

Things of delight here 'turn to death' and, by implication, consume and devour. The verse (*couplet*) comes first: despite the angularity of the solo lines it is vocally delicate and lyrically flexible (*berceur et tendre... souple*). The refrain is then pointedly marked *ff* and *brutal*: the course of this refrain music is unremitting – it carries its force and energy through cumulatively, without interruption, to the end of the 'reprise du Rechant' (score, pp. 39–45; note the intensification and extension in the last three pages). The questioning mood of the coda then registers all the more strikingly, for the listener, against this extended passage of rising intensity. It is clear that the composer has prepared a strong, increasingly intense ending by means of this build-up but in the event has fought shy of it, to sudden dramatic effect. He swerves at (almost) the last moment, and we find ourselves instantaneously 'within' – rather than simply 'confronted by' – the mysterious ending.

The high point of the cycle is to be found instead in the central 'Rechant III', and the mood of resolution and calm joy reached at the end (the striking 'tous les philtres' coda) is carried over and continued, in a different and now less forceful way, celebratory and *joyeux*, in the following number ('Rechant IV', finishing 'mon bouquet rayonne').[30] If 'Rechant III' is in some sense the psychological and emotional crux, not just a midpoint but the fulcrum around which the work revolves, then its positioning and dramatic weight within the cycle were the result of a quite conscious technical, as well as expressive, decision. There is absolutely no vagueness here on the composer's part. Having once more asserted the primacy of rhythm and its governance over the whole work, he noted in particular this vital passage of rhythmic growth and development (score, pp. 17–28; see the reiterations at 17–18, 19–21, 22–4):

> Rhythm here has great importance, and entirely governs both poetry and music. Beyond the use of Hindu rhythms, we should observe the effect of the non-retrogradable rhythm developed by augmentation of the central durations in 'Rechant III', which is certainly the most original passage in the whole work.[31]

This commentary is decisive. It not only justifies but clarifies the positioning of 'Rechant III' as a high point, and underlines its contribution to the narrative of the work as a whole. Its dramatic energy is channelled with absolute precision through three reiterations of the verse (marked *Vif*, and with the long, developing non-retrogradable rhythms referred to in Messiaen's commentary), and the two interjections of the 'troubadour Viviane' refrain (marked *Un peu vif*) are kept short specifically so as not to weaken this cumulative effect. Though it is typical of Messiaen that he should focus solely on the technical aspects of the passage, its expressive substance is what matters most to our understanding of the piece and its 'power to mean'. Like the 12 singers of the ensemble, we are invited to revel in this music, to 'inhabit' its sonorities and rhythms, and thereby receive its imaginative and expressive impact beyond words. If we follow the course of the music fully and attentively, assimilating ourselves to it as we go, we shall be able to come fully alive through the strength of its climactic and cathartic process. The fact that the elements of verbal text function as rhythm and articulation, as colour and image, rather than as discourse or as lyric message in any explicit sense, greatly aids this type of intensive listening. Such effects can be seen as part of the artistic purposes of surrealism, when taken over into music. The example of 'Rechant III' thus shows us something subtle, yet compositionally very concrete,

---

[30] There is effectively only unison writing in 'Rechant IV': the music of the refrains is entirely monodic (in octaves, therefore), and there are just a few accompanimental effects added to the solo lines in the verses. All the refrains are identical: ten bars in length, rhythmically incisive and marked *Très vif, joyeux*. This throws the luscious harmony of the brief cadence into G major with an added sixth for 'mon bouquet rayonne' (score, p. 35) into sharp relief.

[31] *Traité I*, p. 355.

about Messiaen's highly individual understanding of the surrealist potential of his chosen aesthetic.[32]

What, then, are we to understand by 'spiritual violence' in Messiaen's world? More generally even, what can the contemplation of spiritual violence tell us about life and art? Such a question goes to the heart of the expressive reach of Messiaen's music in the sense that it asks how, and where, the language of hyperexpressivity, of struggle and darkness, stands in a complementary relation to that of celebration and light. This then serves to inform our understanding not just of the overtly passionate and at times anguished world of the song cycles and the Tristan works of the 1940s, but of other areas of his output, too: areas where striving and astringency function as a necessary preliminary – as a pathway, indeed – to the exultancy of arrival. More generally, a musical emotion of violent and cumulative intensity can embrace anguish and fulfilment together, as part of the same developing process. The result is complex and mixed, in a psychological and expressive sense: by embodying the conflictual nature of this larger process, it gives us in richly imagined form the mutual interdependence of suffering and joy. This is a polarity that can be found, in varying degrees, within his larger orchestral and other types of works more or less throughout his life.

Messiaen's own struggles were long and arduous, his achievements generally hard won. There was little in his life that was easy, or that brought him easy fulfilment (apart perhaps from what he thought of as his great good fortune to have been born a 'natural believer'). But the idea of spiritual violence is in any case not really a confessional or private one. Rather, it is a *figura,* a representation – expressive and immediate, rather than merely intellectual or philosophical in character – of an archetypal condition. And this remains true, I shall suggest, even when Messiaen is at his most personal. He has not only the wish but the will to enter into the objective, the supra-personal state, and to remain there, at the very moment when his own personal concerns are at their strongest and most insistent. (Recall, for example, his desire to disappear behind the birds at the Donaueschingen première of *Réveil des oiseaux* in 1953).[33] This is his characteristic response to the awkward and often painful vicissitudes of life. It speaks to the seeming irresolvability of his own conflicts. And it is one absolutely crucial aspect of his Christianized sense of the need for catharsis – only through catharsis, of one kind or another, does (self-)

---

[32]　The surrealist dimension of Messiaen's music has both a literary and a specifically compositional aspect. Messiaen himself alluded to it reasonably often, almost always in connection with poetic text and imagery, and by implication with a general aesthetic outlook. Much less thought has been given to what the musical and compositional specificities of a surrealist approach might be. This calls for a larger, more sustained investigation. The present example shows one possible step towards a more radically musical understanding of Messiaen's approach, and in particular the technical-compositional dimension of his aesthetic in its surrealist dimension.

[33]　PHNS, p. 208: 'Don't include my biography, or any personal or musical information...: I'm anxious to disappear behind the birds.'

transcendence begin to become a possibility, a potential reality. Artistically it helps him to envisage a musical language that is able to embrace, at the same time, an extreme subjectivity and a keen sensibility with a grand and sometimes austere impersonality. This rich combination is one of his music's greatest strengths.

The phrase 'violence spirituelle' is first encountered, so far as we can tell, in the short La Jeune France manifesto of 1936: 'It is music's vocation to bring to all who love it its spiritual violence and its generosity of response .... La Jeune France will have diverse tendencies and aspirations ... which will combine to produce and disseminate a living music in a single gesture of sincerity, generosity and artistic self-awareness.'[34] It was obviously an idea with a shared resonance for all four members of the group. And the linking of a certain kind of musical idiom, the strength and intensity of which might border on the violent, with the necessary realities of spiritual experience was certainly common to Messiaen and Jolivet, for example, despite the evident dissimilarity of their respective styles and their very different understanding of the nature of religious ideals and practices. The present study has taken the phrase 'violence spirituelle' as indicative of a more general phenomenon, namely of a strong undercurrent in Messiaen's music of a darker, at times more anguished and violent, kind of intensity that is complementary (I would say *necessarily* complementary) to the joyous and the celebratory towards which he habitually strove.

Messiaen, I shall suggest, was too much of a psychological realist, and had experienced far too much himself, to take the achievement of serenity and transcendence for granted. Even if he himself fought shy of putting it in quite these terms, it is clear that he needed to feel he was creating a musical language that would make a real psychological and spiritualizing process experientially possible. He envisaged music's expressivity as one that could be made to embody, metonymically, the full range of human emotion, while at the same time having the – where necessary, savage – beauty and stylization appropriate to (specifically) modern art. His wish to embody theological virtues – truths, even – was clear and lifelong: to bear witness, in effect, through music to the reality of the world as he understood and believed it, humanely and spiritually, to be. This involved darkness and anguish, unavoidably, in order to arrive at a place or a condition of fulfilment – such was his acceptance, his accepted vocation, in life as in art.

If his sense of dazzlement and light does in the end prevail, in life as in art, then it happens all the more strongly and effectively in contrast to the tension and the phases of passion and struggle out of which it has emerged. His identity as a 'musicien de la joie' was maintained in a state of creative tension *against* the darkness and the suffering that were always there, whether close or distant. In erotic as in spiritual love, the fluctuating process and the phases of anguish,

---

[34]   '[L]a Musique se doit d'apporter sans répit à ceux qui l'aiment sa violence spirituelle et ses réactions généreuses ... Les tendances [de la Jeune France] seront diverses ... [et] s'uniront pour susciter et propager une musique vivante dans un même élan de sincérité, de générosité, de conscience artistique' (printed 'La Jeune France' pamphlet, 1936).

however occasioned, are part of the meaning of the whole experience, and, over time, of its enduring 'power to mean'. The ability to endure, without bitterness of heart, is necessary. And art is one of the embodied forms in which the possibility of such endurance is most positively (and cathartically) present, and thus perpetually 'available'.

This shows the value of 'spiritual violence' (by whatever name it is known) as a mode of response and self-realization – as a mode of resistance, a way of confronting the experiences of life idealistically, yet at the same time pragmatically, not in bitterness, but with resilience and in a state of possible hope. The artist works hard, at the same time, to make all this freely available through the enduring presence and interpretive potential of his music. This is its communicative purpose – its force of change and transformation, or, to put it at its simplest and strongest, its power of utterance. Such an aspiration therefore also becomes a function of craft, of artistic judgement and, finally, of a certain kind of perfection of musical form: a composer such as Messiaen works on the largest and the smallest scale simultaneously. The obsessive technical working and the aesthetic generosity are ultimately part of the same artistic gesture, the same 'project'. The expressive drive, or impulse, and the craftsman-like perfectionism are in the last resort one and the same – or perhaps better, they are two conjoined aspects of the same enterprise.

A Closer and a Larger View (By Way of Conclusion)

Messiaen's declared view of his 'trois Tristans' as a group gives us authority to regard them as a kind of trilogy or triptych. And it is (needless to say) a source of endless fascination to consider what the nature of their complementary interrelations might be, even where we may disagree with the composer on points of detail, or even of substance, as well as to interrogate the aesthetic and psychological specificity of each work. It is more than a little characteristic of Messiaen that he should have thought of the subject and significance of these pieces – on the face of it extraordinarily unlike and diverse! – in so carefully integrated a fashion: that is, as representing complementary angles on an important, fundamental myth, while being at the same time very individual and distinct as to musical character and elaboration, sonic and expressive treatment, genre, formal layout, and so on. We might perhaps find his insistence on such a degree of integration between the three a little excessive; and it clearly responded to a deep psychological need of some kind on his part. He even went so far as to suggest that a knowledge of *Harawi* and *Cinq Rechants* might be useful, even necessary, for a full understanding of *Turangalîla*:

> In order to understand the *Turangalîla-Symphonie* we must not forget that the piece is framed by *Harawi* and the *Cinq Rechants*. These [works] represent three different aspects of a single 'Tristan and Yseut' [myth] that is one and the same ....

> The texts of *Harawi* and *Cinq Rechants* contain particular words and phrases
> that serve as an explanation of *Turangalîla*.[35]

The various narrative and symbolic aspects of the three versions of the Tristan
idea complement one another, and also hint at a larger canvas beyond. Put in very
general terms, we might say that *Harawi* offers a dense network of Tristanesque
motifs in intimately poetic form, closely woven together and tied into Messiaen's
(re)imagining of the impassioned 'colloque sentimental' of the two Peruvian lovers
(the unnamed male and the exotic Piroutcha).[36] *Turangalîla* is conceived and
written on the largest scale, and clearly embraces the widest sonic and expressive
range – while lacking (as the quotation above admits) anything explicitly dealing
with the functioning and imagery of the myth, or the very individual interpretations
Messiaen places upon it. By contrast, the *Rechants* present a dense network of
referential names and other textual elements that are much broader in range and
scope than what we find in the other two pieces: a relatively full spectrum of
images and symbols related – centripetally *and* centrifugally, we might say – to the
main Tristan idea. The fact that the textual elements are assembled in fragmentary,
compressed form is a striking – and typically modernist as well as mysterious,
even secretive – effect. The 'freely associative' kind of collage in which they
flow by, at one with the voices' powerful ongoing stream of rhythm, relates also
to a certain temporal (that is, structural as well as psychological) compression
within the work, over and above its programmatically surrealist character. It is,
so to speak, part of the technical 'method' of Messiaen's version of surrealism.
Most important of all, it corresponds to his desire to show the driven, fiercely
impassioned shortness of human life, a drama of conflict and impermanence over
which only the eternal presence of the Beloved stands guard, or has any effective
redemptive power:

> Despite the work's quick tempo, and despite the dramatic shortness of human
> life which this evokes, what dominates every technical aspect of rhythm, music
> [and] text, dominating even Death itself (like the 'Ligeia' of Edgar Allan Poe),
> [there is] the Beloved standing above and beyond Time, while '[her] eyes travel
> in the past, in the future....'[37]

The biographical question to ask would be: Who is this Beloved? Which of the
women in Messiaen's life? The larger question to ask would be (bearing in mind,

---

[35]	*Traité II*, p. 151.

[36]	Messiaen thinks of his Piroutcha as a Peruvian Yseult (Isolde). The plot archetype
underlies the very varied manifestations of the story, the cultural details and 'colour' of
which, at the surface, are so dissimilar. The exotic setting offers him rich poetic and musical
possibilities to exploit compositionally: the 'colombe verte' metonym, the girl's dance-
song, a new variety of colours and rhythms, 'magic realist' nature imagery and so on.

[37]	Messiaen, 'Note de l'auteur'.

too, that Messiaen had a very specific citation from *Harawi* inscribed upon the headstone of his grave at Saint-Théoffrey in Petitchet, 'Tous les oiseaux des étoiles'):[38] In what dimension, and in what role, does this *Bien-aimée* exist? What is her universal or particular nature?

Perhaps, just perhaps, it is the mythic ideal, the transcendent symbol (*figura* or *Gleichnis*) of the Beloved that is active here. We may still choose to see *Harawi* as relating primarily to Claire and the *Rechants* to Loriod. But this, on its own, may be to diminish the experience of the work and to miss the largeness and connectedness of Messiaen's thinking – which in turn informs the largeness of expression (range and reach) of each of the three Tristan pieces individually. In the final analysis, an important part of this thinking lies in the archetypal value of the experiential process made available to us in and through the music – not in underplaying or undervaluing the human present, nor the often disarming contingencies of life 'as it is', but yet seeing its outcome in larger terms, looking towards the beyond (beyond time, beyond transience). This interrelation between the contingent and the absolute is one of the underlying reasons for the very particular use of symbol, metonymy and other (visual and kinetic) imagery within symbolist and surrealist artistic method. It gives a language well able to capture (or at least evoke) the drama of being and becoming. We see – and hear – this type of interrelation as it informs much of Messiaen's thinking, writing and music not just in the Tristan works. It allows us to view in a clearer light both his commitment to the here-and-now of human life and his still greater impulse towards transcendence – via the cathartic and perhaps the ecstatic. A strong, dynamic and fluid language built on a complex play of imagery and rhythm enables these different layers and objects of experience to commingle.

This, then, is all part of the flux and flow of images encompassed within the composer's sense of the poetic. The symbolic references within the *Rechants* texts are, however, in turn subsumed (Messiaen implies) into a larger aspiration. This aspiration is dynamic and strongly directional, and thus highly susceptible to being embodied within a specifically musical process. It is expressed in terms of a powerful sense of movement towards a higher kind and level of emotion – hoped for, looked for, but only sporadically intuited – that overcomes all else. The mythic dimension of the *Rechants* story and its aura of mystery work as an initiation into a journey of just this sort, the journey itself being accomplished – in a sense enacted – through the dynamic and unfolding quality of our experience of the music. In so doing, the mythic frame and the compositional power of the piece together offer a fully Messiaenesque version of the aesthetic category of the sublime, leading

---

[38]   *Harawi*, score, pp. 84–7. Photos of the headstone on Messiaen's grave are widely available (see, for instance, the cover of Christopher Dingle's *Messiaen's Final Works* (Farnham: Ashgate, 2013). The song is the only one in the cycle in F♯ major (Messiaen's key of divine perfection): it seems to articulate the hope (and possibility) of supra-personal experience and self-transcendence in poetic-musical terms (see below, Appendix 1 of this chapter, 'Comparison with *Harawi*').

through a strong experience of catharsis into quite new regions – where our perceptions are carried by specifically musical means. (If this journey of ascent is already notionally expressed – or better, shown by implication – within the compass of the two vocal works, then it is writ large in every sense over the course of the symphony.) The physical energy and emotional vitality of the experience do not, in Messiaen's terms, run counter to its transcendent, essentially spiritual character. On the contrary, they serve to reinforce it:

> But these fleshly symbols are not sufficient to give a true account of *Turangalîla*.
> The nostalgia and fatality of *Harawi*, the mysterious tenderness of the *Rechants*
> are surpassed and transcended: *Turangalîla* is a hymn to joy – the transcendent,
> supernatural Joy of the unique, everlasting love that is a reflection of the other
> Love.[39]

The graphic – especially the overtly visual – elements of the *Rechants* texts are symbolically powerful and effective in themselves, on their own terms. Their rhythmic character is of course fundamental to the whole musical effect, and their evocative potential serves to conjure up the mythic dimension of the Tristan idea. But their larger purpose (Messiaen insists) is to convey through the idea of fatality, even of death – and within the deeper medium of music – the paradoxical triumph of joy. The motifs and elements that supply the symbolic thread are the expected ones: the irreversible drinking of the love potion ('philtre à deux voix' in *Harawi*; 'Tous les philtres sont bus' in 'Rechant III'),[40] the fatal step of opening the doors in Bluebeard's castle (Perrault, Maeterlinck, Dukas, Bartók), Orpheus's 'exploratory' descent into the underworld, the 'flying lovers' (Chagall) and the ever-vigilant Brangäne (Wagner; by association also the medieval *alba*), Viviane's prison in the air, within which she entraps her lover Merlin, Hieronymus Bosch's crystal sphere in which he encloses his lovers (thereby sealing them within their inner world, cutting them off from the outside) and the disturbingly ambiguous figure of Perseus with the severed head of Medusa, which casts a shadow over the fifth and final *Rechant* (echoing the violent images of blood and decapitation in 'Katchikatchi les étoiles', the nightmarish 11th song of *Harawi*: 'Coupez ma tête... Roule dans le sang').[41] The idea of fatality and the proximity of death – its imminence, as well as our unsuspecting closeness to it – form an integral part of this thematic complex. Eros in its highest form is revelatory, bringing with it an experience both of blinding intensity and of new insight. But the latter is in fact a type of *un*knowing ('knowledge through unknowing'); and that of which we are unaware is, precisely, the sphere of fatality into which we have unwittingly entered.

---

[39]   *Traité II*, p. 153.

[40]   This famous passage is an independent lyric version of one of the 'love motifs' from *Turangalîla*. More famously, it reappears in *Catalogue d'oiseaux* ('Le Loriot', Livre 1er) in an obviously Loriod-related context.

[41]   See *Harawi* score, pp. 92–3, marking a violent conclusion to the song.

The governing function here is that of perspective, or rather, loss of perspective. When confronted by the immensity of an overwhelming experience, we lose ourselves in it. We thereby lose our grasp of distance and measure, and with it our sense of perceptual relativity, hence also our powers of differentiation and cognition. Our capacity to observe is submerged beneath a tide of feeling, coming from we know not where. Existing only in the moment, *this* moment, we are also at the same time somehow beyond ourselves – indeed, very nearly beyond the experience itself. This notion of the beyond is what joins the extremity of absolute love (especially, in the present context, absolute erotic love) to the ineluctability of death. And the joining is decisive. Intensity on this scale provokes a new moment of recognition, one that is flooded with energy and meaning but also shuts out all else. Although the lovers are as if illuminated, the broader light beyond is occluded (hence Tristan and Yseult/Isolde's longing only for night, for oblivion, as countermeasure and corollary to their erotic illumination). Extreme love irradiates and brings a new state of awareness: this is well conveyed (Messiaen implies) through music's power to arouse and overwhelm without loss of articulacy (that is, without stumbling into inarticulacy). But the price of this transcendent awareness, however freely attained, is death.

Close to death, we no longer see death; our gaze becomes wide and yet unseeing, filled with something larger than it can grasp. This, Messiaen suggests, is one crucial aspect of Rilke's 'opening onto eternity' expressed in the *Duino Elegies*; another is the lovers' blindness to the outside world, brought about not through negligence or self-indulgence, but through a state of irresistible possession by a transcendent emotion:

> For close to death we can see death no more,
> But stare before us with a creature's open gaze:
> Lovers, if the Other did not block their
> Sight, are close to it, and marvel.

Denn nah am Tod sieht man den Tod nicht mehr	Car près de mourir nous ne voyons plus la mort:
und starrt hinaus, vielleicht mit großem Tierblick.	Dans nos yeux fixes s'ouvre alors, peut-être,
Liebende, wäre nicht der andre, der	Le grand regard animal.
die Sicht verstellt, sind nah daran und staunen…	Les amants – n'était l'autre qui masque
(Rilke, *Duineser Elegien* (1922), Elegy 8)	La vue – en sont tout proches et s'étonnent.

This is the image, and the linkage of ideas, that Messiaen needs. The lovers are dazzled, blinded, and reach a state of being in which they are struck into submission by a higher kind and degree of feeling than they can control or understand, or even fully apprehend. They are in that sense close to death – not the death of a confining and lightless abyss, a mere extinguishing of life, but that self-transcendence, through death, which brings access to an illuminated beyond:

Very close, indeed. They launch themselves towards one another and lose themselves, like a leap into infinity. No longer is there *this* man, *this* woman, but a single creature, unique and exceptional .... Through this quest, disorientated, struck down by love, overwhelmed by an emotion that is too great for them and of which they are themselves the blameless, unwitting protagonists, they attain [a state of] dazzlement, of unseeing: the complete and irreversible lightning-strike of Joy.[42]

On an imaginative scale *Cinq Rechants* is an immense work, for all its modest dimensions (by Messiaen's standards) and its 'restricted' performing forces. It stands at the very heart of the twentieth-century vocal – not just 'choral' – repertory; and it intersects with general post-war modernist developments in a myriad of ways. By the standards of 1948 – even, some might say, of today – it radiates 'difficulty' in a creative and productive way, and stands as a beacon of advanced musical thinking.[43] The performers, too, surely have their place within this creative matrix. If the Beloved, or even the unreachable song of Love itself, may be seen as the 'onlie begetter' of the *Rechants*, Marcel Couraud, with the enlisted help of his singers, remains an essential genetic factor: however strong the myth of modernist autonomy may be, their trace remains somewhere hidden within Messiaen's sounds and textures. Modernist art is still an art of the possible, but its possibilities are forward-looking, dynamic and (above all) set out to stretch the boundaries of the musically potential in ways which will work their effect on

---

[42]   *Traité II*, p. 153. The extract from Rilke's 'Elegy 8' is given by Messiaen only in French. I have supplied the German original, and also given an English version. The translation of the *Duineser Elegien* by Joseph François Angelloz (1893–1978) was first issued in 1936 and then republished in 1943, under the Occupation, in parallel text format. Rilke's main French translator was Maurice Betz (1898–1946), who published a volume of translations entitled *Poésie* in 1938 (Émile-Paul Frères), which was also reissued during the war. Émile-Paul Frères also published *Fantôme de Rilke*, by the symbolist poet Léon-Paul Fargue (1876–1947), in 1942. The English translation, by the present author, was made from the German.

[43]   The *Cinq Rechants* and Jolivet's *Épithalame* share what we can perhaps call the 'virtue of extreme difficulty' that Daniel-Lesur's *Cantique des Cantiques*, for example, lacks (though it is an obviously beautiful and finely wrought piece in its own right). Other works that approach a similar level of difficulty might include certain Schoenberg choruses, the *Deutsche Motette* op. 62 by Richard Strauss, some Poulenc choral music (parts of the Mass in G, the wartime cantata *Figure humaine*) and a great deal of later music written in the wake of *Cinq Rechants* and often calling on the new professionalism of modern salaried radio chamber choirs or other specialist ensembles. A full, in-depth history of virtuoso ensemble and choral music in the mid-to-late twentieth century, in the modern-to-modernist dimension, has yet to be researched and written. For a considered study of modernist and avant-garde approaches to vocal *écriture*, see Marie-Raymonde Lejeune Löffler, *Les mots et la musique à l'exemple de Darmstadt, 1946–1978* (Paris: L'Harmattan, 2003).

the performers and listeners of today and tomorrow. It may, in time, redefine the nature of the musically actual.

Cinq Rechants set the marker for the new, virtuosic type of vocal ensemble writing and for what a choral piece of 'cantata dimensions' could become in the modern world – a marker which was of seismic impact in the 1950s and 1960s, and still remains contemporary today in a very nearly (if not quite) timeless way.[44] The particularity of the technical and aesthetic challenge of fitting the 'Messiaen style' to an inhabitual musical grouping forced – or if you prefer, enabled, brought out – solutions of *écriture* that would never have seen the light of day otherwise.

We do not, perhaps, have to share Messiaen's deep-seated, even obsessive need to see the completion of *Harawi* and the *Cinq Rechants* in *Turangalîla*. It may be thought just as fruitful, and perhaps more realistic, to preserve a keen sense of the individuality and genius of each. On balance the argument is well made that *Cinq Rechants* expresses Messiaen's gift and vision uniquely, in a fashion not quite like that of any of his other works, illuminating his sonic and psychological world in an irreplaceable way. And it has a special contribution to make to our view of the composer in a larger sense. For despite the evident range and diversity of his output, our image of Messiaen, our grasp of his persona and activity, have a tendency to crystallize around ideas that still remain too narrow, too predictable. The image of him during the 1930s as an otherworldly Catholic composer tied to theology, modality (both traditional and advanced), a modernist style of mysticism and above all the organ loft is belied by the substantial – and to a dispassionate eye, surely persuasive – evidence that the main emphasis lay elsewhere: that extended vocal works, and above all orchestral works, were in fact the driving force behind his musical (and, in a positive cultural way, spiritual) ambition at that time.[45]

If the great sequence of mature orchestral pieces, from *Chronochromie* to *Éclairs sur l'Au-Delà...*, resoundingly confirms the view of the centrality of the twentieth-century symphony orchestra to Messiaen's artistic world later on in life, the position of the human voice in that world is far more difficult to assert.[46]

---

[44]   There can be little doubt that *Épithalame*, for example, first drafted in 1952–53, came to be as it did partly through the example of the *Rechants* themselves and of the achievements of the Couraud vocal ensemble. Put at its simplest, Messiaen showed what was possible and extended the compositional horizons of the available vocal resources, which could then be further explored, and of course extended, by others. Jolivet's sound-world remains, of course, completely his own, and on any reading stands on an entirely equal musical footing with that of the *Rechants*.

[45]   Christopher Dingle, 'Forgotten Offerings: Messiaen's First Orchestral Works', *Tempo*, 241 (July 2007): pp. 2–21.

[46]   Even his closest musical approaches to the conceptual and ideational world of the liturgy may have been couched, compositionally, in terms of the symphony orchestra: the rather vaguely projected 'Credo' for chorus and orchestra, the *action sacrée* for choir and orchestra (associated with the early ideas for *La Transfiguration*) and the 'symphonie liturgique (pour grand orchestre)'; see PHNS, pp. 169, 243, 286).

Only *La Transfiguration* and *Saint François* have vocal forces within their make-up. These are, of course, enormously important large-scale works, which occupy a major position within Messiaen's output, but even so, the apparent lack of engagement with human vocality outside these monumental pieces is difficult to account for. This is a larger and more difficult question than can be addressed here;[47] it is alluded to simply in order to highlight the extraordinary nature and achievement – and perhaps, too, the unrepeatability – of the *Cinq Rechants*.

I say 'unrepeatability' with a certain misgiving, yet also advisedly – for at the start of 1969, *en pleine Transfiguration*, Messiaen had been thinking about a possible new work, projected for the 1971 Royan Festival, to be written for Couraud's (by then) ORTF singers and a very striking mixed instrumentarium (flutes, trombones, piano, ondes, percussion).[48] This piece, had it ever come into existence, would surely have presented something close to a secular 'ritual' work as a smaller-scale pendant to *La Transfiguration*, in a broadly similar way to the *Rechants* in their relation to *Turangalîla*. This, to be sure, is the stuff of fantasy. But what a piece it would surely have made! *Inter alia*, it might well have made more explicit Messiaen's musical relation to a piece he rarely mentioned, but had in mind all his life and which he famously took with him to war – Stravinsky's *Les Noces*.[49] And the very reason we can imagine the Royan piece, surely, as one of the most tantalizing of all his many unrealized projects is, precisely, the extraordinary expressive and imaginative power of the *Rechants* themselves – in particular, the sense we have on hearing it (or even just reading the score) that, although it is perfectly worked out, and of a perfect length for its ideas and material, not quite everything has yet been said.

---

[47] The question will be addressed at greater length in the present author's *Messiaen and the Voice* (in progress).

[48] Diary entry, 30 January 1969, PHNS, p. 280: 'Voices: spoken, sung, noises and onomatopœia, with two sets of bells, two flutes, three trombones, bass trombone, onde, piano, gongs and tam-tam' [for Royan].

[49] On the relation of *Les Noces* to *Trois Petites Liturgies*, see Matthew Schellhorn, '*Les Noces* and *Trois Petites Liturgies*: An Assessment of Stravinsky's Influence on Messiaen' in Christopher Dingle and Nigel Simeone (eds), *Olivier Messiaen: Music, Art and Literature* (Aldershot: Ashgate, 2007).

Appendix 1
Formal Layout and Strophic Arrangement of *Cinq Rechants*

This table (in which parts of the text have been omitted, for greater clarity) shows the overall balance and relational structure of sections, and does not include the internal repetitions of rechant and couplet within each movement.

INTRODUCTION			CODA
I. hayo kapritama la li la li la li la ssaréno	RECHANT les amoureux s'envolent Brangien… t k t k t k t k ha ha ha ha ha soif! l'explorateur Orphée trouve son coeur dans la mort	COUPLET miroir d'étoile château d'étoile Yseult d'amour séparé bulle de cristal d'étoile… (Barbe-bleue château de la septième porte)	hayo kapritama la li la li la li la ssaréno
II.	COUPLET ma première fois terre terre l'éventail… lumineux mon rire d'ombre […] solo de flûte berce les quatre lézards en t'éloignant	RECHANT mayoma kapritama ssarimâ	mano mano nadja lâma krita […] solo de flûte berce…
III. ma robe d'amour mon amour ma prison d'amour faite d'air léger lîla lîla ma mémoire ma caresse…	COUPLET oumi annôla… sari sari floutî yoma robe tendre toute la beauté paysage neuf…	RECHANT troubadour Viviane Yseult tous les cercles tous les yeux…	tous les philtres sont bus ce soir encore
IV.	RECHANT niokhamâ palalan soukî mon bouquet tout défait rayonne […] les volets roses Ha amour amour du clair au sombre Ha	COUPLET roma tama tama tama ssouka rava kâli vâli…	roma tama tama tama mon bouquet rayonne
V. mayoma kalimolimo tes yeux voyagent (mystérieux:) dans le passé	COUPLET losangé ma fleur toujours philtre Yseult rameur d'amour fée Viviane… […] hayo hayo Persée Méduse l'abeille…	RECHANT fleur du bourdon tourne tourne tourne à mort quatre lézards…	mayoma kalimolimo (lointain:) dans l'avenir

The question of how and to what extent these texts may represent a 'real' narrative, lying beyond or behind the words, remains an open one. Working from an account by Antoine Goléa, Michèle Reverdy offered a scenario in her apparently unpublished analysis of the *Rechants*.[50] My own feeling is that a slightly less

---

[50]   PHNS, pp. 182–3.

specific narrative frame, of archetypal character, serves the needs of the piece better: I. Fateful first step: entering into the dark, mysterious domain of love II. Meeting/'betrothal' of the lovers. III. Union of the lovers (ecstatic). IV. Fulfilment, radiance (*joyeux*). V. Fatality, turn to death, possible hope: transcendence, beyond time, of the Beloved.

Comparison with Harawi

The narrative of *Harawi*, by comparison, is less obscure, less mysterious – though still latent, beyond the explicit surface of the text, and with layers of allusion and imagery both verbal and musical. Messiaen himself gives a short, telescoped version of the story (First gaze – Union – Death)[51] and also a larger, song-by-song account that is more detailed and explicit,[52] which may be integrated with the following:

1. First glance: the gaze of love (*premier regard*), G major.
2. Greeting ('Bonjour toi'), mode 2/E♭ major (Beloved as 'colombe verte' = 'the spring girl'; *chants d'oiseaux* in piano 'verses').
3. Mountains, nature ('vibrations de l'atmosphère, en haute montagne').
4. Dance-song, highly rhythmicized, celebratory: (i) framing 'Doundou tchil' sections with extended piano 'couplets'; (ii) long middle section centred on mode 2/E♭ major (score, pp. 22–6, see especially the three-flat key signatures at 'Piroutcha te voilà ô mon à-moi' at pp. 22 and 24).
5. ('L'amour de Piroutcha') Dialogue between the two lovers ('doux et tendre'), G major.
6. Elemental nature: cries, calls, incantations in the forest, tumultuous representation of the mythic creation of the world.
7. First separation of the lovers: loss, distance, intimation and first experience of death ('Adieu toi'), E♭ major; funeral bells in the piano sections: *Un peu vif* (*comme des cloches*).
8. 'Magic syllable' game: recalling the (now absent) girl through the 'chanson de la colombe verte' and alluding to the dance-song, no. 4 ('Colombe verte... Piroutcha mia... doundou tchil'), the refrain being heard very distantly and quietly, in G major ('très loin, tout bas').
9. Reunion – physical union, visionary emotion ('exaltation en un grand cri d'amour'): *Vif, joyeux et passionné*, in E♭ major from 'tes tempes vertes, mauves, sur du temps, comme la mort' (score, pp. 72, 75, 82).
10. Spiritual union, intimation of transcendence ('chaînes tombantes, vers les étoiles, plus court chemin de l'ombre au ciel'): 'Amour oiseau d'étoile', in F♯ major.

---

[51]   See *Traité I*, p. 151.
[52]   *Traité III*, pp. 279–81.

11. Violent, agitated nightmare: the stars leap and dance, but in this terrifying context, not for joy (key signature of E♭ major nevertheless).

12. Death of the Beloved (Messiaen says, of both lovers, since the man dies in calling to her). Textually and musically, this song represents a grand, tragic, yet cathartic reprise, coloured by the presence of death: 'Les mots "très loin, tout bas" (déjà pronouncés dans le 8e chant) prennent ici un sens déchirant et définitif qui est la mort',[53] E♭ major.

---

[53]   Ibid., p. 281.

Appendix 2
Cinq Rechants: A Discography

Ensemble Le Madrigal, dir. Jean-Paul Kreder, Philips Modern Music Series A00579 L ABL. 3400 (1961) with Daniel-Lesur, *Cantique des Cantiques*, reissued *Olivier Messiaen: Portrait* Accord 480 0856 (2008); also in Complete Edition DG 480 1333 (32 CDs).

John Alldis Choir, dir. John Alldis, Argo ZRG 523 (1967) with Bruckner, Schoenberg, Debussy, reissued DECCA 478 0352 (2008).

Solistes des choeurs de l'ORTF, dir. Marcel Couraud Erato STU 70457 (1968), rec. Studio 103, ORTF, Paris (April 1968) with Xenakis, *Nuits* and Penederecki, *Stabat Mater*, reissued Warner 2564 62162-2 (18 CDs).

Solistes des choeurs de l'ORTF, dir. Marcel Couraud, Festival de Royan, 28 April 1968, radio broadcast transmission, recording available at www.ina.fr/audio/PHD07008712/festival-de-royan-olivier-messiaen-5-rechants-pour-choeur-mixte-a-douze-voix.fr.html.

New Music Choral Ensemble, dir. Kenneth Gaburo, Ars Nova Ars Antiqua AN 1005 (1969)

Stockholm Chamber Choir (Kammarkör), dir. Eric Ericson, 'Virtuoso French Choral Music' EMI CDM 769817 2, original release EMI 1C 165-30 796 (1978), rec. Rundfunk, Stockholm, 25 August 1978.

Groupe Vocal de France, dir. Michel Tranchant, Arion ARN 68084 (1989, rec. 1984), with *O sacrum Convivium* and Xenakis, *Nuits*, reissued 2010.

London Sinfonietta Voices, dir. Terry Edwards, Virgin 61916 (1991), with *Trois Petites Liturgies, O sacrum Convivium!*, reissued in EMI 2174662 (2008).

The Sixteen, dir. Harry Christophers, Collins COLL 14802 (1996) 'La Jeune France' with Jolivet, *Epithalame* and Daniel-Lesur, *Cantique des Cantiques*, reissued as Coro COR 16023 (2004).

Danmarks Radiokor (Danish National Radio Choir), dir. Jesper Grove Joergensen, Chandos CHAN 9663 (1999) rec. Danish Radio, 1996, with Stockhausen, Xenakis.

BBC Singers, dir. Stephen Cleobury, 'Love Sacred, Love Profane' BBC Music Magazine BBC MM 85 (1999) rec. St Paul's, Knightsbridge, 1 April 1998.

SWR Vokalensemble Stuttgart, dir. Rupert Huber, Hänssler Classic HAEN 93055 (2003).

RIAS-Kammerchor Berlin, dir. Daniel Reuss Harmonia Mundi France HMC 901834 (2004).

Ensemble Sequenza 9.3, dir. Catherine Simonpietri, Alpha ALPHA 112 (2008).

Det Norske Solistkor, dir. Grete Pederson (2012) BIS BIS-1970.

Note: The discography is as complete as I, with help from friends and in particular from Christopher Dingle, have been able to make it. It is, as far as possible, in chronological order by date of recording. Online performances, from a variety of sources including radio archives, are also available.

Appendix 3
Messiaen's 'Appoggiatura Chords'

Strikingly positioned at the end of the Introduction in 'Rechant III' there is a short but very beautiful sequence of chords (score, p. 16, second system), immediately preceding the grand middle section with its famous passage of rhythmic development and climax (pp. 17–25, 26–8). The harmonies on p. 16 are highly characteristic 'appoggiatura chords', as I shall call them for the moment. There is in truth a fairly extensive use of appoggiatura-type relationships between chords within Messiaen's harmonic practice. They all entail some kind of linear and sequential dependency of one harmony upon another, though it is often more a question of Messiaen's composerly manipulation of phrase-contours, rhythm and accentuation that generates this sense of progression than of any intrinsic harmonic force. This is naturally an open and interestingly debatable point, and calls for a wide-ranging type of investigation – one that is grounded in musical observation of a detailed, comparative kind. This larger discussion will take place elsewhere; here, it is sufficient to draw attention to this particular harmonic usage as it appears in 'Rechant III'.

In *Technique de mon langage musical* these harmonies are styled simply 'accords sur la dominante' (Ch. 14, exx. 201–7); whereas in *Traité VII* they are given the more unwieldy (but more accurate) title 'accords à *Renversements Transposés* sur la même note de basse' (pp. 235–47). The basic formation is of a dominant major ninth, with the tonic substituting for the leading note: above this are located dissonant 'appoggiaturas' (usually in pairs, a perfect fourth apart), which sometimes resolve melodically, at other times remain *in situ* as colourful dissonant 'notes ajoutées' for distinctive timbre and resonance. (There are various permutations available: the 'base chord' can be presented in any inversion, judicious singling out of held bass notes joining two or more chords engenders a variety of harmonic effects, while carefully plotted shifts in the bass note itself will also enable a new repertoire of longer harmonic phrases to be created – all of which results in a potentially very wide range of textural-harmonic colour.)

The historical situation of these particular chord-types is that they emerge out of a period of experimentation and evolution as Messiaen was building up and developing his sense of his own harmonic language over the course of the later 1930s and early 1940s, fuelled no doubt in particular by a long and fruitful period of reflection during his wartime captivity. He himself identified examples in *La Nativité*, in 'Liturgie de cristal' (*Quatuor pour la fin du Temps*), in 'Psalmodie de l'Ubiquité' (*Trois Petites Liturgies*) and in a wide range of post-war pieces, most especially of all *La Fauvette des jardins*. But there are others. Along with the chords of contracted resonance and the pivotal 'accords tournants', they richly deserve a more extended, comparative investigation. By this means their context and purpose – functional, colouristic, expressive-rhetorical – within Messiaen's musical language over a broad span of time can be fruitfully and realistically studied. The reason for drawing attention to this particular passage in the *Rechants*

Example 14.2   *Rechant III*, end of introduction, showing 'appoggiatura chords'
                with changing harmonies above a bass pedal

is that, given the technical constraints of writing for 12 independent voices, it shows
with special clarity the expressive melodic potential of the 'notes ajoutées', here
treated as 'classic' vocal appoggiaturas in parallel perfect fourths (Example 14.2).

Chapter 15

Messiaen in Retrospect

Hugh Macdonald

On an upper shelf in my basement I keep a row of worthless books published in the late nineteenth century with titles like *Great Musical Composers*, *Studies of Great Composers*, *Imaginary Conversations with Great Composers*, and more in the same strain. These generally start with Palestrina and move directly from there to Bach and Handel. Even when Wagner is last in the line, the assumption is that Great Composers are here to stay and that we would see yet Greater ones in the future. When Stravinsky died in 1971 I remember the thought being expressed by musicians young and old that he was the last of the Great Composers, and that we would not look upon his like again. My enthusiasm for contemporary music being then more pronounced than it is now, I cherished the opinion that at least three men might still be candidates for an exalted and historic role, the three being Britten, Shostakovich and Messiaen. All sorts of reasons were put forward why none of them measured up to Stravinsky's high standing, but when, within a few years, Britten and Shostakovich both disappeared (as the French so tactfully put it), Messiaen seemed to me and many others to be without a rival as the keeper of the seal of Greatness.

I have for many years been convinced that some of the best music comes from composers who enjoy little celebrity with the public and little space in the dictionaries, and that we devote too much of our attention to the handful of composers who dominate the repertoire. I am unhappy with the notion of greatness, and even more with the notion of un-greatness that flows from it. I object to the skimming off of a canon of standard works that seems to be the universal method of teaching music history. But Messiaen is uniquely placed since it requires no great concession to place him at the highest level of musical achievement, yet there is no danger of his music ever being over-exploited and becoming over-familiar. Can one imagine *Saint François d'Assise* alternating in provincial opera houses with the *Barber of Seville* or *Carmen*?

Messiaen's music is complex, richly overlaid with meaning, and very difficult to perform. Yet audiences have little difficulty grasping the individuality of its sonority, the sincerity of its faith and the high craftsmanship that we demand of all great artists. He never hid behind a screen of jargon and technical mystification. As a teacher he believed profoundly in expounding music and explaining how it works. The areas in which he developed a fantastic expertise, such as Greek meters, Hindu rhythms and ornithology – a match for professionals in all those fields – these he regarded as fundamentally accessible to anyone prepared to put in the necessary study. 'What's the problem?' he might have said. He wrote and spoke about his music in the most open manner, neither boasting of its brilliance nor veiling its meaning. Even his faith, which must be the most inaccessible part of his make-up to unbelievers, he treated as if it had no complication or mystery for anyone. This is naïveté of a fine and noble kind, for it went hand in hand with an optimism that drew him away from the darker aspects of life. 'Sin and dirt are not interesting', he said.[1] His faith opened up the prospect of salvation, of transfiguration, of resurrection, of glory and of the certainty of the afterlife.

Messiaen was surely a happy man, secure in his faith, and manifestly thrilled by his studies, his teaching, his duties as an organist and, of course, by composing. He was never troubled by doubt. It was Milhaud who gave his autobiography the title *Ma Vie heureuse*, but it might have served for Messiaen, had he written his. We are so accustomed to enumerating the twentieth-century's record of evil and despair that it has become much easier to grasp Shostakovich's persistent expression of emptiness and struggle than to relate to a figure who inoculated himself against the world's atrocities by effortlessly focusing on the beauties of nature and on the divine.

Because of his early facility for music, Messiaen's tastes were formed by the somewhat serendipitous array of music that came his way in his childhood. He discovered *Pelléas et Mélisande* at the age of ten before the move to Paris. One year later, on entering the Conservatoire, he might have encountered sceptical voices that decried impressionism as passé. But it was too late; his passion for Debussy was firmly entrenched; he was not ashamed of composing Debussy-like preludes, and he resented Cocteau's pithy attacks on his hero. *Don Giovanni* was another early encounter that sealed his admiration for Mozart even though many people must have been puzzled by his insistence that Mozart stands out as a colourist and as a rhythmist when elsewhere Messiaen displayed little interest in classical parlance. If he had been more familiar with Beethoven's piano sonatas in the 1920s and 1930s he would not have described the fact that a German officer gave him a copy in 1940 as so revelatory, as if this opened his eyes to their treasure. 'I recognized them as the miracles of structure that they are', he told Claude Samuel.[2] So Mozart's concertos and Beethoven's sonatas became a central study in his analysis classes at the Conservatoire, while the formal conventions of the classical period found no echo in his work. From studying his music alone we would have little idea that either Mozart or Beethoven meant very much to him at all.

That is not the case with Berlioz, since connections between the two composers can readily be heard, even without Messiaen's lifelong admiration for, particularly, the *Damnation de Faust*, another score that miraculously came his way in childhood, and which he played on the piano imagining the orchestral richness that he could only discover later. As colourists Berlioz and Messiaen stand out in the history of French music. In addition they both wrote important treatises that were

---

[1]　*Music and Color*, p. 213.

[2]　Ibid., p. 175.

designed as books of instruction but that we value instead as informative guides to their authors' craft. Messiaen recognized Berlioz as the 'father of orchestration', a rather fanciful simplification, as we know, but one that meant much to him and contributed to his fastidious concern for instrumentation. The quest for the right sonority, the essential goal of Berlioz's treatise, is a fundamental feature of all Messiaen's orchestral works. They both regarded routine orchestration as a failure of a composer's duty, citing Rossini as an offender. Bach's interchangeable instruments were an insult to their sense of the rightness of a given choice, although it has to be said that Berlioz allowed substitutions if necessary, oboe for cor anglais, or clarinet for bass clarinet, for example, driven by his experience as a practical musician in the face of inadequate resources. Messiaen particularly commended the choice of bells in the *Symphonie fantastique*, even if Berlioz himself was so accustomed to substituting a piano for unobtainable bells that he printed the part in the full score as for piano. Sharing roots in the southern part of France, Messiaen assumed that Berlioz loved nature as much as he did. But this was not so. Berlioz was a city dweller, rarely seeking rural surroundings except for tranquillity and repose, not for the fragrances, sounds and colours that bewitched and inspired Messiaen.

They also shared an absorbing interest in rhythm. Both were shocked that the Conservatoire had no class in rhythm. Both detested the commonplace use of four-square pulses. Works such as *Harold en Italie* and *Benvenuto Cellini* display an inventive concern for rhythm that includes additive procedures that Messiaen was later to develop much more comprehensively. But Berlioz would never have explored rhythm so systematically as Messiaen did, nor would he have been the least interested in the rhythmic intricacies of remote cultures, all of which he dismissed as primitive.

Both composers attached importance to spatial concerns and the matching of music to the place where it is performed. There is a sublime grandeur in both composers, often reaching out to infinite spaces, from the canyons to the stars, that challenges our imagination as performers and listeners. Heine's comparison of Berlioz with the apocalyptic paintings of John Martin is particularly apt here. Messiaen used to improvise on themes from *Roméo et Juliette* (and I greatly regret that in my student years in Paris I never went to hear him improvise), and when he played for a memorial mass for Berlioz in 1969 at his own church, the Trinité, he must have remembered that Berlioz's funeral was held there only a few years after it had been built.

Wagner was another composer whose scores appeared early on Messiaen's piano and who thus remained embedded in his artistic consciousness throughout his life in a very complex fashion, as Wagner always tends to be. Messiaen did not share the neoclassicists' disdain for Wagner. His disdain was visited, rather, on the neoclassicists themselves, including Stravinsky's works after *Les Noces*. Despite growing up at a time when hostility to Germany was pervasive in France, he was not anti-German. His main objection to Bach was his rhythmic regularity, overlooking the subtlety of Bach's phrasing and treating the Italianate element in baroque music as rhythmically uninteresting. I have the impression that Bach's organ music did not appear often at the console of the Trinité church, and that it was overshadowed by music of the French school and of course his own. At least Bach's faith, like Messiaen's, was unquestioned. He too was certain of the afterlife, but much more weighed down, as a good Protestant, by the contemplation of sin, and more drawn to the passion of Christ than to the splendour of angels and saints in glory.

Brahms meant little or nothing to Messiaen and did not reach him in his childhood. His orchestration alone would have been contrary to Messiaen's beliefs. But the French often have trouble appreciating Brahms (think of Lalo's horrified reaction to the Violin Concerto).

Messiaen's attachment to colour is surely unique. But he is not the culmination of the long haphazard history of associating music with colour. The eighteenth-century experiments that Telemann was involved with, the flurry of strange instruments that emerged in the late nineteenth century attempting to create a new art-form out of colours (and sometimes smells), the poetic faith in the equivalence of colour and music posited by Hoffmann, Baudelaire and others – none of this prognosticates Messiaen's fundamental delight in colour in parallel with his love of birdsong and his Catholic faith. He did not want to project colour during his music. He had no desire to follow the course suggested by Skryabin's *Prometheus* and Schoenberg's *Die glückliche Hand*. The mention of these works sent him straight back to the entrance of the Commendatore's statue in *Don Giovanni*. Mozart's score makes no mention of lighting or colour, but the orchestration and harmony at that moment struck Messiaen as the supreme expression of colour-control. He heard colour not only in Wagner and Debussy, as we might expect, but also in the music of Mozart and Chopin. Notice that the music whose colour he most admired is by the very same composers who made the first impact on the boy Olivier. In other words his love of colour and his love of music, both intensely felt at an early age, identified one with another and overlapped. He was not wrong in classing Mozart as a source of colour-pleasure, he was simply pursuing a deep instinct that was never dislodged. This was so personal that we, whether his students, disciples or admirers, cannot be expected to share that view, just as we probably cannot expect to share his faith.

Electronic music, in which infinite colour choices are theoretically possible, appalled him, despite his dalliance in *musique concrète* with *Timbres-durées*. He especially loved the colours of nature, in birds above all, also stained glass (he always mentioned the Sainte Chapelle in Paris and Chartres cathedral), while in music colour was for him more a function of harmony than of orchestration. No one would deny the richness of his orchestration and few can resist resorting to traditional colour metaphors when describing it, yet for him colour emerges from harmony, and harmony emerges from modes. He explicitly denied synaesthetic experience. He did not associate individual notes or keys with colours.

The kinship with Skryabin has often been remarked upon, yet I feel it probably illuminates Skryabin's music more than Messiaen's. Skryabin's late music is so prophetic, so swollen with suggestions for later developments – alas denied by his early death at the age of 43 – that it is tempting to connect Skryabin's love of systematic modal harmony, at least, with Messiaen's. Both composers loved to linger in the key or on the chord of F♯ major. Skryabin too created melody out of harmony, in the late sonatas for example; he too allowed harmony to serve a formal function; he too treated time in a radical way. By abandoning functional harmony and allowing chords to exist without horizontal connections, much like in Debussy, Skryabin weakened the sense of forward motion in his music. His sense of pulse had always been loose, and in his later music it seems to disappear altogether. Lacking pulse and direction, his pieces consequently had to be brief. Beginnings sound like middles, which sound like ends. Time effectively ceases to exist.

Some of this applies to Messiaen too. But he would never acknowledge a loss of pulse. The listener may be unaware of the complex rhythmic relations in the music and sometimes imagine that time has stopped. Messiaen's pieces can be extremely slow and immobile. But because in his ear, unlike in Skryabin's, the rhythm is always active, however slow the pulse, the pieces can be very long, often working out complex permutations like a bell-ringer's changes. Skryabin was systematic with his harmony, but not with his rhythm.

Skryabin's legacy included a group of composers in the 1920s who sometimes seem to belong to Messiaen's world. Obukhov has often been cited as a kindred spirit. He was resident in Paris from 1918 until his death in 1954. He composed an immense amount of music, most of it still unpublished and unperformed; he planned some works, notably the enormous *Livre de vie*, on a vast scale; he was driven by a profound religious faith and was much drawn to mysticism; he exploited an early electric instrument, the 'Croix sonore', not unlike the ondes Martenot; he wrote for the ondes Martenot too; he barred his music to reflect musical phrases, not in regular time signatures.

In all these respects, except perhaps in his attachment to mysticism, Obukhov resembles Messiaen. What he lacked was the practical sense that Messiaen sustained through his work as an organist and teacher. What could be more practical than composing the *Quatuor pour la fin du Temps* for the instrumentalists he found in the prison camp? While Obukhov faded into obscurity, piling up endless scores written in a notation that only he could read, Messiaen worked steadily towards world celebrity and recognition. Of Obukhov it is even said that he entered bar numbers in his scores not in red ink, but in his own blood.

Lourié was another Russian resident in Paris from 1924 on, much indebted to Skryabin, avant-garde by instinct, drawn to exploring unusual modes, and devoutly Catholic. His music has a rich harmonic vocabulary and a fondness for bell-like sounds. Perhaps that is as far as resemblances to Messiaen go. Other Russian composers chronicled in Larry Sitsky's invaluable survey seem to have been similarly sympathetic both to Skryabin's and to Messiaen's ways of thinking, including Krein, Protopopov and Melkikh, all of them innocent of anything beyond marginal posthumous survival.[3] They all shunned the Satie-

---

[3]   See Larry Sitsky, *Music of the Repressed Russian Avant-Garde, 1900–1929* (Westport, CT and London: Greenwordd Press, 1994).

esque aesthetic that Parisians adored in the 1920s and they were untouched by the rage for machine music that gripped Honegger, Prokofiev and a group of Soviet composers at this time. Yet Messiaen had no contact, as far as I am aware, with any of these émigrés except Wyschnegradsky, whose speciality was microtones. Yvonne Loriod performed some of his music and Boulez showed some interest, while Messiaen himself, beyond a few early experiments for ondes Martenot, had no use for microtones in his own music.

If we add the *Rite of Spring* and, by extension, Rimsky-Korsakov to the mix, not to mention Mussorgsky, who makes notable appearances in *Technique* and the Samuel interviews, there is a substantial Russian element in Messiaen's music. We might bracket Messiaen with those many Russians who, having attached themselves to an appealing idea, however unworkable, persist in it to the bitter end. Familiar examples are Dargomyzhsky's pursuit of recitative, Tolstoy's pursuit of peasanthood, and of course the Soviet pursuit of Marxism, all of which had failure built in from the start. Messiaen's dedication to what he identified as his four driving instincts – colour, rhythm, birdsong and faith – has a similar obsessive quality about it, and he pursued these studies relentlessly in long, large works to the end of his life. Yet none of them are on the face of it doomed to fail, in fact he insisted, in his attractively optimistic way, that they were the keys to his success as a composer and as a man, and perhaps also the keys to heaven. Let us then acknowledge Messiaen's unswerving loyalty to his ideals and recognize that he failed in none of them.

If the Russian heritage is a real presence in Messiaen's music, what about the French heritage much closer to home? As we have seen, he acknowledged his debt to Berlioz and especially to Debussy. As his teacher at the Conservatoire Dukas was obviously a major figure in his development. Messiaen regarded him with respect and gratitude, although it is hard to point to direct links between their works. It is customary to cite the emphasis in *Ariane et Barbe-bleue* on the colours that stream from the six doors as they are successively opened in Act I. Each door reveals jewels, in turn amethysts, sapphires, pearls, emeralds, rubies and diamonds, each resplendent in their respective colours, literal and orchestral. Dukas as a master-orchestrator knew how to make such scenes brilliantly effective, but this was not the primary attraction of Maeterlinck's play; the subtle intertwining of Perrault's tale and the Ariadne myth, the desire to put Offenbach firmly in his place, and the feminist overtones of the libretto all supplied sufficient motives for Dukas to set to work. In any case the six colour-scenes work in a highly decorative way, not as something that emerges implicitly from the music itself, as it would in a work by Messiaen, even though the scene made a deep impression on him when he first heard it at the age of 18.

What Dukas instilled in Messiaen, if indeed he needed it instilled, was the indispensibility of technique. In the field of orchestration, obviously, Dukas could be a superb teacher, and all students, especially if they are pianists and organists, have a lot to learn in this area. But if you were following Satie's career in the early 1920s you could be forgiven for thinking that craftsmanship was regarded as of no account. Dukas must have been horrified at Milhaud's prolixity in a language whose rules were so loosely defined. He was a conservative musician, not impressed by the array of experimental modern styles that attracted young composers and even some older ones, such as Ravel. Messiaen was modern, but not a rebel. He was deaf to trends, listening only to his inner ear, and applying Dukas's principles of consummate craftsmanship and artistic integrity. Wherever we look in Messiaen's music, the prevalence of technical procedures – in rhythms, in modes, in *valeurs*, in *intensités*, in permutations – is as obvious as in a Bach fugue.

Messiaen was more fortunate than his teacher, for he did not suffer from the destructive self-criticism that caused Dukas to leave us only a tiny handful of works. Of course there are some who wish Messiaen had more often opted for brevity and amputated at least some of his longer works. In Dukas's case, all his pieces, few as they are, are of superb quality, but we should surely give a lot for more *Sorcerer's Apprentices*, more overtures of the solidity of *Polyeucte* or more ballets such as *La Péri*. How strange is the contrast between Dukas's diffidence and Messiaen's confidence, the one the creator of a small, exquisite œuvre, the other responsible for oceans of music, none of it despised by its composer, scarcely any of it ever subjected to revision, all of high technical quality, the fruit of some 60 years of unrelenting productivity. Perhaps it should be said that Messiaen's fertility was not yet on display in the years when Dukas presided over his studies; that seems to have grown exponentially, especially after the war and his emergence into the international arena.

What about Franck, Messiaen's obvious precursor as organist-teacher-composer? There are many parallels between them. The authorities at the Paris Conservatoire resisted giving either of them responsibility for the composition class. Franck never taught composition, only the organ class, while Messiaen had a succession of harmony and analysis classes before becoming professor of composition late in his career in 1966. But both were the most influential composition teachers of their time and both had distinguished students in the next generation. Both were devout, both dedicated to their churches, both generously recognized by their contemporaries. Both found new sounds in the resources of the splendid Cavaillé-Coll organ, both disdained the baroque organ. Both explored the sound of mixture stops that give the organ such a brilliant sonority. Perhaps the repertoire of organ music that Messiaen played at the Trinité, especially the tradition initiated by Franck, would be a fruitful line of research. Surely he played Vierne and Dupré and Franck, even Widor? Or was that only during his student years? But as far as I can tell, he had little to say about this great ancestor in the organ world.

He had even less to say about Gounod and Massenet, perhaps because he shared the general contempt in which both composers languished for the greater part of the twentieth century. He should surely have admired Massenet's discipline, his craftsmanship and his complete understanding of the world of opera. Admirers of *Wozzeck* find it hard to love *Manon*, alas, and so Messiaen can perhaps be forgiven for thinking that Massenet's music had nothing to contribute to his own. But

Gounod was driven by genuine religious fervour and he served the Catholic church well. His versatility and success made him a prominent player, like d'Indy, in the Catholic revival of the late nineteenth century. It would not have surprised anyone if Messiaen had declared Gounod to have been the transmitter of a certain kind of musical truth, but perhaps because Messiaen grew up at a time when Gounod's successes were already beginning to fade, the connection was never made.

So much of the Third Republic's energies went into the salon and into opera that most of their work can have meant little to a young composer growing up between the wars with little interest in either, even to one who turned away from trends. Bizet, Delibes, Saint-Saëns, Chabrier, Fauré – none of them opened any doors for Messiaen to step delightedly through.

But what of the more abstract qualities that are traditionally ascribed to French music? Bruneau defined the French tradition as based on 'la mesure, la clarté, l'esprit, le cœur, la franchise et l'audace', which might be rendered as 'control, transparency, wit, feeling, openness and daring', all nicely vague terms. Taking up the call of the French heritage, Debussy proclaimed: 'Couperin, Rameau – those are real Frenchmen! French music, it's all transparency, elegance, and simple, natural declamation'. Even recognizing that 'clarté' does not mean clarity, it is hard to reconcile the term with impressionism, whose purpose was in part at least to disguise outlines and eschew strong formal gestures. In Messiaen's music, certainly, we find control, feeling, openness and daring, and the kind of *clarté* that suggests brightness. Maybe not elegance, maybe not wit. Neither Bruneau nor Debussy included in their lists two qualities that have much more frequently been identified as French, namely colourfulness and literacy. Colour, as everyone acknowledges, plays a fundamental part in Messiaen's music, even if not in the same sense as most other composers would apply it. Couperin, Rameau, Berlioz, Chabrier and many others pass this test of Frenchness. As for literacy, or at least a fondness for leaning over towards poetry, drama and the other arts, there are few French composers who do *not* conform to that model. The closest is Chopin, and he was not very French. Meanwhile Germans such as Cornelius and von Bülow considered Berlioz to be fundamentally German in character. I think most of us would recognize Messiaen as typically French even if we did not know that his birth, upbringing, language, religion and citizenship were all 100 per cent French.

I venture to suggest that a blind test such as that might easily provoke the suggestion that he was Russian. In another sense he shows a Russian proclivity. I have elsewhere pointed out that of the three watchwords of the French Revolution – liberty, equality and fraternity – the one that was least often invoked in the nineteenth century and even during the Revolution itself was fraternity. The French are a nation of individualists who love to squabble. Think how studiously Alkan and Debussy avoided the company of other musicians. There have been groups or *cénacles* dedicated to a particular cause or banding together in self-defence. The Russians liked to form groups and handfuls and in particular to work together one-to-one, interfering in each other's scores in a way that an unsympathetic posterity has found artistically unacceptable. In France the most famous is, of course, the

Groupe des Six, whose identity is impossible to erase from our consciousness even though everyone agrees that it has little meaning in terms of style or history. Messiaen's group La Jeune France was formed some 15 years later, in part to propagate a diametrically different aesthetic, hostile to frivolity and the cult of Satie. The grouping did little to promote the careers of any of the four, although at least it has kept the names of the other three in the dictionaries. Messiaen was probably thinking that the group was a reincarnation of the camaraderie in 1830 that Berlioz's biographer Boschot described, using the name La Jeune France, which as far as I know was completely unknown to Berlioz himself.

Fraternization comes about automatically from the social nature of music-making, and occasionally groups are formed around charismatic individuals. This was the case with Franck's pupils, with Nadia Boulanger's pupils, and certainly with Messiaen's pupils, among whom are many of the foremost names of the later twentieth-century avant-garde. Few of them wrote music that resembles their teacher's music in any recognizable way, and that surely is the mark of a selfless, thoughtful teacher. Those thrice-weekly, four-hour sessions at the Conservatoire in the Rue de Madrid must have been absorbing exchanges that tested the determination, the brains and the ears of everyone who attended. Messiaen never resented a single minute of his teaching time and regretted the retirement forced on him by French law. And all the while he was composing long works that demanded minute attention to every detail, not forgetting his weekly duties in church. At least he did not have to concern himself much with a choir, as is always the case for his Protestant counterparts.

My first memory of Messiaen's music is the broadcast by the BBC of the *Turangalila* symphony in the early 1950s. I don't know if it was the first performance in Britain or not – it probably was – but I clearly recall my own astonishment at the sound of the music, thinking as I then did that Menotti represented the most advanced musical language, and I also recall the booing that greeted its conclusion. Now that it's established as a twentieth-century classic it no longer gets booed, but it will always test an audience's response. My own local orchestra, the St Louis Symphony Orchestra, has presented it twice in recent years. In the first case, it was conducted by the Dutch conductor Hans Vonk, and the hall was seen to be losing its occupants some time before the end. More recently it has been conducted by David Robertson, a committed champion of Messiaen, who weeded out the faint-hearted by delivering a 50-minute analytical talk not before the concert but as part of the concert itself, before the music began.

The other great Messiaenic moments for me came with *Chronochromie* ten years later, the work that I tenaciously consider his masterpiece, and with the concert performance in 1986 of three scenes from *Saint François d'Assise* at the Royal Festival Hall in London, conducted by Ozawa in Messiaen's presence. I envy those who have had the opportunity to hear the full work performed in the manner the composer intended.

So when Messiaen died in 1992, who was next to inherit the mantle of Greatness that he had worn for a full 20 years? For a short while I clung to the idea that the only candidate was Tippett, whose mind and music resembled Messiaen's in many interesting ways, but even he did not live forever. Certainly none of Messiaen's pupils have equalled their master's range and stature. We live in an era that has no space and no taste for Great Composers. In theory, at least, this might mean that more modest talents might enjoy a brief glimpse of the sun, but in fact it's the sun that shines less brightly on classical music, not the lack of talent or ambition on the part of those who seek it. Messiaen's achievement, meanwhile, was unarguably monumental, and his legacy is a body of music that will continue to provoke the kinds of questions this book and its sister volume have attempted to answer and also to move and inspire audiences for many generations to come.

Appendix
Yvonne Loriod Discography

Christopher Dingle

This discography lists the commercially released recordings by Yvonne Loriod.[1] The first section is, as far as possible, in chronological order by date of recording (rather than release). The intention is not only to provide information on Yvonne Loriod's recorded legacy in as comprehensive a manner as possible, but also to provide a sense of how it developed across her career. This is discussed in my chapter, 'Yvonne Loriod as Source and Influence' which appears as the Intermède between the two parts of this book. The entries provide the available information for each distinct recording date, then list record company details and catalogue numbers for the first known release and significant later reissues. Information is only given for newly recorded performances involving Yvonne Loriod on each release (accompanying re-released recordings are not listed again). Material included from earlier recordings or works on which she does not play are not listed. Some dates and locations are uncertain, as no recording information has been provided on either the original release or subsequent releases. Audio recordings are listed first, followed by the small number of filmed appearances to have been made available commercially. After the discographical listing of recordings, the second section lists the works recorded. These appear in alphabetical order by composer, then work, with numbers referring to the entries for the recordings in the first section.

?	denotes uncertain or unconfirmed date.
DL	indicates the suggested dating is based on the *dépot légal* copy at the Bibliothèque National de France.
*	denotes a recording not originally intended for commercial release (usually a live radio broadcast), but which has recently been made available either on CD or by download.

---

[1]   For a corresponding discography of recordings featuring Messiaen, see Christopher Dingle, 'Messiaen as Pianist: A Romantic in a Modernist World', in Scott McCarrey and Lesley Wright (eds), *Perspectives on the Performance of French Piano Music* (Farnham: Ashgate, forthcoming).

I. Discography Listed by Date of Recording

1. Messiaen: 'Les Sons impalpables du rêve…' (no. 5), 'La Colombe' (no. 1) and 'Le Nombre léger' (no. 3) from *Préludes*
Yvonne Loriod (pno), rec. 20 April 1944, Paris, Studio Albert
> Pathé (NB Not released), Matrix nos: CPTX 582 (nos 1 & 3), CPTX 583 (no. 5)[2]

2. Messiaen: *Trois Petites Liturgies de la Présence Divine*
Yvonne Loriod (pno), Ginette Martenot (ondes), Chorale Yvonne Gouverné, Orchestre de la Société des Concerts du Conservatoire, Roger Désormière (cond.), rec. c. 21 April 1945, Paris, Salle de l'Ancien Conservatoire
> Pathé PDT 190/PDTS194 (78s – 9 sides), Matrix nos: PDT 190 – SOFX 1008-1 (side 1), SOFX 1009-1 (side 2), PDT 191 – SOFX 1006-1 (side 3), SOFX 1007-1 (side 4), PDT 192 – SOFX 1001-1 (side 5), SOFX 1002-1 (side 6), PDT 193 – SOFX 1003-2 (side 7), SOFX 1004-2 (side 8), PDT 194 – SOFX 1005-1 (side 9)
> Dante LYS 310

3. Messiaen: 'Le Baiser de l'Enfant-Jésus' (no. 15) from *Vingt Regards*
Yvonne Loriod (pno); rec. 19 June 1946, Paris
> Pathé (78 rpm) PDT 113, Matrix nos: CPTX 633-1 (side 1), CPTX 634-1 (side 2)
> EMI France 0946 385275 2 7 (2 CDs)

4. Messiaen: 'Regard de l'Esprit de joie' (no. 10) from *Vingt Regards*
Yvonne Loriod (pno), rec. 19 June 1946, Paris, Studio Albert
Pathé PDT 170 (78 rpm) Matrix nos: CPTX 748-1 (side 1), CPTX 749-1 (side 2)
> EMI France 0946 385275 2 7 (2 CDs)

5. Bach: Fugue in C♯ Minor BWV 849; Prelude in C♯ Major BWV 848; Prelude in C♯ Minor BWV 849 [*Well-Tempered Clavier I*]
Yvonne Loriod (pno), rec. 19 June 1946, Paris, Studio Albert
> Pathé (78 rpm) PDT110, Matrix nos: CPTX 631 (side 1), CPTX 632 (side 2)

6. Messiaen: 'Les Sons impalpables du rêve…' (no. 5), 'La Colombe' (no. 1) and 'Le Nombre léger' (no. 3) from *Préludes*
Yvonne Loriod (pno), rec. 12 November 1947, Paris, Studio Albert
> Pathé (78 rpm) PDT 132, Matrix nos: CPTX 635-1 (side 1 – no. 5), CPTX 636-2 (side 2 – nos 1 & 3)
> EMI France 0946 385275 2 7 (2 CDs)

7. Bach-Busoni: 'Chaconne' from Partita for Solo Violin no. 2 in D Minor, BWV1004

---

[2]   The source for this recording is the CHARM online discography, available at www. charm.kcl.ac.uk/discography/disco.html. Assuming this information is correct, Loriod's first recording was not the *Trois Petites Liturgies* in 1945, but this unreleased set. She re-recorded them in 1947.

Yvonne Loriod (pno), rec. 12 December 1946, Paris, Studio Albert

> Pathé PDT 149, PDT 150 (78 rpm 4 sides), Matrix nos: CPTX 673 (PDT149 side 1), CPTX 674 (PDT149 side 2), CPTX 675 (PDT150 side 1), CPTX 676 (PDT150 side 2)

8. Chopin: Barcarolle in F♯ Major, op. 60

Yvonne Loriod (pno), rec. 22 October 1947, Paris, Studio Albert

> Pathé (78 rpm) PDT152, Matrix nos: CPTX 731 (side 1), CPTX 732 (side 2)

9. Messiaen: *Visions de l'Amen*

Yvonne Loriod and Olivier Messiaen (pianos), rec. 1949

> Contrepoint CO 1/2/3/4/5/6 (78 rpm, 6 sides)
>
> Dial 8
>
> FMR FMRCD120-L0403
>
> EMI France 0946 385275 2 7 (2 CDs)

10. *Messiaen: *Turangalîla-Symphonie* [rehearsal excerpt]

Yvonne Loriod (pno), Ginette Martenot (ondes), Boston Symphony Orchestra, Leonard Bernstein (cond.), (live) rec. 28 November 1949, Boston, Symphony Hall, Boston Symphony Centenary Archive Set

> Boston Symphony Orchestra BSO CB 100 (CB112) (12 CDs)

11. *Messiaen: *Turangalîla-Symphonie*

Yvonne Loriod (pno), Ginette Martenot (ondes), Orchestre national de la RTF, Roger Désormière (cond.), (live) rec. 25 July 1950, Aix-en-Provence (European première)

> INA Mémoire Vive IMV078 (6 CDs)

12. *Messiaen: *Turangalîla-Symphonie*

Yvonne Loriod (pno), Ginette Martenot (ondes), Sinfonieorchester des Südwestfunks Baden-Baden, Hans Rosbaud (cond.), (live) rec. 23–24 December 1951 Baden-Baden, Hans Rosbaud-Studio

> Wergo 286 401-2

13. Schumann: *Novelette*, no. 8, op. 21

Yvonne Loriod (pno), rec. 13 April 1950, Paris, Studio Albert

> Pathé (78 rpm) PD117/PD118, Matrix nos: CPT 7624-25 (side 1), CPT 7626-27 (side 2)

14. *Messiaen: *Réveil des oiseaux*

Yvonne Loriod (pno), SWR Sinfonieorchester Baden-Baden und Freiburg, Hans Rosbaud (cond.), (live) rec. 6 October 1953 [NB recorded before the première]

> Col Legno 31911
>
> Hänssler CD 93.078

15. Messiaen: *Trois Petites Liturgies de la Présence Divine*

Yvonne Loriod (pno), J. Loriod (ondes), Ensemble Vocal Marcel Couraud, Orchestre de Chambre André Girard, Marcel Couraud (cond.), rec. 25–26 November, 1954, Paris, Théâtre Apollo

> Ducretet-Thomson 270C075
>
> EMI France 0946 385275 2 7 (2 CDs)

16. Messiaen: *Oiseaux exotiques*; Henze: *Concerto per il Marigny*[3]
Yvonne Loriod (pno), Orchestre du Domaine Musical, Rudolf Albert (cond.),
(live) rec. 10 March 1956 (world première), Paris
    Véga C 30 A 65
    Accord 4769209 (4 CDs); Accord 480 1045 (7 CDs)

17. Messiaen: *Vingt Regards sur l'Enfant-Jésus*
Yvonne Loriod (pno), rec. 13 March 1956, Paris
    Véga C 30 A 60/61/62; Véga 8.500/1/2
    Adès 14112-2
    Accord 480 1045 (7 CDs)

18. Barraqué: Sonate
Yvonne Loriod (pno), Rudolf Albert (cond.), rec. 29 October 1957, Paris
    Véga C30A180; Véga C31A87

19. Stravinsky: *Petrouchka*
Yvonne Loriod (pno), Orchestre des Cento Soli, Rudolf Albert (cond.), rec.
1 November 1957, Paris, Salle Wagram
    Club Français du Disque 114
    Accord 476 8957

20. Albéniz: *Iberia*
Yvonne Loriod (pno), rec. 1957, Paris
    Véga C30A127 (2 LPs)
    Adès 132722: ADE 650; Adès 140712: ADE 680 (Excerpts)

21. Manuel de Falla: *Nuits dans les jardins d'Espagne*
Yvonne Loriod (pno), Orchestre du Théâtre National de l'Opéra, Manuel Rosenthal
(cond.), rec. 2 May 1958, Paris, Salle Apollo
    Véga C30A192
    Adès 132722: ADE 650; Adès 20.250-2

22. Messiaen: *Préludes*
Yvonne Loriod (pno), rec. 18 June 1958, Paris, Studio Magellan
    Boîte à Musique BAM LD 050 (10-inch 33⅓ rpm discs)

23. Messiaen: *Cantéyodjayâ*
Yvonne Loriod (pno), [?live] rec. 1958, Paris
    Véga C30A139; Véga 19 200 (3 LPs)
    Adès AD 13 233-2; Adès 203 142
    Accord 465 791-2; Accord 476 9209 (4 CDs); Accord 480 1045 (7 CDs)

24. Schumann: *8 Novelettes*, op. 21
Yvonne Loriod (pno), rec. ?1958 (DL), ?Paris
    Véga C30S170

25. Messiaen: *Catalogue d'oiseaux*
Yvonne Loriod (pno), rec. 20–26 May 1959, ?Paris
    Véga VAL11 (C30A257, C30A258, C30A259); Véga 19 200 (Excerpts)

---

[3]   Henze withdrew the *Concerto per il Marigny*, but it was later partially reworked as his Requiem.

Adès 14057/ADE 380 (Excerpts)

Accord 480 1045 (7 CDs)

26. Schoenberg: Suite, op. 29

Yvonne Loriod (pno), Marcel Naulais (E♭ cl), Guy Deplus (cl), Louis Montaigne (bcl), Jacques Ghestem (vn), Serge Collot (va), Jean Huchot (vc), Pierre Boulez (cond.), rec. 1959, Paris

Véga C30A271

Accord 476 8862 (4 CDs)

27. Mozart: 4 Fantaisies; Sonata in A, K. 331; Rondo in D, K. 485

Yvonne Loriod (pno), rec. 1959, ?Paris

Adès 132042: ADE 650 (record); Adès 141812 (coffret): ADE 694 (K. 331, K. 397, K. 485 – 5 CDs); Adès 13-204-2

28. Berg: Sonata; Webern: Variations, op. 27; Boulez: Sonate no. 2

Yvonne Loriod (pno), rec. 18 May 1961, ?Paris

Véga C30A 309

Accord 476 8862 (Berg/Webern – 4 CDs); Accord 476 9209 (Boulez – 4 CDs)

29. Messiaen: *Turangalîla-Symphonie*

Yvonne Loriod (pno), Jeanne Loriod (ondes), Orchestre National de la RTF, Maurice Le Roux (cond.), rec. 11 & 13 October 1961, Paris

Véga VAL127 (C30X339/C30X340), Véga 28001

Adès-Radio France 204792

Accord 465 802-2; Accord 480 1045 (7 CDs)

30. *Boulez: *Structures II*

Pierre Boulez and Yvonne Loriod (pianos), rec. 21 October 1961 (world première), Donaueschingen

Col Legno WWE20509

31. Messiaen: *Visions de l'Amen*

Yvonne Loriod and Olivier Messiaen (pianos), rec. 1962, Paris

Véga 8.509; Véga 19 200 (3 LPs)

Adès AD 13 233-2; Adès 203 142

Accord 465 791-2; Accord 480 1045 (7 CDs)

32. Mozart: Concerto no. 1 in F Major for piano and orchestra, K. 37; Concerto no. 2 in B♭ Major for piano and orchestra, K. 39, Concerto no. 3 in D Major for piano and orchestra, K. 40; Concerto no. 4 in G Major for piano and orchestra, K. 41

Yvonne Loriod (pno), Orchestre du Domaine Musical, Pierre Boulez (cond.), rec. 1962, ?Paris

Véga C30A353/354 (2 LPs)

33. *Messiaen: *Turangalîla-Symphonie*

Yvonne Loriod (pno), Reiko Honshô (ondes), NHK Symphony Orchestra, Seiji Ozawa (cond.), (live) rec. 24 July 1962, NHK Symphony Orchestra Studio, Tokyo. Included in set 'The NHK Symphony Orchestra: Live Recordings since 1926'

King Records, NHK K20Z–1–26 (26 LPs)

34. Chopin: Études op. 10, nos 3, 5 and 12, op. 25 nos 1, 2, 3, 5, 6, 8, 9 and 11,
    op. post. no. 3; Liszt: Sonata in B Minor
Yvonne Loriod (pno), rec. ?1963 (DL), ?Paris
    Véga 30 MT 10176; 30 MT 10259

35. *Messiaen: *Oiseaux exotiques*
Yvonne Loriod (pno), Symphonieorchester des Bayerischen Rundfunks, Pierre
Boulez (cond.), (live) rec. 17 April 1964, München, Herkulessaal der Residenz
    Col Legno WWE 2 CD 20084-2 (2 CDs)

36. Messiaen: *Sept Haïkaï*
Yvonne Loriod (pno), Les Percussions de Strasbourg, Orchestre du Domaine
Musical, Pierre Boulez (cond.), rec. 1964, ?Paris
    Adès MA30LA1006; Adès 14022: ADE 380; Adès 140732: ADE 680;
    Adès 202902
    Accord 476 9209 (4 CDs); Accord 480 1045 (7 CDs)

37. Messiaen: *Trois Petites Liturgies de la Présence Divine*
Yvonne Loriod (pno), J. Loriod (ondes), Maîtrise et orchestre de chambre de la
RTF, Marcel Couraud (cond.), rec. February 1964,[4] Église Notre-Dame du Liban
    Erato STU 70.200; Erato ECD 71580 (17 CDs)
    Warner 2292-45505-2/VII; Warner 4509-92007-2; Warner 2564 62162-2
    (18 CDs)

38. Messiaen: *Couleurs de la Cité céleste*
Yvonne Loriod (pno), Groupe Instrumentale à Percussion de Strasbourg,
Orchestre du Domaine Musicale, Pierre Boulez (cond.), rec. January 1966,
Paris, Église Notre-Dame du Liban
    Erato SBRG 72471; Erato STU 70302; Erato ECD 71580 (17 CDs)
    Warner 2292-45505-2/III; Warner 4509-91706-2; Warner 2564 62162-2
    (18 CDs)

39. *Messiaen: *Sept Haïkaï*
Yvonne Loriod (pno), Orchestre National de l'ORTF – Seiji Ozawa, (live) rec.
20 October 1966, radio broadcast, ?Paris
    INA download available at www.ina.fr

40. Messiaen: *Oiseaux exotiques*; *Réveil des oiseaux*; 'La Bouscarle' (*Catalogue
    d'oiseaux*)
Yvonne Loriod (pno), Czech Philharmonique Orchestra, Vaclav Neumann (cond.),
1966
    Supraphon SUA ST 50749
    Crest 1000 COCO-73019

41. *Messiaen: *Turangalîla-Symphonie*
Yvonne Loriod (pno), Jeanne Loriod (ondes), Netherlands Radio Philharmonic,
Jean Fournet (cond.), (live) rec. 24 April 1967, Concertgebouw, Amsterdam
    Q Disc 97019 (8 CDs)

---

[4]   The CHARM catalogue gives 19 January. February is given on several Erato releases.

42. Messiaen: *Turangalîla-Symphonie*
Yvonne Loriod (pno), Jeanne Loriod (ondes), Toronto Symphony, Seiji Ozawa (cond.), rec. 1967
>RCA-Victor 645094, 645095; RCA Red Seal ARL21143; 74321 846 012 (2 CDs)
>Sony 88697 486802 (4 CDs)

43. Charles Chaynes: Concerto pour Piano et Orchestre de Chambre
Yvonne Loriod (pno), Orchestre de Chambre de l'ORTF, Serge Baudo (cond.), rec. ?1968 (not before 1966)
>Erato STU70451 (LP)

44. Debussy: Douze Études
Yvonne Loriod (pno), rec. 9 January 1968, Paris, Église Notre-Dame du Liban
>Erato STU 70432

45. Messiaen: *Préludes*; *Quatre Études de rythme*
Yvonne Loriod (pno), rec. 12 January 1968, Paris, Église Notre-Dame du Liban
>Erato STU 70433; Erato OME 1; Erato STU 70875; Erato ECD 71580 (17 CDs)
>Warner 2292-45505-2/V, Warner 2564 62162-2 (18 CDs)

46. *Bach: Concerto in D Minor, BWV1052; Messiaen: *Réveil des oiseaux*
Yvonne Loriod (pno), Orchestre National de l'ORTF, Marius Constant (cond.), (live) rec. 16 April 1969, radio broadcast
>INA download available at www.ina.fr

47. *Messiaen: *Trois Petites Liturgies de la Présence Divine*
Yvonne Loriod (pno), Jeanne Loriod (ondes), la Maîtrise et l'Orchestre de Chambre de l'ORTF, Jacques Jouineau (cond.), (live) rec. 23 August 1968, Paris, Grand Auditorium de la Maison de l'ORTF, radio broadcast
>INA download available at www.ina.fr

48. *Florilège du Piano: Mozart to Messiaen*
Mozart: Fantaisie in D Minor, KV 397; Mendelssohn: Song Without Words in E Major; Beethoven: Sonata in B♭ Major, op. 106; Albéniz: 'El Polo' and 'Lavapies' (*Ibéria*); Chopin: Étude in A Minor, op. 25, no. 11; Debussy: Étude 'pour les huit doigts'; Messiaen: 'Le Loriot' from *Catalogue d'oiseaux* and 'Par Lui tout a été fait' from *Vingt Regards sur l'Enfant-Jésus*
Yvonne Loriod (pno), rec. ?1970[5]
>Erato STU70555/6 (2 LPs)

49. Messiaen: *Catalogue d'oiseaux*
Yvonne Loriod (pno), 1 March 1970, Paris, Église Notre-Dame du Liban
>Erato STU 70595-8; Erato OS 2561; Erato OME 1; Erato ECD 71580 (17 CDs)
>Warner 2292-45505-2/VI (3 CDs); Warner 2564 62162-2 (18 CDs)

---

[5]   It is unclear whether the Debussy is extracted from Loriod's complete recording of the Études (item 44).

50. Messiaen: *La Transfiguration de Notre-Seigneur Jésus-Christ*
Yvonne Loriod (pno), Janos Starker (vc), Wallace Mann (fl), Loren Kitt (cl), Frank A. Ames (mar), John A. C. Cane (xyba), Ronald Barnett (vib), Westminster Symphonic Choir, National Symphony Orchestra, Antal Dorati (cond.), rec. 28 April 1972, Washington DC, Constitution Hall
    Decca HEAD 1-2; 425161-2 DM2 (2 CDs), Decca 478 0352 (6 CDs)

51. Messiaen: *La Fauvette des jardins*; *Sept Haïkaï*
Yvonne Loriod (pno), Ensemble Ars Nova, Marius Constant (cond.), Yvonne Loriod, rec. 8 February 1973, Paris, Église Notre-Dame du Liban
    Erato STU 70796; Erato OME 1 [*La Fauvette* only]; Erato ECD 71580 (17 CDs)
    Warner 2292-45505-2/VI [*La Fauvette* only] (3 CDs); Warner 2292-45505-2/II [*Sept Haïkaï*] Warner 2564 62162-2 (18 CDs)

52. Messiaen: *Des Canyons aux étoiles...*
Yvonne Loriod (pno), Ensemble Ars Nova, Marius Constant (cond.), rec. July 1975, Paris, Église Notre-Dame du Liban
    Erato STU 70974/5; Erato ECD 71580 (17 CDs)
    Warner 2292-45505-2/II; Warner 256460427-2 (2 CDs); Warner 2564 62162-2 (18 CDs)

53. Messiaen: *Vingt Regards sur l'Enfant-Jésus*
Yvonne Loriod (pno), rec. October 1973, Paris, Église Notre-Dame du Liban
    Erato OME 1; Erato ECD 71580 (17 CDs)
    Warner 2292-45505-2/I (2 CDs), Warner 2564 62162-2 (18 CDs); Warner 2564 69986-5 (2 CDs)

54. Messiaen: *La Dame de Shalott*; *Fantaisie burlesque*; *Pièce* (*pour le Tombeau de Paul Dukas*); *Rondeau*; *Cantéyodjayâ*
Yvonne Loriod (pno), rec. ?1975 (DL), ?Paris, released as part of set of complete piano works 'Olivier Messiaen: Intégrale L'Œuvre Pour Piano' with earlier Erato recordings (entries 44, 49, 51 and 53)
    Erato OME 1 (8 LPs)
    Music Heritage Society MHS 4423 [Just these five works]

55. *Messiaen: *Trois Petites Liturgies de la Présence Divine*
Yvonne Loriod (pno), Jeanne Loriod (ondes), Women of the Tanglewood Festival Chorus, Boston Symphony Orchestra, Seiji Ozawa (cond.), broadcast 7 October 1978, Boston, Symphony Hall, Boston Symphony Centenary Archive Set
    Boston Symphony Orchestra BSO CB 100 (CB 108) (12 CDs)

56. Messiaen: *Trois Petites Liturgies de la Présence Divine*
Yvonne Loriod (pno), Jeanne Loriod (ondes), Ensemble Vocal A Coeur Joie, Ensemble Instrumental de Grenoble, Stéphane Cardon (cond.), rec. April 1983, Grenoble, Salle Olivier Messiaen
    Forlane UM6507; Forlane UCD 16504/05 (2 CDs)

57. Messiaen: *Turangalîla-Symphonie*
Yvonne Loriod (pno), Jeanne Loriod (ondes), Orchestre Symphonique de Radio-Tele-Luxembourg, Louis de Froment (cond.), rec. ?1983, Luxembourg, Grand Auditorium RTL Villa Louvigny
 Forlane UCD 16504/05 (2 CDs)
58. Messiaen: *Oiseaux exotiques*
Yvonne Loriod (pno), Symphonieorchester des Bayerischen Rundfunks, Karl Anton Rickenbacher (cond.), rec. 24 January 1985, München, Herkulessaal
 Koch Schwann 3-1123-2 H1
59. Messiaen: *Vingt Regards sur l'Enfant-Jésus*
Yvonne Loriod (pno), (live) rec. 27 October, 1985, Radio Bremen
 Schwann AMS 5201 (2 records)
60. Messiaen: *Petites Esquisses d'oiseaux*
Yvonne Loriod (pno), rec. October 1987, Paris, Église Notre-Dame du Liban
 Erato OME 1; Erato STU 70.433; Erato ECD 71580 (17 CDs)
 Warner 2292-45505-2/V; Warner 2564 62162-2 (18 CDs)
61. Messiaen: *Trois Petites Liturgies de la Présence Divine*
Yvonne Loriod (pno), Jeanne Loriod (ondes), Pavel Kühn Female Chorus, Bambini di Praga, Prague Symphony Orchestra, Bohumil Kulínský (cond.), rec. 5–6 December 1987, Prague, Dvořák Hall of the House of Artists
 Supraphon 11 0404-2 231
62. Messiaen: *Couleurs de la Cité céleste*; *Sept Haïkaï*; *Un Vitrail et des oiseaux* (world première); *Oiseaux exotiques*
Yvonne Loriod (pno), Ensemble Intercontemporain, Pierre Boulez (cond.), (live) rec. 26 November 1988, Paris, Théâtre des Champs-Élysées, from composer's 80th birthday concert
 Disques Montaignes XXIIII
 naïve 782131; naïve MO 782170 (6 CDs)
63. Messiaen: *Harawi*
Rachel Yakar (sop), Yvonne Loriod (pno), rec. February 1988, Studio 107, Paris, Radio France
 Erato ECD 71580 (17 CDs)
 Warner 2292-45505-2/IX; Warner 2564 62162-2 (18 CDs)
64. Messiaen: *Poèmes pour Mi*; *Chants de terre et de ciel*
Maria Oràn (sop), Yvonne Loriod (pno), rec. May 1988, Studio 107, Paris, Radio France
 Erato ECD 71580 (17 CDs)
 Warner 2292-45505-2/X; Warner 2564 62162-2 (18 CDs)
65. Messiaen: *Quatuor pour la fin du Temps*; *Thème et variations*
Christoph Poppen (vln), Manuel Fischer-Dieskau (vc), Wolfgang Meyer (cl), Yvonne Loriod (pno), rec. 19–21 November 1990, Paris, Église Notre-Dame du Liban
 EMI CDC 7 54395 2; EMI 50999 2 17466 2 8 (14 CDs); EMI 50999 2 06867 2 7 (2 CDs)

66. Messiaen: *Turangalîla-Symphonie*
Yvonne Loriod (pno), Jeanne Loriod (ondes), Orchestre de la Bastille, Myung
Whun Chung (cond.), rec. October 1990, Paris, Opéra de Paris-Bastille
> DG 431 781-2; DG 480 1333 (32 CDs)

67. Messiaen: *La Transfiguration de Notre-Seigneur Jésus-Christ*
Yvonne Loriod (pno), Arturo Muruzabal (vc), Martine van der Loo (fl), Harmen de
Boer (cl), Peter Prommel (mar), Ruud Stotÿn (vib), Henk de Vlieger (xyba), Koor
van de BRT Bruxelles, Groot Omroepkoor & Radio Symfonie Orkest Hilversum,
Reinbert de Leeuw (cond.), rec. 29 June 1991, Amsterdam, Concertgebouw
> Auvidi Montaigne MO 782040
>
> naïve MO 782179 (2 CDs); naïve MO 782179 (6 CDs)

68. Messiaen: *Un Vitrail et des oiseaux*; *La Ville d'En-Haut*
Yvonne Loriod (pno), Rundfunk-Sinfonieorchester Berlin, Karl Anton
Rickenbacher (cond.), rec. 21–23 January 1993, Berlin, Saal 1, Funkhaus
> Koch Schwann 3-1123-2 H1

69. Messiaen: *Concert à quatre*
Catherine Cantin (fl), Heinz Holliger (ob), Yvonne Loriod (pno), Mstislav
Rostropovich (vc), Orchestre de l'Opéra Bastille, Myung-Whun Chung
(cond.), rec. September 1994, Paris, Opéra Bastille, Salle Gounod
> DG 445 947-2; DG 480 1333 (32 CDs)

70. Messiaen: *Trois Petites Liturgies de la Présence Divine*; *Réveil des oiseaux*
Yvonne Loriod (pno), Jeanne Loriod (ondes), Maîtrise de Radio France,
Orchestre National de France, Kent Nagano (cond.), rec. 20–21 December
1994, Paris, Radio France, Studio 103
> Erato 0630-12702-2
>
> Warner 2564 62162-2 (18 CDs) [*Réveil des oiseaux* only]

71. *Messiaen: *Chant des déportés*
Yvonne Loriod-Messiaen (pno), BBC Symphony Orchestra and Chorus, Andrew
Davis (cond.), (live) rec. 22 March 1995, London, Royal Festival Hall
> JADE 7432167411-2; DG 480 1333 (32 CDs)

72. Messiaen: *La Transfiguration de Notre-Seigneur Jésus-Christ*
Yvonne Loriod (pno), Silke Uhlig (fl), Oliver Link (cl), Michael Sanderling
(vc), Peter Sadlo (xyba), Edgar Guggeis (mar), Tobias Schweda (vib), NDR-
Chor, Rundfunkchor Berlin, Rundfunk-Sinfonieorchester Berlin, Karl Anton
Rickenbacher (cond.), rec. April 1996, Konzerthaus Berlin
> Koch Schwann CD 3-1216-2 (2 CDs)

73. Messiaen: *Pièce* (*pour le Tombeau de Paul Dukas*); *La Mort du Nombre*;
    Prélude (1964); *Le Merle noir*; *Chant dans le style Mozart*; *Pièce* (pour
    piano et quatuor à cordes); *Feuillets inédits*
Yvonne Loriod-Messiaen (pno), Jeanne Loriod (ondes), Christian Lardé (fl),
Guy Deplus (cl), Françoise Pollet (sop), Hervé Lamy (ten), Agnès Sulem-
Bialobroda (vn), Quatuor Rosamonde, rec. 3–4 January 1999, Paris, Église
Notre-Dame du Liban
> JADE 7432167411-2; DG 480 1333 (32 CDs)

Film

74. **Au coeur de la musique*
Mostly dialogue, but includes performances of Mozart: Fantaisie in D Minor, KV 397; Albéniz: 'Lavapies' (*Ibéria*); Debussy: Études 'pour les huit doigts' and 'pour les Arpèges composés'; Messiaen: 'Le Loriot' from *Catalogue d'oiseaux*
Yvonne Loriod (pno), Olivier Messiaen and Bernard Gavoty, TV broadcast, 25 November 1969.
> INA video download available at www.ina.fr

75. 'Olivier Messiaen: Improvisation & Works'
Compilation of three films from series G. Bessonnet présent Personnages de la Touche for TV broadcast. Includes Messiaen: 'Le Baiser de l'Enfant-Jésus' (no. 15) and 'Regard de l'Esprit de joie' (no. 10) from *Vingt Regards*
Yvonne Loriod (pno), rec. 1983
> Videodisc, Amadeo PHLK-5008[6]

76. *Olivier Messiaen: Man of Faith*
Film made for The South Bank Show, London Weekend Television programme broadcast on Good Friday, 5 April 1985, directed by Alan Benson. Includes excerpts of Yvonne Loriod playing 'Les Sons impalpables du rêve...' (no. 5) from *Préludes*; 'L'Alouette Calandrelle' from *Catalogue d'oiseaux*; 'Amen du Désir' (no. 4) from *Visions de l'Amen* (with Roger Muraro)
> Films for the Humanities and Sciences VHS video tape, FFH10323

77. Olivier Mille (dir.), *Les Leçons d'Olivier Messiaen: le cheminement, la virtuosité, humour de sa pensée musicale*
Includes Loriod playing 'Le Rouge-gorge', no. 3 from *Petites Esquisses d'oiseaux* (from the manuscript); excerpts from a performance of *Trois Petites Liturgies* and rehearsing *Chants de terre et de ciel* with Maria Oràn, recorded July 1987
> Artline Films Video 577822 – EDV 21

78. *François Manceaux (dir.), *Yvonne Loriod: Pianist & Teacher – A Film by François Manceaux*, TV programme filmed 1990–91.
Contains master classes, interview clips with Loriod and Messiaen, discussion between Loriod and Roger Muraro, and performances of Messiaen, 'Résurrection' (no. 6) from *Chants de terre et de ciel*; 'Noël' (no. 13) from *Vingt Regards*
Agnès Robert (sop), Yvonne Loriod (pno), with Nicholas Angelich, Kei Saotome, Yoko Kaneko and Masaaki Yasuda (pno)
> Harmonia Mundi DVD HMD 9909032

79. Olivier Mille (dir.), *Olivier Messiaen: La Liturgie de Cristal*
Includes clips of Messiaen describing birdsongs, with illustrations by Loriod, an interview with Loriod and excerpts of her in performances of *Oiseaux exotiques*; *Trois Petites Liturgies*
> Idéale Audience International DVD DVD9DS44

---

[6]   Also released unofficially on Encore DVD 2489.

80. 'Yvonne Loriod-Messiaen'

Interview (video) with Bruno Serrou (6 hours 24 minutes) [NB dialogue only, no performance] in the INA Musique Mémoires series, rec. 12–13 September 2002, Paris, INA

> INA video stream available at www.ina.fr/grands-entretiens/video/ Musique/Loriod

II. List of Works Recorded

Composer/Work	Ref. no. in Section I
Albéniz	
Iberia	
Complete:	20
Excerpts:	
'El Polo'	48
'Lavapies'	48, 74
Bach, J. S.	
Prelude in C♯ Major, BWV 848 [Well-Tempered Clavier I]	5
Prelude and Fugue in C♯ Minor, BWV 849 [Well-Tempered Clavier I]	5
Concerto in D Minor, BWV 1052	46
Bach-Busoni	
'Chaconne' from Partita for Solo Violin no. 2 in D Minor, BWV 1004	7
Barraqué	
Sonate	18
Beethoven	
Sonata in B♭ Major, op. 106	48
Berg	
Piano Sonata	28
Boulez	
Piano Sonata no. 2	28
Structures II	30
Chaynes	
Concerto pour Piano et Orchestre de Chambre	43
Chopin	
Barcarolle in F♯ Major, op. 60	8
Études op. 10, nos 3, 5 and 12	34
Études op. 25, nos 1, 2, 3, 5, 6, 8 and 9	34
Étude op. 25, no. 11	34, 48
Étude op. post., no. 3	34
Debussy	
Douze Études	
Complete:	44
Excerpts:	

Composer/Work	Ref. no. in Section I
'pour les huit doigts'	44, 78
'pour les Arpèges composés'	74
Falla	
Nuits dans les jardins d'Espagnes	21
Henze	
Concerto per il Marigny	16
Liszt	
Sonata in B Minor	34
Messiaen	
Cantéyodjayâ	23, 54
Catalogue d'oiseaux	
Complete:	25, 49
Excerpts:	
no. 2 'Le Loriot'	48, 74
no. 8 'L'Alouette calandrelle'	76
no. 9 'La Bouscarle'	40
Chant dans le style Mozart	73
Chant des déportés	71
Chants de terre et de ciel	
Complete:	64
Excerpt:	
no. 6 'Resurrection'	78
Rehearsal:	77
Concert à quatre	69
Couleurs de la Cité céleste	38, 62
La Dame de Shalott	54
Des Canyons aux étoiles...	52
Quatre Études de rythme	45
Fantaisie burlesque	54
La Fauvette des jardins	51
Harawi	63
Le Merle noir	73
La Mort du Nombre	73
Oiseaux exotiques	16, 35, 40, 58, 62
Excerpts:	79
Petites Esquisses d'oiseaux	
Complete:	60
Excerpt:	
no. 3, 'Le Rouge-gorge'	77
Pièce (pour piano et quatuor à cordes)	73

Composer/Work	Ref. no. in Section I
Pièce (*pour la Tombeau de Paul Dukas*)	54, 73
Poèmes pour Mi	64
Prélude (pno), 1964	73
Préludes	
Complete:	22, 45
Excerpts:	
no. 1 'La Colombe'	1, 6
no. 3 'Le Nombre léger'	1, 6
no. 5 'Les Sons impalpables du rêve…'	1, 6, 76
Quatuor pour la fin du Temps	65
Réveil des oiseaux	14, 40, 46, 70
Rondeau	54
Sept Haïkaï	36, 39, 51, 62
Thème et variations	65
La Transfiguration de Notre-Seigneur Jésus-Christ	50, 67, 72
Trois Petites Liturgies de la Présence Divine	
Complete:	2, 15, 37, 47, 55, 56, 61, 70
Excerpts:	77, 79
Turangalîla-Symphonie	
Complete:	11, 12, 29, 33, 41, 42, 57, 66
Rehearsal:	10
La Ville d'En-Haut	68
Vingt Regards sur l'Enfant-Jésus	
Complete:	17, 53, 59
Excerpts:	
no. 6 'Par Lui tout a été fait'	48
no. 10 'Regard de l'Esprit de joie'	4, 75
no. 13 'Noël'	78
no. 15 'Le Baiser de l'Enfant-Jésus'	3, 75
Visions de l'Amen	
Complete:	9, 31
Excerpt:	
no. 4 'Amen du Désir'	
Un Vitrail et des oiseaux	62, 68
Messiaen (arr. Loriod)	
Feuillets inédits	73
Mendelssohn	
Song Without Words in E Major, op. 19, no. 1	48
Mozart	
Concerto no. 1 in F Major for Piano and Orchestra, K. 37	32

Composer/Work	Ref. no. in Section I
Concerto no. 2 in B♭ Major for Piano and Orchestra, K. 39	32
Concerto no. 3 in D Major for Piano and Orchestra, K. 40	32
Concerto no. 4 in G Major for Piano and Orchestra, K. 41	32
Fantasia in C Major, K. 394	27
Fantasia in C Minor, K. 396	27
Fantasia in D Minor, K. 397	27, 48, 74
Fantasia in C Minor, K. 475	27
Rondo in D, K. 485	27
Sonata in A, K. 331	27

Schoenberg
  Suite, op. 29   26

Schumann
  8 Novelettes
    Complete: 24
    Excerpt:
      no. 8, op. 21   13

Stravinsky
  Petrouchka   19

Webern
  Variations, op. 27   28

Select Bibliography

Alten, Michèle, *Musiciens français dans la guerre froide* (Paris: l'Harmattan, 2000).

—, 'Le Conservatoire de musique et d'art dramatique: Une institution culturelle publique dans la guerre, 1940–1942', *L'education musicale*, available at www.leducation-musicale.com/conservatoire.pdf.

Anderson, Julian, 'Messiaen and the Notion of Influence', *Tempo*, 63/247 (January 2009): 2–18.

Bail, Karine Le, *Musique, pouvoir, responsabilité: La politique musicale de la radiodiffusion française, 1939–1953*, PhD diss. (Paris: Institut d'études politiques de Paris, 2005).

Balmer, Yves, *Comment compose Messiaen? Analyse génétique des brouillons de* Visions de l'Amen, research thesis under the direction of Michaël Lévinas (CNSMDP, 2008).

—, *Edifier son œuvre: Génèse, médiation, diffusion de l'œuvre d'Olivier Messiaen*, PhD thesis (Université Charles-de-Gaulle Lille 3, 2008).

—, 'Religious Literature in Messiaen's Personal Library', in Andrew Shenton (ed.), *Messiaen the Theologian* (Farnham: Ashgate, 2010).

Balmer, Yves and Murray, Christopher Brent, 'La classe de Messiaen: Retour aux sources', in E. Ducreux and A. Poirier (eds), *Une musique française après 1945?* (Lyon: Symétrie, forthcoming).

—, 'Olivier Messiaen en 1941: À la recherche d'une année perdue' in M. Chimènes and Y. Simon (eds), *La musique à Paris sous l'Occupation* (Paris: Fayard/Cité de la musique, forthcoming).

Barbier, Pierre and Schaeffer, Pierre, *Portique pour une fille de France* (Paris: Chiron, 1941).

Barraqué, Jean, *Écrits*, ed. Laurent Feneyrou (Paris: Sorbonne, 2001).

Benitez, Vincent P., 'Simultaneous Contrast and Additive Designs in Olivier Messiaen's Opera *Saint François d'Assise*', *Music Theory Online*, 8/2 (August 2002).

—, *Olivier Messiaen: A Research and Information Guide* (New York and London: Routledge, 2008).

Bergès, Michel, *Vichy contre Mounier* (Paris: Economica, 1997).

Berlière, Jean-Marc, 'L'autre Maurice Toesca', letter, *Le Monde* (13 February 1998).

Bertrand, Paul, 'Le Concours de Rome', *Le Ménestrel* (10 July 1931): 303.

Boivin, Jean, *La classe de Messiaen* (Paris: Bourgois, 1995).

—, 'Musical Analysis According to Messiaen: A Critical View of a Most Original Approach', in Christopher Dingle and Nigel Simeone (eds), *Olivier Messiaen: Music, Art and Literature* (Aldershot: Ashgate, 2007).

Boulez, Pierre, *Stocktakings from an Apprenticeship*, trans. Stephen Walsh (Oxford: Clarendon, 1991).

Bozza, Eugène, 'This History of the "Prix de Rome"', *Hinrichsen's Musical Yearbook*, 7 (1952): 487–94.

Bradbury, Ernest, 'The York Festival 1957', *Musical Times* 98/1375 (August 1957): 445.

Brady, I. C., 'St. Bonaventure', in *New Catholic Encyclopaedia*, Vol. 2 (New York: McGraw Hill, 1967): 661.

Brasillach, Robert, *Le Procès de Jeanne d'Arc*, nouvelle version présentée et ordonnée par Robert Brasillach, (Paris: Alexis Bredier, 1932).

Broad, Stephen, 'Messiaen and Cocteau', in Christopher Dingle and Nigel Simeone (eds), *Olivier Messiaen: Music, Art and Literature* (Aldershot: Ashgate, 2007).

—, *Olivier Messiaen: Journalism 1935–39* (Farnham: Ashgate, 2012).

Bruhn, Siglind (ed.), *Messiaen's Language of Mystical Love* (New York: Garland Publishing Inc., 1998).

—, *Messiaen's Contemplations of Covenant and Incarnation: Musical Symbols of Faith in the Two Great Piano Cycles of the 1940s* (Hillsdale, NY: Pendragon Press, 2007).

—, *Messiaen's Explorations of Love and Death: Musico-Poetic Signification in the 'Tristan Trilogy' and Three Related Song Cycles* (Hillsdale, NY: Pendragon, 2008).

—, *Messiaen's Interpretations of Holiness and Trinity: Echoes of Medieval Theology in the Oratorio, Organ Meditations, and Opera* (Hillsdale, NY: Pendragon, 2008).

—, 'Traces of a Thomistic *De musica* in the Compositions of Olivier Messiaen', *Logos: A Journal of Catholic Thought and Culture*, 11/4 (2008): 16–56.

Brussel, Robert, 'Le Concours de Rome', *Le Figaro* (6 July 1931): 5.

Campos, Rémy and Poidevin, Aurélien, '"Nous entrerons dans la carrière…": Le prix de Rome, concours d'entrée des compositeurs dans la profession? 1906–1968', in Julia Lu and Alexandre Dratwicki (eds), *Le concours du prix de Rome de musique, 1803–1968* (Lyon: Symétrie, 2011).

Carroll, Mark, *Music and Ideology in Cold War Europe* (Cambridge, Cambridge University Press, 2003).

Catechism of the Catholic Church (Dublin: Veritas, 1994).

Chabrol, Véronique, 'L'ambition de "Jeune France"', in Jean-Pierre Rioux (ed.), *La vie culturelle sous Vichy* (Brussels: Editions Complexe, 1990).

Chancerel, Léon, *Mission de Jeanne d'Arc, célébration par personnages* (Paris: La Hutte, 1938).

CHARM online discography, available at www.charm.kcl.ac.uk/discography/disco.html.

Cheong, Wai Ling, 'Buddhist temple, Shinto shrine and the invisible God of Sept Haïkaï', in Andrew Shenton (ed.), *Messiaen the Theologian* (Farnham: Ashgate, 2010).

Chion, Michel, *Pierre Henry* (Paris: Fayard, 2003).

Clark, Walter Aaron, *Isaac Albéniz: Portrait of a Romantic* (Oxford: Oxford University Press, 1999).

Clarke, T. E., 'Consubstantiality', in *New Catholic Encyclopaedia*, Vol. 4 (New York: McGraw Hill, 1967): 251–2.

Clifford, Richard J., SJ, and Murphy, Roland E., O. Carm, 'Genesis', in Raymond E. Brown et al., *The New Jerome Biblical Commentary* (London: Chapman, 1997).

Cogniat, Raymond, 'En zone non-occupée', in Michel Florisoone, Raymond Cogniat and Yves-Bonnat, *Un an de théâtre, 1940–1941* (Lyon: Les éditions de la France nouvelle, 1942).

Couturier, Père Marie-Alain, *Dieu et l'art dans une vie* (Paris: Cerf, 1965).

Crispin, Judith (ed.), *Olivier Messiaen: The Centenary Papers* (Newcastle upon Tyne: Cambridge Scholars Publishing, 2010).

Cross, Jonathan, *The Stravinsky Legacy* (Cambridge: Cambridge University Press, 1998).

CTS New Daily Missal Standard Edition (London: Catholic Truth Society, 2012).

Delamain, Jacques, *Why Birds Sing*, trans. Ruth and Anna Sarason (London: Victor Gollancz, 1932).

Dingle, Christopher, 'La statue reste sur son piédestal: Messiaen's *La Transfiguration* and Vatican II', *Tempo*, 212 (April 2000): 8–11.

Dingle, Christopher, *The Life of Messiaen* (Cambridge: Cambridge University Press, 2007).

—, 'Forgotten Offerings: Messiaen's First Orchestral works', *Tempo*, 241 (July 2007): 2–21.

—, 'Frescoes and Legends: The Sources and Background of *Saint François d'Assise*', in Dingle and Simeone (eds), *Olivier Messiaen: Music, Art and Literature* (Aldershot: Ashgate, 2007).

—, *Messiaen's Final Works* (Farnham: Ashgate, 2013).

—, 'Messiaen as Pianist: A Romantic in a Modernist World', in Scott McCarrey and Lesley Wright (eds), *Perspectives on the Performance of French Piano Music* (Farnham: Ashgate, forthcoming).

Dingle, Christopher and Simeone, Nigel (eds), *Olivier Messiaen: Music, Art and Literature* (Aldershot: Ashgate, 2007).

Dratwicki, Alexandre, 'Une histoire du prix de Rome de Musique', in Julia Lu and Alexandre Dratwicki (eds), *Le concours du prix de Rome de musique, 1803–1968* (Lyon: Symétrie, 2011).

Eigeldinger, Jean-Jacques, *Chopin Pianist and Teacher*, ed. Roy Howat, trans. Naomi Shohet, Krysia Osostowicz and Roy Howat (Cambridge: Cambridge University Press, 1986).

Eliade, Mircea, *Images et Symboles: Essais sur le symbolism magico-religieux* (Paris: Gallimard, 1952).

Elswijk, H. C. Van, 'Richard of Saint-Victor', *New Catholic Encyclopaedia*, Vol. 23 (New York: McGraw Hill, 1967): 483.

Emmanuel, Maurice, *Essai sur l'orchestrique grecque: Étude de ses mouvements d'après les monuments figurés* (Paris: Hachette, 1895), Eng. trans. 1916.

Fabre, André, 'Portique pour une fille de France', *Lyon-Soir* (7 May 1941): 3.

Fallon, Robert, *Messiaen's Mimesis: The Language and Culture of the Bird Styles*, PhD diss. (University of California, Berkeley, 2005).

—, 'The Record of Realism in Messiaen's Bird Style', in Christopher Dingle and Nigel Simeone (eds), *Olivier Messiaen: Music, Art and Literature* (Aldershot: Ashgate, 2007).

—, 'Two Paths to Paradise: Reform in Messiaen's *Saint François d'Assise*', in Robert Sholl (ed.), *Messiaen Studies* (Cambridge: Cambridge University Press, 2007).

—, 'Birds, Beasts, and Bombs in Messiaen's Cold War Mass', *Journal of Musicology*, 26/2 (Spring 2009): 175–204.

—, 'La spiritualité gothique de Messiaen et le renouveau catholique', in Sylvain Caron and Michel Duchesneau (eds), *Musique, Art et Religion dans l'Entre-deux-guerres* (Lyon: Symétrie, 2009).

—, 'Dante as Guide to Messiaen's Gothic Spirituality', in Andrew Shenton (ed.), *Messiaen the Theologian* (Farnham: Ashgate, 2010).

Faugier, Stéphane, 'Portique pour une fille de France', *Le Journal* (9 May 1941): 2.

Fauser, Annegret, '"Fighting in Frills": Women and the *Prix de Rome* in French Cultural Politics', in Jane A. Bernstein (ed.), *Women's Voices across Musical Worlds* (Boston: Northeastern University Press, 2004).

Fellot, Henry, 'La Partition de MM. Yves Baudrier, Léo Preger et Olivier Messiaen', *Lyon Soir* (14 May 1941): 3.

Ferraton, Yves, *Cinquante ans de vie musicale à Lyon: Les Witkowski et l'Orchestre Philharmonique de Lyon, 1903–1953* (Trevoux: Editions Trevoux, 1984).

Flem, Paul Le, [review of *Hymne au Saint-Sacrement*], *Comœdia* (27 March 1933).

Florand, François, [editorial] No. 6 'Problèmes de musique sacrée', *Les Cahiers de L'Art sacré* (1946).

Ford, Andrew, *Composer to Composer* (London: Quartet Books Ltd., 1993).

Forman, Edward, '"L'harmonie de l'Univers": Maurice Toesca and the Genesis of *Vingt Regards sur l'Enfant-Jésus*', in Christopher Dingle and Nigel Simeone (eds), *Olivier Messiaen: Music, Art and Literature* (Aldershot: Ashgate, 2007).

Forte, Allen, 'Debussy and the Octatonic', *Music Analysis*, 10/1–2 (March–July 1991): 143–144, 153.

Fulcher, Jane, 'The Politics of Transcendence: Ideology in the Music of Messiaen in the 1930s', *The Musical Quarterly*, 86/3 (2002): 449–471.

Gaucher, Pierre, *De la Spirale à la Jeune France, 1935-1945: Les tourments d'une avant-garde musicale*, PhD thesis, Université de Tours, 2001.

—, *La Jeune France, 1936-1945: Une ambition collective* (Lyon: Symétrie, forthcoming).

Gilbert, David, 'Prix de Rome', in Stanley Sadie (ed.), *The New Grove Dictionary of Music and Musicians*, 2nd edition (London: Macmillan, 2001), Vol. 20, 385–7.

Gillies, Malcolm (ed.), *The Bartók Companion* (Faber and Faber: London, 1993).

Gillock, Jon, *Performing Messiaen's Organ Music: 66 Masterclasses* (Bloomington: Indiana University Press, 2009).

Goehr, Alexander, *Finding the Key: Selected Writings*, ed. Derek Puffett (London: Faber and Faber, 1998).

Gourret, Jean and Giraudeau, Jean, *Dictionnaire des chanteurs de l'Opéra de Paris* (Paris: Albatros, 1982).

Gribenski, Jean, 'L'exclusion des juifs du Conservatoire', in Myriam Chimènes (ed.), *La vie musicale sous Vichy* (Brussels: Éditions Complexe, 2001).

Griffiths, Paul, *Olivier Messiaen and the Music of Time* (London: Faber and Faber, 1985).

—, '*Saint François d'Assise*', in Peter Hill (ed.), *The Messiaen Companion* (London: Faber and Faber, 1995).

—, 'Messiaen, Olivier', in Stanley Sadie and John Tyrrell (eds), *The New Grove Dictionary of Music and Musicians*, 2nd edition (London: Macmillan, 2001): Vol. 15, 491–504.

Grosset, Joanny, 'Inde', in Albert Lavignac (ed.), *Encyclopédie de la musique et dictionnaire du Conservatoire*, Première Partie, *Histoire de la musique, Antiquité-Moyen âge* (Paris: Delagrave, 1913), 301–4.

Hamer, Laura, *Musiciennes: Women Musicians in Interwar France*, PhD thesis (Cardiff University, 2009).

Harcourt, Marguérite and Béclart d', Raoul, *La musique des Incas et ses survivances* (Paris: Paul Geuthner, 1925).

Healey, Gareth, 'Messiaen: Bibliophile', in Christopher Dingle and Nigel Simeone (eds), *Olivier Messiaen: Music, Art and Literature* (Aldershot: Ashgate, 2007).

—, *Messiaen's Musical Techniques: The Composer's View and Beyond* (Farnham: Ashgate, 2013).

Healy, Nicholas M., *Thomas Aquinas: Theologian of the Christian Life* (Aldershot: Ashgate, 2003).

Heller, Karin, 'Olivier Messiaen and Cardinal Jean-Marie Lustiger: Two Views of the Liturgical Reform according to the Second Vatican Council', in Andrew Shenton (ed.), *Messiaen the Theologian* (Farnham: Ashgate, 2010).

Hill, Camille Crunelle, 'Saint Thomas Aquinas and the Theme of Truth in Messiaen's *Saint François d'Assise*', in Siglind Bruhn (ed.), *Messiaen's Language of Mystical Love* (New York: Garland, 1998).

Hill, Peter (ed.), *The Messiaen Companion* (London: Faber and Faber, 1995).

—, 'Interview with Yvonne Loriod', in Peter Hill (ed.), *The Messiaen Companion* (London: Faber and Faber, 1995).

—, 'Piano Music I', in Peter Hill (ed.), *The Messiaen Companion* (London: Faber and Faber, 1995).

Hill, Peter and Simeone, Nigel, *Messiaen* (New Haven and London: Yale University Press, 2005). [PHNS]

—, *Olivier Messiaen:* Oiseaux exotiques (Aldershot: Ashgate, 2007).

—, *Messiaen*, French trans. Lucie Kayas (Paris: Fayard, 2008). [PHNS, fr. edn]

Hill, William J., *The Three-Personed God* (Washington, DC: Catholic University of America Press, 1982).

Howat, Roy, *The Art of French Piano Music* (New Haven and London: Yale, 2009).

Hsu, Madeleine, *Olivier Messiaen, the Musical Mediator: A Study of the Influence of Liszt, Debussy, and Bartók* (Madison, NJ: Fairleigh Dickinson University Press, 1996).

Jaquet-Langlais, Marie-Louise, *Jean Langlais: Ombre et lumière* (Paris: Combre, 1995).

Jean de la Croix, Saint, *Poésies* (Paris: Flammarion, 1993).

Johnson, Robert Sherlaw, *Messiaen*, second paperback edition, updated and additional text by Caroline Rae (London: Omnibus Press, 2008; first published 1975). (Note: Pagination is identical to the 1st (1989) paperback edition up to p. 195.)

Kandinsky, Wassily, *Über das Geistige in der Kunst* (Munich, 1911); English edition, *Concerning the Spiritual in Art*, trans. M. T. Sadler (New York, 1977).

Karkoschka, Erhard, *Notation in New Music* (New York: Praeger, 1966).

Kayas, Lucie and Murray, Christopher Brent, '*Portique pour une fille de France*, un mystère du xxᵉ siècle', in Martin Kaltenecker and Karine Le Bail (eds), *Pierre Schaeffer, Constructions impatientes* (Paris: CNRS éditions, 2012).

Kelly, Barbara L. (ed.), *French Music, Culture and National Identity, 1870–1939* (Rochester, NY: University of Rochester Press, 2008).

Kutsch, K. J. and Riemens, Leo, *Großes Sängerlexikon, Vierte, erweitere und aktualisierte Auflage* (Munich: K. G. Saur, 2003).

Lambert, Constant, *Music Ho!* (London: Faber and Faber, 1934).

Landormy, Paul and Loisel, Joseph, 'L'Institut de France et le prix de Rome', in Albert Lavignac and Lionel de La Laurencie (eds), *Encyclopédie de la musique et dictionnaire du Conservatoire*, Part 2 (1920), 3491.

Leaver, Robin A., 'The Mature Vocal Works', in John Butt (ed.), *The Cambridge Companion to Bach* (Cambridge: Cambridge University Press, 1997).

Le Jeune, Claude, *Le Printemps*, 3 vols, ed. Henry Expert, Les Maîtres Musiciens de la Renaissance Française, 12–14 (Paris: Leduc, 1900–01; New York: Broude Bros, 1963).

Lesure, François (ed.), *Debussy on Music*, trans. Richard Langham Smith (London: Secker & Warburg, 1977).

—, 'The Music Department of the Bibliothèque Nationale, Paris', *Notes*, 35/2 (December 1978): 251–68.

Lockspeiser, Edward, *Debussy: His Life and Mind* (London: Casell, 1962).

Löffler, Marie-Raymonde Lejeune, *Les mots et la musique à l'exemple de Darmstadt, 1946–1978* (Paris: L'Harmattan, 2003).

Loriod, Yvonne, 'Étude sur l'œuvre pianistique d'Olivier Messiaen', in Catherine Massip (ed.), *Portrait(s) d'Olivier Messiaen* (Paris: Bibliothèque nationale de France, 1996). (Note: Author given as Yvonne Loriod-Messiaen.)

Lu, Julia, 'Les origines du prix de Rome de musique: Genèse et fonctionnement sous l'Empire', in Julia Lu and Alexandre Dratwicki (eds), *Le concours du prix de Rome de musique, 1803–1968* (Lyon: Symétrie, 2011).

Lu, Julia and Dratwicki, Alexandre (eds), *Le Concours du prix de Rome de Musique (1803–1968)* (Lyon: Symétrie, 2011).

Maas, Sander van, *The Reinvention of Religious Music: Olivier Messiaen's Breakthrough Toward the Beyond* (New York: Fordham University Press, 2009).

Marchal, Béatrice, *Les chants du silence: Olivier Messiaen, fils de Cécile Sauvage ou la musique face à l'impossible parole* (Paris: Editions Delatour, 2008).

Mari, Pierrette, *Olivier Messiaen* (Paris: Editions Seghers, 1965).

—, *Henri Dutilleux* (Paris: Editions Zurfluh, 1988).

Marie, Jean-Etienne, *Musique vivante, introduction au langage musical* (Toulouse: Presses Universitaires de France, 1953).

Maritain, Jacques, *Art and Scholasticism with Other Essays*, trans. J. F. Scanlan (London, 1930).

Marmion, Dom Columba, *Le Christ vie de l'âme* (Namur, Belgium: Abbaye de Maredsous, 1914).

—, *Le Christ dans ses mystères: Conférences spirituelles* (Namur, Belgium: Abbaye de Maredsous and Paris: Desclée de Brouwer, 1919).

—, *Le Christ idéal du moine: Conférences spirituelles sur la vie monastique et religieuse* (Namur , Belgium: Abbaye de Maredsous and Paris: Desclée de Brower, 1922).

—, *Christ in His Mysteries: Spiritual and Liturgical Conferences* (St Louis, MO: Herder, 1931), available at www.cin.org/marmion.html.

Marmontel, Antoine, *Les pianistes célèbres* (Paris: Heugel, 1878) available via Project Gutenberg download at www.gutenberg.org, E-Book no. 37654.

Martin, Marie-Pauline, 'Ouvrir le prix de Rome à la musique ou l'émulation des arts réunis: Enjeux et réalité d'une idée reepublicaine', in Julia Lu and Alexandre Dratwicki (eds), *Le Concours du prix de Rome de Musique, 1803–1968* (Lyon: Symétrie, 2011).

Mason, Colin, 'Messiaen's "Vingt Regards Sur L'enfant Jesus" [sic]: Yvonne Loriod at York Festival', *Manchester Guardian* (1 July 1957): 7.

Massardier-Kenney, Françoise, *Gender in the Fiction of George Sand* (Amsterdam, Rodopi, 1999).

Massin, Brigitte, *Olivier Messiaen: Une poétique du merveilleux* (Aix-en-Provence: Alinea, 1989).

Massip, Catherine (ed.), *Portrait(s) d'Olivier Messiaen* (Paris: Bibliothèque nationale de France, 1996).

McDannell, Colleen, *Material Christianity: Religion and Popular Culture in America* (New Haven and London: Yale University Press, 1995).

Messiaen, Olivier, '*La Nativité du Seigneur*, neuf méditations pour orgue, d'Olivier Messiaen', *Tablettes de la Schola Cantorum* (January–February 1936).

—, 'Charles Tournemire: Précis d'exécution de registration et d'improvisation à l'orgue', *Le Monde musical* (30 June 1936): 186.

—, 'Billet Parisien: Le Mana de Jolivet', *La Sirène* (December 1937): 8–10.

—, 'Derrière ou devant la porte?... (Lettre ouverte à M. Eugène Berteaux)', *La Page musicale* (26 February 1937): 1.

—, 'Musique religieuse', *La page musicale* (19 February 1937): 1.

—, 'Autour d'une Œuvre d'orgue', *L'Art sacré* (April 1939): 123.

—, 'De la Musique sacrée', *Carrefour* (June–July 1939 [double issue]): 75.

—, *Technique de mon langage musical*, 2 Vols (Paris: Alphonse Leduc, 1944; single volume edition published 1999).

—, 'Note de l'auteur', in *Vingt Regards sur l'Enfant-Jésus* (Paris: Durand, 1947).

—, *The Technique of My Musical Language*, 2 Vols, trans. John Satterfield (Paris: Alphonse Leduc, 1956; single volume edition published 2001).

—, 'Expériences musicales: Preface', *La revue musicale*, 244 (1959): 5.

—, 'Des Paroles d'esprit: Entretien avec Olivier Messiaen', in Michel Casenave and Olivier Germain Thomas (eds), *Charles de Gaulle* (Paris: Editions de l'Herne, 1975).

—, 'Grand jeu pour la Trinité', in *La politique de la mystique: Hommage à Mgr Maxime Charles* (editor unacknowledged) (Limoges: Criterion, 1984).

—, *Les 22 Concertos Pour Piano de Mozart* (Paris: Librairie Seguier, 1990).

—, *Traité de rythme, de couleur, et d'ornithologie – Tome I* (Paris: Alphonse Leduc, 1994) [*Traité I*].

—, *Traité de rythme, de couleur, et d'ornithologie – Tome II* (Paris: Alphonse Leduc, 1995) [*Traité II*].

—, *Traité de rythme, de couleur, et d'ornithologie – Tome III* (Paris: Alphonse Leduc, 1996) [*Traité III*].

—, *Traité de rythme, de couleur, et d'ornithologie – Tome IV* (Paris: Alphonse Leduc, 1997) [*Traité IV*].

—, *Traité de rythme, de couleur, et d'ornithologie – Tome V, 1er Volume – Chants d'Oiseaux d'Europe* (Paris: Alphonse Leduc, 1999) [*Traité V:1*].

—, *Traité de rythme, de couleur, et d'ornithologie – Tome V, 2ème Volume – Chants d'Oiseaux Extra-Européens* (Paris: Alphonse Leduc, 2000) [*Traité V:2*].

—, *Traité de rythme, de couleur, et d'ornithologie – Tome VI* (Paris: Alphonse Leduc, 2001) [*Traité VI*].

—, *Traité de rythme, de couleur, et d'ornithologie – Tome VII* (Paris: Alphonse Leduc, 2002) [*Traité VII*].

—, 'The Life and Works of Jean Lurçat (1892–1966)', in Christopher Dingle and Nigel Simeone (eds), *Olivier Messiaen: Music, Art and Literature* (Aldershot: Ashgate, 2007).

Messiaen-Loriod, Yvonne – see Loriod, Yvonne.

Murray, Christopher Brent, *Le développement du langage musical d'Olivier Messiaen: Traditions, emprunts, expériences*, PhD thesis (Université-Lumière Lyon 2, 2010).

—, 'A History of *Timbres-durées*: Understanding Olivier Messiaen's Role in Pierre Schaeffer's Studio', *Revue de musicologie*, 96/1 (2010): 117–29.

—, 'Nouveaux regards sur le soldat Messiaen', in David Mastin and Marine Branland (eds), 'De la guerre dans l'art, de l'art dans la guerre' special issue, *Textuel: Revue de lettres arts et cinéma de l'Université Paris VII*, 63 (2010): 243–55.

Music and Color – see Samuel, Claude, *Olivier Messiaen: Music and Color*.

Nardelli, Zdzisław, *Otchłan ptaków* [Abyss of the Birds] (Katowice: Wydawn, 1989).

Nichols, Roger, *Messiaen*, 2nd edition (Oxford: Oxford University Press, 1986; first published 1975).

—, 'Messiaen: *Éclairs sur l'Au-Delà...*', *Musical Times*, 135/1812 (February 1994): 116–17.

—, *The Harlequin Years: Music in Paris, 1917–1929* (London: Thames and Hudson, 2002).

Nord, Philip, 'L'Expérience de Jeune France', in Karine Le Bail and Martin Kaltenecker (eds), *Pierre Schaeffer, les constructions impatientes* (Paris: CNRS Editions, 2012).

O'Malley, John W., *What Happened at Vatican II* (Cambridge, MA: Belknap-Harvard, 2008).

Périer, Alain, *Messiaen* (Paris: Seuil, 1979).

Perret, Simon-Pierre and Ragot, Marie-Laure, *Paul Dukas* (Paris: Fayard, 2007).

Pétain, Philippe, 'Réforme de l'éducation nationale', *La revue des deux mondes* (15 August 1940).

Petersen, Nils Holger, 'Messiaen's *Saint François d'Assise* and Franciscan Spirituality', in Siglind Bruhn (ed.), *Messiaen's Language of Mystical Love* (New York: Garland, 1998).

PHNS – see Hill, Peter and Simeone, Nigel.

Pople, Anthony, *Messiaen: Quatuor pour la fin du Temps* (Cambridge: Cambridge University Press, 1998).

Potter, Caroline, *Henri Dutilleux; His Life and Works* (Aldershot: Ashgate, 1997).

Pozzi, Raffaele, '"Le rythme chez Mozart": Alcune osservazioni analitiche di Olivier Messiaen sull'accentuazione ritmica in Mozart', in Rudolph Angermüller, Dietrich Berke, Ulrike Hofmann and Wolfgang Rehm (eds), *Bericht über den Internationalen Mozart-Kongreß Salzburg 1991* (Kassel: Bärenreiter, 1992): 613–24.

Pruvot, Samuel, *Monseigneur Charles: Aumônier de la Sorbonne, 1944–1959* (Paris: Éditions du Cerf, 2002).

Rabaud, Henri, *L'Appel de la mer, drame lyrique en un acte sur la pièce* Riders to the Sea *de J. M. Synge*, French text and music by Henri Rabaud (Paris: Max Eschig & Cie, 1923).

Rae, Caroline, *The Music of Maurice Ohana* (Aldershot: Ashgate, 2000).

—, 'The Works of Messiaen's Final Years', in Robert Sherlaw Johnson, *Messiaen*, 2nd paperback edition, updated and additional text by Caroline Rae (London: Omnibus Press, 2008).

Rahner, Karl, *The Trinity*, trans. Joseph Donceel (New York: Crossroad, 2010).

Rémond, René, *Notre siècle* (Paris: Fayard, 1991).

Rischin, Rebecca, *For the End of Time: The Story of the Messiaen Quartet* (Ithaca, NY: Cornell University Press, 2003).

—, *Et Messiaen composa...* trans. Emilie Akoka and Guillaume Marlière (Paris: Ramsay, 2006).

Rilke, Rainer Maria, *Poésie*, nouvelle édition, French trans. Maurice Betz (Paris: Émile Paul: 1941).

—, *The Selected Poetry of Rainer Maria Rilke (1975–1926)*, trans. and ed. Stephen Mitchell (London: Picador, 1987).

Rößler, Almut, *Contributions to the Spiritual World of Olivier Messiaen with original texts by the composer*, trans. Babara Dagg and Nancy Poland (Duisburg: Gilles und Francke, 1986).

Rubin, William S., *Modern Sacred Art and the Church Of Assy* (New York and London, 1961).

Ryder, Andrew, SCJ, *The Spirituality of the Trinity* (Dublin: Carmelite Press, 1982).

Sablonnière, Marguerite, *Le Conservatoire de musique de Paris pendant l'entre-deux-guerres*, PhD thesis (École Nationale des Chartes, 1996).

Sacred Music: A Translation of the Encyclical 'Musicae Sacrae Disciplina' (London: Challoner, 1957).

Samazeuilh, Gustave, 'Le Concours de Rome 1930: Ce qu'il pourrait être, ce qu'il est', *Courrier musical* (15 July 1930): 477.

—, 'Le Prix de Rome', *Le Courrier musical* (15 July 1931): 461.

Samson, Jim, *The Music of Chopin* (London: Routledge & Kegan Paul, 1985).

Samuel, Claude, *Entretiens avec Olivier Messiaen* (Paris: Pierre Belfond, 1967).

—, *Conversations with Olivier Messiaen*, trans. Felix Aprahamian (London: Stainer and Bell, 1976).

—, *Musique et couleur: Nouveaux entretiens avec Claude Samuel* (Paris: Pierre Belfond, 1986).

—, *Olivier Messiaen: Music and Color: Conversations with Claude Samuel*, trans. E. Thomas Glasow (Portland, Oregon: Amadeus, 1994).

—, *Permanences d'Olivier Messiaen* (Arles: Actes Sud, 1999).

Saunders, Francis, *Who Paid the Piper, the CIA and the Cultural Cold War* (London: Granata, 2000).

Sauvage, Cécile, *Œuvres* (Paris: Mercure de France, 1929).

Schaeffer, Pierre, *À la recherche d'une musique concrète* (Paris: Seuil, 1952).

—, 'Vers une musique expérimentale', *La Revue musicale*, no. 236 (1957): 18.

—, *Les antennes de Jéricho* (Paris: Stock, 1978).

Schellhorn, Matthew, '*Les Noces* and *Trois petites Liturgies*: An Assessment of Stravinsky's Influence on Messiaen', in Christopher Dingle and Nigel Simeone (eds), *Olivier Messiaen: Music, Art and Literature* (Aldershot: Ashgate, 2007).

Schloesser, Stephen, 'The Charm of Impossibilities: Mystic Surrealism as Contemplative Voluptuousness', in Andrew Shenton (ed.), *Messiaen the Theologian* (Farnham: Ashgate, 2010).

Shadle, Douglas, 'Messiaen's Relationship to Jacques Maritain's Musical Circle and Neo-Thomism', in Andrew Shenton (ed.), *Messiaen the Theologian* (Farnham: Ashgate, 2010).

Shanley, Brian, OP, *The Treatise on the Divine Nature: Summa Theologiæ I, 1–13* (Indianapolis: Hackett, 2006).

Shenton, Andrew, *Olivier Messiaen's System of Signs* (Aldershot: Ashgate, 2008).

— (ed.), *Messiaen the Theologian* (Farnham: Ashgate, 2010).

Sherlaw Johnson, Robert – see Johnson.

Sholl, Robert, 'Love, Mad Love and the "*point sublime*": The Surrealist Poetics of Messiaen's *Harawi*', in Robert Sholl (ed.), *Messiaen Studies* (Cambridge: Cambridge University Press, 2007).

— (ed.), *Messiaen Studies* (Cambridge: Cambridge University Press, 2007).

Simeone, Nigel, *Olivier Messiaen: Catalogue of Works* (Tutzing: Hans Schneider, 1998).

—, 'Messiaen and the Concerts de la Pléiade: "A kind of clandestine revenge against the Occupation"', *Music and Letters*, 81/4 (November 2000): 551–84.

—, 'Offrandes oubliées 2', in *Musical Times*, 142 (Spring 2001): 21.

—, '"Chez Messiaen, tout est prière": Messiaen's Appointment at the Trinité', *The Musical Times*, 145/1889 (Winter, 2004): 36–53.

—, 'Messiaen in 1942: A Working Musician in Occupied Paris', in Robert Sholl (ed.), *Messiaen Studies* (Cambridge: Cambridge University Press, 2007).

Sitsky, Larry, *Music of the Repressed Russian Avant-garde, 1900–1929* (Westport, CT: Greenwood, 1994).

Smalley, Roger, 'Debussy and Messiaen', *Musical Times* 109/1500 (February 1968): 128–31.

Thérèse de l'Enfant-Jésus, *Manuscrits autobiographiques* (Paris: Seuil, 2006).

Tierney, Neil, *The Unknown Country: A Biography of Igor Stravinsky* (London: Hale, 1977).

Timbrell, Charles, *French Pianism: A Historical Perspective*, 2nd edn (London: Kahn and Averill, 1999).

Toesca, Maurice, 'La Nativité', *La revue hommes et mondes,* no. 39 (January 1949): 119–38.

—, *Cinq ans de patience* (Paris: Emile-Paul, 1975).

—, *Mémoires dactylogaphiées* (Caen: IMEC, Fonds Toesca, n.d.).

Tyrrell, John, *Janáček: Years of a Life, Volume 2, 1914–1928: Tsar of the Forests* (London: Faber and Faber, 2007).

[Ugolino di Monte Santa Maria, Brother], *Les Petites Fleurs de Saint François*, trans. André Pératé, illustrations by Maurice Denis (Paris: Librairie de l'art catholique, 1926).

[Unsigned], 'Pour Jeanne d'Arc à Vienne', *Lyon Soir* (9 May 1941).

[—], *Le Progrès* (12 May 1941).

[—], 'Japanese Baritone's Lieder Recital', *The Times* (28 November 1966): 6.

[—], *Hommage à Olivier Messiaen* (Paris: La Recherche artistique, 1978).

[—], 'Maurice Toesca: Essayiste et romancier', obituary, *Le Monde* (3 February 1998): 11.

Vallas, Léon, *Claude Debussy: His Life and Works*, trans. Maire and Grace O'Brien (New York: Dover Publications, 1973).

Whittall, Arnold, 'Messiaen and Twentieth-century Music', in Robert Sholl (ed.), *Messiaen Studies* (Cambridge: Cambridge University Press, 2007).

Wolff, Christoph, *Johann Sebastian Bach: The Learned Musician* (Oxford, Oxford University Press, 2000).

Wu, Po-Yi (Nelson), 'Messiaen's Dynamic Mozart', in Judith Crispin (ed.) *Olivier Messiaen: The Centenary Papers* (Newcastle upon Tyne: Cambridge Scholars Publishing, 2010).

Xenakis, Iannis, *Alliages* (Paris: Casterman, 1979).

Discography

For recordings featuring Yvonne Loriod, please see the Appendix, which provides a complete discography of her commercial recordings.

Bayle, François (presenter), *Acousmathèque: Musique Concrète, Musique Électroacoustique* radio broadcast on France Musique, 5 February 1985, conserved in the INA archives (www.ina.fr).

Koch, Ludwig, *Songs of British Birds*, rec. December 1952 and January 1953; HMV B 10473-6 (78 rpm discs).

Manceaux, François, *Yvonne Loriod: Pianist & Teacher – A Film by François Manceaux*, TV programme filmed 1990–91, DVD, Harmonia Mundi HMD 9909032.

Messiaen, Olivier, *Quatre Études de rythme* [*Île de feu 1*; *Mode de valeurs et d'intensités*; *Neumes rythmiques*; *Île de feu 2*], Olivier Messiaen (pno), rec. Paris, 30 May 1951, Pathé LFX 998/999 (78rpm) Matrix Nos.: LFX 998 – CLX 2843-21 (side 1) CLX 2844-21 (side 2) LFX 999 – CLX 2845-21 (side 3) CLX 2846-21 (side 4)); FMR FMRCD120-L0403; '*Les rarissimes de Olivier Messiaen*' [sic] EMI France 0946 385275 2 7 (2 discs).

—, *Fête des belles eaux*, Sextuor Jeanne Loriod, rec. Paris, ?1983, Adès 14.035 (vinyl); DG 480 1333 (32 CDs)

—, *Entretien avec Claude Samuel*, rec. rue Marcadet, Paris, October 1988; Erato ECD 75505; Warner 256462162-2 (18 discs).

Messiaen, Olivier and Samuel, Claude, *Musique de Notre Temps: 'Où va la musique?*, Radio broadcast, 25 January 1966.

Mille, Olivier (dir.), *Olivier Messiaen: La Liturgie de Cristal*, DVD, Ideale Audience International DVD9DS44.

Nicholson, E.M. and Koch, Ludwig, *Songs of Wild Birds*, rec. 1936; Parlophone E 7771-4 (78 rpm discs).

Samuel, Claude, *Interview d'Olivier Messiaen*, rec. Paris, October 1961, 10″ disc (VAL 027); Vega 30 BVG 1364; C35X340; Accord 472 031-2 (1964).

Serrou, Bruno (dir.), 'Yvonne Loriod-Messiaen', interview (video), INA Musique Mémoires series, rec. 12–13 September 2002, Paris, INA, INA video stream, available at www.ina.fr/grands-entretiens/video/Musique/Loriod.

Notes on Contributors

Julian Anderson is Senior Professor at the Guildhall School of Music and Drama in London. Born in London in 1967, his teachers have included John Lambert, Alexander Goehr and Tristan Murail. He attended the Centre Acanthes Summer Course around Olivier Messiaen in July 1987, during which he attended Messiaen's musical analysis lectures, the last class teaching Messiaen did. Since his 1990 score *Diptych* won an RPS Prize, he has continued to attract the attention of the musical community as composer and teacher. He has been Composer in Residence to Sinfonia 21, the City of Birmingham Symphony Orchestra, the Cleveland Orchestra, and currently the London Philharmonic Orchestra. Between 2002 and 2010 he directed the Philharmonia's Music of Today series. Before his current post he was Professor of Composition at the Royal College of Music, London (1996–99), then Head of Composition at the same institution (1999–2004) and Harvard University (2004–07).

He has received commissions from such bodies as the BBC Proms, the Nash Ensemble, the Cheltenham Festival, the London Sinfonietta, the Asko Ensemble and the Cleveland Orchestra. His music has been played at international festivals such as the ISCM, Agora (IRCAM), Ultraschall, Aldeburgh Festival and the Helsinki Biennale, which in 2005 mounted a major festival of his output. He wrote the opening work, *Alleluia*, for London's recently refurbished Southbank Centre and his piece *Book of Hours*, for ensemble and electronics, won the 2006 RPS Award for Large Scale Composition. The NMC recording of the same work was in the final list of the 2007 Gramophone Award, which was won by his CD *Alhambra Fantasy* the same year. Anderson's music has also frequently been used for dance. *Poetry Nearing Silence* (1997), originally a commission from the Nash Ensemble, was later choreographed by Mark Baldwin with whom Anderson also collaborated on the prize-winning ballet *The Bird Sings with its Fingers* (2001). In 2009 Anderson and Baldwin collaborated again on a new ballet, *The Comedy of Change*, based on Darwin's *On the Origin of Species*, which toured widely throughout the UK. More recently, in 2012, Mark Baldwin choreographed a new dance work using Anderson's viola solo *Prayer*.

Anderson has been very active in the world of choral music: his *Four American Choruses* (2003) were premiered by the Groot Omroepkoor at the Concertgebouw and *Bell Mass* (2010) was premiered by the Choir of Westminster Abbey, London, to great acclaim: 'People should soon be singing this piece up and down this land and many others' wrote Martin Anderson in *Tempo* magazine (October 2010). In 2011 *Bell Mass* won a BASCA award in the liturgical category, and the same year Anderson's orchestral odyssey *Fantasias*, written for the Cleveland Orchestra, won the BASCA award for orchestral music. Anderson's largest work to date, the oratorio

Heaven is Shy of Earth won the BASCA Large Scale Choral Work award in 2007. His most recent work, *The Discovery of Heaven*, a co-commission by the New York Philharmonic and the London Philharmonic Orchestra, attracted significant critical attention and has just been recorded on CD with *Fantasias*. Anderson's current project is an opera on the Oedipus trilogy for English National Opera. He also starts a post as Composer in Residence with the Wigmore Hall, London, in October 2013.

Yves Balmer is both a musician and a musicologist. He is a *maître de conférences* (associate professeur) and chair of the Arts Department at the École Normale Supérieure in Lyon and professor of musical analysis at the Paris Conservatoire. His doctoral dissertation on Olivier Messiaen (*Edifier son œuvre: Genèse, médiation, diffusion de l'œuvre d'Olivier Messiaen*) was based on a number of new sources including the Loriod-Messiaen archives at the Bibliothèque nationale de France where he was an associated researcher from 2004 to 2006. Balmer was recently appointed as Editor-in-chief of the *Revue de musicologie*.

Stephen Broad is Head of Research at the Royal Conservatoire of Scotland. He undertook interdisciplinary studies at the Universities of Glasgow (MA, Music and Physics) and Oxford (DPhil, Historical Musicology). His research interests include: Olivier Messiaen, especially his early career and writings; music and ideas in 1930s Paris; mythologies in biography and autobiography; problems in twentieth-century history. In addition, Broad pursues research interests across music education policy and the philosophy of practice-based research. Broad's publications include an edition of Messiaen's little-known journalism, *Olivier Messiaen: Journalism 1935–1939* (Ashgate, 2012), a chapter on Messiaen and Cocteau in Dingle and Simeone (eds), *Olivier Messiaen: Music, Art and Literature* (Ashgate, 2007), and articles in a range of journals and yearbooks. He was also the co-author of *What's Going On?* (Scottish Arts Council, 2003), an examination of young people's music-making in Scotland. This work led to the establishment of the Youth Music Initiative, which has disbursed around £100 million to support youth music-making in Scotland since its inception in 2003.

Christopher Dingle is Reader in Music and Co-ordinator of Research Degrees at Birmingham Conservatoire, UK. A specialist in the life and music of Olivier Messiaen, he is author of the acclaimed biography *The Life of Messiaen* (Cambridge University Press, 2007) and *Messiaen's Final Works* (Ashgate, 2013). He co-edited *Olivier Messiaen: Music, Art and Literature* (Ashgate, 2007) and is contributing two chapters to McCarrey and Wright (eds), *Perspectives on the Performance of French Piano Music* (Ashgate, forthcoming). He was the organizer of the Messiaen 2008 International Centenary Conference hosted by Birmingham Conservatoire in June 2008, having previously conceived and organized the Messiaen 2002 International Conference in Sheffield.

Dingle is also a specialist in the history and practice of music criticism. He is the editor of the *Cambridge History of Music Criticism* (Cambridge University Press, forthcoming), and co-author with Chris Morley of *The Cambridge Introduction to Music Criticism* (Cambridge University Press, forthcoming). He is also working on a research project exploring evolutions in British newspaper criticism since the Second World War. He is a member of the review panel for *BBC Music Magazine*, broadcasts on BBC Radio 3 and has written for *Tempo, Music & Letters, The Guardian, The Independent, The Herald* and *Organists' Review*. He was a member of the jury for the *BBC Music Magazine Awards* in 2011 and 2008.

Robert Fallon is Assistant Professor and Coordinator of Musicology at Carnegie Mellon University School of Music in Pittsburgh, Pennsylvania. His research interests include nature and theology in Messiaen's music and thought, ecocriticism, the pressures of globalization and place on musical composition, and aesthetic and social issues affecting contemporary music in France, the United States and Turkey. He has previously edited *Ars Lyrica: Journal of the Lyrica Society for Word-Music Relations.* His book chapters on Messiaen appear in *Messiaen the Theologian* (Ashgate, 2010), *Musique, arts et religion dans l'entre-deux-guerres* (Symétrie, 2009), *Messiaen Studies* (Cambridge University Press, 2007), *Olivier Messiaen: Music, Art, and Literature* (Ashgate, 2007) and *Jacques Maritain and the Many Ways of Knowing* (Catholic University of America Press, 1999). He has also contributed articles to the *Grove Dictionary of American Music* and published in the *Journal of the American Musicological Society*, the *Journal of Musicology*, the *Journal of the Society for American Music*, *Modern Fiction Studies, Music & Letters, Tempo* and *Notes*. He has provided programme notes or pre-concert talks for the Pittsburgh Symphony, San Francisco Opera, New York City Opera, Carnegie Hall and the Kennedy Center and is a frequent contributor to The Allegheny Front radio programme on music and the environment.

Fallon is co-founder of the AMS Ecocritical Musicology Study Group and is the 2004 recipient of the Paul A. Pisk Prize for most outstanding paper by a graduate student read at the annual meeting of the American Musicological Society. He holds a PhD from the University of California at Berkeley.

Laura Hamer is Lecturer in Music at Liverpool Hope University, UK. She studied music at Brasenose College, Oxford University, Cardiff University, and the Université de Paris– Sorbonne. Her research interests lie in women in music, nineteenth- and twentieth-century French and Austro-German music, and reception and criticism studies, and she has published various articles and books chapters on these areas. After completing her PhD, she worked as a post-doctoral Research Assistant at Birmingham Conservatoire on the British Music Criticism since 1945 Project, and still plays an active role in this research. She is also a member of the Francophone Music Criticism Project. Prior to joining Liverpool Hope University in 2012, she was a Lecturer in Music at the Open University. She was programme committee chair of the Eighth International Music since 1900 Conference at Liverpool Hope University in September 2013.

Peter Hill has had a long association with the music of Messiaen. As a pianist he recorded all of Messiaen's solo piano music (originally on Unicorn Kanchana, re-released by Regis and recently by Brilliant Classics), receiving the support and encouragement of the composer, with whom he studied in Paris. The recording won numerous awards and distinctions, and has been described as 'one of the most important solo recording projects of recent years' (*New York Times*). Among other recordings are CDs of Bach (Delphian), Stravinsky (Naxos) and of Beethoven's *Diabelli Variations* (Unicorn-Kanchana). His CD of the complete solo piano works of Schoenberg, Berg and Webern (Naxos) was a recording of the year in *Classic CD* and *The Sunday Times*, and Editor's Choice in *Gramophone*.

The invitation from Messiaen's widow, Yvonne Loriod, to research in the private Messiaen archive in Paris led to a biography of the composer (*Messiaen*), published by Yale University Press in 2005, and reissued in translation in Germany (Schott) and in France (Fayard). *Olivier Messiaen: Oiseaux exotiques* (Ashgate) was published in 2007. Much in demand for lectures and master classes, recent appearances include the University of Western Australia, University of Chicago, Boston University, New York University, the Juilliard School of Music, Carnegie Hall, and the Library of Congress. In 2008 Peter was awarded the annual prize for musical scholarship by the Académie des Beaux-Arts in Paris. In 2009 he was appointed Professor Emeritus of Performance and Musicology at Sheffield University, and in 2011 a Fellow of the Royal Northern College of Music.

Lucie Kayas works in parallel as an author and editor, having recently translated Peter Hill and Nigel Simeone's seminal *Messiaen* into French. She has two books published by Actes Sud. The first, which she edited, is a portrait of André Jolivet. Her second, an annotated edition of the unpublished broadcasts of Francis Poulenc, was commended by the jury of the Prix des Muses at Musicora. She also published a biography of Jolivet (Fayard, 2005) and compiled the catalogue of his works within her doctorate.

After studying piano and chamber music at the École Normale de Musique de Paris, she studied musicology at the Conservatoire National Supérieur de Musique de Paris, where she is now teaching musical culture. She worked for Deutsche Grammophone in Hamburg as French Editor and, on her return to Paris, she worked for Avant-Scène Opéra, and the festivals of Radio France and Montpellier. She then took up a post in the publications department of the Théâtre du Châtelet with responsibility for the Education Department of the Châtelet and developed initiatives to introduce opera to new audiences until August 2012. Taking inspiration from the British approaches to collaboration between with artists and teachers, Lucie developed her department's artistic activities through pan-European exchanges.

Anne Mary Keeley is completing a doctorate on Messiaen's organ cycle *Méditations sur le mystère de la Sainte Trinité* at University College Dublin. She has spoken on the composer at several conferences, notably the Messiaen

2008 International Centenary Conference at Birmingham Conservatoire, the joint SMI–RMA conference at the Royal Irish Academy of Music, Dublin in 2009, and the 50th International Eucharistic Congress 2012 Theology Symposium at St. Patrick's College, Maynooth, Ireland. She has written on the composer for *The Musicology Review*. Her most recent conference paper focuses on the Eucharist in Messiaen's music and is published in *50th International Eucharistic Congress: Proceedings of the International Symposium of Theology*.

Hugh Macdonald is Avis H. Blewett Professor Emeritus of Music at Washington University, St Louis, MO, USA. He was the General Editor of the 26-volume *New Berlioz Edition* (Bärenreiter, 1967–2006) and has published books on Skryabin and Berlioz. His collection of essays *Beethoven's Century* was published by the University of Rochester Press in 2008, and his *Music in 1853: The Biography of a Year* by Boydell Press in 2012. He is well known as a lecturer and broadcaster in Britain and the United States.

Christopher Brent Murray defended his doctoral dissertation *Le développement du langage musical d'Olivier Messiaen: Traditions, emprunts, expériences* at the Université-Lumière Lyon 2 in 2010. He also holds degrees in analysis and composition from New York University's Graduate School of Arts and Sciences and the Eastman School of Music. From 2011 to 2013 Murray was a postdoctoral research fellow at the Université Libre de Bruxelles where he is studying musical life in Brussels during the twentieth century. He is a *chargé de recherches* with the FRS-FNRS, the Francophone Belgian National Fund for Scientific Research.

With co-authors Yves Balmer and Thomas Lacôte, Murray will soon publish a book-length study of Messiaen's composition techniques and use of pre-existing musical materials; with Yves Balmer, Murray is working on a second book project re-examining Messiaen's studies and teachings at the Paris Conservatory. Murray's research and reviews have been published in the *Revue de Musicologie*, the *Revue Belge de Musicologie*, *Notes*, and *Opera Quarterly*.

Sigune von Osten, soprano, is one of the most important singers of music of the twentieth and twenty-first centuries internationally. She has worked with composers such as John Cage, Olivier Messiaen, Luigi Nono, Giacinto Scelsi, Krzysztof Penderecki, and Cristobal Halffter, and has been a guest at international music festivals in Berlin, Vienna, Salzburg, Donaueschingen, Venice, Paris, Madrid, Lisbon, Warsaw, St. Petersburg, Tokyo and Shanghai.

Initiator and dedicatee of many world premieres, she has undertaken concert tours, radio and television recordings and music theatre productions in Europe, the United States, South America, Japan, and recently in China. Among her CDs are interpretations of *Harawi* by Olivier Messiaen (ITM), Satie, Ives, Cage (ITM) and *cageAnimations* (WERGO), a personal approach to John Cage.

Von Osten was professor for voice at the Musikhochschule Würzburg for ten years and gives international workshops and master classes for voice and interpretation of new music. Among her publications are 'La voix qui transcende Messiaen', in Lechner-Reydellet (ed.), *Messiaen l'empreinte d'un géant* (Séguier, 2008), 'L'interprétation en question', in Poirier (ed.) *André Boucourechliev* (Fayard, 2002), and about Giacinto Scelsi, *Lebeweise eines Yogi* (*MusikTexte* 26).

To propagate the music of the twentieth and twenty-first centuries she founded and managed the ensemble Musica Temporale for contemporary music in Dresden, and has been involved in some extraordinary cultural projects at Trombacher Hof, her residence, with the multidisciplinary and multicultural Art Point ensemble. Here she works as an initiator, composer, designer, artistic director, and producer, and she combines music, literature, the fine arts, light, space, movement, and voices in her own projects (e.g. John Cage's *Musicircus* and *Novemberland* with Günter Grass). At Trombacher Hof she also founded and runs the festival Parkmusik Neue Ho(e)rizonte every year.

Caroline Rae is Senior Lecturer in Music at Cardiff University and has been Visiting Lecturer at the universities of Paris–Sorbonne, Paris 8, Rouen and Cologne as well as Visiting Scholar at St John's College Oxford. The author of *The Music of Maurice Ohana* (Ashgate, 2000), editor of the revised and expanded edition of Robert Sherlaw Johnson's *Messiaen* (Omnibus, 2008) and co-editor of 'Dutilleux at 95' for *Contemporary Music Review* (2010), she has published numerous articles on twentieth-century music in France, as well as on the writings and musical activities of Alejo Carpentier. She is currently preparing a new study of André Jolivet and an interdisciplinary monograph *Magic Realism, Music and Literature*, both forthcoming with Ashgate. Also a pianist, she has performed internationally as well as in the UK and gives lecture-recitals relating to her research interests. A pupil of Dame Fanny Waterman, she later studied with Yvonne Loriod-Messiaen under a French Government Scholarship in Paris, as well as at the Hochschule für Musik und Theater in Hanover. She maintained a two-piano duo with the late Robert Sherlaw Johnson for many years, their programmes focusing on French repertoire, notably Messiaen's *Visions de l'Amen*. She broadcasts for BBC Radio 3, discussing twentieth-century French music, and with the BBC National Orchestra of Wales was co-organizer of the 2008 BBC Discovering Dutilleux Festival, which took place in the presence of the composer, as well as the André Jolivet Composer Portrait and the Paul Sacher Perspectives season 2011–12. She is also programming consultant for the Philharmonia Orchestra of London. Caroline is the sister of the composer and writer Charles Bodman Rae.

Philip Weller has a long-standing interest in Debussy and Messiaen, and in French music of the twentieth century more generally. He has worked on aesthetic, technical and philosophical aspects of the French tradition, and in particular has made a special study of the vocal and operatic repertory. His translation of *L'Âme en bourgeon*, the garland of poems written for Messiaen by his mother before he was born, formed the centre-piece of Dingle and Simeone (eds), *Olivier Messiaen: Music, Art and Literature* (Ashgate, 2007), and he is currently working on an extended study of Messiaen and the voice. Philip has also published on specific areas of sacred music in the late-medieval and renaissance periods, and has collaborated on research-led performance projects and recordings in this field. Other research interests include the development and character of French opera as a distinctive national tradition from the time of Lully, Campra and Rameau; the study of art and visual culture in their musical dimension; the field of music and language; and the related topics of the Lied and *mélodie*.

Index

Académie des Beaux-Arts 15–16, 19, 25, 26
Agoult, Marie Comtesse d' 31
Albéniz, Isaac 199, 235–7, 242, 244,
        247–50, 255–6
    Ibéria 199, 201, 248–50, 255
Allais, Maurice 92
Amy, Gilbert 199
Anderson, Julian 227
Aprahamian, Felix 200
Arche, L' 270, 273
Arnoult, Louis 25
Arrieu, Claude 46
Association Jeune France 45–8, 52–3, 63, 91
Aubin, Tony 19, 21, 47
Aubray, Laurence 55–6
Augustine, St 179

Bach, J. S. 183, 199, 202, 207, 271, 273–4,
        277–8, 315, 319
    Well-Tempered Clavier 199, 257
Bachelet, Alfred 25
Baïf, Jean-Antoine de 291
Balmer, Yves 128–9, 228
Banville, Théodore de 19, 31–3, 37–8
Barbier, Pierre 45, 48, 58, 62
Barraine, Elsa 42–3, 91
Barraud, Henry 90–91
Bartók, Béla 91, 200, 238, 302
    Second Piano Concerto 200
    Piano Sonata 91
Basil of Cæserea, St 189
Baudrier, Yves 45, 49, 60–61, 277
Béclart d'Harcourt, Marguérite 103–4
Béclart d'Harcourt, Raoul 103–4
Beethoven, Ludwig van 199, 201, 219, 314
    Piano Sonata in B♭ Major, op. 106,
        'Hammerklavier' 199
Benitez, Vincent 2
Benjamin, George 238
Berg, Alban 227

    Wozzeck 319
Berio, Luciano 104, 119
    Sequenza III 104, 119
Berlioz, Hector 14, 42, 219, 222–3, 230,
        236, 314–15
    Benvenuto Cellini 315
    Damnation de Faust 314
    Harold en Italie 315
    Roméo et Juliette 315
    Symphonie fantastique 315
Bertrand, Paul 27
Bibliothèque Nationale de France 69–70,
        74, 143
Bizet, Georges 14, 38, 320
    Carmen 313
Björk 2
Bloch, André 25, 47–8
Bloy, Léon 270, 272
Bosch, Hieronymus 302
Boulanger, Nadia 25, 33, 321
Boulez, Pierre 1, 38, 82, 153, 166,
        199–200, 218, 289
    Second Piano Sonata 199–200
Bourdariat, René 91
Bousquet, Francis 47
Brahms, Johannes 230, 257, 316
Brasillach, Robert 48
Britten, Benjamin 313
Bruckner, Anton 257
Bruhn, Siglind 2, 85, 100
Bruneau, Alfred 25, 38, 320
Bunlet, Marcelle 104

Cage, John 119, 130
cahiers de notations de chants d'oiseaux
        see Messiaen, Olivier: *cahiers de
        notations de chants d'oiseaux*
Catholic Art 30, 189, 225, 269–70, 272,
        274, 276, 279–306, 320
    l'art sacré 269–78

Catholic Church 221, 275–7
  Second Vatican Council 177, 180–81
Chabrier, Emmanuel 28–9, 38, 237, 239,
    241–2, 320
Chagall, Marc 269, 302
Chailley, Jacques 47, 49
Challan, Henri 23, 26
Challan, René 23, 26
Chancerel, Léon 48, 52
Charles, Monsignor Maxime Marcel
    176–82, 191–3
Charpentier, Gustave 25
Chaynes, Charles 199
Chen, Pi-hsien 121
Chopin, Frédéric 200–201, 207, 222, 230,
    235–47, 253–6, 316, 320
  Ballade in A♭ Major, op. 47: 244
  Barcarolle in F♯ Major, op. 60: 207, 242
  Études, op. 10: 244–5, 256
  Études, op. 25: 243, 245
  Piano Sonata in B♭ Minor, op. 25: 256
  Preludes, op. 28: 242–4
Ciampi, Marcel 236
Cocteau, Jean 92, 314
Conservatoire [C. N. S. M. D. P.] see Paris
    Conservatoire
Cortot, Alfred 91, 236, 248
Costantini, Celso Cardinal 275
Couperin, François 237–8, 320
  Le rossignol en amour 237
Couraud, Marcel 280, 288–90, 293, 304, 306
Couturier, Marie-Alain, O.P. 269–70, 272–3
Crispin, Judith 3
Crossley, Paul 207

Daniel-Lesur 277, 280, 304
Daniélou, Jean Cardinal 178
Daquin, Louis-Claude 237
  Le coucou 237
Dargomyzhsky, Alexander 318
Dautremer, Marcel 23
De Chirico, Giorgio 53, 87, 98
Debussy, Claude 13–14, 35, 37–8, 42, 61,
    91, 199, 207–8, 218–19, 222–3,
    227, 229–30, 236–7, 239, 241–2,
    249, 314, 316–17, 320
  Estampes 240
  Etudes 91, 199, 207

  Pelléas et Mélisande 36–7, 207, 222
Delamain, Jacques 123, 129, 145–6,
    148–9, 168
  Pourquoi les oiseaux chantent [Why
    Birds Sing] 145
Delapierre, Guy-Bernard 88–9, 91, 145
Delbos, Claire 15, 31, 43, 58, 143, 203,
    260, 266, 282
Desnos, Robert 88
Desportes, Yvonne 17–18, 21, 23, 26–7, 34
Diémer, Louis 236–7
Dingle, Christopher 260
Domaine Musical, Le 153, 240, 289
Donaueschingen (Germany) 152, 170, 297
Doncœur, Père 48
Dukas, Paul 19–23, 28–9, 42–3, 224,
    241–2, 248, 302, 318–19
  L'apprenti sorcier [Sorceror's
    Apprentice] 224, 318
  Ariane et Barbe-bleue 224, 318
  Peri, La 319
  Polyeucte 319
Dupont, Jacques 21, 23, 27
Dupré, Marcel 14, 36, 319
Durand (publisher) 2, 18, 70, 165, 208–9

Eminger-Sivade, Nelly 199
Emmanuel, Maurice 14, 28–9, 291

Fabre, Lucien 284
Falkenberg, Georges 241
Falla, Manuel de 199
Fallon, Robert 143, 223
Favre, Georges 21, 23–4
Fellot, Henry 60–63
Fleming, Renée 1
Florand, Père François 277–8
Fonds Messiaen 10, 99, 354, 346
Fontainebleau, Palais de 16–17, 19, 23
Forman, Edward 11, 85
Franck, César 218, 319, 321
  Prélude, choral et fugue 199
  Symphonic Variations 218
Francis of Assisi, St 86, 207, 221, 263
  Fioretti 86
François, Samson 200

Gallon, Noël 19

Gaubert, Philippe 25
Gaulle, Charles de 65–7
Giardino, Jean 49
Gillock, Jon 2
Gluck, Christoph Willibald 241
Goléa, Antoine 124–5, 131–2, 307
Gounod, Charles 14, 319–20
Gourmont, Jean de 264–5
Goya, Francisco 110
Green, Julien 92
Griffiths, Paul 2
Grimaud, Yvette 48
Guénot, Louis 25

Haas, Monique 200
Halle, Adam de la 76
Hamer, Laura 227
Haskil, Clara 238
Hautecœur, Louis 47
Haydn, Joseph 230, 257
Healey, Gareth 3
Hello, Ernest 83
Hemmer, Curé 30
Henry, Pierre 123–6, 129–31, 135, 139–40
    Symphonie pour un home seul 124
Hindemith, Paul 271–2
Horowitz, Vladimir 238
Hsu [Forte], Madeleine 245
Hüe, Georges 19, 25, 259

impressionism 171, 314, 320
Institut de France 15–16
Institut National de l'Audiovisuel (INA)
    12, 124–5

Janáček, Leoš 257–8, 263, 266–7
    Capriccio 258
    Sinfonietta 258
Janowski, Marek 218
Jeune France, La 14, 49, 236, 298, 321
Joan of Arc 45, 48–9, 51–2, 54, 56, 61–3,
    65–7
John of the Cross, St 97, 100
Johnson, Robert Sherlaw 2–3, 175
Jolivet, André 91, 227, 238, 251, 280, 298
    Épithalame 293, 304–5
    Mana 251
    Trois danses rituelles 91

Kandinsky, Wasily 270
Kayas, Lucie 61
Kessel, Joseph 92
Koch, Ludwig 157–8, 165–6
Kodály, Zoltán 91
    Four Pieces, op. 3 91
Koussevitsky, Serge 201

Lack, Théodore 241
Lacôte, Thomas 228
Lambert, Constant 239
Landormy, Paul 16
Le Courbusier 269
Le Flem, Paul 272–3
Le Jeune, Claude 218, 290–92
    Le printemps 218, 290–91
Le Moal, Jean 53–5
Lekander, Gunnar 159
Lévy, Lazare 199, 236, 238
Lipchitz, Jacques 269, 272
Liszt, Franz 31, 199, 236–7, 244, 247–9,
    251, 253–6
    Années de pèlerinage 248, 251–3
    Deux légendes 237, 254
    Harmonies poétiques et réligieuses 253
    Piano Sonata in B Minor 199, 251
Loisel, Joseph 16
Loriod, Yvonne 11–12, 47–8, 71, 91, 99–121,
    143, 147, 153, 163–5, 167, 169, 170,
    177, 197–216, 218, 227, 235–6, 238,
    240, 246, 248, 250–51, 255, 260,
    282–3, 285–6, 289, 301, 318
    concerts 69, 91, 100–101, 197–8, 200,
        202, 205, 250
    pianistic technique 99, 197–200, 202,
        205, 236, 238, 246–7, 249
    relationship with Messiaen *see*
        Messiaen, Olivier: biography:
        relationship with Yvonne Loriod
    recordings 9, 11–12, 91, 101, 103, 119–
        21, 206, 208, 236, 250, 323–38
    teaching 206–7, 236
Lourié, Arthur 317
Lurçat, Jean 269
Lustiger, Jean Cardinal 178

Maas, Sander van 2
Machaut, Guillaume de 257

Maderna, Bruno 218
Maeterlinck, Maurice 302, 318
Magaloff, Nikita 238
Maillard, Pierre 19, 21
Mangeot, Auguste 16
Marcelin, Émile 19, 21, 23, 26–7
Marchal, André 14
Marchal, Beatrice 264–6
Marie, Jean-Étienne 130
Marmion, Dom Columba 85–7, 89, 93–8
　　Le Christ dans ses mystères [*Christ in
　　　His Mysteries*] 86, 89, 96–8
Marmontel, Antoine-François 236–7, 241,
　　237
Martenot, Maurice 91
Martin, Louis 218
Massenet, Jules 14, 38, 215, 319
Mathias, Georges 236, 241
Mathieu, Georgette 25
Matisse, Henri 269
Mauduit, Jacques 291
Maurois, André 92
medievalism 45–67, 165, 180, 182, 292, 302
Mendelssohn, Felix 202, 230
　　Songs Without Words 202
Mendès, Catulle 23, 38
Menotti, Gian Carlo 321
Messiaen, Alain 265
Messiaen, Olivier
　　biography
　　　Prix de Rome entry 13–15, 18–31,
　　　　43, 260
　　　rehearsing 101–21
　　　relationship with Claire Delbos 15,
　　　　31, 43, 58, 143, 153, 159, 170,
　　　　204, 260, 266, 282–3, 285–6,
　　　　288, 301
　　　relationship with Yvonne Loriod 5,
　　　　99–100, 119–21, 164–5, 167,
　　　　170, 197–210, 247, 251, 260,
　　　　265, 282–3, 285–6, 301
　　　Second World War 46–7, 58, 306
　　　teaching 145, 149, 207, 210, 225,
　　　　227, 240, 314, 321
　　birdsong 10–11, 85, 100, 116, 123,
　　　129, 132, 143–73, 186, 202–3,
　　　205–6, 209, 218, 222, 237, 249,
　　　256–7, 267, 276, 278

recordings 11, 132, 143–4, 152–62,
　　165–6, 168–70, 206
　　see also Messiaen, Olivier: *cahiers
　　　de notations de chants d'oiseaux*
*cahiers de notations de chants
　d'oiseaux* 10–11, 129, 132,
　　143–73, 209, 247, 277
colour 3, 98, 102, 128, 130, 134, 141,
　　144, 157, 229–31, 260, 314, 316, 320
communicable language *see* Messiaen,
　　Olivier: *langage communicable*
form 33–4, 40, 71–83, 136, 144, 155,
　　175, 218–19, 299–300, 307–9
　　chiasmus 182–4
　　fugue 19, 71–2, 259
　　permutation 124, 129, 133–7, 140,
　　　262, 267
　　symmetry 133–6, 138, 140, 179
harmony 34–5, 37–8, 40, 62, 79–80,
　　128, 166, 207–8, 219, 230, 237,
　　239, 242, 245, 249–50, 311–12
　　chord 35, 40–41, 79–80, 82, 128,
　　　131, 157, 164, 166, 231–2,
　　　252–3, 311–12, 317
　　mode 35, 38, 41, 70, 79, 150, 170,
　　　245, 263, 284, 308
　　see also Olivier, Messiaen: colour
historiography 1–3, 9–13, 45–6, 61,
　　69–71, 74, 82–3, 85, 87, 100–102,
　　123–4, 143–4, 162, 172–4,
　　197–201, 206–10, 213–15, 217,
　　224, 226–7, 229, 232, 257–8, 264,
　　266–8, 292, 313, 321–2
langage communicable 175, 182, 184,
　　186–7, 264, 266, 293
melody 35, 37, 40, 62, 72, 74–83, 99,
　　118, 148, 157, 162, 184, 186–91,
　　200, 218, 225–7, 239, 245–6, 251,
　　253–5, 259, 261, 284–5
nature 76, 83, 98, 127, 129–32, 145–6,
　　148, 164, 167–8, 169–70, 189,
　　229, 235, 254, 258–9, 262, 308,
　　314–5 *see also* Messiaen, Olivier:
　　birdsong
performance practice 101–21, 235–56,
　　280, 305
plainchant 61–2, 71, 97, 225, 255 *see
　　also* Messiaen, Olivier: melody

rhythm 71, 76–7, 111, 123, 126, 128–41, 145, 147, 166, 169, 170, 186, 201–2, 219, 228–9, 250–51, 267, 291–3, 296, 315

serialism 128, 133–4, 140–41, 166–7, 170, 262–3, 267

theology *see separate entry*

timbre 102–21, 126–30, 132, 134, 136, 138, 141, 154–55, 160–61, 166, 168, 170, 203, 206, 222, 230, 242, 246, 253, 256–7, 263, 275, 280, 293, 319

WORKS

Apparition de l'Église éternelle 57

L'Ascension 224

Banquet céleste, Le 11, 262

Banquet eucharistique, Le 11, 18

Cantéyodjayâ 133, 170, 205, 256, 288

Catalogue d'oiseaux 132, 143–5, 149, 152–3, 158–70, 198, 204, 235, 256, 260, 262, 285

Chant des déportés 13, 40–41

Chants de terre et de ciel 101

Chœurs pour une Jeanne d'Arc see *Portique pour une fille de France*

Chronochromie 126–8, 157, 169, 171, 205, 260, 262, 267–8, 305, 321

Cinq Rechants 164, 205, 215, 279–312 discography 310

Concert à quatre 204, 208–9, 218, 226–7, 235, 238

Corps glorieux, Les 276

Couleurs de la Cité céleste 201, 204, 276

Des Canyons aux étoiles... 204, 222, 261

Éclairs sur l'Au-Delà... 205, 208–9, 218

L'Ensorceleuse 23–4, 31

Et exspecto resurrectionem mortuorum 276

Fantaisie 35

Fantaisie burlesque 258

Fauvette des jardins, La 169, 204, 311

Fête des belles eaux 254, 258–60

Fugue pour le Concours de Rome 19, 31, 259

Harawi 101–21, 204, 247, 260, 279, 281, 283–4, 287, 299–302, 305, 308

Hymne au Saint-Sacrement [*Hymne*] 272

Jeunesse des vieux, La 23, 38–41

Livre d'orgue 128, 134, 140–41, 169, 171, 262, 276

Méditations sur le mystère de la Sainte Trinité 173–93, 222, 257

Merle noir, Le 132

Messe de la Pentecôte 275–6

Nativité du Seigneur, La 72, 85, 273–4, 276, 311

O sacrum convivium! 281

Offrandes oubliées, Les 13, 40–41, 229, 260

Oiseaux exotiques 132, 144, 152–7, 165, 170–71, 200, 204, 256

Petites Esquisses d'oiseaux 204–5

Pièce (piano and string quartet) 204, 258

Pièce (*pour le Tombeau de Paul Dukas*) 208

Poèmes pour Mi 101, 121, 288

Portique pour une fille de France [*Chœurs pour une Jeanne d'Arc*] 45–67

Préludes 21–2, 90–91, 201, 235, 242–4, 246–9

Quatre Études de rythme 133, 141, 171
    Mode de valeurs et d'intensités 233, 258, 261, 262, 266
    Neumes rythmiques 233
    Île de feu 2 134

Quatuor pour la fin du Temps 35, 88, 146, 171, 229, 254, 259–61, 281, 311, 317

Réveil des oiseaux 129, 132, 143–4, 146, 148, 151–2, 157, 160, 165, 170–71, 175, 202, 204, 297

Rondeau 258, 260

Saint François d'Assise 4, 86, 144, 206, 221, 223–4, 229, 231–2, 247, 263, 306

Sainte-Bohème, La 19, 31–8, 40–41

Sept Haïkaï 204

Sourire, Un 205, 218, 220, 223, 233, 239

Timbres-durées 123–41, 262–3, 316 spatialization 123, 139–40

Tombeau resplendissant, Le 209

Transfiguration de Notre-Seigneur Jésus-Christ, La 204, 222, 276, 305–6

*Trois Petites Liturgies de la Présence
     Divine* 13, 35, 41, 89, 148, 204,
     278, 283, 306, 311
Trois Tâla 287
Turangalîla-Symphonie 88, 129,
     200–201, 204–5, 224, 260, 279,
     281, 285, 287, 299–300, 302,
     305–6, 321
Ville d'En-Haut, La 204
Vingt Regards sur l'Enfant-Jésus
     85–100, 197–9, 201–4, 235, 245,
     247, 249–53, 255, 283
Visions de l'Amen 69–83, 88–9, 129,
     202, 204, 226, 235, 239, 247, 249,
     251–53, 255
Vitrail et des oiseaux, Un 204, 208
Vocalise-étude 260
Writings and pedagogical works
     Technique de mon langage musical
          11, 37, 58, 71, 76, 78–9, 81,
          136, 138, 239, 310, 318
     *Traité de rythme, de couleur, et
          d'ornithologie* 10, 78–81, 85,
          98, 140, 165, 169, 208, 218,
          221, 225, 231–2, 240, 243,
          245, 310
     Vingt leçons d'harmonie 38
Michelangelo Buonarotti 87, 100
Milhaud, Darius 153, 206, 215, 223, 314, 319
Milkina, Nina 238
Miramon Fitz-James, Bérenger de 14
Mirouze, Marcel 23
modernism 30, 60–62, 222, 254, 269, 272,
     275, 277, 279–80, 282, 289, 300,
     304–5
Mozart, W. A. 79–81, 199–201, 207, 210,
     217–33, 238–41, 247, 251, 314, 316
     Don Giovanni 217, 220, 223–4,
          229–33, 314, 316
     Magic Flute, The 217, 223, 230
     Marriage of Figaro 80, 218, 223,
          226–7, 239–40
     Piano Concerto in E♭ Major, KV. 271:
          220
     Piano Concerto in F Major, KV. 413: 221
     Piano Concerto in C Major, KV. 415: 221
     Piano Concerto in B♭ Major, KV. 450:
          222

     Piano Concerto in G Major, KV. 453:
          220
     Piano Concerto in B♭ Major, KV. 456:
          220
     Piano Concerto in E♭ Major, KV. 482:
          220, 230
     Piano Concerto in A Major, KV. 488: 220
     Piano Concerto in C Major, KV. 503:
          200, 221
     Piano Concerto in D Major, KV. 537: 221
Muraro, Roger 207–8
Murray, Christopher Brent 32, 38, 227–8
musique concrète 123–41, 262, 318
Mussorgsky, Modest 227, 266, 318
     Pictures at an Exhibition 253, 248–9

Nabokov, Nicolas 125
Nagano, Kent 233
Nardelli, Zdzisław 10
Neussargues (France) 48, 58
New York Philharmonic 1
Nichols, Roger 1–2

Obukhov, Nikolai 317
Offenbach, Jacques 318
Ohana, Maurice 238, 280
Ollivier, Albert 91
Ozawa, Seiji 321

Pagnol, Marcel 92
Palmér, Sture 159
Paris Conservatoire 2, 11, 13, 18–19, 21–3,
     28, 34, 37, 46–7, 49, 69, 125, 218,
     233, 236, 238, 240–42, 259–60,
     290–91, 314–15, 319, 321
Pelliot, Alice 47–8
Penrose, Roland 116
Perrault, Charles 302, 318
Pétain, Maréchal Philippe 45, 49–51, 63,
     65, 67
Petersen, Nils Holger 233
Petichet (France) 143, 163, 167, 169, 288
Petrassi, Goffredo 280
Pichard, Joseph 270
Pierné, Gabriel 25
Pius XII, Pope 275
Pléiade, Concerts de la 69, 78–9
Poe, Edgar Allan 300

Pozzi, Raffaele 223
Preger, Léo 45, 49, 59–62
Prix de Rome 13–43, 260
Prokofiev, Sergei 199, 218, 318
Puig-Roget, Henriette 23
Py, Fernard 270, 273

Quef, Charles 14, 23

Rabaud, Henri 24–5
Rachmaninov, Sergei 247, 253–5
radio 45, 52, 61, 85, 90–92, 100, 124–5, 159
Radiohead 2
Rae, Caroline 202
Rameau, Jean-Philippe 76, 235, 237–8,
    320, 359
Ravel, Maurice 150, 199, 223, 235–7, 240,
    242–5, 249, 254, 319
    Gaspard de la nuit 150, 201, 240, 243–4
    Jeux d'eau 254
    Miroirs 150
Recordings
    see Discography; of birds,
    see Messiaen, Olivier: birdsong; by
        Yvonne Loriod,
    see Appendix
Rémond, René 63
renaissance, the 99, 291, 359
Reverdy, Michèle 72, 307
Richard of St Victor 180, 191–3
Rilke, Rainer Maria 221–2, 303–4
    Duino Elegies 221, 303
Robertson, David 321
Roget, Henriette 23, 26–7
Roland-Manuel 277
Romains, Jules 92
romanticism 30–31, 83, 99, 202, 215, 235–56
Rößler, Almut 176
Rubin, William S. 274
Rubinstein, Arthur 248

Sacré-Coeur de Montmatre 176, 178–9
Saint-Saëns, Camille 33, 320
Samazeuilh, Gustave 21–2, 28
Samuel-Rousseau, Marcel 25
Sand, George 31
Sauvage [Messiaen], Cécile 264–6
    L'Âme en bourgeon 265

Scarlatti, Domenico 199, 235, 238
Schaeffer, Pierre 45, 48, 52, 58–9, 62–3,
    91–2, 100, 124, 126, 139–41
Schmitt, Florent 91
Schoenberg, Arnold 119, 316
    Die glückliche Hand 316
Schola Cantorum 31, 272
Schumann, Clara 198
Schumann, Robert 198–200, 218
Second Vatican Council *see* Catholic Church
Selva, Blanche 248
Shakespeare, William 264
    Macbeth 127
Shenton, Andrew 2–3
Sherlaw Johnson, Robert *see* Johnson,
        Robert Sherlaw
Sholl, Robert 2
Shostakovich, Dmitri 313–14
Six, Les 321
Skryabin 227, 316–7
    Prometheus 316
Société Nationale de Musique 14, 28–9, 43
Spirale, La 14
Stockhausen, Karlheinz 166, 257, 267
Stravinsky, Igor 201, 218, 221, 230, 271–2,
    306, 313, 315
    Les noces 306, 315
    Le sacre du printemps [*The Rite of
        Spring*] 218, 289, 318
surrealism 98, 116, 242, 279, 281–2,
    285–6, 296–7, 300–301

Tcherepnin, Alexander 199
theology 66, 96, 175–82, 189, 191–3, 222,
    305
    Ressourcement 180, 182
    Scholasticism 180–81
    Trinitarian 180, 189, 191–3
Theresa of Lisieux, St 86–7, 99–100
Thomas of Aquinas, St 85, 176, 179–80,
    191, 193
    Summa Theologiæ 176, 181
Toesca, Maurice 85–93, 96, 98, 100
    Cinq ans de patience 87–8
    Douze regards 86–7, 90, 92, 96, 98
    La Nativité 87, 89
Tournemire, Charles 14, 227, 270–71
    L'Orgue mystique 270, 272

Traber, Hans 159
Trinité, Église de la (Paris) 11, 14–15, 23,
    30, 43, 176–9, 193, 275, 315–6, 319
Tristan (legend) 164, 279, 282–5, 287,
    299–300, 302–3

Vatican II *see* Catholic Church
Vaubourgoin, Marc 21, 23
Vichy France 47–50, 57, 63, 65, 67, 91
Villa-Lobos, Heitor 215
Villa Médicis [Académie de France]
    14–15, 42
Vitrac, Roger 272

Vonk, Hans 321
Vuillermoz, Jean 21, 23

Wagner, Richard 60, 104, 219, 221, 230,
    239, 241, 292, 302, 313, 315–16
    Tristan und Isolde 292
Webern, Anton von 225
Widor, Charles-Marie 14, 22, 25, 319
Witkowski, Jean 49, 58–61
Wyschnegradsky 318

Xenakis, Iannis 140, 280

Contents of *Messiaen Perspectives 2: Techniques, Influence and Reception*

Introduction
Christopher Dingle and Robert Fallon

PART I   TECHNIQUES

Perspectives on Techniques
Christopher Dingle and Robert Fallon

1   Sacred Machines: Fear, Mystery and Transfiguration in Messiaen's
     Mechanical Procedures
     Christopher Dingle

2   *La Fauvette des jardins* and the 'Spectral Attitude'
     Roderick Chadwick

3   Aspects of Compositional Organization and Stylistic Innovation in
     Petites Esquisses d'oiseaux
     David Kopp

4   Messiaen's Counterpoint
     Christoph Neidhöfer

Intermède 1

5   A Catalogue of Messiaen's Birds
     Robert Fallon

PART II   INFLUENCE

Perspectives on Influence
Christopher Dingle and Robert Fallon

6   Messiaen and Ohana: Parallel Preoccupations or Anxiety of Influence?
     Caroline Rae

7   The Messiaen–Xenakis Conjunction
    Anne-Sylvie Barthel-Calvet

8   From France to Québec: Messiaen's Transatlantic Legacy
    Heather White Luckow

9   Messiaen and the Spectralists
    Marilyn Nonken

Intermède 2

10 The Tombeaux of Messiaen: At the Intersection of Influence and
    Reception
    Robert Fallon

PART III   RECEPTION

Perspectives on Reception
Christopher Dingle and Robert Fallon

11 The Reception of Messiaen in Italy: A Historical Interpretation
    Raffaele Pozzi

12 Three Decades of Messiaen's Music in Spain: A Brief Survey,
    1945–1978
    Germán Gan-Quesada

13 Placing Mount Messiaen
    Robert Fallon

14 Genesis and Reception of Olivier Messiaen's *Traité de rythme,
    de couleur, et d'ornithologie*, 1949–1992: Toward a New Reading
    of the Composer's Writings
    Jean Boivin

Appendix: A Critical Catalogue of Messiaen's Musical Works
      1. Complete List of Messiaen's Works
         i. Acknowledged Works
         ii. Other Pieces
      2. Messiaen's Works, Listed by Year of Première
      3. Messiaen's Acknowledged Works, Listed by Instrumentation
      4. Annotations
      Christopher Dingle and Robert Fallon

Made in the USA
Middletown, DE
08 September 2023

38203953R00219